CLASSIC MARQUES

The A-Z of Three-Wheelers

A definitive reference guide

ELVIS PAYNE

NOSTALGIA ROAD

First published by Crécy Publishing Ltd 2013

A CIP record for this book is available from
the British Library

ISBN 9781908 347169

Printed in China

**Nostalgia Road is an imprint of
Crécy Publishing Limited**
1a Ringway Trading Estate
Shadowmoss Road
Manchester M22 5LH
www.crecy.co.uk

Front cover: *The 2011 Morgan SuperDry Edition that was limited to 200 vehicles
and included SuperDry branding, orange wall tyres and quilted leather seats.*
Morgan Motor Co

Front cover inset left: *For its time the Framo Stromer had an extremely stylish
streamlined body that tapered off at the rear end.* Maximilian Busch

Front cover inset middle: *The Aptera was a hybrid vehicle stated to achieve
330mpg (0.8-litre/100km) whilst travelling at 65mph (104km/h) though the
company went into liquidation before full production started.* Aptera Motors

Front cover inset right: *Recognised by its covered front wheels, this particular
photo of a Messerschmitt KR175 was taken in Paris in 1955.* Allan Hailstone

Back cover main left: *Described as a 'crossover between sports car and motorcycle',
the Volkswagen GX3 used an engine from the Volkswagen Lupo GTi.* Volkswagen

Back cover main right: *Designed by General Motors in 1969, the Chevrolet Astro III
was a concept vehicle that was planned to use a Model 250-C18 gas-turbine
engine.* General Motors

Back cover inset clockwise from top left:

*The 'Butler Petrol Cycle' was completed in 1890 though plans for it were shown as
early as 1884 by Edward Butler who is also credited to be the first to use the word
'Petrol'.* Jane Neil

*The Coventry Victor Luxury Sports model featured a full leather interior, a folding
hood, dynamo lighting, front and side screens and even an electric horn.* John Lloyd

*Built in Spain the Delfin was made under licence to New Map though used a
different engine to the New Map Solyto.* Hans Bodewes

*With its futuristic shape compared with other vehicles on the road in 1947 the
Davis was an eye catcher and as a result over 300 franchises were created that
were all waiting for vehicles to be delivered.* Hal Schmidt

*When assembled, the Zascka was a folding car that had a tubular steel frame with
a body consisting of fabric stretched over it.* Author's Collection

With its DVC system, the Carver was able to tilt up to 45° each side when cornering.
Harry Kroonen

CONTENTS

Charles Morgan aboard a replica of the 1909 Morgan Runabout fitted with a Peugeot V-Twin Engine.
Morgan Motor Co

Foreword by Charles Morgan

It is a great honour for me to write a Foreword for the book of the three-wheeler. This history by Elvis Payne is an important reference guide.

My experience of three-wheelers started with my Grandfather, H F S Morgan, who was the inventor of the Morgan Runabout. He passed on to me his love of mechanical contraptions that had an elegant simplicity but a giant killing performance. When I knew him he had retired from running the Morgan Motor Co, but was still constructing pedal cars for his grandchildren in his favourite shed. I learnt to drive in one of his designs, an F4 three-wheeler, built in 1935, which belonged to my Grandmother. At the time it was possible to obtain a licence for the road at 16 years of age. I quickly learnt that the combination of light weight and stability meant brisk performance and good fuel economy.

When the Morgan three-wheeler was launched it was one of the first lightweight cars. Arguably it was also one of the most successful in terms of numbers built and for the reliable miles of travel it provided. In fact the Morgan three-wheeler was so successful a separate factory was built in Paris to manufacture the car in France under the name 'Darmont Morgan'. Morgan three-wheelers were the first experience of freedom for many drivers and families at an affordable cost, and in a reliable manner. What was so clever was that the Morgan three-wheeler (with minimal modifications) could also become such a successful racing machine. The Morgan three-wheeler went on to win many land speed records and regularly lapped Brooklands race track at an average of over 100mph.

The illustrious history of the Morgan three-wheeler provided the company with the perfect excuse to relaunch the Morgan three-wheeler in 2011, a year after celebrating our Centenary. The new Morgan three-wheeler has proved almost as popular as the 'Runabout' and brought back the sense of freedom and fun that the original car provided.

There are of course many other three-wheelers that have been designed and built by other manufacturers. They have all good features and clever specifications, but perhaps none has brought quite the same smile to the face of the driver as the Morgan three-wheeler. Like many others, I am so grateful to my Grandfather, H F S Morgan, for having the ingenuity and vision to invent one of the greatest ways of getting from A-B that there has ever been conceived by an engineer.

Charles Morgan

Chairman,
Morgan Motor Co,
19 April 2013
www.morgan-motor.co.uk

Introduction

Love them or loathe them the three-wheeler, Cycle-car or even Tri-car has had an important impact in the development of the present day motorcar. From the beginnings of the Industrial Revolution to the Concept cars of the future, these vehicles can hold their headlamps up with pride. They were present at the birth of motoring and possibly may well be the answer to the future with the constant depletion of the earth's energy resources.

The three-wheeler, therefore, has truly made its impact in history and, as this book will show, three-wheelers are not just limited to specific manufacturers of three-wheel vehicles. Over the years almost all of the major manufacturers of four-wheel vehicles have dabbled with three-wheelers at some point: General Motors, Ford Motor Co, Maserati, Subaru, Mazda, Volkswagen, Peugeot and many more have a three-wheeler tucked away somewhere in their archives.

One of the largest benefits of the three-wheeler is economy as many three-wheelers are light vehicles that are powered by small engines, which provide a very good power to weight ratio and give a fairly respectable performance for family vehicles up to eye watering performance in some of the sportier vehicles. In the UK especially one of the main advantages about owning a three-wheeler is that all three-wheelers that weigh less than 450kg are classed as tricycles and thus come under a much lower tax bracket than their four-wheeled counterparts. Three-wheelers could also be driven on a motorcycle licence* in the UK, which, for generations of old where the only family vehicle was a motorcycle and side car, being able to drive a three-wheeler offered many families a true family car. This was something numerous three-wheel manufacturers — especially in the UK — depended upon, resulting in three-wheelers consistently evolving with each one an improvement on the last. In other countries, such as France and Italy, small three-wheelers were favoured as no driving licence at all was required to drive them on the roads. Further afield, in parts of Asia and India, thousands of three-wheelers earned their crust serving as economical delivery vehicles and taxis.

One of the main criticisms about three-wheelers — ironically often made by people who have never driven one let alone owned one — is that they are unstable and you only have to sneeze abruptly to end up gambolling down the road. This isn't something new; even in the early years of motoring three-wheelers were verbally whipped for their apparent inadequacies and it was thanks to vehicles like the Morgan three-wheeler that completely turned such beliefs on their head, showing three-wheelers could be both speedy and stable — so much so that in 1924 they were banned from competing against four-wheelers as they kept beating them. Some three-wheelers, however, were slow, and there are models that are easier to tip over than others (though this all comes down to design).

All three-wheelers in their design form a triangle from the centre points of each wheel; from these designs most three-wheelers adhere to two basic formats: the Delta or the Tadpole. A Delta format applies to a vehicle that has two wheels parallel to each other at the back and one at the front whereas a Tadpole format is the opposite and applies to a three-wheeler that has two wheels parallel to each other at the front and one at the back. As with most things there are always exceptions. This is demonstrated by vehicles like the 1921 Scott Sociable that had three-wheels though the front and offside rear wheel were in line with both rear wheels being parallel to each other. Perhaps the strangest of layouts was the 1913 Condor in which the front and rear wheels were in line with each other and the third wheel was in the middle at the side of the body. In this case the front and rear wheel steered and the middle wheel was the one that was driven.

Naturally the basic format is just the start of it; the placement of the engine within the triangle is the key factor as to where the centre of gravity sits within the vehicle and thus determines how it will behave. One of the most stable of three-wheel designs is the Tadpole with the weight of the engine between the front two wheels. On fast cornering the weight is transferred onto one of the front wheels. When it comes to Deltas, like the infamous Reliant three-wheeler, the engine is positioned behind the single front wheel and so in fast cornering the weight is thrown sideways and there is nothing there to control it. Deltas that have the engine at the back of the vehicle — like the Bond 875 — are theoretically more stable as the weight is distributed between the rear wheels. Even so, being a Reliant owner myself for many years, a Reliant does not roll as easy as the media and numerous tales would suggest.

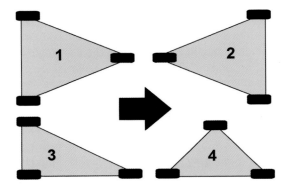

Examples of three-wheel layouts. Diagram 1 and 2 show the most popular layouts of the three-wheeler with two wheels at one end with a single wheel at the other. Diagram 3 shows the unusual layout of having the front and one rear wheel in alignment with each other and the third wheel in alignment with the nearside rear wheel (eg: The 1921 Scott Sociable). Finally diagram 4 displays a layout used on the 1913 Condor with the front and a rear wheel in alignment and the third wheel positioned between them on the opposite side of the body. Author's Collection

One of the main reasons that most early vehicles were three-wheelers and were Delta in design was due to issues making two wheels at the front steer. With a horse and carriage it was easy, as the front wheels were attached to a central pivot point that turned the whole axle and a horse would just pull the carriage in the right direction. With self-propelled vehicles, however, this became more of an issue as this configuration suffered from the fact that any shock load applied to either wheel had substantial leverage on the steering direction, thus making vehicles extremely hard to control. Using one wheel, therefore, eliminated this issue and was also easier to build. Steering with two wheels was something that was not solved until 1817 when Rudolph Ackermann designed a double-pivot method whereby two front wheels could be steered at equal angles. In addition early three-wheelers were steered by tillers — essentially a lever that was pushed or pulled in the opposite direction you wished to go — as it was not until 1894 that the first steering wheel appeared.

Another oft-quoted remark about three-wheelers is that they do not have a reverse gear. Certainly this was true for a great number of vehicles as many were powered by engines from motorcycles where a reverse gear was not required. In the UK, only people with a full car licence could have a reverse gear on a three-wheeler. Motorcycle licence holders with no car licence had to have the reverse gear disabled if it was fitted. This, however, changed as a result of several meetings between Tom Scott from the Reliant Motor Co and the Minister of Transport at the time, Ernest Marples. In 1963 the law was amended and anyone could have a reverse gear on a three-wheeler.

Whilst some may idolise the virtues of a three-wheeler and others curse their existence like a bulldog chewing a wasp, one thing is sure, the three-wheeler is not going to go away any time soon. Even with the dawn of a new Millennium new manufacturers of three-wheel vehicles continue to appear, all aiming to be super-efficient or super-sporty, whilst others, like the mighty Reliant, finally close their doors for good. Perhaps you could say, as one door closes, another door opens...

* In the UK when motorcyclists passed a motorcycle test they would automatically have a B1 category added to their licence that permitted them to drive a three-wheeler weighing up to 450kg. The category definitions changed in 2001 and the B1 category was abolished so this was no longer the case. Further changes were made in January 2013, which, for tests taken after this date, allow a person with a full category A1 motorcycle licence to ride motorised three-wheelers up to a 15kW power output, and a full category A motorcycle licence to ride three-wheelers with a power output exceeding 15kW. (Those with a physical disability are able to drive three-wheelers with a provisional A and B category.) In all cases enquiries should be made with the DVLA for the latest regulations.

About this Book

After riding motorcycles for several years, in 1990 I got my first car — a three-wheel 1974 Reliant Robin — and since then I have just been fascinated by all things three-wheeled. Whilst at University I needed to write a history project that explored the development of a particular subject. Being a Reliant owner and living in Tamworth with the Reliant Motor Co on my doorstep, I thought this would be easy. However, it was whilst researching Reliant that other three-wheelers started to make themselves known and the project turned into the history of the three-wheeler with about 10 times more research than I planned; I even ended up spending beer money on visits to museums to gather more information. At the time I had gathered much more information than I needed and I was not able to use it in the project so, in 2000 when the Internet was becoming established and everyone was buying domain names like there was no tomorrow, I set up www.3-wheelers.com and uploaded all the three-wheel information I had at that point. The response was overwhelming with more and more three-wheelers coming to light and, from that point, I knew that one day I wanted to write a book on three-wheelers. It has taken a long time to get there and so I am, therefore, forever indebted to Crécy Publishing for its belief in such a project and giving this book the green light to go ahead.

Over the years I have been contacted by some wonderful people, many of whom were personally involved with the three-wheelers listed in this book. In fact so many people have contributed to this book that a separate section at the back has been added to include all their names with thanks. Sadly some are no longer with us, including the late John Cleve Graham whose fascination for three-wheelers was parallel to my own and he handed over copious amounts of his own research to assist me with mine. Living in Australia, he even once went on a world tour and stopped by the UK for two days just to visit me and then flew out again.

Initially it was planned that this book would be a definitive list of every three-wheeler known to man (and woman) kind, though as the research intensified more and more vehicles were emerging, many of which I was unable to find information about and, if I am honest, some of them I could not even pronounce as I was unable to translate them. Numerous sources of information have been referred to and I have tried as best as I can to ensure that the information contained within is accurate. I have been fortunate enough to talk to many people actually involved with the vehicles, though for other vehicles I am at the mercy of information already published. Whilst I always seek parallels between various sources, even then this is not always correct as I found with a couple of vehicles after contacting the original designers and indeed as I discovered from the Lane Motor Museum in the USA whilst researching the Martin Martinette, even information published several times over can be wrong. The aim of this book is to still be as concise as possible offering a comprehensive A-Z and also as diverse as possible covering three-wheelers from the early steam-powered monsters to the most innovative of three-wheelers powered by nothing but air. I have also come across the fact that not all three-wheelers have three-wheels; throughout history there have been a few three-wheelers that actually had a fourth wheel hidden away somewhere. In most cases the end with a single wheel is sometimes formed by two wheels either bolted together or set very closely together. As these vehicles were often classed as three-wheelers I have also included these as well.

It took me a while to decide whether vehicles should be listed by their name or by manufacturer, as some vehicles are better known by their model name. However, listing vehicles by model names would have resulted in models from a single manufacturer being scattered throughout the book. After much deliberation, I decided to list them by manufacturer, detailing the models under each heading. For some models the name of the manufacturer is not necessarily that well known and so both models and manufacturers have been detailed separately in the index at the back of the book. It goes without saying that all the old favourites are here but also hopefully a few that you may have never seen before as well.

A Special Thank You

This book was very nearly not completed; two and a half months before the deadline I was struck with an infected forehead cyst combined with facial cellulitis, which is life threatening and, around the eye (which is where mine started), can result in permanent loss of sight. After being hospitalised, it's thanks to all the doctors and nurses who looked after me in the Military Ward at the New Queen Elizabeth Hospital in Birmingham — with special thanks Dr Farya Domah of the Maxillofacial Surgery Unit — that I was discharged alive and well and this book was able to be concluded.

My heartfelt thanks also go to Caroline, my wife, for always being there at my side and to my son, Harvey, for the continued enjoyment he brings into our life.

Elvis Payne
Tamworth, UK
April 2013.

The author with his son Harvey in a 2013 Morgan Three-Wheeler.
Caroline Payne

A

A V Roe & Co Ltd

1921 — Harper Runabout

Designed as a cheap vehicle the Harper Runabout was able to achieve 90-100mpg. This particular vehicle is a 1921 version in the Air & Space Hall at the Museum of Science & Industry, Manchester. UK. MOSI — Museum of Science & Industry, Manchester

The Harper Runabout first appeared in Manchester, UK in 1921. It was designed by Robert Harper and was made in the A V Roe & Co Ltd aircraft factory. The vehicle had an integral body and chassis that was constructed from plywood strengthened by metal castings and had an option of a windscreen for an extra two guineas. It was fitted with a centrally mounted 2.5bhp, two-stroke, single-cylinder, 269cc Villiers engine with a three-speed gearbox and was controlled by motorcycle handlebars. The vehicle featured quarter-elliptic leaf springs attached to all three wheels and offered 90-100mpg (3.1-2.8-litre/100km) at a speed of over 40mph (64km/h). A confidential memorandum sent to agents for the Harper Runabout suggested that, whilst the machine was mechanically capable of carrying two people, it should be sold as a single-seat machine as the makers did not guarantee that the passenger would have the same level of comfort. The Harper Runabout was, therefore, a single-seater with provision for an emergency passenger who sat in tandem behind the driver. Although they were not officially able to compete, two Harpers took part in the Scottish six-day trial in 1922 and are said to have impressed many with their performance in poor weather conditions and steep gradients. In addition to the passenger version, a parcel-carrying model was also created, in which the emergency seat was replaced with a box. Production of the Harper Runabout ceased in 1926 with *circa* 500 vehicles believed to have been made.

A W Wall Ltd

1911 — Tricar

Financed by Sir Arthur Conan Doyle, famous for his Sherlock Holmes' novels, the Wall Tricar was manufactured in Tyseley, Birmingham, UK, by A W Wall Ltd from 1911. As manufacturers of the Roc motorcycle, Wall experimented with a number of unorthodox designs. The Wall Tricar — nicknamed the Roc Egg — had a sidecar type body that was mounted onto a tubular steel chassis and used tiller steering though, in 1914, this was replaced by a more conventional steering wheel. The Tricar had two engine options available: an air-cooled, single-cylinder, 4.5bhp Simplex engine or a twin-cylinder, 6bhp Precision engine that were also used in the company's motorcycles and provided drive to the rear axle. Brakes were fitted on the rear wheel hubs and also on the transmission shaft, the latter operating independently. Production of the Tricar ceased in 1915 and, at present, only two survivors are known to exist.

Nicknamed the 'Roc Egg' the 1911 Wall Tricar was little more than a sidecar body attached to a chassis and running gear. Author's Collection

AC

1904 — Auto Carrier

Established in 1901 as Autocar & Accessories, AC is one of the oldest car manufacturers in the UK. The AC — Auto Carriers Ltd — name came from the name of its first commercial three-wheeler — the Auto Carrier — that was designed and manufactured by John Weller (who was financially backed by John Portwine; a very wealthy butcher). Weller previously had his own business in south London in 1903, making the Weller car, but this was not a great success. The Auto Carrier was built from 1904 as a small delivery vehicle with a large carrying compartment mounted between the two front wheels. It was powered by a 5.6bhp, 648cc, air-cooled, single-cylinder engine that drove the single rear wheel via a two-speed gearbox. The Auto Carrier became very successful and it became very fashionable at the time for companies to have at least one Auto Carrier as a delivery van; Harrods and the General Post Office were amongst the first customers to use them.

A 1910 Auto Carrier delivery vehicle; it was from this model that the name AC derived. Built from 1904 it became very successful. Author's Collection

1907 — Sociable

In 1907 a new a passenger version that was called the AC Sociable was introduced. The name came from the fact that the passenger and driver's seat were side-by-side and not in a tandem design as with many other three-wheelers at the time. It was also the first time that the initials AC were used. The British Army used AC Sociables as a result of their reliability; they were fitted with customised bodywork and acted as machine gun carriers. The AC Sociable continued production up until 1915. During World War 1, AC continued to produce vehicles as well as shells and fuses. For the next few years AC turned to producing four-wheel vehicles.

The AC Sociable, so named as the vehicle featured side-by-side seating, something many other three-wheelers of the time did not have. John Napper

1950 — All Weather Tricycle/All Weather Tricycle Mk II

The AC All Weather Tricycle was introduced in 1950 and was an invalid carriage designed to offer weather protection. Built on a tubular steel chassis with a steel and aluminium body, the vehicle was a single-seater that was fitted with an air-cooled, 249cc BSA C10 engine. The rear of the vehicle was equipped with a large boot that was able to accommodate a folded wheelchair. In 1951 an improved Mk II version was introduced, though production ceased a year later. At present only a single survivor is known to exist.

The AC All Weather was the first invalid carriage built by AC and with it the company attempted to offer full weather protection for its occupant. Stuart Cyphus

Seating two adults the AC Petite — this is a 1954 model — was also advertised as a family car as if only one adult sat inside it then two children could sit in the front. Author's Collection

Whilst having a slight resemblance to the AC Petite, the AC Acedes was a totally different vehicle that was designed as a single-seat invalid carriage. RUMCar News

1953 — Petite/Petite Mk II

In 1953 AC introduced a new three-wheeler in the form of the Petite, which had a steel chassis and a fully enclosed aluminium body that had a roll-back fabric hood. The Petite was powered by an 8.5bhp, single-cylinder, two-stroke, 346cc Villiers Type 27B engine that drove the rear wheels via a three-speed plus reverse gearbox. The interior of the Petite had a large single bench seat that seated two adults or one adult and two children with luggage space available behind the seat. In 1955 a Petite Mk II version was introduced, which had a few minor changes and was powered by a slightly more powerful Villiers engine. The cars (and their van derivatives) were not, however, a great success. Despite a price of £255, plus £53 13s 9d Purchase Tax, the car was said to look like the government-sponsored invalid cars that AC also made and so the Petite were not widely accepted. Production continued until 1958.

1957 — Acedes/Acedes Mk 14/ Acedes Mk 15

In 1957 the AC Acedes was announced that, whilst having a slight resemblance to the AC Petite, was a totally different vehicle and designed as an invalid carriage. Fitted with a steel chassis, the vehicle had a fully enclosed aluminium body — with a convertible version also available — and was powered by a 197cc Villiers Mk 9E engine that was

then uprated to a Villiers Mk 11E engine in 1961. In 1958 an electric model was also introduced; this was driven by a 72V electric motor. In 1967 the Acedes was replaced with the Acedes Mk 14 that now had a full fibreglass body. The Acedes Mk 14, using the same Villiers Mk 11E engine, introduced a 'drop-open' sliding door that pulled outwards and then slid forwards allowing greater access to the vehicle. An Acedes Mk 15 model then followed shortly afterwards, which provided improvements to the rear suspension. Production ceased in 1971.

1971 — Model 70

Arriving in 1971, the AC Model 70 invalid carriage is, perhaps, to many the most memorable invalid three-wheeler. Fitted with a steel chassis and a fibreglass body that had a 'drop-open' sliding door, the interior of the vehicle was adapted to meet the requirements of the individual with options of a tiller, handlebars or a steering wheel. It was powered by a flat-twin, 493cc Steyr-Puch engine with Salisbury variable belt transmission and, as a result, provided a quicker and smoother ride than its predecessors. The vehicle was manufactured until 1978 with the closure of the Department of Health & Social Security Invalid Vehicle Service.

Acoma

1973 — Mini Comtesse (Type 73 and 730E)

Production of the Acoma Mini Comtesse started in Angers, France, in 1973. Powered by a 2.5bhp, 47cc Saxonette engine and started with a pull string, the engine sat on top of the front wheel and so turned with it. The single-seater had a fibreglass body with two types of doors: a standard side opening door on one side and a 'gull-wing' (porte papillon) type on the other. At just 135kg with brakes to the rear wheels only, the vehicle was extremely light and, as a result, was reported to tip over easily. To help stabilise things a pair of 'training wheels' were attached either side of the front wheel. Despite its size, the Mini Comtesse was very successful and Acoma became one of the major microcar manufacturers with a 30% share of the French microcar market. The law in France was also favourable for such vehicles, as a licence was not required to drive them.

The Acoma Mini Comtesse was a single-seater that featured a standard door one side and a gull-wing door that lifted upwards on the other. Hans Bodewes

1977 — Mini Comtesse (Type 770 E2)

The Type 770 was an 'improved' version of the Mini Comtesse and was introduced in 1977 with a different style of body. Again a single-seater, the Type 770 was powered by a 3bhp, 48cc, two-stroke Motobecane engine with a top speed of 24mph (39km/h). An electric version, the Electro-Comtesse, was also introduced. In 1978 the Comtesse became a Super Comtesse with the addition of a fourth wheel. Production of the three-wheelers stopped in 1980 although a number of other four-wheeler variants were also made and produced until around 1984.

Actividades Industriales

1952 — Aisa

Created by Marti Marti and built by Actividades Industriales in Barcelona, Spain, in 1952, the Aisa was powered by a 2bhp, 197cc Hispano-Villiers air-cooled engine. This drove the single rear wheel via a three-speed gearbox and provided a top speed of around 49mph (80km/h). Production ceased in 1957.

Adler

1890 — Der Maikäfer

Adler originally started as a bicycle manufacturer in Frankfurt-am-Main, Germany, in 1880 and supplied wheels to the Benz company for the latter's three-wheeler. In the 1890s Adler produced a number of three-wheelers for Max Cudell, who had the licences from France to build De Dion-Bouton engines though did not have the facilities to build them and so approached Adler. The company then produced a number of four-wheelers; however, in 1930 a three-wheeler called Der Maikäfer ('The May Bug') was introduced. The vehicle was only marketed for a short time before it was abandoned, although it is believed that the vehicle inspired Carl F Borgward to design the three-wheeled Goliath Pioneer in 1931. Adler then concentrated on motorcycles and four-wheelers.

Advance Motor Co

1907 — 6bhp Forecar

Initially the Advance Motor Co in Northampton, UK, started life in 1902 as a bicycle shop that hired out old motorcycles with wicker trailers. The company then started to make its own motorcycles and then in 1907 introduced the 6bhp Forecar. Almost a motorcycle in design with handlebar steering, the Advance Forecar was powered by a 6bhp, 744cc, air-cooled V-twin engine that provided power to the rear wheel via the 'Advance Adjustable Pulley' that had been invented and patented in the same year. The device was said to aid the ascent of steep hills, though the Forecar was also available with an option to have a two-speed gearbox and chain drive.

1907 — 6bhp/9bhp Tricar

Whilst the 6bhp Tricar used the same engine as the Forecar, the 9bhp Tricar was powered by a 1,145cc water-cooled V-twin engine,

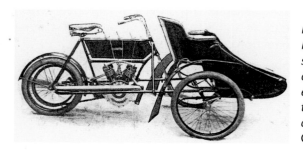

In 1907 the Advance Forecar had a design similar to many other vehicles of its era though was said to be a good hill climber. Author's Collection

which, through a large clutch, powered the rear wheel via two chains. The controls for the vehicle — ignition, air and throttle — were all contained in the steering wheel whilst the front brakes were foot-operated. The Tricar also had a sprung chassis that used semi-elliptical springs and, in addition, both rear and front seats were also sprung. In 1912 the company moved to larger premises and production of motorcycles and Tricars ceased in favour of producing engines and components. The company retained its name in one form or another up until 1979, when it was purchased by the British engineering company GKN plc.

Aermacchi

1947 — Aermacchi

Built at the Macchi aircraft factory in Italy from 1947, the Aermacchi was powered by a flat-twin 750cc engine. The vehicle had eight forward gears and two reverse gears with power going to the rear wheels. From 1950 the engine was uprated to a 973cc two-cylinder, air-cooled diesel engine. The vehicle still had a fully enclosed two-seat cabin and had a variety of bodies that allowed a carrying capacity of 1.5 tons. In 1960 the company was acquired by Harley Davidson and renamed Aermacchi Harley-Davidson SpA. Shortly after that another takeover saw the name change again, this time to AMF-Harley-Davidson Varese SpA. In 1970 the three-wheel division was sold to Fratelli Bennan and three-wheelers continued production as the Bremach.

Able to carry 1.5 tons of cargo the Aermacchi had eight forward and two reverse gears. Author's Collection

Aero Cycle Cars

2003 — BRA CV3

Having purchased the full rights to the BRA CX3 and BRA MG3 — see BRA for more information on these models —Aero Cycle Cars was formed in 2003 in East Sussex, UK, by Arthur Rayner. The company then also went on to purchase the rights to the Citroën-powered BRA CV3 as well and then, following the MSVA — Motor Cycle Single Vehicle Approval — that came into force in August 2003, worked closely with the MSVA authority to ensure that the vehicles complied with the new legislation. For this, a number of changes were made to the chassis design whilst further safety and aesthetic changes were incorporated. The company continues to sell kits for the BRA CV3.

2012 — Aero Merlin

Created by Arthur Rayner in 2012, the Aero Merlin is a classic handmade replica of the Morgan three-wheeler and is made either as a Beetleback — rounded rear end — or Barrelback — sloping rear end — model. The Aero Merlin has a space frame chassis that is clad in aluminium along with various fibreglass components and is powered by a V-twin air-cooled Moto-Guzzi engine with a choice of 850, 950, or a 1,064cc engine. The vehicle is sold either as a complete car in turn-key guise that is fully tested and registered or either a rolling chassis or as a kit to build the vehicle from scratch. The Aero Merlin is available at the time of writing.

The record breaking California Commuter pictured with its financer, Bill Long, and his wife Peggy. Bill was going to drive the vehicle for the Guinness world record attempt though, following a motorcycle accident, the honour was then passed over to the vehicle's creator Doug Malewicki, who set a new world miles per gallon record for both petrol and diesel engines. Doug Malewicki

AeroVisions Inc

1980 — California Commuter (CC)

Created in 1980 by the inventor Doug Malewicki in California, USA, the California Commuter was designed to set a new world record for miles per gallon whilst being driven at legal freeway speed limits. Financed by Bill Long, the CC weighed just 230lb and had a light steel space frame with a single-seat fibreglass body that incorporated a lift-up hatch to gain access. Once in the vehicle, the driver was almost horizontal and used joystick steering controls that included a twist grip throttle, clutch handle and front-brake handle. The rear brake and shifting were foot controlled. With a top speed of 82mph (132km/h), the vehicle was powered by a modified Honda 90cc motorcycle engine that drove the

The handmade 2012 Aero Merlin that features vintage looks with modern mechanics. Aerocycle Cars

Side profile of the Aero Merlin showing a Beetleback rear end and exhaust that runs down the side of the body. Aerocycle Cars

rear wheel by chain. In 1980, the California Commuter set a Guinness world record when it achieved 157.192mpg (1.797-litre/100km) at 55mph (88.5km/h) travelling from Los Angeles to San Francisco on its way to the San Francisco International Auto Show. Travelling 451.3 miles (726.30km) the CC used just 2.87gall of fuel. In 1981, the vehicle then achieved another Guinness world record, this time for a diesel engine when it travelled from Anaheim, California to Las Vegas, Nevada for the Specialty Equipment Manufacturers Association (SEMA) Show and achieved 156.53mpg at 56.3mph (90.6km/h). On this occasion it travelled 263.4 miles (423.90km) and used 1.68gall of diesel. In the same year do it yourself plans were released for the CC that were available — and remain available at the time of writing — from AeroVisions Inc. A 125mpg (2.3-litre/100km) California Commuter II was also designed that could carry three people though, due to other projects, it never reached the prototype stage.

2013 — Electric California Commuter (eCC)

The Electric California Commuter is currently in development in Southern California and is planned to set a new world record in electric mileage efficiency at road legal speed limits. Whilst sharing a similar body design to the CC, the eCC has 25% less aerodynamic drag with an advanced composite carbon fibre monocoque body. The monocoque version will be incredibly strong and will feature an Indy Car/Formula 1 type driver protective cell for enhanced safety. It is estimated to offer an equivalent of more than 400mpg (0.70-litre/100km) at a steady freeway speed of 65mph (104.6km/h) and have a top speed of 90+mph (144.8km/h). At the time of writing, it is

hoped a new energy efficiency record will be set in 2013 with the ultimate aim to set a record that is the equivalent of around 500mpg equivalent (0.56-litre/100km). At this level of efficiency, a small affordable solar panel collector system that delivers useful energy all day long to deep cycle storage batteries can be used to recharge the eCC at night. The goal is to be totally off the grid and never again have to use fossil fuels for commuting or ever waste time at a petrol station.

AF Cars

1969 — AB1/Spider

The first AF was created in 1969 by Alexander Fraser though it was not until a few years later that he formed AF Cars. Working for Antique Automobiles, Fraser created the first AF prototype, which was initially called AF AB1, in his kitchen. The idea was that the car would have the character of a vintage three-wheeler but would be practical enough for everyday use. Having experience of the Mini Cooper, the AF was based around a Mini front sub-frame, engine unit and running gear. Apart from a fabricated mounting for the rear trailing arm, the rest of the car was made out of wood with a hardwood frame, finished with aluminium panels and mahogany-faced marine ply board. The prototype was fitted with a 1,275cc engine that was left exposed and a Shorrocks supercharger. It had a 22gall alloy fuel tank, tow bar and was generously equipped with dashboard instruments. Despite the model's excellent handling and speed, it was too heavy at the time to be classed as tricycle in the UK tricycle taxation class. The production model of the AF Spider, as it now became known, was then created but was different in a number of ways in a bid to reduce weight and get it into the tricycle taxation class. The 22gall tank was replaced by a 9gall tank, the dashboard had fewer instruments and fibreglass panels were used in place of aluminium. In addition the vehicle had lower wings and smaller running boards.

The AF Spider was a two-seater based around a Mini front sub frame, engine and running gear and featured large wooden running boards. Peter Frost

With more conventional looks, around five AF Grand Prix vehicles were built from 1969 to 1980 with some using a highly tuned Cooper 'S' engine. Peter Frost

1969 — Grand Prix

As the looks of the AF Spider were criticised by some, a new Grand Prix model was made. This had a similar construction to the Spider but, amongst other changes, now featured mudguards instead of wings, a different rear end and an altered windscreen. The Grand Prix was powered by 850-1,275cc Mini engines with some having a highly tuned Cooper 'S' engine that gave the vehicle a top speed in excess of 100mph (161km/h). In 1980 AF Cars started to make four-wheelers, and Alexander Fraser then went on to form Lion Omnibuses that specialised in producing scale (two thirds) replicas of vintage trucks and buses. In total around seven Spiders and five of the Grand Prix model were made between 1969 and 1980.

Aichi Kigyo Co Ltd

1947 — Cony AA11/ AA12/ AA13/AA14/ AA15/AA24/AA25/ AA26/AA27/AA28

Manufactured from 1947 in Nagoya, Japan, Aichi Kokuki KK built three-wheelers under the name of Cony. A number of three-wheel commercial vehicles were made with engines varying from a 359cc two-cylinder engine in the lighter vehicles to a 1.5-litre, water-cooled, four-cylinder engine in a two-ton three-wheel truck. Production started with the Cony AA11 in 1947, which was built in varying versions through to the AA15 in 1959. Using the same base structure, each had slight differences in style or length of the rear bed. The AA15 was followed by the Cony AA24, which was made from 1959 and evolved into the AA26 and the AA28 in 1960. In 1959 the Cony AA27 pick-up truck was introduced; this was fitted with a two-cylinder, horizontally-opposed, air-cooled, OHV 359cc engine. The company was absorbed into the Nissan group in 1965 though the AA27 continued in production until 1970.

The Cony AA27 was a lightweight delivery truck that had a single-seat cabin. Author's Collection

Aimers McLean & Co Ltd

1960 — Gnat

Designed for golf courses, forestry grounds, estates and parks, the Gnat was a three-wheel cross-country vehicle introduced in 1960 and manufactured by Aimers McLean & Co Ltd in Scotland. The author also had an email about one being used at a research station in the sub-Antarctic. The vehicle was the pre-cursor to the three-wheel ATV trikes that took off in the 1970s. The Gnat was an open two-seater with a steel tube chassis and frame that was controlled by tiller steering and powered by a 400cc, 10bhp, air-cooled, Briggs & Stratton four-stroke engine. This drove the rear wheels independently by chains through a three-speed Albion gearbox. In addition to eight-inch disc brakes, each wheel has wide tyres measuring 14in across to improve traction in muddy areas. This combined with a 12in ground clearance meant the Gnat could climb a 1 in 1 gradient with a stability of sideways tilt in excess of 30°. The vehicle proved to be a true workhorse being able to carry 650lb and pull up to 950lb on its tow bar. The Gnat could reach 25mph (40km/h) though a Gnat Mk 2 model was also introduced that was governed to just 15mph (24km/h), which resulted in many owners replacing the engine for a more powerful one. Production ceased in the late 1970s.

1960 — Gnat (New Zealand)

From 1960 to 1976 the Gnat was also made by A J Cameron Lewis & Co Ltd in Christchurch, New Zealand with the same specifications as the Gnat though initially fitted with an air-cooled, 160cc, Villiers engine.

Airomobile

1937 — Airomobile

The Airomobile was a one-off prototype that, although stimulating great interest, never made it into production. Plans for the Airomobile were first drawn up in 1934 by Paul Lewis in the USA. Lewis believed that the three-wheel configuration would meet his needs for streamlining and economy. After many technical problems were sorted out with the vehicle, it was eventually built in 1937. The vehicle was powered by a horizontally-opposed, 129cu in, OHV, air-cooled four-cylinder unit (57bhp) created by the Dorman Marks Engine Co.

The body was created from steel and was very aerodynamic, trailing to the rear and having two large fish like fins. The Airomobile did have a very low centre of gravity and was said to take corners faster than any four-wheeler at the time. Lewis toured the USA on

Said to corner faster than any four-wheeler, the Airomobile was extremely aerodynamic for its time. Pete Shirk

a promotional tour with the Airomobile covering over 45,000 miles (72,400km). Prospective dealers were told that they would not be able to follow the Airomobile for one mile over rough terrain without damaging their driving mechanism. Lewis would then drive through ploughed fields and ditches without the need to slow down and return to show no damage had been sustained to the vehicle. As a result many dealers became interested in the Airomobile and Lewis was able to establish possible dealers throughout the USA.

In 1938 the Airomobile was slightly redesigned with a new front section that included the lights being moved from the top of the wings and built into them. Lewis again toured the USA but interest in the vehicle had diminished and plans to put the vehicle into full production were squashed with the onset of World War 2 and so the vehicle never became anything more than a prototype. The vehicle still survives and currently lives at The National Automobile Museum in Reno, Nevada, USA.

Whilst the aeronautical themed rear plane type wings are the most eye-catching things at the back of the Airomobile, the mind also wonders how easy it was to refuel with the centrally positioned fuel cap on the top.
Pete Shirk

All Cars

1974 — Charly

The Charly was an Italian car sold in France from 1974 and was designed by the beach buggy maker Autozodiaco; it was also sold under the name of All Cars Snuggy. The Charly was a two-seat vehicle that was powered by a 49cc four-speed Moto Morini engine. The body was made from fibreglass and unusually all vehicles were equipped with right-hand drive. From 1977 a Charly II version was available with a larger Motori BCB 125cc engine and then, from 1982, the range was updated with the Charly III that now offered automatic transmission for both the 49cc and 125cc models.

1974 — Charly Camel

Powered by the same 49cc engine, the Camel was fitted with large wheels thus almost becoming a dune buggy version.

The All Cars Charly was also sold under the name of Snuggy that perhaps describe the interior with large adults on board. Pol de Carnières

Showing the company's beach buggy heritage the All Cars Charly Camel had the same specification as a standard model though was fitted with large knobbly tyres. John Lloyd

1974 — Charly Tobruk

The Tobruk was a convertible version of the Charly that was powered by the 125cc engine. The rear of the body on the Tobruk was almost vertical and, whilst the roof had been cut away, it was fitted with a detachable canvas top and sides that again were much squarer in shape and so offered more internal space compared with other models with the roof on. The Tobruk also had a spare wheel that was fastened to the rear. All the three-wheel range was manufactured until 1985 when they were then replaced with the four-wheel Charly 4.

Allard

1953 — Clipper

The Allard Clipper was first created in south London, UK, in 1953 by the sports car maker Sydney Allard. Despite winning the 1952 Monte Carlo Rally in a sports car of his own design, the sales of Allard sports cars were swamped by manufacturers like Jaguar and so Sydney Allard decided to design an economical car. The Allard Clipper was designed by David Gottleib and was said to have an 'indestructible' fibreglass body that was impregnated with colour throughout and made by Hordern-Richmond Ltd. The first vehicle was registered and licensed on 15 April 1954 and this made it the first production car in the UK to have a fibreglass body. It was fitted with a 346cc Villiers single-cylinder, two-stroke engine that powered the left rear wheel by a chain via a Burman gearbox. Unfortunately the Allard Clipper was to suffer from many problems; these included cooling and weak drive shafts and so manufacture ceased in 1955. Initially the original

production plan was to have a run of 100 vehicles though only 22 were made. It is believed at present that only two vehicles still exist.

Alta

1967 — 700

Manufactured from 1967 in Greece. The Alta 700 truck was an all-purpose three-wheeler that had a number of bodies ranging from a pick-up to a van. Powered by a 35bhp BMW two-cylinder horizontal engine mounted at the rear, the Alta 700 is described as being one of the most successful three-wheelers in Greece. It had a fibreglass cab that contained two seats and, with its combination of rear bodies, boasted a payload of up to 800kg. In 1970 a passenger vehicle under the name of Alta was also produced under licence from Fuldamobil. This was also a two-seater powered by a 198cc Fichtel & Sachs engine. Alta also produced some BMW 700s under licence in the 1980s. Production of the Alta A700 ceased in 1982.

Altona

1947 — Condor

The Altona Condor was built in Hoboken, Antwerp, Belgium, in 1947 at the Altona factory. The owner of the factory — Mr De Belder — was an ex-engineer of the famous Minerva car factory and only one prototype of the Condor was ever built. The vehicle had a canvas roof

Made by the sports car maker Sydney Allard, the Allard Clipper was an attempt to break into the economy car market though only 22 were made. Author's Collection

Said to steer like a cow whilst braking is futile, the Altona Condor was a one-off prototype built at the Altona factory. A-1 Classic Cars, Maastricht

whilst the body was made from steel that was attached to a wooden frame. It was powered by a 20bhp 800cc two-cylinder air-cooled engine that powers the rear wheel via a chain. The Condor still exist today though it reportedly 'Steers like a cow whilst braking is futile and it accelerates in increments of metre/minute.'

American Microcar Inc

1979 — Microcar

Introduced in 1979 in New York, USA, the Microcar — also called the Tri-Ped — was built by American Microcar Inc, a company that also used the name of American Tri-Ped Corp. It was fitted with an air-cooled, single-cylinder, two-stroke, 49cc engine — the earlier vehicles had Minarelli engines and later ones used Tomos engines — that drove the rear wheels via a two-speed gearbox. To start the vehicle the driver had to pedal until the centrifugal clutch started the engine. Built around a light tubular steel frame, the vehicle had handlebars and a bench seat for two people; it was also provided with a windscreen and a canvas roof. Optional side curtains were also available. Production is believed to have ended in 1985.

A 1979 advertisement for the American Microcar that was also known as the Tri-Ped on account of the driver needing to pedal to start the 49cc engine. Author's Collection

Ammar Motor Co

1990 — K-SL1/K-SL2/K-SL3/ K-SL4/K-SL5/K-SL6

Under the leadership of Haider Bilgrami, the Ammar Motor Co, based in Karachi, Pakistan, started development of three-wheelers in 1990; these are produced along with a range of four-wheelers. The new three-wheelers were designed whilst assisting the government of Pakistan in its efforts to phase out noise and atmospheric pollution. The vehicles — built both in Pakistan and in China by Shandong Pioneer Motorcycle Co Ltd — all have eco-friendly, fuel-efficient engines. The 650cc, four-stroke, water-cooled engine combined with a five-speed gearbox is used throughout the three-wheel range. The vehicles were available in numerous body types, including the following models:

- The K-SL1: A fully enclosed five-door vehicle.
- The K-SL2: A fully enclosed four-door vehicle.
- The K-SL3 and K-SL4 range: A four- or five-seat open vehicle with fold down roof.
- The K-SL5 range: A fully enclosed cab with a pick-up truck type rear.
- The K-SL6 range: An open cab (no doors) with a pick-up truck type rear.

Whilst manufacture ceased in Pakistan during the first decade of the 21st century, production continues at the time of writing in China. The range is also distributed throughout the USA as the Wildfire.

Aptera Motors

2007 — Aptera Hybrid/ Aptera 1e/Aptera 1h

Designed by Accelerated Composites, California, USA, the 'Aptera hybrid' started development in January 2006 when the company stated that the vehicle was to be a 330mpg (0.8-litre/100km) vehicle capable of 65mph (104.6km/h) using a diesel 12bhp engine combined with a 25bhp electric motor. With a planned weight of 850lb the two-seat coupé — with a centre mounted infant seat — was estimated to have a 0-60mph (0-96km/h) time of 11sec with a top speed, electronically limited, of 95mph (152.8km/h). The shape of the Aptera came from extensive optimisation in a virtual wind tunnel that produced a vehicle with a drag coefficient of 0.15. In 2007 the Aptera Typ-1e and Typ-1h were officially launched. Both versions were front-wheel drive — unlike previous versions that had a belt driven rear wheel — and, whilst the Aptera 1e was an all-electric model with a reported range of 120 miles (193km), the Aptera 1h was a petrol/electric hybrid that gave 300mpg (0.9-litre/100km) though, due to concerns over emissions, the diesel engine was dropped. Solar cells in the roof powered the 'always-on' climate control system. Both the 1e and the 1h had a planned 2008 delivery date though by 2009 no vehicles had been delivered.

2008 — Aptera 2e/Aptera 2h

The company enhanced the electric version with the Aptera 2e in 2008. Enhancements included wider door openings, aerodynamic side mounted mirrors, LED lighting inside and out, GPS navigation, RFID key fob and a 0-60mph (0-96km/h) time of less than 10sec. An Aptera 2h was also developed that was a series hybrid; this meant the engine — a small water cooled EFI petrol engine coupled with a 12kW generator — would have been used to recharge the batteries rather than power the vehicle. It was claimed that with a tank capacity of five gallons of fuel that the Aptera 2h would have a range of around 600-700 miles (965-1,125 km). It was hoped that there would be 100,000 electric Apteras on the road by 2015; however, on 2 December 2011 the company went into liquidation. The production rights, patents, tooling and equipment were then purchased by Zaptera USA Inc in 2012. The new owners plan to build the vehicles in conjunction with the Zhejiang Jonway Group in China. The latter will be building the composite chassis and then exporting them to the USA for final assembly. In 2012, an Aptera 2e, under the name of Zaptera, was displayed at the Beijing Auto Show in China with an announcement that the Zaptera would enter production by 2013. At the time of writing no further announcements have been made.

The Aptera was a hybrid vehicle stated to achieve 330mpg (0.8-litre/100km) whilst travelling at 65mph (104km/h) though the company went into liquidation before full production started. Aptera Motors

Manufactured in Turkey in the 1960s the Arçelik Triportör was a lightweight goods vehicle designed for narrow crowded streets. Anthony Phillipson

Arçelik

1960s — Triportör

The Arçelik Triportör was produced in Turkey in the late 1960s by the Turkish consumer goods manufacturer Arçelik. The vehicle was based on Italian Lambretta scooter mechanicals and was available with either a 125cc or 250cc single-cylinder engine. The body was made from fibreglass and, as the vehicle was very slim, it was a popular solution to the problem of urban delivery in narrow and crowded streets.

Ariel

1896 — Tricycle

Ariel was established in 1870 by James Staley and William Hillman in Birmingham, UK, shortly after they invented the tensioned wire spoke wheel. At first the company produced penny-farthing bicycles under the tradename Ariel but, by 1896, it had ventured into motorised transport. Considered to be the best tricycle available at the time, the Ariel Tricycle was a single-seater that initially had a 2.25bhp 239cc De Dion-Bouton engine mounted behind the rear axle. This, however, caused a tail-heavy vehicle that would topple backwards in certain situations and so the rear frame was extended with the result that

A 1904 advertisement for the Ariel Tri-Car powered by an air-cooled 3.5bhp engine. Grace's Guide

the engine (now 1.75bhp) could sit forward of the rear axle. The vehicle had a cylindrical tank fitted behind the seat that formed part of the water-cooling system that circulated water around a cast passage that sat on top of the engine. With a top speed of around 20mph (32km/h) the vehicles proved to be very popular but eventually fell out of favour due to its inability to carry passengers.

1905 — Tri-car

Ariel was also manufacturing quadricycles alongside its three-wheeler and, by 1905, the tricycle had evolved into the Tri-car. The Tri-car, powered by a 3.5bhp air-cooled engine, followed the trend for such vehicles at the turn of the century with a motorcycle type body and a passenger seating located in between the two front wheels. By 1910 Ariel created a four-wheeler that replaced all existing models and then went on to concentrate on cars and motorcycles. In 1944 Ariel was taken over the BSA group though the Ariel name was used once more in 1970 for a 50cc two-stroke moped that was launched called the Ariel 3 (see BSA on page 48 for more information).

Available as a two-seater or a truck, the Moto-Cor was featured acetylene headlamps and an oil lamp at the rear. Author's Collection

Armino Mezzo

1920 — Moto-Cor

Available with a number of bodies ranging from a two-seat passenger version to a 4.5cwt tip truck the Moto-Cor was first built in 1920 and was manufactured by Armino Mezzo in Turin, Italy. It was fitted with an air-cooled, twin-cylinder, 575cc engine and then, from 1921, an OHV, 745cc engine was also available. Both engines provided drive to the single rear wheel by a chain through a three-speed gearbox with reverse. Lighting was provided through two methods: the headlights were acetylene and the tail lamp was an oil lamp. In 1924 the vehicles were replaced with a four-wheel version though, due to the lack of funds, it did not go into production and the company closed down.

Arola

1976 — Type 10/11/12

Arola started to produce three-wheelers in France in 1976. The first generation of three-wheelers was the Type 10 and 11, which were powered by a 3bhp 47cc Fichtel & Sachs Saxonette engine with two automatic gears, whilst the Type 12 had a 50cc Motobécane engine that also had a reverse gear. The body of the vehicle was made from fibreglass whilst the doors were made completely in Plexiglas. A single-seater, the Type 10 and 11 could reach 25mph (40km/h) whilst the Type 12 could reach 40mph (64km/h). Apart from the engine, the Type 11 and 12 were essentially the same as the Type 10 with slight cosmetic differences and were manufactured until 1978.

1978 — Arola SP (Super Pratique)

Introduced in 1978, the Super Pratique was a pick-up version of the Type 12. This was almost the same as the Type 12 though slightly longer with the addition of a rear loading area and was produced until 1982.

At the time these vehicles could be driven in France without a car licence. From 1982 Arola continued to make further models that were all based on four wheels. In 1983 the company was acquired by Aixam that continue to make four-wheel micro-cars at the time of writing.

Arrowhead

1936 — Arrowhead

Designed by Wellington Everett Miller in 1936, the Arrowhead was a one-off custom vehicle built for the Arrowhead Spring Water Co in the USA. As sales were being hit by the depression at that time, the company decided on a vehicle that would advertise itself. Built by the Advance Body Co in Los Angeles, USA, the design of the Arrowhead was shaped like a drop of water with a tapered end and a dorsal fin at the top of the car carrying the company's name. The design of the body was very advanced for its time and it was advertised as 'America's first fully streamlined automobile'. Powered by a Ford V8 engine the Arrowhead was perhaps the only three-wheeler that had an engine at the rear, which drove the front wheels

With a body made of fibreglass the Arola had side doors made completely in Plexiglas that offered good all round visibility. Author's Collection

Made in 1936 as a one-off custom vehicle built for the Arrowhead Spring Water Co the Arrowhead was advertised as 'America's first fully streamlined automobile'. Alden Jewell

Arzens
1942 — L'Oeuf

Created in Paris, France, in 1942 the Arzens L'Oeuf (Arzens Egg) is noted as being the world's first true bubble car. Designed and built by Paul Arzens, the vehicle was constructed from hand-formed aluminium with a windscreen and curved side doors made of Plexiglas. (Plexiglas at the time was a new material.) Initially the L'Oeuf was electric-powered, supplied from five 12V 250amp batteries that powered an electric motor on the single rear wheel. After World War 2 this was

via a prop shaft. As a result the front wheels were fixed and steering was done via the rear wheel that turned almost 360°. The body consisted of a wooden frame that was covered with aluminium that was complete with teardrop-shaped headlights. Inside the vehicle the driver sat in the middle. It is believed that the vehicle was badly damaged in a crash in 1937 and its ultimate fate is unknown.

replaced with a 125cc engine. The vehicle was used by Arzens up until his death aged 87 in 1990; it is now in the Transportation Museum in Mulhouse, France.

Built by Paul Arzens in 1942 the Arzens L'Oeuf was built from hand formed aluminium and had a curved windscreen and side doors made of Plexiglas. Robert Iveson

With a large Plexiglas type dome Arzens L'Oeuf was the world's first true bubble car. Robert Iveson

Ateliers de Construction de Janville

1924 — Villard (Sports/Touring/Commercial)

After the Columbe Cyclecar (see page 59) went out of production in 1924, M Villard redesigned the vehicle, incorporating a number of improvements and reintroduced it using his own name in the same year. The Villard was manufactured in Oise, France, from 1924 and had a steel chassis with a body made from metal sheets. It was powered by a single-cylinder, two-stroke, 346cc Harissard engine that drove the single front wheel via a six-speed friction transmission and single chain. The Villard came in two versions: the first was a two-seat touring model capable of 35mph (56km/h) and the second was a sports model that could reach 50mph (80.4km/h). A number of customised versions were also made for handicapped victims from World War 1. By 1927 Villard also began to make four-wheelers and, by 1931, the three-wheeler was built as a light delivery van powered by a 350cc Chaise engine. It was in this form that the most three-wheelers were sold. Construction of Villard three-wheelers stopped in 1935.

Atomette

1921 — Atomette

First built in 1921 by Allan Thomas of Cleveland Street, Wolverhampton, UK, the Atomette was a single-seat vehicle of which only a few prototypes were built. In 1922 a two-seat model, powered by a 3.5bhp, 343cc Villiers two-stroke engine, was introduced. The engine was mounted just in front of the single rear wheel and drove a chain through a Burman three-speed gearbox that had a final drive via a belt. Weighing 280lb the vehicle had a top speed of 30mph (48km/h). The only weather protection afforded to its occupants was the vertical windscreen as it had no doors and real body to speak of. The Atomette had an ingenious device that allowed adjustment of the steering column rake. Production ceased in 1922 with few vehicles being sold.

Auto Body Craft

1969 — ABC Tricar

Originally called the Trimini, the ABC Tricar from Auto Body Craft of Brierley Hills, Staffordshire, UK, is believed to be the first three-wheeler to be based on the Austin Mini. Designed and built from 1969 by Bill Powell and Ken Heather, the vehicle used the complete front end of a Mini but with the rear end cut away whilst retaining the floor pan with a strengthened sub-frame. The two-seater had a fibreglass body and is believed to have been in production until around 1974, with 25 to 30 vehicles being built.

Auto Mirage

1976 — Mirage 3

The Mirage 3 was first manufactured in 1976 by Auto Mirage in Bologna, Italy, and locally did not require a licence to drive it. The vehicle was powered by a 49.9cc Motori moped engine that drove the single rear wheel. The fibreglass body featured seats for both driver and a very small passenger.

Despite having a 49cc engine the Mirage 3 featured two seats for a driver and a very small passenger. Pol de Carnières

Left: *The Atomette offered very little in terms of protection against the weather though did have an ingenious device that allowed the driver to adjust the steering wheel.* Author's Collection

The Auto Mirage SR3 fitted with a 125cc engine. Thomas Tutchek

1981 — SR3

In 1981 the SR3 was introduced; this had a much squarer body and was fitted with a 125cc BCB engine. The vehicle sold very well until production ceased in 1985. A SR4 version then introduced was a four-wheeler.

Autoette Electric Car Company Inc

1947 — Autoette Cruise About

The Autoette Cruise About was first manufactured in 1947 in Long Beach, California, USA, by the Autoette Electric Car Co Inc (AECC) that was founded by Royce Seevers. The Cruise About was a two-seat electric vehicle that was initially driven by a converted 24V Dodge 1.5bhp electric starter motor though, later in the vehicle's life, a proprietary motor was built

Powered by an electric motor, this 1960 Mobilette has more than a passing similarity to the Autoette.
Larry Fisher

that drew its power from either three or four 6V batteries. With a range of around 30 miles (48km) on a single charge, the motor powered the rear wheels through a three-speed with reverse gearbox and provided a top speed of up to 16mph (26km/h). The vehicle had a steel chassis and an open steel body, and also found favour as an Invalid Carriage as a result of its ease of use and tiller steering. The Cruise About was produced in various forms until the early 1970s.

1948 — Pick-up Truck/Golfmobile

The Autoette was also available as a Pick-up Truck; this was a single-seater that had a slightly higher back allowing it to carry up to a ¼ton. It also served as a Golfmobile, specifically designed for carrying two people and their clubs across the course. Both versions were made until the early 1970s.

1960 — Mobilette

The company later purchased Mobilette Electric Car Sales & Service of Long Beach, California, which made the Mobilette that was a competitor to the Autoette. The Mobilette was very similar to the Autoette with a number of parts for it actually being made by AECC. Production of the Mobilette ceased in 1969.

B & B Speciality Co

1946 — Brogan

B & B Speciality Co was established in Ohio, USA, in 1946. Its first three-wheeler was the Brogan, which took its name from its designer and builder, Frank Brogan, whose first product had been a beer pump. The Brogan evolved from a motor scooter and so was a small two-seat car with a five-foot wheelbase and was less than four feet high to the top of the windscreen. Powered by an air-cooled, rear-mounted, 10bhp engine, the vehicle could reach 45-50mph (72.4-80.4km/h) at 65-70mpg (4.3-4-litre/100 km). The vehicle was modified over the years and came in many different forms, including a passenger car with a hard top and a light delivery truck with an open back that had a load carrying capacity of 500lb.

1946 — Broganette

A Broganette model was also manufactured in 1946; this was classed as a motor-scooter with a scooter type seat. It had handle bar steering and was powered by a 3bhp engine producing speeds of around 35-40mph (56-64km/h) at 85mpg (3.3-litre/100km). By 1951 the vehicle became the Broganette Deluxe and had completely changed, becoming more car like with two wheels at the front and a 10ft (three-metre) long body. The engine was also up rated to a 10bhp Onan engine. Production of all vehicles ceased in 1952.

Above: Made under licence to the Reliant Motor Co, the B & N Plastics Robin BN-1 was built from 2001 and featured many updates compared with its Reliant counterpart. Author's Collection

B & N Plastics

2001 — Robin BN-1

Led by Les Collier, B & N Plastics began production on 30 April 2001 in Suffolk, UK, and, under licence from the Reliant Motor Co Ltd, started to manufacture the Reliant Robin under the model's new name: the Robin BN-1. The new vehicles, whilst sharing many of the components found in Reliant's vehicles, had many new features, including a reengineered gearbox and axle for increased power along with a completely new interior. The vehicle strongly followed Reliant's original and Reliant provided the running chassis. This consisted of an 850cc aluminium air-cooled engine attached to a galvanised chassis giving the Robin BN-1 a fuel economy of around 80mpg (3.3-litre/100km). The body of the Robin BN-1 was made from fibreglass, as in the original, and was officially launched on 12 July 2001.

2001 — Robin BN-2

On the day of the BN-1's launch, a Robin BN-2 was also announced; this was finished in light reactive paint so that the vehicle changed colour. This was also the first Reliant Robin in history to feature electric windows and CD player as standard. A small handful of these new vehicles were shipped to Reliant dealers in January 2002. In July 2002 the company announced plans to make an electric-powered Robin that would have a range of 50 miles (80km) between charges and a top speed of 50-55mph (80.4-88.5km/h). Due to various problems, production of all vehicles was put on hold in October 2002 and no further vehicles have been made by the date of writing.

B & Z Electric Car Co (Electric Car Co)

1961 — Model 167

Founded in 1961 in Long Beach, California, USA, the B & Z Electric Car Co made a number of electric vehicles, both three- and four-wheelers. The model 167 was a two-seater that had tiller steering with a single wheel at the front. The body was low cut and, whilst having a roof, there were no side windows.

1963 — Electra King

The Electra-King was perhaps the company's best-known vehicle and was first introduced in 1963. A two-seater, the vehicle had many uses ranging from golf buggy to trucks, with a number of body designs that were mainly used at airports and factories. As a result there were numerous models based around the Electra-King, including a four-wheel version that was built from 1968 to 1970.

Prior to 1972 vehicles were powered by a 1bhp DC electric motor that gave a top speed of around 18mph (29km/h) with a range of 45 miles (72km). Some are known to have been powered from army surplus tank turret motors. From 1972 four new motors were introduced with the most powerful giving the vehicle a top speed of 36mph (58km/h). Early vehicles had four batteries whilst later ones had six.

Production ceased in 1980, though at the time of writing the company still sells a range of imported electric cars; the business is now called the Electric Car Co.

B E Dickinson Toledo Engineering Works

1903 — Morette

The Dickinson Morette was manufactured by B E Dickinson Toledo Engineering Works from 1903 in Aston Brook Lane, Birmingham, UK. The single-seat machine was powered by a 1.5bhp engine whilst the 'sociable' two-seater was powered by either a 2.5bhp or a 4bhp two-cylinder engine. Both variations provided power to the front wheel by chain. Despite being very high, the car was unique for its day in that it could be started from the driver's seat by means of a flexible chord that fitted into a groove in the flywheel. When the chord was pulled this would then fire up the engine. A pulley on the crankshaft was then brought into frictional driving contact with a rubber covered wheel on a lay shaft by lowering the steering tiller. This gave the Morette a top speed of around 12-15mph (19-24km/h). Lifting the tiller would lift the engine out of action whilst braking applied a double brake and cut off the fuel supply to the engine.

The body and seat of the Morette were constructed from steel tubing whilst the floor of the vehicle was made from wood carried across the steel tubes. The wheels were all the same size and so were completely interchangeable; they featured 'specially thickened driver tyres' that helped prevent the risk of punctures and prolong the life of the tyre. Production of the Dickinson Morette ceased in 1905.

Badsey Bullet

1979 — Badsey Bullet

Equipped with a Yamaha 1,074cc motorcycle engine, the Badsey Bullet had a top speed of 150mph (241km/h) and a 0-60mph (0-96km/h) time of 4.6sec. It was first created in 1979 by Bill Badsey in South Africa; production subsequently moved to California, USA. The Bullet

Featuring twin cockpits, the Badsey Bullet lived up to its name with a top speed of 150mph whilst a Silver Bullet version was claimed to reach more than 180mph.
Dave Norton

featured a unique fibreglass body that had separate cockpits with forward opening fighter-style cockpit canopies between which the engine sat. Power was provided to the rear wheel by means of a shaft drive and the vehicle had two gear levers that gave it 20 forward and five reverse gears. A Silver Bullet version with a turbo-charged Yamaha 1,200cc Russ Collins Engineered engine that offered 200bhp and a claimed 180mph+ (290km/h) was also created. Around eight vehicles were sold in South Africa and the USA between 1979 and 1983.

Bajaj

Bajaj was founded in 1926 by Jamnalal Bajaj in Pune, Mumbai, India, though it was not until 1950 that the first Bajaj three-wheeler appeared built under licence from Piaggio/Vespa. All vehicles were mechanically the same but featured many different bodies; available models included taxis, vans and pick-up trucks. In 1963 Bajaj took over the Tempo/Hanomoh range (see Vidal & Sohn Tempo-Werke GmbH on page 269 for more information) of three-wheelers and added medium sized trucks to its range of light three-wheelers. In 1985 Bajaj joined forces with the Hindalco Aluminium Co and designed a three-wheel enclosed car with an aluminium body. High production costs, however, saw very few vehicles made.

Bajaj passenger vehicles are imported all over the world, this particular one being used for carrying goods and spotted by the author whilst in Kenya in 2009. Author's Collection

Like the first vehicles, modern Bajajs still have many different body configurations from bare bones chassis, through rickshaws to fully enclosed vans, with differing gross vehicle weights. The pressed steel chassis of the Bajaj has an electro deposited anti-rust base coat.

1950 — Goods Carriers: GC Max Series/RE600

The GC Max series was designed as a range of commercial vehicles with a ladder chassis and twin shock absorbers to allow a higher load capacity of up to 600kg. Powered by either a 416cc Japanese Kubota diesel engine (GC Max Diesel) or a 200cc four-stroke petrol engine (GC Max CNG/RE600) commercial vehicles are available with either a pick-up or full van body.

1950 — Passenger Carriers: RE25 Series

Bajaj manufactures a wide range of passenger vehicles that are designed for more comfort when carrying passengers. The engines come in many configurations running on petrol, CNG, LPG or diesel and range from a 145.45cc, two-stroke, air-cooled petrol engine to a 173.52cc, four-stroke, air cooled engine as well as a 416cc diesel version.

Another Bajaj, this one a passenger version serving as a taxi in Katmandu in 1994. John Cleve Graham

The Bajaj is exported all over the world with the USA being a significant market. The vehicles have passed some of the world's strictest emission standards and, for the US market, a number of improvements have been made; these include a full, laminated glass wraparound windscreen, dual headlights, a fully hydraulic braking system, an anti-dive front end and a limp home system if the vehicle is running low on fuel. As a significant manufacturer of motorcycles, Bajaj is currently ranked as the world's fourth largest manufacturer of two- and three-wheelers,

Baldet

1957 — Bluebird

Andre Baldet was the main agent for Isettas in the Midlands during the 1950s and 1960s in addition to selling various other microcars and scooters through the Moto Baldet dealership. Created in 1957 by Baldet, the Baldet Bluebird used an Isetta chassis and engine and was built from a vehicle that had been written off in an accident. The Bluebird used the front end of a Renault Dauphine including front panel, bonnet and wings with separate small folding windscreens for the driver and passenger. The rear of the vehicle was made from fibreglass with a rounded section that covered the single rear wheel.

Baldi Mini Auto

1971 — Amica

Based in Ravenna, Italy, Baldi Mini Auto (BMA) started to manufacture three-wheelers in 1971 with the Amica. This was built from 1971 to

Although not present in this image the BMA Amica also featured detachable gull wing canvas doors.
Nagy Róbert

1980 and had an ABS body with detachable gull-wing canvas doors attached to a tubular chassis. The vehicle was a two-seater powered by a 223cc engine. The Amica was also exported to France from 1976 under the William brand and was powered by a 125cc engine.

1979 — Brio

Introduced in 1979, the BMA Brio was a single-seat tricycle that used a handlebar for steering. It was powered by a 47cc Fichtel & Sachs engine, giving a top speed of around 25mph (40km/h). The Brio was also imported to France by William with a 47cc Saxonette engine. The Brio was produced in Italy until 1984.

1980 — Nuova

Replacing the Amica in 1980, the BMA Nuova was not only powered by a choice of air-cooled two-stroke petrol engines — 49cc and 125cc along with a two-cylinder, three-stroke 250cc — but was also available with a 359cc diesel engine. There was again a French version powered by a 125cc engine only. With a more streamlined body, the Nuova was produced until 1991 when the company was absorbed by Grecav, which then continued with the Nuova renaming it Nuova Amica.

Bamby Cars Ltd

1983 — Bamby

After building a replica Peel P50, Alan Evans felt inspired to build a modern equivalent and designed and built the Bamby in Hull, UK, in 1983. Evans created the Bamby after being made redundant from a building firm in 1982. The vehicle was a single-seater with a fibreglass body that had a single gull-wing-type door. It was powered by an air-cooled, single-cylinder, 50cc Yamaha or Suzuki moped engine. Around 50 vehicles were built before production ceased in 1985 when the project was sold and subsequently dissolved.

2011 — Bamby P50

In 2011 the company was re-established by Alan Evans and his daughter, Emma, with the intention of building a range of replica classic microcars using modern components. Built as an updated replica of the Peel P50, the Bamby P50 has a fully-reinforced fibreglass monocoque body shell and is fitted with a 50cc four-stroke engine. Whilst following the same lines as the original P50, all components, including hydraulic disc brakes on all wheels and safety glass, are updated.

The Bamby P50 was a 50cc vehicle that drew its inspiration from the Peel P50 and offered a modern equivalent with a single gull-wing door. Author's Collection

2011 — MiniMicros: Schmitt KR

Minimicros are a range of ²/₃rd scale fully-operational replicas of classic microcars. They are powered by a 49cc, two-stroke engine with centrifugal clutch. The Schmitt KR is a ²/₃rd scale Messerschmitt replica with a top speed of around 20mph (32km/h). Built on a welded steel chassis, which incorporates a steel framework on to which to attach the fibreglass body panels, the Schmitts have a lift-up canopy like the original to allow access into the vehicle. The vehicles are available at the time of writing.

Basson's Industries

1954 — TRI CAR Delivery Van

In 1954 Basson's Industries of New York, USA, in conjunction with the Tri Car Corporation of America, set about creating a light delivery van. A prototype van with a fibreglass body and rear-mounted engine was created. The vehicle loosely resembled the TRI CAR (see page 250) but Tri Car did not want to use Basson's design and so the project was abandoned.

1956 — Basson Star

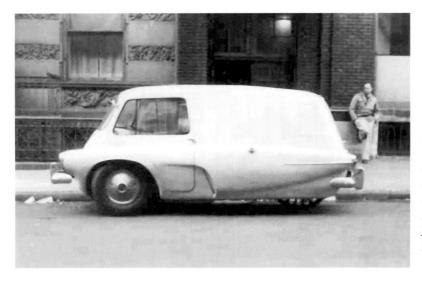

Built in conjunction with the Tri Car Corporation the rear-engined Basson Delivery van progressed no further than a prototype.
H Roy Jaffe

In 1956 the Basson Star was introduced. This was an open two-seat vehicle fitted with a fibreglass body that had a large carrying area at the rear. Powered by a 10bhp, single-cylinder, two-stroke engine, the Basson star featured 12V electrics, independent rear wheel suspension, hydraulic brakes, disc wheels and an 'airplane-type steering wheel'. The body was open with no doors or a roof. Perhaps as a result of its $999 price tag, very few production vehicles were actually built.

With an open body and a price tag of $999 in 1956 the Basson Star was not the cheapest of three-wheelers for its time. RUMCar News

Beeston Cycle Works

1896 — Humber Tricycle

Introduced in 1896 the Beeston tricycle was manufactured by Beeston Cycle Works in Beeston, Nottingham, UK. Powered by a 400cc engine, the Beeston tricycle was the only motorcycle/tricycle to make it from London to Brighton in the 1896 Emancipation Day Run to celebrate the raising of the speed limit to 12mph (19km/h). In 1898 the Duke of York — later King George V — was the first royal to ride one.

1898 — Motette

The Beeston Cycle Works had factories in Nottingham, Coventry and Wolverhampton in the UK. In 1898 the Beeston Motette was introduced; this was built at the company's Coventry factory. The Motette was a 'car version' of the tricycle and was powered by a 1.5bhp 'Electric Spark Motor'. This was quoted as being: 'a petrol motor developing from 0.7 to 1.5 horse power the charge in which is ignited by an electric spark.' The engine had three speeds: 5, 15 and 20mph (8/23/32km/h). The price for the Motette was 160 guineas. Production ceased in 1908 following financial problems.

Benz

1885 — Motorwagen

Accepted as the inventor of the motorcar, Karl Benz first unveiled his Benz Motorwagen in 1885 at Mannheim, Germany. The vehicle was powered by a 1.5bhp, water-cooled gas engine that was driven by the vapour of ligroin or benzene. The rear wheels received the power via a pulley and belt that were attached to a transmission shaft whilst the water cooling was by water evaporation in a jacket round the cylinder. The Benz had a top speed of *circa* 6-9mph (9.6-14.4km/h). The engine was increased to 2bhp in 1888. Despite inventors like Gottlieb Daimler, who worked on four-wheel designs, Benz stuck to a three-wheel design for many years, producing many vehicles. However, in the days before tarmac streets, many roads consisted of two rutted tracks left by horse drawn coaches. Whilst the four-wheeler normally ran in these ruts, the front wheel of a three-wheeler ran on uneven ground, thus creating a bumpy ride and placing great stress on the structure of the vehicle itself. Benz had initially designed his vehicle as a three-wheeler to overcome problems with steering.

Although other petrol vehicles are known to exist earlier, Karl Benz is generally accepted as the inventor of the motorcar with his Motorwagen in 1885 that ran on the vapour of ligroin or benzene. Ursula Haigh

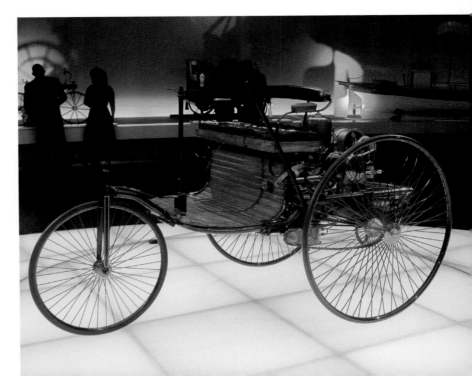

In 1888 Karl Benz started to advertise his three-wheeler but the public refused to buy it. It was after his family — wife and two sons — stole the car one night and drove it from Mannheim to Pforzheim (approximately 65 miles [105km]) that the public became fascinated by it and the model started to sell. From 1893 Benz then converted his vehicle to a four-wheel design — the Benz Viktoria. Benz then later merged with Daimler to become Daimler-Benz with its products known as Mercedes-Benz (although the company name remained Daimler-Benz until 1998 when, following a merger with Chrysler, it became DaimlerChrysler AG. In 2007, following the sale of Chrysler, the company was renamed Daimler AG).

Berkeley

1956 — T60

Berkeley Coachworks was a caravan maker based in Biggleswade, Bedfordshire, UK. It was approached by Lawrence Bond — the designer of the Bond three-wheeler — in 1955 with the concept of building a new micro sports car. When Charles Panter of Berkeley agreed, Bond built three prototypes and, as a result, in 1956 the company introduced its first four-wheel sports car. In August 1959, a three-wheel version was announced as the Berkeley T60.

The T60 was powered by an Excelsior Talisman 328cc, twin-cylinder engine and had a top speed of around 60mph (96.5km/h). It had a streamlined fibreglass body, which incorporated an aluminium-alloy chassis that was bonded into the body. The primary drive of the car was through a multi-plate wet clutch with the secondary drive being by chain to a differential and then through Hardy Spicer universal joints and half shafts to the front wheels.

The T60 came in two forms —a hard or a soft top — and as a standard or Deluxe model, the latter featuring extra dashboard instruments and a spare wheel. The vehicle had a bench-type seat at the front of the vehicle for two with an occasional seat for two children in the rear.

Introduced in 1959 the Berkeley T60 looked like a proper little sports car maintaining all the character from Berkeley's four-wheel sports cars.
Author's Collection

1960 — T60/4

A T60/4 version was introduced in September 1960; this had stronger suspension and a redesigned rear end, creating additional space for two small seats and thus making it a four-seater. Due to the company's financial problems, Berkeleys were only manufactured until 12 December 1960, when the company then ceased trading with just over 1,700 three-wheelers built.

Berkeley Bandini

1993 — Berkeley Bandini

When Berkeley Coachworks closed in 1960, the Berkeley Enthusiasts Club set about sourcing spares for existing vehicles. Dave Ratner, who was also the chairman of the club for a number of years, was able to acquire the moulds for the Berkeley T60 and, in 1991, these were sold to Andy Argyle who was also a Berkeley enthusiast.

In the same year Argyle set up a new Berkeley Cars company based in Queniborough, Leicestershire, UK, and began to sell replacement body panels and offered a service restoring T60s. By 1993 things had moved along and Berkeley Cars started to sell complete body/chassis units that included a chassis to fit a Mini engine with a rear end that used a Mini's swinging arm with coli-over shock absorber. The Mini engine was something that owners of Berkeleys used to convert their vehicle before the original Berkeley closed down. Along with the Mini-powered version, there were also options for a T60 powered by either a Kawasaki two-stoke, 750cc engine or a Citroën 2CV engine.

The Mini-powered T60 was called the Bandini with engines ranging from 850cc to 1,300cc. The most obvious external difference between the original T60 and the Bandini was the front wheel arches as they are 2½in wider to accommodate the Mini wheels. By 2005 the company had ceased trading and the T60 moulds were sold on.

Favoured by the Berlin Police force, the BEF had an electric motor mounted directly above the front wheel that provided drive via a vertical cardan transmission. Author's Collection

Even whilst the Berkeley T60 was in production many vehicles were soon modified with more powerful engines and found their way on to the racetrack. Spike

With wider front wheel arches the Berkeley Bandini was in essence a beefed up T60 powered by a variety of Mini engines ranging from 850-1,300cc. Marc Le Beller

Berliner Elektromobil-Fabrik

1907 — BEF

Built by the Berliner Elektromobil-Fabrik, the BEF was an electric vehicle built both as a commercial van and private vehicle. Designed by Victor Harborn, it was first built in 1907 in Berlin, Germany. The vehicle had front-wheel drive with vertical cardan transmission to the hub. The 4bhp

33

electric motor rotated in grease within a circular dustproof case above the front wheel. Steered via a rod the BEF had a top speed of around 15mph (24km/h). It found favour with the Berlin Police for use as an ambulance although production ceased in 1914.

Bernardi

1894 — Bernardi

Introduced in 1894 the Bernardi was the first vehicle to run on the roads of Italy. Professor Enrico Bernardi had researched the Internal Combustion Engine at the University of Padua where he was Professor of Hydraulic & Agricultural Machinery. On 5 August 1882 he developed the 'Motrice Pia', the first petrol combustion engine, and then, in 1884, he produced his first engine. This was a small engine that was demonstrated by powering a sewing machine and was then fitted to his son's tricycle. From 1889 Bernardi became interested in motorised vehicles and so started to build an engine that could propel a vehicle. In 1894 Bernardi introduced his first three-wheeler. Powered by a 3.5bhp, 624cc, single-cylinder, four-stroke engine with overhead valve, the vehicle had an interesting feature in that the throttle was a bulb mounted on the handlebars; this had to be squeezed and closed to control the speed of the vehicle.

A new company, La Società Miari & Giusti (see page 158), was established to build and sell the vehicle and patents were obtained in several countries including Britain. When the company closed down in 1899, Bernardi formed his own company — Società Italiana Bernardi — and produced the Bernardi until 1901.

Blackjack Trikes

1995 — Avion

Blackjack Trikes have been producing three-wheelers since 1995. Based in Cornwall, UK, it was founded by car designer Richard Oakes, who had previously worked for the Ford Motor Co and freelanced for Aston Martin and JCB. In the 1970s Oakes designed a Mini-engined Midas, followed by subsequent models in the 1980s, along with the GTM cars, Rossa, K3, Libra and Libra Spyder. The business is run by Oakes and his wife with the first three-wheeler designed being the Blackjack Avion

The Blackjack Avion was offered as either a whole vehicle or in a kit form. Using pre-war racing Morgans as its inspiration, the Avion was an open two-seat vehicle based on the Citroën 2CV powertrain and front suspension with vertically mounted dampers. The rear suspension had a swinging arm with a spring and damper unit. The body was made from a polyester moulding with subframes mounted to a ladder frame chassis and had a moulded windscreen. Around 69 vehicles were built.

2005 — Zero

The Blackjack Zero was initially designed as a prototype in 2004 and, in March 2005, became the first kit car to pass the Single Vehicle Approval (SVA) Test at Exeter, UK, at its first attempt. As with the Avion, the Zero was designed by Richard Oakes. Available in kit form, the Zero is powered by a Type 1 Volkswagen 1,300-1,800cc engine with big valve heads fitted with a large volume oil pump and the crankcase drilled and tapped for an external oil filter. This, along with a few other tuning recommendations, is added to a Volkswagen gearbox originally fitted in

The 2008 Blackjack Zero powered by a V-twin 1,100cc Moto-Guzzi engine. Blackjack Trikes

the 1302S Beetle (1970-1972). Keeping to the Volkswagen theme, the brakes and front suspension are modified from a Volkswagen Golf GTi. The body has a steel chassis, whilst the main body tub with reinforced bulkheads and panels is made from fibreglass, helping to keep the weight of the vehicle down to 450kg. In 2008 a new derivation of the Blackjack Zero was introduced, using the air-cooled Moto-Guzzi 1,100cc V-twin engine. As with earlier models, the 2008 version is front-wheel drive. Blackjack Trikes remain in production at the time of writing.

BMW

1957 — Isetta (UK)

Founded as an aircraft company during World War 1 by Herr Bayer, BMW (Bayrische Motoren Werke) went on to produce motorcycles. In the 1930s BMW started to produce motor vehicles and in 1932 created prototypes of a three-wheel car as both a delivery vehicle and a car. The delivery vehicle being an open single-seat vehicle with a loading area between the front two wheels whilst the car version was more car like with side-by-side seating and a collapsible pram type hood. Both vehicles used either a 200cc or 400cc four-stroke engine and were built until 1934.

By 1953 the company were on the brink of bankruptcy when one of their executives spotted the ISO Rivolta Bubble concept car from Italy and contacted ISO. After a deal was struck, ISO then sold the design and the manufacturing rights to BMW to build the machine and the BMW Isetta was born. Although the main elements of the vehicle remained intact, BMW did much to redesign the vehicle adding its own engine and modifying parts so they were not interchangeable with the original ISO vehicle. The first BMW Isetta (the Isetta 250) was introduced in April 1955 and, whilst it appeared to be a three-wheeler at first glance, it was actually a four-wheeler with two rear wheels set 48cm apart. The Isetta soon became the Isetta 300 when the engine was replaced with a 300cc engine.

In 1957 the BMW Isetta reached the UK and was manufactured by 'Isetta of Great Britain Ltd.' at the Southern Locomotive works in New England Street, Brighton. The Isetta however was not popular mainly due to the high road tax cost of the four-wheeler in the UK and so sales were hampered until the first three-wheel version arrived in 1958.

The Isetta was one of the true 'bubble cars', having a bubble-shaped body made from steel and bolted to a separate tubular chassis and, like its four-wheeler counterpart, it used the 298cc,

Initially released in the UK as a four-wheeler, the BMW Isetta was not popular due to the extra road tax incurred and so in 1958 a three-wheel version arrived that became an instant hit. Wilfried Dibbets

A BMW delivery van from 1932, which at first glance looks as though the back should be the front. Author's Collection

four-stroke BMW engine. Access to and from the car was via a large door at the front of the Isetta; this also incorporated a unique feature in that the steering column was attached to the door and by using a universal joint the steering column would swing away with the door allowing easier access to and from the vehicle. The British versions were modified so that they were right-hand drive and the door hinged from the right-hand side of the vehicle. The interior of the vehicle featured a single bench type seat that was said to seat up to three adults. The Isetta also featured a canvas sun roof that was fitted partially as a means of escape should the vehicle be involved in a head on collision which obstructed the door and prevented it from opening. In total over 200,000 Isetta's were manufactured worldwide until it was discontinued in 1964.

The BMW Isetta had a single front door that had the steering wheel and dashboard attached to it so when the door was opened both would swing away with the door. Robert Grounds

1991 — C1

BMW returned to three-wheelers in 1991 with a concept vehicle called the C1 that, although a non-runner, would have been powered by either an air-cooled 800cc or 1,000cc engine. The vehicle used motorcycle technology and would tilt up to 45° when cornering. In essence, it was a covered three-wheel motorcycle with handlebar steering.

2009 — CLEVER

In 2009 BMW unveiled the CLEVER (Compact Low Emission Vehicle for Urban Transport) concept vehicle. With an enclosed two-seat cabin the CLEVER was powered by a 230cc BMW engine fuelled by natural gas that was stored in two removable gas bottles. The combination offered a predicted 188mpg (1.5-litre/100km) whilst also providing a range of up to 93 miles (150km) and a top speed of around 50mph (80.4km/h). As the vehicle was only one metre wide it had a Direct Tilt Control (DTC) system, designed by the University of Bath, which allowed it to tilt up to 45° when cornering. Whilst the cabin and front wheel both lean to one side, the rear two wheels remain horizontal. To date research for this project is still ongoing.

Bond Cars Ltd

1949 — Mk A

Lawrence 'Lawrie' Bond was an aeronautical designer for the Blackburn Aircraft Co and, having designed a new three-wheeler, needed somewhere to manufacture it. Sharps Commercials Ltd was a company based in Preston, UK, that was contracted by the Ministry of Supply to rebuild military vehicles. Bond knew the contract was due to expire in 1948 and contacted them, asking to rent the company's factory to build his three-wheeler. Sharps Commercials Ltd refused, though the company said it would manufacture the vehicles. As a result, an agreement was made and full production started in 1949. The company changed its name to Bond Cars Ltd in 1963.

The first Bond Minicar Mk A appeared in 1949; this was a two-/three-seater powered by a Villiers 10D 122cc air-cooled engine. The Bond Mk A initially was a very basic vehicle with a stressed skin aluminium body and no doors. Whilst the front of the vehicle had a girder type suspension, the car had no rear suspension whatsoever. The car also only had brakes on the back wheels and gear changing was by means of a lever on the dashboard. Under the dashboard there was a handle that was connected to a modified kick starter for starting the vehicle. The vehicle had 6V electrics, though the windscreen wiper had to be manually operated.

A Deluxe Tourer model of the Bond Mk A was introduced in December 1949; this was almost identical, though had a more powerful Villiers 6E 197cc engine. The Deluxe Tourer was improved further in October 1950 with a Triplex glass windscreen replacing the old Perspex one. Rack and pinion steering was used, replacing the bobbin variety used on all variations. A total of 1,973 Mk A Bonds were made.

A 1951 Bond Minicar Mk A that had no rear suspension and aluminium body with no doors. Wikipedia — Mighty Antar

1951 — Mk B

Arriving in April 1951, the Bond Minicar Mk B retained many features found on the Mk A, including the same Villiers 6E 197cc air-cooled engine. Where the Mk B differed was that it now featured coil spring rear suspension, which gave a much more comfortable ride. In 1952 a Sharps Minitruck appeared; this was a Mk B with a single seat and a larger more upright rear body that provided the vehicle with a payload of 3cwt (or a carrying capacity of 24cu ft). Hot on its heels was the Sharps Minivan, which had a built-in compartment with a door at the rear offering the same loading capacity and a hood and side screens. The final Mk B variation was the Family 'Safety Saloon' that arrived in August 1952. This was the same as the Minivan though equipped with side windows and rear seats. In all, 1,414 Bond Mk Bs were made.

1952 — Mk C

Appearing in October 1952, the Bond Minicar Mk C brought with it a completely new body shape, including dummy wings at the front of the car with headlights incorporated into them. This new body also housed a new steering device that allowed the car to be steered at 180°. At the time for a three-wheeler to be driven on a motorcycle licence it could not have a reverse gear, the 180° steering, therefore, meant that the Bond Mk C could turn around within its own length. At this time aluminium was becoming very difficult to source and so

With 180° steering this 1956 Bond Minicar Mk C Deluxe Tourer was able to turn around in its own length. Wikipedia — Mighty Antar

A 1958 Advert for Bond Minicar Mk E that notes the vehicle has more room and greater comfort as a result of the Mk E's larger restyled body and improved seats. Author's Collection

the rear wings of the Mk C were made from steel. In June 1953 the engine was replaced with a Villiers 8E 197cc engine and the vehicle received several other updates including a redesign of the braking system in 1955. In total 6,399 Bond Mk Cs were built.

1956 — Mk D

The Bond Minicar Mk D that first appeared in May 1956 was virtually identical to the Mk C, though now it used a Villiers 9E 197cc engine. The electrics were also improved with a new 12V system and this model was now also available with a fibreglass hard top. Until now all Bonds had three gears, though, with the Family Tourer in October 1958, a new four-speed gearbox was fitted. Just 3,761 Bond Mk Ds were made.

1957 — Mk E

The arrival of the Bond Minicar Mk E in October 1957 brought along a new restyled body that featured a wrap-around Triplex screen and a steel box-section chassis. Along with a larger fuel tank, improved lighting and new folding seats the Mk E was also two feet longer than its predecessor. In all, 1,189 vehicles were produced.

1958 — Mk F

Introduced in November 1958, the Bond Minicar Mk F was identical to the Mk E, though now it had a more powerful Villiers 31A 250cc engine. In 1960, a Mk F Ranger was also added to the line up with a carrying capacity of 3cwt (31cu ft). This was essentially the Family saloon version but with no rear windows. A single-seat Mk F van was also made from June 1960 but only sold 39 vehicles whereas 6,493 Mk Fs were built.

The Bond Minicar Mk G was powered by an improved 250cc engine and included additional features like adjustable seats and locking door handles.
Nick Greatwood

Banishing the idea the Bond Minicars were slow the Bond 875 burst onto the scene in 1966. It was fitted with a Rootes 875cc engine that provided a top speed of 80-90mph (129-145km/h). Author's Collection

1961 — Mk G

August 1961 saw another new body shape; this introduced quarter light windows and a reverse sloping rear window that was also popular on the Ford Anglia at the time. The Bond Minicar Mk G was powered by a new improved Villiers 35A 250cc engine with a four-speed gearbox. Inside the vehicle seats were now adjustable in length and height, and locking door handles were also included. In May 1962 a Ranger version was built with no rear windows or rear seats that had an increased carrying capacity of 4cwt (42cu ft). In June of the same year, a Mk G Estate was announced with rear seats that could be either laid flat or removed. Later on, in November, the Villiers 4T 250cc twin engine, which was advertised as 60mph (96.5km/h) and 60mpg (4.7-litre/100km), became available as an option. The range was extended again in October 1964 with a Tourer version, which had a rear opening luggage boot. In total 3,253 Mk Gs were built.

1966 — 875

The belief that Bond cars were slow was shattered in April 1966 with the introduction of the 875 model. The 875 had the engine at the rear, which drove the rear wheels, and was fitted with a water-cooled low compression 875cc engine from the Commer van built by Rootes. The 875 used the same layout as the Hillman Imp and included Hillman Imp transmission, rear suspension and rear wheels; this gave the vehicle a top speed of 80-90mph (129-145km/h). The body shell of the 875 was made completely from fibreglass although it had aluminium doors. It was available in a saloon version although a Ranger van form, with a lift up tailgate at the rear, followed in April

1967. In March 1968 the 875 received a restyled body and was released as the Mark II saloon. In total 3,441 875s were built.

With its increased engine size the Bond was now in direct competition with the 700cc Reliant Regal and, even though Bond was only manufacturing 1,500 three-wheelers a year compared with Reliant's 15,000, it was enough to make the Reliant Motor Co take over Bond in February 1969.

1970 — Bond Bug

In August 1970 Reliant ceased manufacture of all Bond models but prior to this, the new owners had commissioned Ogle Design Ltd — their design consultants — to produce a sports three-wheeler for the 'young' generation. This was to be sold under as the Bond Bug. Introduced in June 1970, the early Bond Bugs were manufactured at the Bond factory in Preston but, shortly afterwards when the factory closed, Bug production was moved over to Reliant at Tamworth, UK. (See Reliant Motor Co on page 210 for more information on this model.)

Although Bond is mainly known for its range of three-wheel vehicles, it had also made over the years a Bond Sea Ranger speedboat in 1960, a four-wheel sports car in 1963 (the Bond Equipe), and Bond P1-P4 scooters from 1957. It is interesting to note that many parts from the Bond three-wheelers were used to make the scooters.

Covered with 18swg light alloy panelling the Bonallack Minnow was a sturdy vehicle though also a fairly heavy one for its class at 500lb.
RUMCar News

Bonallack & Sons Ltd

1951 — Minnow

The Bonallack Minnow was built by Bonallack & Sons Ltd in London, UK, from 1951. It was fitted with a 250cc Excelsior Talisman twin-cylinder two-stroke engine. The engine sat at the rear of the vehicle and drove the single rear wheel by a chain via a four-speed gearbox. The chassis was made of heat-treated channel-section alloy runners

through the length of the vehicle. The chassis was braced with runners whilst the body was coach built with 18swg light alloy panelling and had a single 6V headlamp at the front. Louvres were formed at the rear of the body to draw in air to cool the engine. The vehicle had a vertical windscreen and a bench for a front seat along with a convertible hood and side curtains. At 500lb the Minnow was on the heavy side for a three-wheeler and was priced at £300 plus £168 3s 4d Purchase Tax. Top speed was around 45-50mph (72-80km/h) and a fuel consumption of around 70mpg (4-litre/100km). Production ceased in 1952.

Bonnington Roadster

2007 — Bonnington Roadster

Designed and built by automotive designer Brad Bonning in Queensland, Australia, in 2007, the Bonnington Roadster was developed from a pedal-powered car that Bonning had produced for driver training. The main concept behind its development was to create a vehicle that could consume not only petrol but also alternative fuels like hydrogen and methanol derived from household waste.

The Bonnington was a two-seater constructed from aluminium, giving the car a total weight of just 400kg. Powered by a motorcycle-derived engine, it is said to have phenomenal acceleration, and a top speed of approximately 125mph (201km/h). To date only the prototype exists.

Appearing in 2007 as a prototype, the Bonnington Roadster not only feeds on petrol but also alternative fuels derived from household waste. Michael Barnard

Borgman

1951 — Bubblecar

Very few three-wheelers can claim that there were built in a living room; this was the case, however, for the 1951 Borgman Bubblecar. Designed and built by Hendrikus Hildebrand Borgman in Zaltbommel, The Netherlands, the vehicle was designed for his personal use and was made in the living room as he did not have a garage. As a result the car could only be 80cm high so that it would fit though the front door on its side and could also get through the garden gate. With a chassis made from 4mm iron tubes, the body was made from 3mm plywood whilst the bonnet was made from steel. To help minimise the height, the windscreen would fold down and the soft-top was detachable. It was initially powered by a 125cc JAP engine, but this was underpowered and so it was replaced with a 150cc ILO engine with forced air-cooing providing a top speed of approximately 43mph (70km/h). The engine was attached to the front-wheel suspension and not only turned with the single front wheel but also drove it through a three-speed gearbox. There was no reverse gear; reverse was achieved by sticking an iron tube through a hole in the floor into the gaps between the stones on the street and levering the vehicle along. The interior had four seats, suitable for two adults in the front and two children in the back, whilst the steering wheel was half-moon shaped so that it did not exceed the height of the body when the vehicle was on its side. After five years of faithful service, including a family holiday to Luxemburg, the Borgman Bubblecar was sold on and its ultimate fate remains a mystery.

Built in 1951, the Borgman Bubblecar was a homemade family vehicle with four seats.
Rik Borgman

Built in a living room the Borgman Bubblecar could be no higher than 80cm, which meant that, on its side, it would fit through the front door of the house and through the garden gate.
Rik Borgman

Bouffort

1945 — Bouffort

Created in France in 1945, the Bouffort was designed by Victor Bouffort and was largely based on a Citroën Traction Avant. With Citroën mechanics at the front of the vehicle, the Bouffort was exceptionally streamlined with its long mudguards and aerodynamic body. Seating was for two, side-by-side, and the car had hydropneumatic suspension. It is not known how many vehicles were made, but construction is believed to have ceased around 1960.

The Bouffort Peardrop, so called as a result of its revolutionary shape, which was later to appear in vehicles produced by other manufacturers.
RUMCar News

1952 — Peardrop

The Peardrop was a revolutionary egg shaped three-wheeler created in 1952 with a plastic body. This was also designed by Bouffort and he toured Germany trying to sell the design; however, despite great interest no one purchased it.

1955 — Enville

Another three-wheeler designed by Bouffort was the Enville in 1955. The vehicle was a single-seater with two wheels at the front. There were no side doors as such, just a canvas side that folded forward to allow access to the vehicle.

BRA

1990 — CX3

BRA (Beribo Replica Automobiles) was established in the late 1970s in the UK, producing kit forms for many cars with its kit form of the Cobra replica being its most acclaimed. Beribo came from the names of the company founders, John Berry and Peter Ibbotson.

A BRA CX3 demonstrator vehicle with this particular car fitted with additional chrome and Connolly leather seats. BRA Motor Works

John Berry produced the BRA CX3 Super Sports three-wheeler in 1990. This was a modern interpretation of the classic 1930s three-wheel Morgan. In 1996, when Berry and Ibbotson retired, James Mather brought the CX3 project along with the BRA name. After undertaking a number of design modifications, he then continued to produce the CX3 in North Wales, UK, assisted by his friend and fellow engineer David Wiles, who had joined the company. The CX3 was powered by either a Honda CX500 or CX650 water-cooled V-twin motorcycle engine, which provided power to the single rear wheel by a shaft drive. The body of the vehicle was made from aluminium alloy body panels that were attached to a 16swg steel tubing chassis. Between 1996 and 2002 around 100 cars were sold.

Fitted with a Honda motorcycle engine, the BRA CX3 was a modern interpretation of the classic 1930s Morgan three-wheeler.
BRA Motor Works

1997 — CV3

In the latter part of 1997 James Mather and David Wiles designed the BRA CV3, which, when launched at the Stafford Kit Car Show in March 1998, became an instant success. The CV3 was powered by the Citroën 2CV/Dyane flat twin air-cooled 600cc engine. Unlike the CX3, power was provided to the front wheels. The body was 16swg aluminium alloy sheet attached to a 16swg steel tubing chassis. The CV3 was, therefore, more of a touring machine compared with its high revving CX3 counterpart.

1999 — Leighton

In December 1999, BRA purchased the Leighton project from GCS Hawke. After a number of modifications, which included changes to the shape and cockpit size, the Leighton was launched in March 2000. Powered by a Citroën 2CV/Dyane flat twin 602cc engine, the Leighton had a moulded GRP body attached to a triangulated space frame that was also manufactured by BRA.

2000 — MR3

BRA started to develop an Austin Metro-based MR3 in 2000, though the project was subsequently put on hold.

2001 — MG3

The Moto-Guzzi-based MG3 was introduced in April 2001 with the first photo showing the vehicle released via the author's web site at www.3-wheelers.com. The MG3 was a re-engineered CX3 capable of accepting the Moto-Guzzi engine, gearbox, transmission and rear end. The MG3 could be powered by a range of engines from 850cc to the 1,100i. The MG3 was produced in very limited numbers, with only five MG3 chassis being made. A number of other specials were made to accept other engines, such as the Harley Davidson V-twin and Honda ST100 (Pan European) V4.

In January 2002 the CV3 and the Leighton projects were sold to Martin Philpott of Kent, UK, who traded as the Leighton Motor Co and, in September of the same year, the last CX3 left the BRA factory. In 2003 full rights to build the CX3 and MG3 were sold to Arthur Rayner of Aerocycle Cars, who then also went on to purchase the rights to the CV3. James Mather and David Wiles retained the BRA name — and its variations — and then concentrated on four-wheel, road legal, all-terrain vehicles.

Built in 1923 this Bramham with its intriguing front wheel drive is, to date, the only known survivor. Peter Stanhope

Bramham Motors (Leeds) Ltd

1922 — Bramham (Belt Drive)

In 1922 Stanhope Motors (Leeds) Ltd (see page 234 for more information), which was run by the Stanhope brothers, lost its financial backer and was then financed and taken over by Walter Bramham, who was a wealthy pork butcher. As a result the name of the company was changed to Bramham Motors (Leeds) Ltd and the vehicles became known as Bramham with two models being announced. The belt-drive version was powered by an air-cooled, 8bhp, JAP engine that was bolted immediately behind the front wheel to two tubular cross-members of the chassis. Two Whittle belts then ran over automatic governor pulleys, with drive being sent to the front wheel by sliding forks that also allowed the wheel to steer. The belt-drive model was a two-seater and sold for £160.

1922 — Bramham (Chain Drive)

Fitted with the same engine, the chain drive model was sold for £190 and had a better finish. The vehicles were also sold in a number of variations, including a 5cwt light delivery van and a Sports model. Both vehicles were equipped with acetylene lighting, a hood and side screens.

The specifications of the vehicles continually changed as improvements were made which meant that very few Bramhams were alike. By 1923 a tandem body was also introduced, which was claimed to seat four people, along with a four-speed gearbox. A number of special vehicles were also made to order; these were fitted with a range of four-cylinder, water-cooled engines from Blackburne, Singer and Triumph. Production of three-wheelers ceased in 1924 when Bramham returned to manufacturing pork pies and the Stanhope brothers went on to build four-wheel vehicles.

With a 1.5 ton payload and fitted with a 1,000cc engine the Bremach Motocarro came in a number of guises all aimed at the commercial sector. Patrick Castelli

Although the Brookland Swallow received a lot of interest it was too heavy to be classed as a tricycle and hence was not able to be driven on a motorcycle licence. Iain Ayre

Bremach

1956 — Motocarro

Fratelli Brenna was established in Varese, Italy, in 1956 as a machine shop. In 1970 the company acquired the production rights for a small three-wheel delivery vehicle that was built by Aermacchi (see page 12). Fratelli Brenna made a number of improvements to the vehicle, including a hydraulic braking system and an enclosed cab; the vehicle was then sold as the Bremach Motocarro. The Bremach remained a lightweight vehicle and had a 1.5-ton loading capacity and was powered by a 23bhp 1,000cc two-cylinder petrol engine that drove the rear two wheels via a four-speed gearbox with shaft drive. It proved to be very adaptable model, featuring a number of rear ends that included a tipper truck, fire engine and hydraulic crane. In the mid-1970s Bremach then began to design and manufacture four-wheel vehicles.

Brookland Motor Co

1993 — Brookland Swallow

Designed and created in 1993 by kit car journalist Iain Ayre in the UK, the Brookland Swallow was a kit car based on the Mini. Built around a steel chassis the vehicle used the Mini engine to drive the front two wheels. It had four seats and had a steel body that used Mini doors

and extended Mini wings, a Riley/Wolseley 1500 bonnet, Renault 5 windscreen along with the rear wings off a Volvo P1800 and a Mini trailing arm at the rear. Painted in yellow primer, the completed vehicle was exceptionally strong and sturdy. It attracted much interest, especially from motorcyclists, though it weighed too much to be classed as a tricycle. As a result it was not eligible for a reduced tax rate and thus could not be driven on a motorcycle licence. As a result only one vehicle was built and the project was developed no further.

Brütsch

1954 — 200 Spatz

Founded in Stuttgart, Germany in 1950, Egon Brütsch Fahrzeugbau (often shortened to Brütsch) created a large number of different three- and four-wheelers between 1954 and 1958. The vehicles were all designed by former motorcycle and racing car driver Egon Brütsch. Although a great variety of models was available, each sold in low numbers with an estimated 81 vehicles in total.

Built for just a year from 1954 to 1955, the 200 Spatz was powered by a single-cylinder 191cc Fichtel & Sachs engine with a top speed of 56mph (90km/h). Despite its sporty looks, the vehicle had no chassis and relied on the strength of the fibreglass body to keep everything in place. The strength, however, was overestimated and the design proved to be very weak. This resulted in numerous cracks in the main structure, leading one German judge to rule that the car was illegal. Only five cars were made, though the 200 Spatz was also built under licence by A Grünhut & Co of Switzerland with minor changes and sold as the Belcar. A licence was also sold to Alzmetall in Germany to manufacture the car though, due to the number of faults with the original design, its production model — the Spatz Kabinenroller — ended up very different. Consequently, Brütsch was forced to take Alzmetall to court to ensure payment of his licence fees; however, he lost the case. The 200 Spatz was also re-engineered and sold in the UK as the Bruetsch 300.

1955 — Zwerg

Using the same single-cylinder 191cc Fichtel & Sachs engine as the Spatz, the Zwerg was a two-seater built from 1955 to 1957 with 12 cars being produced. The Zwerg was also built under licence by Air Tourist Sàrl in France and sold as the Avolette with a few minor changes.

1955 — Zwerg Einsitzer

A single-seater powered by a single-cylinder, 74cc DKW Hobby scooter engine was built from 1955 to 1956. Its top speed was around 40mph (64km/h) and four cars were made.

1956 — Rollera

Another single-seater, the Rollera was driven by a single-cylinder 98cc Fichtel & Sachs engine and had a top speed around 50mph (80km/h). Eight vehicles were produced between 1956 and 1958. It was also built under licence by Air Tourist Sàrl of France.

1956 — Mopetta

The Mopetta was an egg-shaped vehicle with a single seat and, at just 170cm long, 88cm wide and 110 cm high, had the distinction of being the world's smallest three-wheeler until 1965 when the Peel 50 was produced by the Peel Engineering Co. Driven by a single-cylinder 49cc engine, the top speed was around 28mph (45km/h). Built from 1956 to 1958, 14 cars were made.

Until the arrival of the Peel P50, the Brütsch Mopetta was the world's smallest production vehicle at just 170cm long, 88cm wide and 110cm high.
Caroline Payne

1956 — Bussard

Manufactured from 1956 until 1958, the Bussard was fitted with a single-cylinder 191cc Fichtel & Sachs engine that gave a top speed of 59mph (95km/h). The model had a fibreglass body, which resembled the original 200 Spatz, attached to a steel tube frame. Eleven cars were produced, most of them being sold in the UK.

Bruetsch Cars (England) Ltd

1955 — 300 Mk 1

Based in Nottingham, UK, from 1955, Bruetsch Cars produced English versions of Brütsch cars. The 300 Mk 1 was essentially the three-seat Brütsch 200 Spatz re-engineered to make it a safer vehicle. It was driven by a more powerful 14.5bhp, 247cc, air-cooled, single-cylinder engine. It was fitted with a four-speed plus reverse gearbox that provided drive to the single rear wheel by a roller chain running in an enclosed metal cover. The 300 had a colour impregnated fibreglass body that, unlike the 200 Spatz, was attached to a tubular steel cross-frame and so was much stronger. Top speed was 60mph (96.5km/h) with petrol consumption at 65mpg (4.3-litre/100km). Bruetsch Cars also produced the Mopetta and Bussard. (See Brütsch above for details of these models.)

BSA

1929 — Standard Model

The Birmingham Small Arms Co (BSA) of Small Heath, Birmingham, UK, was founded in 1861 and was famous for its side arms and bicycles (BSA Cycles Ltd). It began to manufacture cars in 1907, with motorcycles following in 1910. Its first three-wheeler appeared in 1929 and used a Hotchkiss engine — a 1,021cc, air-cooled, overhead-valve V-twin — to power its front wheels. The Standard Model was first publicly announced at the 1929 Motorcycle Show and was admired by many. The car featured all-round weather protection, electric starter, three forward speeds and a reverse gear, independent front suspension and front-wheel drive; the latter was something very rare at the time. The BSA performed well both on the racetrack and on the road, and its success led BSA to produce nearly 2,000 vehicles a year. By the end of 1932, BSA was offering six versions of the vehicle tailored to meet everyone's needs in a serious attempt to rival Morgan. The cheapest of these was the £100 Standard two-seater. The Family version had a family style body with an extra two seats in the rear for children for £105. There was the De-Luxe two-seater for £108, the De-Luxe Family model for £110 and the Special Sports model for £115. In 1933 slight alterations were made to the standard model along with upgraded the engine to 1,100cc

The Bruetsch 300 Mk 1 was a re-engineered British version of the Brütsch 200 Spatz that was fitted with a stronger chassis and a larger engine. Author's Collection

Finding success both on the roads and the race track the BSA became extremely popular in the 1930s with just under 2,000 vehicles a year being built. Alan Styles

A BSA Tourer from 1932 that was available both as a two- and a four-seater that seated two adults and two small children. Simon Baynes

A rare BSA driver's view of the English countryside in the 1930s. Alan Styles

1930 — Sports/Tourer

In 1930 two new models were introduced — the Sports and the Tourer — both of which also had four-seat family model variations; the four-seater had two children's seats behind the main ones with only one of the seats actually having a foot well. Both models were fitted with a four-cylinder engine. In 1934 BSA introduced its new four-wheeler — the Scout — but continued to produce three-wheelers until 1936.

1930 — Commercial van

The BSA three-wheeler was also built as a commercial van with a large covered area to the rear. This was fitted with twin doors at the back. However, it is believed that the interest in this model was very low.

1950s — Ladybird

It was not until the late 1950s that BSA introduced its next three-wheeler: the Ladybird. This, however, was essentially a prototype and never reached mass production. The first prototype had a handmade steel body and was powered by a Triumph Tigress 250cc engine at the rear of the vehicle. The car was very basic and did not feature items such as spare wheel, traffic indicators or a windscreen wiper. Although the vehicle was basic, interest in the Ladybird prompted a second prototype in 1960. This model featured a windscreen wiper, and the half-moon shaped handlebars in the first prototype were replaced by a steering wheel type control with the control resembling the top third of a circle. Sadly, due to the decline in demand in microcars, the Ladybird was abandoned in 1960.

1970 — Ariel 3

In 1944 BSA took over Ariel but it was not until 1970 that the Ariel name was used again with the BSA Ariel 3, a 50cc two-stroke moped. The Ariel 3 was not only different to other mopeds at the time in having three wheels, but it was also a tilting vehicle with two wheels at the rear. The front half of the moped was hinged and so the vehicle could tilt into corners whilst keeping all three wheels on the ground. Production of the Ariel 3 was limited and the moped was dropped along with the Ariel name shortly afterwards. The tilting system used in the Ariel 3 was then licensed to Honda for use from 1981 in the Honda Stream. The Japanese company went on to produce a number of tilting three-wheel mopeds.

BTB Engineering Ltd

1975 — BTB Ant

From October 1975, BTB Engineering of Blackburn, Lancashire, UK, produced a range of Reliant TW9-based vehicles built upon the standard Reliant vehicle. Towards the end of 1977 it purchased the production rights to the TW9 from Reliant and renamed the vehicle as the BTB Ant. Reliant still supplied the main parts. It continued manufacturing the Ant for both the UK and American markets in low numbers. In the UK, the BTB Ant, unlike other Reliant three-wheelers, required a full driving licence as the combined weight of just the chassis and cab alone was 550kg. The vehicle often had a weight that approached 1,350kg with a full body at the rear. A great many of them found favour with local authorities and county councils as road sweepers. Production of the BTB Ant continued until May 1987.

Having purchased the production rights from the Reliant Motor Co, the BTB Ant was made in numerous forms the most popular of which was a road sweeper that was used by local authorities and councils. Kerry Croxton

BubblePuppy

1940s — BubblePuppy

The BubblePuppy (or 'Welpe Luft-Blassen') was first created during World War 2 by Count S von Teleki, who was a Nazi scientist later recruited by the American military to work in New Mexico, USA. Count Teleki, however, subsequently disappeared without trace and so nobody knew what the BubblePuppy was designed to do. The vehicle was lost for a number of years until it was discovered in an old crate in Alamogordo, New Mexico, during the 1980s. The Count's grandson got to hear of the discovery and claimed the vehicle as his rightful property and hired a moving company to transport it from New Mexico to Long Beach, California, USA, telling the drivers that it was a sculpture.

Sean Guerroro, a sculptor of large exhibits made from metal such as parts from vehicles, heard about the discovery of the BubblePuppy and visited the people who found it. The level of secrecy was so high that he was unable to see the vehicle or copy the blueprints but was given a quick glance. From this glance

An economic worker with a wide range of bodies for all purposes.

Built by Count S von Teleki during World War 2, no one actually knows what the BubblePuppy was designed to do as its discovery in the 1980s was shrouded in secrecy. Ace Scott King

The location of the actual BubblePuppy is unknown and so this is a replica of it built by Sean Guerroro after a quick glance at the original blue prints. Ace Scott King

Guerroro built his own BubblePuppy in his garage. The new vehicle has been aged to give it the appearance of being in storage for 50 years and, whilst the machine is as accurate as possible, the cockpit is sheer fantasy as no plans of this were seen. To date the location of the Count's grandson and the original BubbyPuppy are unknown and so the vehicle is once again lost.

body panels, front-wheel drive, suspension components and instrument panel. Optional items were also available; these included the exhaust system, seats and an electric motor that provided a reverse gear. It is believed that the project was abandoned in 1987 with only one vehicle still known to exist. The survivor uses a four-stroke, V-twin, 920cc Yamaha motorcycle engine.

Buchanan Automotive Technology

1983 — Tryker

The Tryker first appeared in 1983 and was a kit-based vehicle sold by Buchanan Automotive Technology of Carpinteria, California, USA. The vehicle was built using the front-wheel drive system from a 1977-1982 series Honda Accord and was able to accept most four-cylinder overheard cam motorcycle engines, especially those made by Honda, Suzuki, Yamaha and Kawasaki. The engine was fitted to an integral five-speed transmission that drove the front wheels. The Tryker had a perimeter chassis made from rectangular steel tubing with an integral steel floor pan and an aluminium body. A basic Tryker kit was available; this consisted of a complete welded chassis,

Using the front-wheel drive system of a Honda Accord, this particular Tryker is fitted with a 920cc Yamaha engine. Tom Carmody

Buckeye Manufacturing Co

1891 — Lambert

Built by John William Lambert in Ohio, USA, in 1891 the Lambert 'horseless carriage' is claimed by automobile historian L Scott Bailey to be the first practical petrol-powered vehicle in the USA. The initial vehicle was designed and built in 1890 and, after testing in January 1891, was advertised to the public. Whilst there was interest in the vehicle none appear to have been sold in that year. The horseless carriage was essentially a one-seat carriage with a single-cylinder, four-stroke engine positioned under the seat. The first model had two forward speeds along with a wipe spark ignition and dry cell batteries as well as a surface vaporizer carburettor with a flexible diaphragm compensator. Steering was achieved by a series of levers whilst the wheels were made from wood with steel rims. The single wheel was at the front.

In 1895 Lambert founded the Buckeye Manufacturing Co in Indiana, USA, and announced that he would soon have a petrol-powered vehicle, to be called the Buckeye, on the market. The Buckeye was based on the original vehicle created in 1891. It was not well received and so was extensively redesigned and developed into the four-wheel Union automobile that was built from 1902.

Buckland

1985 — B3

The B3 was designed and built by Dick Buckland of Newport, South Wales, UK. The first car was built in 1985 and appeared at the Stoneleigh Kit Car Show of that year where it was very well received. Buckland took his inspiration from the Morgan F Type, having successfully modified and raced an F type for many years.

The B3 was designed for handling, speed and lightness. It was based around inexpensive and easily accessible mechanical parts taken from vehicles produced by Ford, Reliant and Datsun to name but a few. The engine and gearbox were 1300 Ford Kent units that provided the B3 with 95bhp and a top speed of 130mph (209km/h). In addition the Ford Escort gearbox provided the benefit of a reverse gear. The chassis — all Buckland's own work — was exceptionally strong and hand crafted from Zintec steel, with weight saving wherever possible whilst the body tub, bonnet and wings were all fibreglass. The rear body tub lifts and hinges at the front to the same angle as the bonnet to facilitate access to the rear wheel and drive train. The single rear wheel was driven by a chain with power leaving the gearbox by a specially made propshaft and torque tube onto a Reliant crown and pinion and then to sprocket and chain. In all, 12 Buckland B3s were built, spanning a period from 1985 to 1998.

2010 — B3 Mk2

In 2010 Penguin Speed Shop acquired the rights to produce the B3. This was developed as the B3 Mk2 (see page 186 for more information on this model).

Budweiser Rocket Car

1979 — Budweiser Rocket Car

Sponsored by Budweiser, the Budweiser Rocket Car was built in 1979 in the USA with the intention that it would be the first land vehicle to break the sound barrier in the 'Project Speed of Sound'. Designed by Stan Barrett and Bill Frederick, the vehicle had two wheels at the rear and was 12m long. It was powered by a rocket engine with a booster from a Sidewinder missile. On 17 December 1979 the vehicle, driven by Stan Barrett, attempted to break the sound barrier, leaving a debate that has been controversial ever since as the final speed of the vehicle has always been disputed. It was believed that the car could exceed the speed of sound but when the vehicle was run no sonic boom was heard.

The speed was estimated from a radar system at 38mph (61km/h) though, unfortunately, the radar had been tracking a large truck in the distance, away from the track that the rocket car had used. Some hours after the run the speed (at the vehicle's peak) was calculated at 739.666mph (1190.38km/h/Mach 1.01). This, however, caused widespread disbelief as the speed was never officially recorded.

Busy Bee

1920 — Busy Bee

Created by engineer Joseph Mills in 1920 at his garage in Mansfield, Nottinghamshire, UK, the Busy Bee was a one-off vehicle that served Mills trouble free for 27 years. The Busy Bee had an aluminium and plywood body that was attached to a tubular steel frame with sliding pillar front suspension and with the single rear wheel mounted in forks suspended on quarter elliptic springs. The engine, initially a 763cc side-valve Stag engine built in 1914, was mounted at the front of the vehicle

Built as a one-off vehicle in 1920, the Busy Bee — pictured here with its creator Joseph Mills — ran trouble free for 27 years before then passing through several further homes finally resting in a private collection. RUMCar News

and drove the single rear wheel. The engine was replaced in 1928 with an AJC 6bhp side-valve twin engine from a motorcycle combination that continued to use the original Sturmey Archer motorcycle-type clutch and gearbox. After Mills died the Busy Bee is believed to have had several homes and now resides in a private collection.

Butler Petrol Cycle

1885 — Petrol Cycle

The Butler Petrol Cycle is accepted by many as the very first British motorcar although, as it never went into production, others regard John Henry Knight's three-wheeler as the first. Although Karl Benz is recognised as the inventor of the modern motorcar, an Englishman named Edward Butler was said to have exhibited plans for a three-wheel vehicle two years earlier than Benz in 1884 at the Stanley Cycle Show, London, UK, and it was also the first design shown at the 1885 Inventions Exhibition, London, UK.

Butler, however, did not patent his vehicle until 1887 — Patent No 15598 (London) — due to British laws on experiments. On the vehicle, the patent read 'Butlers Petrol-Cycle Syndicate Limited Patent'. It also referred to 'F. B. Shuttleworth, Erith, London.' as Butler built the Petrol Cycle in the works of F B Shuttleworth. In 1890 Butler finished his design; the result was a vehicle powered by an engine that used mineral hydro-carbons.

The two-cylinder engine worked by a spray of Benzoline or petroleum product carburetted with air. The configuration saw two 32in wheels at the front that steered the vehicle. This was done through a pair of rocking handles actuating the front wheels that moved on separate pivots. A single rear wheel was powered by a chain whilst a single saddle type seat was positioned in between the front two wheels. A braking device was attached to both front wheels and activated by a foot lever.

Butler refined the vehicle further by using a four-stroke, water-cooled engine that achieved 600rpm. He is credited with first using the word 'Petrol' and inventing the spark plug, magneto, coil ignition and spray jet carburettor. Butler found problems with his invention due to government restrictions and on 12 December 1890 whilst referencing his vehicle wrote the following in the *English Mechanic* journal:

'..the authorities do not countenance its use on the roads, and I have abandoned in consequence any further development of it.'

At the time the maximum speed was 2mph (3km/h) in the city and 4mph (6km/h) in the countryside. In addition, each vehicle had to be attended by three people, of whom one had to walk in front of the vehicle waving a red flag — a consequence of the Locomotive Act (also known popularly as the Red Flag Act; 1865) — to warn other road users and help control horses. This act had originally appeared as a result of the growing number of steam-powered vehicles.

It is possible to see how restrictive this speed limit was for Butler from an article on the Butler Petrol Cycle in the 14 February 1891 edition of the *Scientific American*. This stated that one gallon of petroleum or benzolene was enough to 'furnish sufficient power' to achieve a journey of 40 miles (64km) at a speed ranging from 3-10mph (5-16km/h). The speed of the vehicle was regulated by a throttle valve lever whilst overheating was prevented by water circulating through a radiator over the rear driving wheel. Stopping and starting the vehicle was managed by rising and lowering the driving wheel from the ground by a foot lever, the weight of the vehicle was then spread onto two small castor wheels ahead of the driving wheel.

51

In 1900 Butler penned a letter to *The Autocar*, which was published on 7 April 1900. The letter read:

'Now that public attention is being drawn to the early attempts of the two German pioneers, Benz and Daimler, I trust that you may find space in your journal for an illustration [see image left] of a small petrol vehicle, which I believe was absolutely the first made in this country, and if I could have interested any one to finance it when the drawings were exhibited at the Stanley Show in 1884, and the following year at the Inventions Exhibition, I should have been contemporaneous, if not earlier than either of them.

Although I cannot claim to have done very much in the light of the present enormous development of the automotor trade, it may have been forgotten that I carried out a series of experiments in the perfecting of a motor vehicle at a time when progress was much hindered by the prejudice and want of interest – the motor part of which has been since used in many types of engines for industrial purposes.'

Above: *The 'Butler Petrol Cycle' was completed in 1890 though plans for it were shown as early as 1884 by Edward Butler who is also credited to be the first to use the word 'Petrol'.* Jane Neil

Butler then went on to describe his latest development of an 80bhp vertical compound three-cylinder engine standing at 7ft 6in and weighing six-and-a-half tons

Due to the lack of interest, Butler broke his Petrol Cycle up for scrap in 1896, following which the patent rights were sold to H J Lawson; thereafter the engine continued to be produced for motor boats. Shortly afterwards the Locomotive on Highways Act (1896) was passed that allowed speeds of up to 14mph (22.5km/h). This resulted in an immense change that saw new factories being established and motoring within the UK moving on rapidly.

Edward Butler pictured with his Butler Petrol Cycle in May 1889 at Erith, London. Jane Neil

Available as both a petrol and electric version the Harper Mk 1 was a single-seat invalid carriage that offered full weather protection. Stuart Cyphus

C B Harper Ltd

1954 — Harper Mk 1

After taking over the Stanley Engineering Co, which manufactured Argson invalid carriages, in 1954 C B Harper Ltd dropped the Argson range of vehicles in the UK and, in July 1954, replaced it with the company's own Invalid Carriage in the form of the Harper Mk 1. Both a petrol and an electric version were available; these were fitted with either a rear-mounted, air-cooled, single-cylinder, 197cc Villiers Mk 8E/R engine or a 36V electric motor. Both versions were single-seaters that had a fibreglass body built on a common steel chassis.

1956 — Harper Mk 4

The Harper Mk 4 — there was neither a Mk 2 nor a Mk 3 — was announced in 1956 and, whilst also available in both a petrol version and electric version, it had a redesigned body that was made from depressed mouldings. This not only offered more rigidity in the structure but also featured a wider windscreen that aided visibility.

1957 — Harper Mk 6/ Stanley Mk 7

As a result of new Ministry of Health Standard Specifications for Invalid carriages, the Harper Mk 6 was introduced in 1957. This was much larger than its predecessors and again came in both a petrol and electric version. By 1960 the Mk 6 had been renamed as the Stanley Mk 7 and was now powered with a larger Villiers Mk 11E engine. It had a slightly redesigned body with a higher roofline and glass side windows. Production ceased in 1965.

C W Manufacturing Co

1898 — Auto Tri

Designed by C W Kelsey, the Auto Tri was built in Pennsylvania, USA, from 1898 to 1900. It was fitted with an air-cooled, four-stroke, single-cylinder engine. The vehicle had tiller steering and remained solely a prototype that was used by Kelsey.

The prototype Auto Tri by C W Kelsey that was powered by a four-stroke single-cylinder engine. Author's Collection

1910 — Motorette

The Motorette was introduced in 1910; again it was designed by Kelsey and manufactured in Connecticut, USA. Power was supplied by a two-stroke, two-cylinder engine; this was initially air-cooled in the early models but was switched to water-cooled by 1911. The engine drove the single rear wheel through a two-speed with reverse gearbox whilst steering was controlled by a tiller device. The Motorette was a two-seater that was available with a number of options; these included a folding windscreen, lights, spare wheels, speedometer, folding hood and repair kit. As the first models produced tended to roll on cornering, an anti-sway bar was developed to counteract this. Several hundred vehicles were built and shipped throughout the USA as well as being exported to Denmark, Canada, Mexico and Japan. In addition to the standard version, a delivery van was also created with a payload of 250lb; the cargo area was positioned between the two front wheels. A rickshaw model was also created; this was exported to Japan. Production of all variations ceased in 1912.

Campagna Motors

1994 — T-Rex

The Campagna Corporation was founded in 1988 by Daniel Campagna in the Province of Quebec, Canada. Campagna was once an engineer who supported the F1 driver Gilles Villeneuve and from this gained the experience required to create a three-wheel sports vehicle.

The first generation of the T-Rex appeared in 1994 and went into production a year later. Designed by Daniel Campagna and Paul Deutschman, the T-Rex was a two-seat vehicle that had a body made of a fibreglass reinforced plastic-sandwich construction with a carbon fibre windscreen and headrest on a multi tubular steel roll cage. It was powered by a 1,100cc four-cylinder, two-OHC engine with ram-air that gave the vehicle a 0-60mph (0-96km/h) time of 4.1sec and a top speed of 140mph (225km/h).

The latest generation of the T-Rex is the 14R powered by a liquid-cooled Kawasaki 1,400cc engine and providing 197bhp with a top speed of 144mph (230Km/h). Campagna Motors

2010 — T-Rex 14R/ T-Rex 14RR

The latest generation of the T-Rex is the 14R that was first introduced in 2010 and the limited edition 14RR, the latter being an enhanced version that is deemed to be 'Track Worthy'. Both versions are powered by a Kawasaki 1,400cc inline four-cylinder, liquid-cooled engine offering 197bhp with 0-60mph (0-96km/h) in 3.92sec and a top speed of 144mph (232km/h). Like the original T-Rex, the body panels are made from fibreglass with carbon fibre windscreen and headrest that is attached to a rigid 1.5in tubular steel chassis that has a safety roll-cage and three-points safety belts. Suspension is catered for with unequal opposed triangular arms at the front and a swinging arm with dual shock dampers at the rear. Drive is sent to the rear wheel by chain from a six-speed gearbox. The T-Rex 14RR differs from the 14R in that, whilst remaining street legal, it has been enhanced for track use with a race ready four-point harness, ventilated brake disc on all wheels with braided steel lines along with adjustable rear shocks amongst other features. These include a race oriented rack and pinion with 2.75 turn ratio. The T-Rex 14R and T-Rex 14RR remain in production at the time of writing.

2011 — V-13R

Originally manufactured by Cirbin Inc in Canada, Campagna Motors acquired the rights to build the V-13R in 2011. The two-seat Campagna V-13R is an open top three-wheeler with modern design roadster styling. With a few subtle differences to the Cirbin version, the vehicle remains powered by a 1,250cc Harley-Davidson liquid-cooled Revolution 60° V-twin engine that drives the rear wheel by a belt via a five-speed gearbox. The chassis is made from 1.5in tubular steel with laminated fibreglass body panels whilst suspension is provided for with unequal opposed triangular arms shocks on the front and a mono shock at the rear. The V-13R is available at the present time.

Designed as a modern day roadster the V-13R is built for cruising rather than speed. Campagna Motors

Castle Three Motor Co

1919 — Castle Three

The Castle Three Motor Co was based in Kidderminster, Worcestershire, UK, and was founded in 1906 by brothers Stanley and Laughton Goodwin as a repair business. It was after making gun carriage hubs, shells and aero-engine components during World War 1 that the brothers decided to build cars. In 1919 they produced their Castle Three, described as having 'that proper car look it was aimed at the top end of the market and designed as a rival to the Morgan three-wheeler'. The first 12 Castle Three vehicles were fitted with a four-cylinder, side-valve, water-cooled, 1,094cc Dorman engine. This was then uprated to a four-cylinder, 1,207cc, 9bhp Belgian-made Peters engine that drove the single rear wheel by shaft and bevel gears through either a two-speed epicyclic or three-speed conventional type gearbox.

The car had all the equipment of a 'real car' with dynamo lighting, spare wheel and tyre, and pressed steel artillery wheels instead of the usual wire or wooden disc. The wheels were advertised as being fully interchangeable. The body was an open two-seater that also

Designed to look and feel like a 'real car' the Castle Three contained all the equipment and build of a four-wheeler of its time. Unfortunately in doing so, it exceeded the weight limit to qualify for a lower tricycle tax and so attracted full tax. Joe Turner

Powered by a 192cc engine the Cambro Monocar was one of the cheapest cars on the market in 1921 at £82 19s. Author's Collection

had a dickey seat and featured a nickel-plated radiator. Attempting to create a true car three-wheeler, the vehicle was extremely heavy; this unfortunately meant that it exceeded the weight limit to make it qualify for a lower tax. It was also the most expensive three-wheeler, being priced at £295, and so any advantages a buyer might have gained in buying a three-wheeler were lost in extra fuel consumption, no tax reduction and purchase price.

The transmission on these cars did cause serious setbacks for the company that later, when combined with other problems, caused manufacturing to cease in 1922 after only 350 vehicles were produced. In the same year the company introduced a four-wheeler called the Castle Four though it never entered production. The company then closed and the works were sold to a local carpet maker. In August 2013 the Castle Three Motor Co was reformed and at the time of printing is seeking investors with an aim to produce an updated two-seat version of the original.

Catley & Ayres

1869 — Steam vehicle

In 1869, Catley & Ayres of York, UK, built a small steam powered three-wheeler that was able to carry four passengers. The vehicle had a fire tube vertical boiler mounted at the rear that worked at 120psi, driving the horizontal twin-cylinder engine. It had a single front wheel that was steered with a tiller. Top speed was 20mph (32km/h).

Central Aircraft Co Ltd

1921 — Cambro

The Cambro (Monocar) was one of the cheapest cars on the market in 1921 priced at £82 19s. Manufactured by the Central Aircraft Co Ltd of Middlesex, UK, the vehicle was a single-seater and was fitted with a 192cc two-cylinder, horizontally-opposed, two-stroke engine. The engine was mounted over the single rear wheel, which it drove by a chain through a gearbox that had just one gear with a ratio of 9-5:1. Due to its diminutive proportions the Cambro weighed just 165lb. Later in 1921 a new version was introduced that had a hood for weather protection and a more triangular front end.

Certain

1907 — Tri-Voiturette

Manufactured in France from 1907, the Certain Tri-Voiturette was powered by a Lurquin-Courdert single-cylinder engine. The engine was placed at the driver's feet and drove the single rear wheel by a belt. The driver's seat was a single seat at the rear with a high backrest whilst the passengers sat in a passenger compartment between the two front wheels.

Chang Jaing

1970s — Chang Jaing

This three-wheeler was built in China by the Chang Jaing Motorcycle factory for use as a small truck during the 1970s and 1980s. Powered by a BMW side-valve, four-stroke boxer (R12) engine the vehicle came with different body versions that included a tipper and minibus. With the cabin removed the vehicle had the front end of a motorcycle.

Chevrolet

1969 — Astro III

Chevrolet is not the first name you associate with three-wheelers though, in 1969, it created the Astro III as a concept vehicle. Designed by Bill Mitchell, the Astro III had a sleek fibreglass body that was less than 3ft high. Access to the vehicle was through a canopy that lifted up and forward electrically, the seats also rose to make boarding easier. Once in position both the seats and canopy were lowered at the flick of a switch. Although classed as a three-wheeler, the vehicle actually had four-wheels with the front two wheels sitting side-by-side under the nose, giving the appearance of a single wheel. They were steered by pistol grip lever controls. Power came from a Model 250-C18 gas-turbine engine built by the Allison Division of General Motors. The car's concept was that it would travel on restricted access or systems-controlled interstate highways of the future.

China Engineering Corporation

1948 — Rik-Mobile

Developed by the China Engineering Corporation in San Francisco, USA, in 1948, the Rik-Mobile was designed to be exported to China. With an open body with no roof or doors, the vehicle resembled a large three-wheel scooter with a single seat for the driver at the front and two passenger seats at the rear. With a large fairing that turned with the front wheel, the Rik-Mobile was steered by motorcycle-type handlebars whilst the brakes and accelerator were in the conventional position on the floor board. It was fitted with an air-cooled engine with two gears.

Designed by General Motors in 1969, the Chevrolet Astro III was a concept vehicle that was planned to use a Model 250-C18 gas-turbine engine.
General Motors

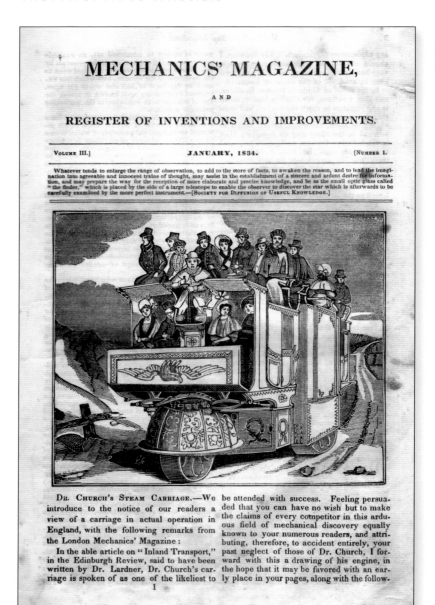

The front page of the Mechanics' Magazine and Register of Inventions and Improvements *for January 1834 featuring Dr Church's Steam Carriage.* Mechanics' Magazine

was detailed as being 60bhp capable of carrying a load of 15 tons. The steam coach was designed to carry 44 passengers, with 22 inside and 22 outside, though it was not popular as passengers were nervous about sitting so close to the boiler. Fitted with three large solid wheels, it was said that the steam coach ran daily between Birmingham and London at an average speed of 14mph (22.5km/h) though in reality it is believed that it was never a going concern. The company planned to have three stations along the route at which the steam coaches would stop and be replaced by a fresh coach so that the old one could be examined and oiled/adjusted as necessary. The scheme, however, is said to never have been practically accomplished as the coaches were constantly failing and the company was dissolved in May 1837.

Cimera

1952 — Boli

Due to government policies in Spain at the time, entrepreneur José Bolinche was not authorised to manufacture four-wheel vehicles and so he built three-wheelers in Valencia. Bolinche is believed to have said: 'that this is not a car with a wheel missing but a motorcycle with an extra wheel.' In 1952 Bolinche created the Boli, which was essentially based on the rear end of a scooter with the front modified to support two wheels between which was an open storage area with wooden sides and a single headlamp at the front. Despite its strong scooter heritage, steering was done through a steering wheel.

1954 — Cimera

The Cimera was made in 1954 and sold both as the Cimera and also as the Boli. Unlike the previous vehicle, this was more car-like with an open two-seat fibreglass body and a hood for weather protection. The body went through a number of restyles during 1954, with the front end becoming more streamlined. Power was provided to the single rear wheel.

Church

1833 — Steam Coach

Born in 1778 William Church was an Amercian inventor who moved to Bordesley Green, near Birmingham, UK, in the mid-1820s. In 1832 he patented his first steam carriage and, following another patent in 1835, the London & Birmingham Steam Carriage Co was set up. Dr Church's three-wheel steam coach was completed in 1833 and

Cirbin Inc

2007 — V-13R

Co-founded by André Morissette and David Neault, Carbin Inc produced its first three-wheel prototype — the VT-Rod — which was taken along to a number of trade shows to gauge interest. Following the input from potential customers, they unveiled the V-13R at the SEMA show in October 2007. Built in Canada, the V-13R was a two-seat, Hot-Rod, retro-styled three-wheeler, powered by a Harley-Davidson liquid-cooled, Revolution 60° V-twin engine of 1,250cc, giving the vehicle 125bhp. The chassis is made from tubular steel with fibreglass body panels giving the V-13R a weight of 1,050lb (475kg). The suspension had adjustable front shocks that were adjustable in both preload and rebound damping along with a fully adjustable motorcycle monoshock at the rear. In 2011 the manufacturing rights of the Cirbin V-13R were acquired by Campagna Motors and at present is sold by them as the Campagna V-13R.

Powered by a 2.5kW electric motor the City-El had a range of 43 to 55 miles (70 to 90km) with a top speed of 40mph (63km/h).
RUMCar News

CityCom A/S

1987 — City-El

The City-El was originally manufactured in Denmark between 1987 and 1995 under the name of Mini-El and built by El Trans A/S (see page 93 for more information). The company was taken over in 1995 by Citycom Denmark A/S and production was moved to Kitzingen, Germany, with between 150 and 200 vehicles being built each year.

The City-El is a single-seat electric three-wheeler, which has an optional rear facing child seat that fits behind the front seat in the engine compartment. The latest City-Els are Series 2 introduced in 2009, with Series 1 having a 36V, 2.5kW electric motor fed by three 80 Ah lead acid batteries offering a top speed of 25-35mph (40-56km/h) and a range of 43 miles (69km). Series 2 have a more powerful 4kW electric motor that provides a top speed of 40mph (64km/h) and a range of 43 to 55 miles (69-89km). The vehicles can be charged from any 220V outlet.

1987 — Basic

The Basic version was discontinued in 2009. The body of the vehicle was made of plastic whilst the whole top half was hinged to allow access to both the front and back seats.

1987 — Targa

The Targa version was the same as the Basic model though it had a removable centre soft top and solid rear windows. This model is also now discontinued.

1987 — Fun

The Fun version is essentially the same specifications as the Basic model though featuring a detachable top. This model is still in production at the time of writing.

Columbe

1920 — Colombe

Available in both one- and two-seat versions, the Colombe was first manufactured in France in 1920. It had a 345cc single-cylinder engine that was attached directly to the single front wheel. The one-seat version set many world records for its class in 1923 in Arpajon, France. It had a metal body with a canvas fold-up roof. Production ceased in 1924, although a redesigned version was introduced under the Villard name in the same year (see page 24).

Combidrive Ltd

1996 — Mouse

In 1996 the Combidrive Mouse three-wheeler set the World record for the lowest petrol consumption at the Shell Mileage Marathon in Northants, UK. Created in the mid-1990s in Wales by Combidrive Ltd, the Mouse was powered by a 265cc single-cylinder, direct injection, 4.8bhp diesel engine and was capable of up to 255.9mpg. (1.1-litre/100km). The single-seat vehicle set a record of 568mpg. (0.5-litre/100km).

Compagnie Française du Cyclauto

1919 — Cyclauto

Introduced in France in 1919, the Cyclauto was built by the Compagnie Française du Cyclauto. Power came from a 487cc, water-cooled, two-stroke, side-by-side, vertical-cylinder Sicam engine that was mounted at the front of the vehicle and drove the rear two wheels by a chain to an epicyclic gear on the counter shaft and then two belts running over pulleys to provide the final drive. Later models were powered by 900cc Ruby four-cylinder engines. The body of the vehicle was a tubular steel frame used for bicycles with steel panels attached to it. It also had a large collapsible hood. Production ceased in 1923.

Condor Motor Co

1913 — Condor Lightcar

The single-seat, three-wheel Condor of 1913, manufactured by the Condor Motor Co in Coventry, UK, was totally unique when it came to three-wheeler design. It had three-wheels aligned in the form of an isosceles triangle, with the wheel at the apex driving the vehicle whilst the front and rear wheel both steered the vehicle. The 4bhp air-cooled engine was attached to a wooden beam and sat midway between the steering wheels; the engine was suspended as a sprung weight off the main frame. The middle wheel was on the opposite side to the engine and was driven by a propeller shaft via two leather universal couplings to an internally-toothed ring on the driving wheel. The vehicle had a tubular frame that was suspended on laminated springs. The steering wheels were connected by long tubular radius rods to the point of attachment of the engine with the driving wheel being braced by tubular members that formed a triangle with the radius rods. Production is believed to have ended in the same year.

Construcciones Acorazadas SA

1957 — Triver

Although at first glance, and by name, the Triver appears to be a three-wheeler, it was actually a four-wheeler with two wheels at the back that were set very close together. Manufactured from 1957 by

The Condor Lightcar from 1913 was different from other three-wheelers in that it was based on an isosceles triangle with the third wheel being half way down the body at the side whilst the front and rear wheels were in line with each other. Author's Collection

The engine on the Condor Lightcar sat directly opposite the centre third wheel on the other side of the body and drove the wheel via a propeller shaft. Author's Collection

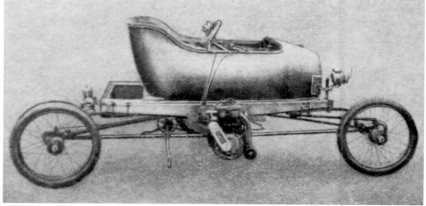

Construcciones Acorazadas SA in Bilbao, Spain, which also made safes and armoured goods, the Triver was built on a steel chassis and had a 3mm thick steel body. It was available as both a passenger car and a van with both versions seating two people. The Triver was powered by a rear mounted 5bhp, air-cooled, twin-cylinder 339cc engine or a 14bhp, twin-cylinder 500cc version that drove the rear wheels with a top speed of 50mph (80km/h). Production ceased in 1960 with around 75 vehicles believed to have built of which a single survivor remains.

Contal et Cie

1905 — Contal

The Contal was built by Contal et Cie in Paris, France, during 1905. Power came from a 4bhp, single-cylinder, water-cooled engine that powered the single rear wheel via a chain. It was available in both passenger and commercial versions with the passenger sitting in front of the driver. The vehicle is probably better known for its entry into the 1907 Peking to Paris race. It was driven by Auguste Pons with mechanic Octave Foucault. The vehicle was the only three-wheeler in the race but struggled through the mud and over mountains. Due to the weight on the front of the vehicle, the rear wheel could not maintain traction and eventually broke down and ran out of fuel in the Gobi desert. The car was abandoned and the pair, almost dead, managed to crawl for several days until they came across an encampment of nomads.

In 1908, the single rear wheel was put on the front of the vehicle with power going to the two rear wheels but the vehicles ceased manufacture in the same year.

Copeland

1881 — Tricycle

Built by Lucius Day Copeland in Pheonix, Arizona, USA, the roots of the first Copeland three-wheeler can be found in 1881 when he began working on steam engines. One of his steam engines managed to power a Columbia bicycle at 15mph (24km/h). As a result Copeland went on to manufacture the Copeland tricycle. Steam-powered, Copeland's Tricycle was a two-seat vehicle that had an automatic oil-fired vertical boiler, which was mounted just in front of the single rear wheel. This transmitted power to the two front wheels, which drove the vehicle whilst steering was via the rear single wheel. In 1884 the Northrup Manufacturing Co was set up in New Jersey, USA, by Copeland to produce the vehicles. To prove the model's worth, Copeland, along with a director of the company, drove a tricycle on a 120-mile round trip to Atlantic City. The vehicle had a range of 30 miles (48km) before needing to stop and then took around five minutes to build up enough steam to continue. Manufacture of the vehicles ceased in 1891 after around 200 vehicles had been built.

Fitted with an automatic oil-fired vertical boiler, the steam powered Copeland Tricycle was able to travel 30 miles before needing to stop for five minutes to build up enough steam again to continue. Kerry Croxton

Although several test vehicles were created the Corbin Merlin Roadster was an open topped vehicle that never managed to reach full production. Dave Vezina

Powered by a Harley Davidson V-twin engine the Corbin Merlin Roadster featured lift-up scissor doors. Dave Vezina

Corbin Motor Co

1999 — Sparrow

The Corbin Motor Co, of California, USA, was formed on 29 March 1999 as a spin-off from the Corbin-Pacific Co, which had been founded in 1996 by Mike Corbin. The Corbin Pacific Co had been working on a single-person electric vehicle since 1996 whilst supplying motorcycle seats, saddles and body styling globally. On 12 April 1999 its first three-wheeler — the Sparrow — passed its final testing for the Department of Transport and later that year the vehicle went into full production. The Sparrow, designed by Mike Corbin, had a 156V electric engine that was powered by 13 12V batteries that give a range of 40 to 60 miles (64-97km) on one battery pack charge and was capable of speeds up to 70mph (113km/h). The Sparrow had a lightweight monocoque chassis and a body made from fibreglass with a top and a bottom section secured together with industrial adhesive. Two-part polyurethane foam was then injected between the two shells in varying thicknesses. The Sparrow also featured disk brakes on all three-wheels, a three-point safety harness and electric windows.

2002 — Merlin/ Roadster

Corbin Motors also designed a second three-wheeler called the Merlin, which was powered by a V-twin Harley Davidson engine and developed alongside an open-top Roadster that Corbin announced would be produced from 2002. Although several test vehicles were built it never saw full production. According to the *Pinnacle News* (Internet edition dated 16 January 2003) fewer than 300 Sparrows were made and many customers never received their vehicles. Of those sold many went back to the factory for repairs. The company filed for Chapter 7 Bankruptcy protection on 31 March 2003. In August 2003 the key to the old Corbin Motors' building was handed over to Ron Huch, who used to be the former Corbin Motors company president, as he was the only individual from more than a thousand creditors who filed a guaranteed $500,000 UCC lien against Corbin Motors just before the company went bankrupt. In 2004 the Corbin Sparrow stock was acquired by Myers Motors (see page 174 for more information).

Coronet Cars Ltd

1957 — Coronet

The 1957 Coronet was a design based on the Powerdrive three-wheeler that had ceased production earlier in the same year (see page 192). It was designed by David Gottleib. Construction by Coronet Cars Ltd was undertaken in Denham, UK, before the company moved to larger premises at West Drayton, London, UK. The chassis consisted of 14-gauge channel-section steel longerons with tubular cross members with the front suspension being unequal length wishbones and Armstrong coil spring/damper units with a single Armstrong coil spring/damper unit at the rear. The two-seat body was made from fibreglass, providing very sporty looks for the time, and the car was

Introduced in 1957, the Coronet looked like a sports car of its era and although it had dummy air intakes at the front, the engine was actually mounted behind the seat. Jeff Green

powered by a 328cc Excelsior twin engine — mounted behind the seat — that drove the single rear wheel by roller-chain via a three-speed plus reverse gearbox. The Coronet was manufactured until 1960.

Costruzioni Meccaniche Casalini Srl

1971 — Sulky/ Sulky Cabriolet

Based in Piacenza in Italy, Costruzioni Meccaniche Casalini Srl is one of the oldest microcar manufacturers in the world. Founded in 1939, the company initially built mopeds and tricycles before introducing the Casalini Sulky in 1971. It featured a tubular-steel chassis and had a metal body with side doors and a door at the rear. It was fitted with either an air-cooled, single-cylinder 50cc or 60cc engine. Early versions of the Sulky had a bench seat designed for one person and handlebar steering, whilst later versions had a steering wheel. A Sulky Cabriolet version was also available; this had no roof or side doors. In the 1970s the Sulky was restyled with a new body that featured ABS bumpers and twin headlights and had an updated interior with dual seats and a steering wheel. Over 10,000 vehicles were built before production ceased in 1994 to be replaced by the Sulky Kore range.

A front cover of a Casalini Sulky brochure that worryingly seems to depict owners in the background taken a Sulky apart. John Lloyd

The Casalini Sulky; this particular model being a later version as it has a steering wheel rather than handlebars. William Brand

1986 — Sulky A16/Sulky A18/ Sulky Diesel/ Sulky SP50 Kore

The Sulky A16 was introduced in 1986 and powered by a two-stroke 125cc engine positioned at the rear of the vehicle that drove the rear wheels with a 'V' belt through an automatic transmission. Like the original Sulky, the A16 had a monocoque steel body shell with a tubular-steel chassis and was a two-seater with separated seats. Fitted with a 'sporting' steering wheel, the A16 was available in both right-hand and left-hand drive versions. Other features included ABS bumpers and spoiler, fog light, reversing light and a two-speed windscreen wiper. The Sulky A18 followed the same specifications as the A16, though was fitted with a twin-cylinder 246cc engine and the diesel version was also the same although powered by a 325cc Lombardini engine. In addition to the fully-enclosed models, an open-top version of each model was also available; these had a roll back canvas roof. In 1994 Casalini introduced a new range of four-wheelers known as the Sulky Kore; amongst them was a three-wheel Sulky Kore (SP50) that replaced all the other three-wheel versions. Whilst essentially the same vehicle, it received a number of updates along with different ABS bumpers, and side bumpers along with an updated interior that gave the vehicle a modern feel when compared with the previous versions. The Kore SP50 was powered by either a Piaggio Ape 50cc engine or a Honda 350cc engine and was manufactured until 1996 when the range was reduced to four-wheelers only.

County Commercial Cars Ltd

1936 — Devon Distributor

Using the Ford Tug as a base (see Ford Motor Co on page 99 for more information), in 1936 County Commercial Cars Ltd of Fleet, Hampshire, UK, created a three-wheel van that was both approved of and marketed by the Ford Motor Co. The Devon Distributor van was an extended version of the Ford Tug. It was modified to accommodate either a 1,250cu ft Lawson Overtype Luton body or a smaller 1,040cu ft version that was also made. The vehicle from the front to the end of the cab was a standard Tug model and then extensions were added to the middle of the chassis to extend it. Production ended in 1938 when Ford stopped manufacturing the Ford Tug.

Using a Ford Tug as its base, the Devon Distributor was fitted with a Luton body that offered 1,250cu ft of space. Colin Pickett

Amongst the listed features on the Coventry Premier was a quick detachable rear wheel that could be removed without disturbing the transmission. Coventry Transport Museum

Coventry Premier Ltd

1919 — Coventry Premier

Introduced in October 1919, the Coventry Premier had listed amongst its features 'a quickly detachable rear wheel'. Built in Coventry, UK, by Coventry Premier Ltd, the vehicle was powered by a Premier 1,055cc, water-cooled, V-twin engine that drove the single rear wheel by chain. The drive was taken from the engine to the three-speed plus reverse gearbox by a leather-to-metal cone clutch. The design of the back wheel meant that the wheel could be removed without disturbing the transmission as a result of the way that the back wheel anchorage was designed. Whilst acetylene

lighting was standard, there was an option of upgrading to electric lighting provided by a dynamo that sat behind the engine and was driven from the main shaft, a pulley already in position on the standard model. For the vehicle's purchase price of £210, standard equipment also included a horn, hood, windscreen, spare wheel and tyre along with tools and a jack. In 1920 Coventry Premier was taken over by Singer and the model continued to be manufactured until 1923 when it was then replaced with a four-wheeler.

Coventry Victor Motor Co

1926 — Standard/ De-luxe/Parcelcar/Sports

Originally called Morton & Weaver, a manufacturer of proprietary engines in Coventry, UK, from 1904, the company changed its name to the Coventry Victor Motor Co in 1911 and then started making engines and sidecars. From 1919 it started to manufacture motorcycles. In 1926 the company launched the Coventry Victory three-wheeler in four versions: the Standard, the De-luxe, the Parcelcar and the Sports. All were initially powered by a water-cooled, twin-cylinder, 688cc engine and used a steel chassis with the engine, which drove the single rear wheel by chain via a two-speed gearbox,

mounted at the front. The engine was enlarged to 749cc and other improvements to the vehicle were made; the engine was again enlarged in 1932 to 850cc; its final capacity was 998cc. Whilst the Standard and Sports models were two-seaters, the De-luxe version was a family version that included two extra seats in the rear for children. The parcel van had a rear van conversion that was available as a three- or 4cwt van and all models were manufactured until 1938 with the company then concentrating on general engineering.

1932 — Avon Sports Coupé/ Luxury Sports

In 1932 the Avon Sports Coupé with an enclosed body was introduced; it was followed by an open Luxury Sports model in 1934 that was powered by an 8bhp water-cooled, twin-cylinder 850cc engine, which offered 70mph (113km/h). A 900cc version was also then announced. Both versions had the single rear-wheel drive via a two-speed plus reverse gearbox. The luxury models included full leather interior and also came with a folding hood, safety glass, side-screens, dynamo lighting, electric horn and a spare wheel amongst other things. Production of all models ceased in 1938, although, in 1949, an attempt was made to revive the Coventry Victor name with several prototypes code-named 'Venus' being created. These were powered by a 747cc flat-four engine but the model did not go into production.

The Coventry Victor Luxury Sports model featured a full leather interior, a folding hood, dynamo lighting, front and side screens and even an electric horn.
John Lloyd

Advertised as being 'in touch with tomorrow' the Ceres had a coefficient drag of 0.18 CD that with its 993cc engine was able to achieve up to 62mpg. Doug Tuttle

Creative Cars Corporation

1983 — Ceres

Manufactured in Rockford, Illinois, USA, in 1983 by the Creative Cars Corporation, the Ceres was a three-wheeler marketed as being 'In touch with tomorrow'. With its sleek fibreglass body, the Ceres had a coefficient of drag that was just 0.18 – something the manufacturers proudly compared with the Audi 5000 (.30) and the Rolls-Royce Spirit (.55). Weighing in at 1,475lb the vehicle was able to achieve 55bhp from its OHC Daihatsu three-cylinder 993cc engine that was mounted between the rear wheels. This was able to provide a top speed of over 90mph (145km/h) and a fuel consumption of 50mpg (5.6-litre/100km) in the city and 62mpg (4.5-litre/100km) on the highway.

Standing just 17in above the road and having a wide wheelbase, the vehicle was said to have superior handling. Additionally 72% of the vehicle's weight was over the rear wheels, thus improving overall traction, especially in snow or on ice. The vehicle had a three-seat interior fitted with a walnut dashboard and optional leather seats. Costing $13,875 for the basic model and $15,270 for a model with air conditioning, AM/FM cassette clock radio, two-tone paint and leather seats, production numbers are believed to have been very low.

The Daihatsu engine of the Ceres was mounted between the rear wheels and so the body had side vents at the rear to help pull in air to cool the engine. Doug Tuttle

Cree AG/SAM Group AG

2001 — Sam

Creation Engineering Ecology (Cree AG) was founded in Switzerland in 1996 with the aim of developing a contemporary vehicle for local use. In 2001 the company unveiled the Sam (Sustainable Automotive Mobility), a three-wheel electric vehicle for two people seated in a tandem style. Powered by 14 lead-acid batteries that provided 168V to a modularised drive system — a synchronous belt providing power to the back wheel — the vehicle had a top speed of around 52mph (84km/h) and a range of 31 to 43 miles (50-69km) between charges. A full recharge took six hours. With two people on board the vehicle could reach 30mph (48km/h) in seven seconds.

Made with a chassis that is 90% recycled steel, a Polyethylene body that is 100% recyclable and powered by an electric motor that can be charged via a solar carport, the Sam is extremely environmentally friendly.
AU Dan Daniels

The Sam had a double-walled plastic body that was composed of four major components and featured gull wing doors that opened upwards. The seats were air-filled thermoplastic that, combined with an aluminium chassis, gave the vehicle an overall weight of 545kg.

Many Sam prototypes were built and the model was tested by more than 30,000 drivers. The vehicle was due to be launched in 2002 but, despite much interest, Cree did not succeed in finding adequate funding with the result that production was delayed until further notice.

2007 — Sam II

In 2007 the SAM Group AG was founded; this had all the rights to the Sam and, by 2008, the first prototype of the Sam II was created and, following numerous tests, was then launched for sale in 2010. The Sam II remains virtually the same vehicle as the Sam though is now driven by a 105V engine powered by a Lithium polymer battery with a top speed of 56mph (90km/h). In addition, the chassis is created from 90% recycled steel whilst the Polyethylene body is 100% recyclable. The Sam can be charged from any 220V socket with a charging time of one hour for 40% or five hours for a full charge. One extra that can be purchased is a solar carport with 8m² roof that produces enough electricity to charge the Sam. At present the Sam is available in Switzerland, Germany and Poland.

Crouch Cars

1912 — Carette

Founded in 1912 in Coventry, UK, by John W F Crouch, Crouch Cars Ltd introduced its three-wheeler — the Crouch Carette — the same year. The model was powered by a 749cc, side-valve, water-cooled Coventry-Simplex V-twin engine (which later became known as the Coventry Climax) that was mounted behind the seats and provided drive to the single rear wheel by a chain via a three-speed gearbox. The chassis and frame were made from Ash with metal sheeting to form the body. By 1913 the three-wheel Carette became a four-wheel version with a larger 906cc engine. The company continued to manufacture four-wheelers until it closed in 1928.

Cugnot

1769 — fardier à vapeur

Nicolas-Joseph Cugnot is recognised as building the first self-propelled vehicle to transport man. Cugnot was at the time an engineer in the French Army. Steam power has been used since the early 18th century for fixed machines that pumped water from mines, or raised heavy equipment. It was not known at the time how to convert the back and forth pass motion of steam power into a rotary movement to make a wheel turn. Cugnot solved this problem and in 1769 built a full-size prototype vehicle based on a model he had made some six years earlier. His Steam Dray (fardier à vapeur) had three-wheels with iron rims, two wheels were at the back with the one wheel in front.

Fitted with the famous Coventry Climax engine, the Crouch Carette was just one of the hundreds of vehicles that were manufactured in Coventry.
Coventry Transport Museum

The world's first self-propelled vehicle was Cugnot's 'fardier à vapeur' that was built in 1769 and designed as a gun carriage. It went on to cause the world's first automobile accident when it demolished a garden wall.
Chuck Andersen

The vehicle carried a front mounted boiler and a two-cylinder engine located over the front wheel. Cugnot's vehicle worked but needed to stop every 10-12min to rebuild enough steam pressure to continue. The vehicle had a top speed of 2mph (3km/h) and eventually caused the world's first automobile accident when it ran out of control and demolished a garden wall. Cugnot's Steam Dray was designed initially as a gun carriage to transport large pieces of artillery and was tested to carry large loads. In July 1771, Cugnot built a second vehicle ready for testing. He had been encouraged in his work by General Gribeauval and the Duke of Choiseul, who were placed very well at the Court of Louis XV. Gribeauval then wrote to the Marquis de Monteynard, the Minister for War, asking him to close the Avenue of Versailles so that Cugnot's vehicle could be tested in secrecy and on uneven land. These tests did not take place as the letter was never answered. It is thought the vehicle was used in the grounds of the Arsenal where it had been built. It survived the Revolution and today is in the National Academy of Arts and Métiers, France, where it has been since 1800.

Louis XV gave Cugnot an annual pension of 600 francs; this ceased after 1789 and as a result the inventor became poor and was exiled to Brussels. Cugnot was also to receive, shortly before his death in 1804, a pension from Napoleon. Napoleon was not interested in steam-powered gun vehicles and so gave the technology little thought. In the following 30 years no inventors worked in France and steam power was developed further in the UK by names like William Murdock, James Watt and Richard Trevithick. (See page 174 and page 250 for more information).

Cushman Motor Works

1952 — Truckster

Cushman was founded in 1901 in Nebraska, USA, as a manufacturer making two-stroke engines for fishing boats. In 1936 the company became The Cushman Motor Works and began to manufacture two-wheel Scooters, including the Cushman Airborne (model 53) that was designed to be dropped by parachute to support airborne troops. In 1952 the company started to build a small, light duty vehicle called the Cushman Truckster. It was powered by an 18bhp engine that provided an average top speed of around 35mph (56km/h) and had a load capacity of 2,000lb. A number of variants of the van have been produced over the years with most of them being used in airports and factories. Since the 1970s, a number of police forces in the USA, including the New York Police Department (NYPD), have used the Cushman. They are mainly used by officers who are on foot patrol as the Cushman assists quick movement around the state and helps them to cover greater distances. These Patrol Trucksters were produced up until 2002.

1955 — Haulster/Golfster

In 1955 Cushman introduced electric-powered three-wheel vehicles for golf — which became the Golfster in 1961 — and industrial use — Haulster — for moving goods around sites. The Golfster was a popular golfing vehicle that was used by figures such as President Eisenhower and a number of celebrities including Bob Hope and Frank Sinatra. Production, however, ceased in 1975 as a result of the imported Polish-built Golf Carts costing less to buy. The Haulster was eventually replaced by a four-wheel variant with the same name that at the time of writing still offers a choice of petrol or diesel engines.

1957 — Mailster

In 1957 Cushman received a contract from the United States Postal Service (USPS) for 1,500 Mailsters. The vehicles were adapted Trucksters and could carry up to 500lb of mail. Powered by a 7.5bhp engine that was positioned below the driver's seat, the driver controlled the vehicle via handlebars. The Cushman Mailster had no doors, having instead a vinyl curtain that was pulled across. This arrangement led many postal workers to complain about their inability to heat the vehicle.

Used by numerous Police forces throughout the USA the Cushman Patrol Truckster was used by officers on foot patrol. This particular vehicle was spotted by the author in New York in 2005 and brought much amusement to the officer as to why it was being photographed. Author's Collection

2011 — Minute Miser

Introduced in 2011 the Cushman Minute Miser is an electric-powered truck that is designed for carrying goods around warehouses, airports, work sites, etc. Powered by a 24V, 1.5bhp electric motor, it has a maximum speed of 10mph (16km/h) and is available with either a tiller or steering wheel to steer the single front wheel. The vehicle is an open single-seater and is able to carry two people, with the back rest from the front seat folded down, or one person and up to 300lb (140kg) on the cargo deck. This vehicle remains in production at present.

Cyklon Co

1902 — Cyklonette

The Cyklonette was first exhibited at the Leipzig Motor Show, Germany, in 1902. Built by the Cyklon Co in Rummelsburg, Germany, which had been manufacturing motorcycles that had an engine fixed on to the front wheel, the model was then transformed into a three-wheeler. The Cyklonette used two engines — a 450cc 3.5bhp, air-cooled, single-cylinder version for the two-seat Cyklonette and a 1,290cc, two-cylinder engine for the four-seat Cyklonette. In both cases the engine was placed directly above the front wheel which it powered by a chain. As the front wheel was turned, using a tiller for steering, the whole engine would also turn. Whilst the mechanics remained the same with engine placement, several body versions were available for the vehicles; these included a passenger vehicle and a delivery vehicle with a van-like section at the back. Manufacture continued until 1929.

The Cyklonette used an air-cooled engine that was mounted directly above the front wheel with both the wheel and the engine built in the same frame. This meant that the engine turned with the front wheel. Maxwell Paternoster

CZ

1961 — Cezeta 505

In 1961 the CZ (Česká zbrojovka) motorcycle factory in Czechoslovakia, which had been established in 1919, produced a commercial three-wheeler. The Cezeta 505 used the front end of a Cezeta scooter attached to a tubular frame with two rear wheels. Powered by a 171cc, single-cylinder, two-stroke, air-cooled engine, the Cezeta 505 came as either an open type scooter or with a completely enclosed fibreglass cabin. There was also a choice of a number of rear bodies, including a flat bed, van body and drop side that provided a load capacity of 200kg. Production ceased in 1963.

D

D & A Vehicles

1983 — Minikin

D & A Vehicles of Minnesota, USA, acquired the rights to the Freeway manufactured by H M Vehicles in 1983. In the same year it introduced a three-wheeler called the Minikin. Mechanically the Minikin was almost identical to the Freeway and was powered by a 16bhp, four-stroke, air-cooled, 453.25cc Tecumseh engine that offered up to 70mpg (4-litre/100km). The single rear wheel was driven by a chain. Unlike the Freeway, however, the Minikin was a two-seat vehicle with side-by-side seats and was a convertible with a 'soft top'. The body was made from fibreglass that had a 'gel coat' finish in yellow, orange or red. Optional extras were available, including towing gear and a cargo carrier. A total of 17 Minikins were manufactured before production ceased in 1986.

Based on the H M Freeway, the Minikin was a two-seat vehicle powered by a 453cc engine that provided up to 70mpg. Author's Collection

Initially built as a hobby, the D R K was powered by a Renault engine. Joseph Hall

D R K

1985 — D R K

The D R K originated in the UK in 1985 and was initially unveiled at the Cheshire Kit Car show in May 1986. As the car proved to be a success, D R K went into business. The name D R K derives from the car's designers and builders: Derek Callister, Robert Callister and Keith Hamer. The D R K was powered by a number of engines, ranging from the Renault Four to the 1,100cc Renault Six, and was dependent on what the owner chose and the donor car that was used. It featured an aluminium body mounted onto a wooden frame that, in turn, was secured to a steel chassis. Until

Although every D R K vehicle was built to a basic specification each one was individually tailored. Pete Skinner

1990 D R Ks were built as a spare-time hobby but, after the business was sold to Callister & Roscoe body repairers (with Derek and Robert Callister as long-term partners), the D R K went into full production, building the model to order. All D R K vehicles were built to a basic specification but were individually tailored for each customer. They left the factory with a fully built and painted chassis with all the components needed. It was then up to the customer to install a suitable engine and gearbox. Production of D R K vehicles ceased in June 1998 after 59 cars were built.

DAF

1941 — DAF-kini

DAF is more usually a company associated with trucks though, in 1941, the founder of the company, Hubert 'Hub' van Doorne created the DAF-kini in The Netherlands. This was nicknamed '(rijdende) regenjas' ('[driving] overcoat') and was designed as a car that you could drive into your house. The vehicle had a 125cc engine but was never put into mass production. The only prototype that existed was purchased by a circus. Today the car is now at the DAF museum in Eindhoven, The Netherlands.

Daihatsu Motor Co

Daihatsu started to make three-wheelers in 1930. The company had been established in Japan in 1907 as the Hatsudoki Siezo Co, manufacturing engines; it was not until 1951 that it became Daihatsu. The company was one of the first to manufacture a motorised tricycle in Japan and the sheer range of the three-wheelers that Daihatsu went on to produce shows not only the popularity of three-wheelers in the country at that time but that Daihatsu was also the leaders in producing such vehicles. The three-wheel boom is also backed up with information from the Ministry of Transportation in Japan that shows in 1945 there were 28,500 new three-wheelers registered. By 1959 this figure had grown to 679,804; this growth is reinforced by the fact that in 1959 there were more new three-wheelers registered than there were of every other vehicle combined just eight years earlier. (In 1951 there were 502,803 new registrations; this figure includes cars, trucks, buses, utility vehicles, three-wheelers and motorcycles and scooters.)

1930 — HA/HB/HD/HT/HS

Daihatsu's first three-wheeler in 1930 was the HA model; this was essentially a three-wheel motorcycle with a single saddle, handlebar

Nicknamed the overcoat the narrow DAF-kini was designed as a vehicle that you could drive straight into your house with and park in the hallway. Jan Barnier

steering and a luggage area located between the two rear wheels. Built around a steel chassis, the vehicle was fitted with a four-stroke, single-cylinder, 498cc side-valve engine that drove the rear wheels via a chain. The vehicles developed over time through various versions, with the first change in the 1931 — the HB — that was closely followed by the HD model in the same year. This now had a car-type transmission with a driveshaft and a differential on the rear axle. In 1933 the HT variation brought along with it a larger 670cc engine and a payload of 500kg. The engine was increased again to a 750cc engine with the HS model in 1934.

1946 — SE/SSE/SH/SK

After World War 2, a new model was announced in 1946 with the SE. This had similar lines to the earlier HT model and also the same engine until 1947 when the SSE model was introduced. The SSE was available with either a 675cc engine or a 750cc engine and, with the SH model in 1949, a V-twin, air-cooled, 1,005cc engine was fitted. This provided an increased payload of 750kg. By 1951, with the SK

model, the vehicles now used the Daihatsu name and attempts were made to build a cab upon the chassis.

1951 — Bee

In 1951 Daihatsu made its first four-seat passenger car — the Daihatsu Bee. Weighing 800kg the vehicle had a steel chassis and a fibreglass body. It was powered by an air-cooled, flat-twin, overhead-valve, 540cc engine that was mounted in the rear of the car and drove the rear wheels. Around 300 vehicles were made before production ceased in 1956 as a result of lack of demand.

1952 — SN/SR/SX

In 1952 the Daihatsu SN featured a body built on to the front of the machine to accommodate the driver. Whilst still having a saddle and

Daihatsu made its first passenger car in 1951 with the Daihatsu Bee. In a land full of three-wheel trucks however there just wasn't the demand for such a vehicle. Hikaru Baba

handlebars, the body was made from flat sheet and shaped by hand until 1953 when the panels were then press formed. Powered by a choice of a V-twin, 736cc engine or a 1,005cc engine, the vehicle had a 750kg payload. The model continued to be updated with the SR model and then the SX model in 1954, which now featured twin headlamps at the front of the body rather than a single central headlight.

1955 — SCA/SCB/SCE/SCO/SKD/SDF/SSDF

As customer demand for three-wheelers grew, so did their needs. As a result the Daihatsu three-wheeler continued to evolve with the Daihatsu SCA in 1955. The SCA had a redesigned cab with two seats and, whilst having no side doors, offered more weather protection than earlier models. Four versions were available with a 750kg version powered by a 736cc engine and the other (the SCB) with a 1,000kg payload capacity fitted with an overhead valve, 794cc engine. Added to these was the SCE model powered by a 28bhp, air-cooled, V-twin 1,135cc engine and a SCO model powered with a water-cooled, 1,480cc engine that also had a modified cab that featured an angled windscreen. In 1956 the SCB model became the SKD when the engine was uprated to a 25bhp, 854cc unit and the SCE became the SDF, being powered by a water-cooled, V-twin, 1,005cc engine. In the same year the SKD model was introduced; this had a cabin that featured side doors. There was also a SSDF version that had an increased 1.5-ton payload.

1957 – RKO/RKF/RKM

The RKO model, introduced in 1957, was the first model to be fitted with a conventional steering wheel in place of the handlebars on earlier versions. The RKO featured a more refined cab and stronger suspension. Following an updated version — the RKF — the RKM model was announced; this was powered by a 35bhp, V-twin, water-cooled, 1,135cc engine that now had a four-speed with reverse gearbox providing a maximum speed of 43mph (70km/h). This made it one of the best performing three-wheelers of this type at the time.

1957 — Midget DKA/Midget DK2 (Standard, Station Wagon, Light Van, Canvas Van, Mail Van)

Along with the heavy commercial three-wheelers, Daihatsu also catered for the other end of the spectrum with the Daihatsu Midget (DKA) that was introduced in 1957. The vehicle had a light steel chassis with a single-seat cab that had no doors. The driver sat in the centre and controlled the vehicle via handlebars. A number of variants were available with a standard pick-up, five-seat station wagon with a canvas roof and drop-down canvas sides, a light van with a metal van rear that was hermetically sealed, a canvas van (as the standard model with a canvas rear end), and a mail van with a rear section that had improved weather protection. Powered by an 8bhp, air-cooled, two-stroke, single-cylinder, 249cc engine that sat behind the cabin and drove the rear wheels, the vehicle had a three-speed plus reverse gearbox. The Midget was so successful that it was copied by other manufacturers and so, in 1959, Daihatsu responded by revising the Midget with the DK2 version. This had the payload increased from 300kg to 350kg.

1958 — Midget MPA/Trimobile

Following on from the success of the Midget model, Daihatsu released the Midget MPA in 1958; this was again available in numerous forms. The Midget MPA featured a revised front end that also had a wider

Although called the Daihatsu Midget MPA in Japan, the vehicle was also exported to the USA and marketed as the Trimobile. John Lloyd

cabin that was fully enclosed with metal doors and a roof. Internally the extra width meant that it could now seat two people and was also updated with upholstered seats instead of a saddle and a steering wheel instead of handlebars. It was powered by a 10bhp, two-stroke, single-cylinder, 249cc engine that was uprated in 1959 to a 12bhp, 305cc engine. The vehicle was also first exported to the USA, where it became known as the Trimobile, in the same year. By 1960 the vehicle had been redesigned and now had a slightly longer wheelbase, increasing the payload to 350kg. Continuous updates were added, including seat belts in 1969, until production ceased in 1971.

1962 — CM/CO/DO/DE

Daihatsu three-wheelers were getting bigger and stronger all the time and, by 1962, with the CM and CO range the vehicles were able to carry a payload of two tons. The vehicles were fitted with a four-cylinder, 1,862cc engine that, when travelling without a payload, provided a maximum speed of 62mph (100km/h). Other engines were also used, dependent on the body type, with V-twin, 1,135cc and 1,490cc units also being employed. The Daihatsu CM models were also the first Daihatsu three-wheelers to be fitted with brakes on the front wheels. The vehicles came in many guises, some with extended flatbeds that meant they were up to 6,065mm in length. In addition to pick-up trucks, there was also a Daihatsu Dump Truck fitted with an hydraulic body that provided a maximum tilt of 60°, the Daihatsu fire engine with a water pump and 1,000gall tank of water, and the Daihatsu Pack Master that had a specially-built body for the collection of waste materials. All of these were fitted with a V-twin, 1,478cc engine. In 1967 the DO and DE range appeared; these were powered by a 65bhp, 2,270cc diesel engine with all variations being manufactured until 1976.

1989 — BC-7

After many years away from three-wheelers, Daihatsu created its BC-7 concept three-wheeler in 1989. This was a short, single-seat car that was powered by a 49cc engine. With handlebar steering, the BC-7 had a single wheel at the front with a lightweight body that had a windscreen and roof with the sides and rear end being open.

Davis Motor Co

1947 — Model 482 (Divan)

The Davis was first introduced in 1947 by Glenn Gordon 'Gary' Davis in the USA. Just after World War 2, Davis bought a small racing car that had been converted into a three-wheeler and named the 'Californian'. Believing it would make a good economy vehicle, Davis built his first

Daihatsu built many heavy-duty three-wheel vehicles this being a Daihatsu CM dumper truck version with a payload of two tons. Author's Collection

After a hard life, a Daihatsu pick-up truck consigned to the scrap heap in Japan. Today's junk, Tomorrow's classic. Kim Scholer

Right: *With its futuristic shape compared with other vehicles on the road in 1947 the Davis was an eye catcher and as a result over 300 franchises were created that were all waiting for vehicles to be delivered.* Hal Schmidt

Below: *Wide enough to seat four adults abreast and powered by a 2,600cc Continental engine, the Davis was possibly the largest production passenger three-wheeler ever made.* Alden Jewell

prototype which he nicknamed 'Baby' (or Davis D-1). The second Davis prototype D-2 (or Davis 'Delta') was also built in 1947, whilst the third prototype became known as Model 482; this became the standard specification for production vehicles. From 1948 the Davis Motor Co then produced 11 Divan models that all featured a removable top. The Davis is possibly the largest production passenger three-wheeler ever made; it was 14ft in length and wide enough to sit four adults abreast. It was powered by a 2,600cc four-cylinder Continental engine — although the first two prototypes used a Hercules engine — and had an aluminium body that was attached directly to a steel chassis with normal cushion body mounts. It was estimated that Davis raised $1,200,000 with over 300 franchises in place, all waiting to receive the vehicles. However, as vehicles were being built, workers were not being paid and the threat of lawsuits loomed from potential dealers and investors. By 1948 with a number of ex-employees filing suit for back wages, Davis was also being investigated for fraud by the Los Angeles District Attorney's office. A few months later the Davis plant was shut down and all assets seized; the business finally resulted in Davis being sent to jail for fraud.

In 1950, after all the assets were sold for tax claims, 16 franchise holders formed the Delta Motor Car Co and, owning car number five and some tooling, tried to salvage the Davis. The fifth Davis was then shipped to the Reliant Motor Co in Tamworth, UK, for 'engineering evaluation' with a hope that Reliant might manufacture the car though, after evaluation, it was never to return. The UK Customs Officers

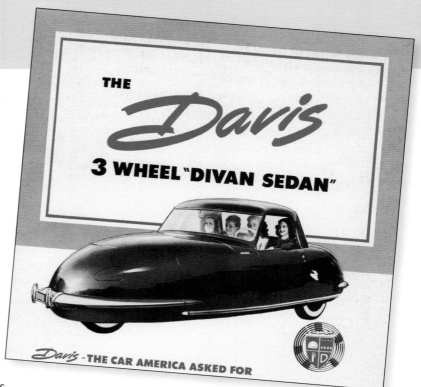

THE *Davis* 3 WHEEL "DIVAN SEDAN"

Davis - THE CAR AMERICA ASKED FOR

demanded that the customs bond be paid for the car to be sent back to America. At the time the company that owned the rights to manufacture the car was not willing or able to pay for return shipment and, as Reliant did not want to pay the customs bond, the company was then required to 'destroy the car under the eyes of the customs agents.'

The Davis Model 494 was a jeep designed for the military and at the request of the Pentagon two such vehicles were sent to the Army for testing at the Aberdeen Proving Grounds in Maryland. Wikipedia — Jaydec

1948 — Model 494 (Military)

Prior to the plant closing in 1948, Davis also produced a utility jeep for military use; this used the same chassis and was in effect a three-wheel jeep version of the Divan with an open body and known as the Model 494. The Pentagon had ongoing arrangements with Davis to test the vehicle at its Aberdeen Proving Grounds in Maryland and, of the three Model 494s that were built, two went sent to the Army for testing.

Marquis Jules-Albert de Dion aboard his steam car that was recorded at 37mph (59.5km/h) in 1887. Author's Collection

Dazin

1936 — Dazinette

The Dazinette was created by the French Inventor, Dazin in 1936. The vehicle was powered by a 1bhp engine mounted above the single front wheel, which provided a top speed of 16mph (26km/h). The body was of basic tubular steel and steering was performed by turning the inner frame that the engine and front wheel were mounted to. The vehicle was originally intended as a means to get its inventor from Paris to Berlin in March 1936.

De Dion-Bouton Automobile

1883 — Steam Car/La Marquise

De Dion produced engines that were so reliable that they powered many early vehicles worldwide. Founded in 1883 by Marquis Jules-Albert de Dion in Paris, France, De Dion along with his partner Georges Bouton (an ex-toymaker) and his brother-in-law, Charles Trépardoux, went on to produce steam engines for boats. Towards the end of 1883 the company fitted one of its small boat steam engines on to a set of wheels and thus created its first steam car. A three-wheeler, the vehicle had the boiler and engine mounted at the front, driving the two front wheels by belts. Steering was by tiller to the single rear wheel. When the first prototype burnt to the ground, a second was built a year later and called *La Marquise* (after de Dion's mother). The new version was rear-wheel drive, had a steering wheel and could seat four people. It was during a motoring competition in 1887 — where the De Dion was the only entrant — that the vehicle was recorded at 37mph (59.5km/h); this was exceptional at the time, bearing in mind that the first official land speed record set in 1898 was 39.24mph (63.15km/h). As a result of the success of the prototypes, the company then started to manufacture steam tricycles that used a three-cylinder engine with the boiler between the two front wheels. In October 2011, an 1884 steam-powered De Dion was sold at auction as the world's oldest car still on the road for £2.9 million.

An 1896 De Dion-Boulton Tricycle that amongst other things featured Michelin pneumatic tyres. Ron Will

1896 — Tricycle/Petite Voiture

With the introduction of a petrol engine, De Dion created the De Dion-Bouton Tricycle in 1896. The Tricycle was built on a bicycle-derived frame that was purchased from Decauville and fitted with a water-cooled, single-cylinder, 137cc engine. The tricycle had a cylindrical tank and radiator mounted behind the rider's seat and a fuel tank that hung from the frame in between the rider's knees. The wheels also featured Michelin pneumatic tyres. In 1896 a 250cc version was introduced. Production of the tricycles ceased in 1902; by this time some 40,000 engines had also been shipped across Europe to be used in other vehicles due to their reliability. De-Dion then concentrated on four-wheelers.

Delfin

1954 — Delfin

Manufactured in by Fabrica Espanola de Motocicetas y Tricyclos Delfin, of Barcelona, Spain, in 1954 the Delfin was essentially the New Map Solyto (see page 176) made under licence. Unlike the New Map Solyto, the Delfin was powered by a larger air-cooled, 197cc Hispano-Villiers engine. The steel body housed two-seats and was able to carry a load of 250kg. It came with a range of bodies and flat beds. The vehicles were built until about 1960.

Built in Spain the Delfin was made under licence to New Map though used a different engine to the New Map Solyto. Hans Bodewes

Deltawerkes Lindner GmbH

1954 — Deltamobil

Constructing furnaces and oil heaters, Deltawerkes Lindner GmbH was based in Munich, Germany, and founded by a Mr Lindner. As a result of many conversations with people he knew, Lindner recognised there was a need for a small vehicle and so contacted his colleague Heinrich Auer and together they started to design one. The result was the Deltamobil that appeared in late 1954. Compared with most other three-wheelers it had an unusual chassis, which consisted of a

Fitted with a chassis that ran around the outside of the wheels the Deltamobil had an all-round bumper under its skin. Author's Collection

tubular steel frame that ran around the outside of the wheels. It was fitted with live axle rear suspension with the axle being cushioned with rubber bands and was powered by a rear mounted 9bhp air-cooled, 200cc Ilo engine that drove the single rear wheel via a three-speed gearbox. The vehicle was a two-seater and had a lightweight aluminium body with a folding hood that also incorporated front and rear flashing indicators as standard. Inside the vehicle the single bench seat consisted of four rubber air cushions that were covered in fabric and could be inflated/deflated depending on the occupant's preference. Eight vehicles had been made when, in 1955, Lindner

hoped to start a production run of the vehicles starting with a further 10 vehicles. The new vehicles were to have been fitted with a more powerful twin-cylinder 250cc Ilo engine; however, Lindner was said to have been unable to provide the finance necessary. By 1955 further three-wheelers were appearing on the German market and so Lindner ceased further development and returned to manufacturing oil heaters.

Degant

1949 — DD

Wishing to replace Vietnamese rickshaws with a safer vehicle so that passengers were not carried in front of the driver, Marcel Degant with Louis Descloitre designed a car and set up a factory in Saigon, Vietnam, in 1949 to produce a three-wheeler called the DD. The DD was available in two forms — as a passenger vehicle and as a pick-up — the only difference between the two being that the passenger vehicle had a slightly higher body at the back with a bench seat for passengers and a hood whilst the pick-up style version had a wooden box between the two rear wheels. In both cases the driver sat on a motorcycle-type seat at the front, controlling the vehicle by handlebars. The DD had a 125cc Jonghi engine and a body made from steel. It is believed that after just six vehicles were made in Vietnam, Degant moved to Marrakech, Morocco, where production of the vehicle continued with a further 36 vehicles being built. Due to financial problems production of the vehicles ceased in 1950.

Initially designed to replace the rickshaw in Vietnam, the Degant DD was built both in Saigon and Morocco. RUMCar News

The Degant DD was also available as a pick-up version with a small cargo area replacing the backseats of the passenger version. RUMCar News

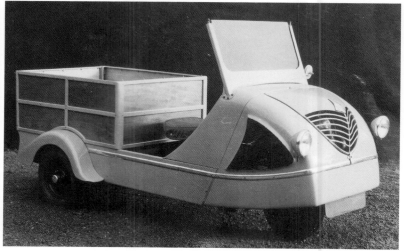

Diable

1919 — Diable

The Diable was first manufactured in Paris, France, in 1919. It was powered by a 1,096 cc, V-twin engine with power going via a shaft to a two-speed plus reverse gearbox with a final chain drive to the rear wheel. Production of the vehicle ceased in 1924.

Diablo Kleinauto GmbH

1922 — Diablo

Driven by an 1,100cc Motosacoche engine that drove the single rear wheel by a chain, the Diablo was introduced in Stuttgart, Germany, in 1922. The vehicle had a metal body with two seats and a hood. Production ceased in 1927.

Dolly Cyclecar

1919 — Dolly

The Dolly Cyclecar was a two-seater that, notable for its time, was fitted with an automatic clutch. Designed by P H Bergasse in Sussex, UK, and announced in 1919, the vehicle was fitted with an 8bhp,

water-cooled JAP engine. It had a tubular chassis with sheet steel forming the body. Produced as a prototype, it is not known whether the vehicle entered production as anticipated.

Dolphin Vehicles

1980s — Vortex

The Vortex is a DIY car for the home enthusiast to build from the ground up from plans that are purchased from the company. It was created by Dolphin Vehicles in the USA in the mid-1980s. The Vortex has a monocoque chassis that is made from plywood and fibreglass with a metal sub-frame to hold the rear drive unit and independent front suspension. Due to the design of the modular chassis the Vortex can be powered by either an electric motor or a petrol motorcycle engine such as the 1,000cc Honda engine. The body is made of foam and covered with fibreglass. It features a removable sunroof and gull-wing type passenger doors that open up and forward. The plans are still available at present.

Believed to exist only as a prototype the Dolly Cyclecar from 1919 was fitted with an automatic clutch, something quite rare for its time. Author's Collection

Doran Motor Co

1980s — Doran

The Doran was designed in the USA by Rick G Doran who spent six years developing, refining and testing the design in the 1980s. It is a self-build vehicle, made from plans, and can be powered by either an electric motor or petrol engine. The petrol version of the Doran uses an 1,800cc engine from a 1980-89 Subaru Hatchback. In addition to the Subaru engine it also utilises the entire drive train from the Subaru including the five-speed manual gearbox. The vehicle is front-wheel drive and will accelerate from 0-60mph (0-96km/h) in 8.7sec with a maximum speed of 125mph (201km/h). Its body has a backbone frame that runs down the centre of the vehicle made from a fibreglass/urethane foam composite that houses a two-seat cabin. The body is initially built from foam and then fibreglassed over to create a strong rigid body. With double wishbone front suspension, the vehicle is said to have the handling agility and overturn resistance similar to that of many modern sports cars.

1980s — Doran EV

The electric version uses deep discharge 12V batteries to power its motor and a transistor chopper for smooth speed control. This gives the Doran a range of approximately 50 miles (80km) before the vehicle needs to be recharged. The recharging can be done overnight. Accelerating from 0 to 60mph (0-96km/h) in 10.9sec with a maximum speed of 60mph (96.5km/h), the Doran EV won a number of races and electric vehicle range contests and rallies in the 1990s. Like its petrol counterpart, it also uses the drive train from a Subaru. At the time of writing, the plans are still available for both models.

Dot Cycle & Motor Manufacturing Co

1932 — Motor Truck

The Dot Cycle & Motor Manufacturing Co was established in 1903 by Harry Reed in Salford, Manchester, UK. From 1906 up until 1932, when it temporarily ceased building them, the company produced motorcycles. Under the new ownership of Burnard Scott Wade in the same year, the company broke into the three-wheel market. Initially its three-wheelers were pedal-powered and developed for niche markets like milk delivery and ice cream vending. During World War 2, Dot was awarded a contract to build economy delivery vehicles and the idea of the vehicle being powered by an engine soon developed.

The Dot Motor truck was essentially the rear half of a Dot motorcycle with a modified front section. The vehicle was powered by a 197cc Villiers two-stroke, air-cooled engine that provided power to the back wheel via a chain. The front of the vehicle was modified in several ways so that it could accommodate various bodies, including a truck, ice cream van and motorised rickshaw. The rickshaw featured a large body at the front that two passengers could sit in with a large windscreen. Production of the three-wheelers ceased in the late 1950s and the company ceased trading all together in the 1960s.

DS Malterre

1955 — DS Malterre

Founded in France in 1922, DS Malterre manufactured motorcycles. In 1955 it created its first three-wheeler, a vehicle powered by a 125cc two-cylinder Ydral engine that was located in the rear of the vehicle and drove the single rear wheel. Only a few prototype vehicles were built before the project was dropped in 1958.

Using a Subaru drive train the Doran was a self-build vehicle that could be built using either a Subaru engine or an electric motor. Robert Occhialini

Dumas

1902 — Dumas

The Dumas was first manufactured in France in 1902 by M A Dumas. It was powered by a Buchet 4.5bhp engine that sat behind the front wheel. Power from the engine was fed to the front wheel by a chain. Compared to other three-wheelers at the time, the Dumas has a distinctive car look to it with its engine being housed under a bonnet, a two-seat body and steering wheel. Production ceased one year later in 1903.

Dunkley

1915 — Dunkley Cyclecar

Dunkley of Jamaica Row, Birmingham, UK, was established in 1878 and, in 1896, invented a vehicle powered by compressed gas. By 1914 it had become a manufacturer of perambulators, bath chairs, circus roundabouts and flying machines to name just a few items from its catalogue. The Dunkley Cyclecar introduced in 1915 was a lightweight vehicle weighing in at under 3cwt and was advertised by the fact that, due to its weight, it came within the £1 tax bracket. Priced at £98 17s 6d, it was powered by a 5bhp, twin-cylinder, air-cooled JAP engine. It had a rectangular frame built up of standard tubes and lugs with a tubular front axle. The single rear wheel was driven by a chain that was adjusted by moving the Jardine four-speed gearbox backwards to tighten the chain. The engine controls were mounted onto the tube containing the steering pillar so that they did not turn with the steering wheel. The vehicle was started by a chain and pedal device acting through the gearbox, replacing the need for a kick starter. To appeal to motorcyclists, it was possible to remove the engine, gearbox, back wheel and one front wheel and use them in a motorcycle frame. Production of the Dunkley Cyclecar ceased in the same year, though Dunkley as a company survived until 1959 when it was then taken over by M G Holdings Ltd.

One of the advertising points of the Dunkley Cyclecar was that you could remove the engine, gearbox, back wheel and one front wheel and use them in a motorcycle frame. Author's Collection

Duryea Motor Wagon Co

In 1893 the Duryea brothers — Charles E and J Frank —created one of America's first petrol-powered cars in Springfield, Massachusetts. Up until then the brothers had built bicycles in Peoria, Illinois, USA, but Charles wished to build an automobile and so, whilst he designed it, his younger brother Frank built the first prototype. This first vehicle was a four-wheeler, being no more than a horseless carriage with metal tyres and a water-cooled, four-stroke, 4bhp engine. In 1895 the Duryea Motor Wagon Co was established and a second vehicle was built. This was entered in the first motorcar race — the *Chicago Times-Herald* Race — in America. Due to weather conditions only six vehicles turned up with three of those being Benz vehicles imported from Germany. At 7mph (11km/h), the Duryea, driven by Frank came first and won the $2,000 prize. In 1896 Duryea built 13 identical Duryea Motor Wagons fitted with 8bhp engines, making them the first US company to manufacture multiple vehicles of the same design for sale. Two of these entered the London to Brighton Emancipation run in the UK and the one driven by Frank came first beating its nearest rival by 75min. This was obviously frowned upon by the British at the time as Frank was awarded a trophy for his 'prompt arrival'. In the same year, in the Cosmopolitan race, a Duryea was involved in the first recorded US automobile accident when motorist Henry Wells hit a cyclist with his new Duryea. The rider suffered a broken leg whilst Wells spent a night in jail.

1898 — Trap/Light Delivery

From 1898 Duryea also built three-wheelers that came in a number of variations, all with the single wheel at the front. The Trap was a passenger vehicle that had an open body that seated four people, with two facing forwards and two facing backwards. It had tiller steering,

Built from 1898 the Duryea three-wheeler came in many variations that included a four-seat passenger version and a light delivery van.
Author's Collection

1900 — Phaeton

In 1900, the three-wheel Phaeton was introduced; this had a steel frame with a tall upright hood and seating for two. It was powered by a 12bhp, three-cylinder, 214cc engine. The vehicle had tiller-type steering in which moving the lever left or right steered the vehicle whilst twisting it activated the gear selector and throttle. The vehicle was speedy for its time with a top speed of 30mph (56km/h) whilst averaging around 23mpg (12-litre/100km). Commercial models were also available with the driver sitting further forward and a van type rear. Duryea vehicles were manufactured until 1907.

large spoke wheels and was powered by a three-cylinder engine. A light delivery version was also made, which came with an open body that had a cargo area behind the seat or a van version in which the driver sat further forward in the open with a van body at the back that had a roof that extended over the driver to provide some weather protection. In 1899 a Duryea three-wheeler was developed for military purposes into a gun carriage by Royal Page Davidson of the Northwestern Military Academy. This had a Colt .30 calibre automatic machine gun mounted to it with a gun shield to protect the driver. However, further development then went on to use a four-wheel design.

D'Yrsan

1923 — D'Yrsan

Containing many refinements that were not standard on even four-wheel cyclecars at the time, the D'Yrsan was first manufactured from 1923 in France. The company, Les Cyclecars D'Yrsan, was founded by Raymond Siran — who also used the pseudonym Cavanac Siran — and it also built motorcycles and four-wheelers.

The three-wheeler was fitted with either a 750cc, four-cylinder, water-cooled, overhead valve Ruby engine or an 1,100cc Ruby engine that drove the single rear wheel by a shaft. This was through a three-speed and reverse gearbox. The D'Yrsan had a steel tube chassis/frame and a steel body with independent front suspension using its own design. In addition to brakes operating on all three wheels, an electric starter was also available as an optional extra.

1923 — Type T Grand Tourer

Built for comfort, the Type T Grand Tourer model had runner boards down the side of the vehicle, and twin windscreens for driver and passenger.

1923 — Type DS Sport

The Type DS Sport model was lower to the ground than the conventional model and was lighter with shorter wheel arches and no windscreen resulting in a top speed of around 60mph (96.5km/h). The Sport model was also more expensive, costing 10,500 francs in 1924 compared with 9,650 francs for the touring model. In the UK at the time this equated to around £120. Manufacture of all vehicles ceased in 1928.

A 1927 D'Yrsan Type DS fitted with a 1,100cc Ruby engine. Robert Pichon

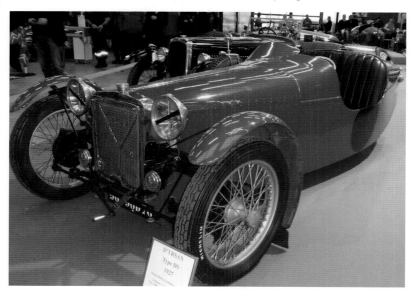

Dymaxion

1933 — Dymaxion

In the late 1920s experiments were being undertaken to test aerodynamics. Richard Buckminster Fuller — an inventor, engineer, and designer amongst many other things — conducted wind-tunnel test on three-wheel teardrop shapes with a V-shaped groove running under the vehicle. A rudder was also added to the vehicles and Fuller intended that this would unfold from the upper side of the tail and provide stability. In 1933 Fuller hired Starling Burgess, a naval architect, and a crew of expert sheet metal workers, woodworkers, former coach builders and machinists. They designed and built Dymaxion car number one, which was shown publicly in July 1933. 'Dymaxion' was selected as a portmanteau word of dynamic, maximum and tension. Able to carry 11 passengers, the vehicle was 20ft (6.1m) long and had a chassis of chrome-molybdenum steel, an aluminium body with wraparound bumpers and ⅛in-thick aircraft glass windows. As a result of enclosing all the chassis and wheels in a streamlined shape, Fuller is reported to have driven the vehicle at 120mph (193km/h) with a 90bhp engine. A conventional 1933 car would have required, Fuller estimated, at least a 300bhp engine. Fuller also claimed that fuel consumption of the Dymaxion car number one was 30% less than a conventional car at 30mph (48km/h) and 50% less at 50mph (80km/h). The two front wheels of Dymaxion car one were driven by a Ford V-8 engine. The single wheel at the rear was steerable and so it could do a U-turn in its own length.

On Dymaxion cars two and three an angled periscope was provided to help compensate for the lack of a rear window. Initially the car created vast attention wherever it went. However, in 1933 a British auto enthusiast flew to Chicago to examine the Dymaxion car and, when he was injured and his driver killed, after the Dymaxion collided with another car on the way to the Chicago World Fair, the headlines in the press referred to the vehicle as a 'freak car' and blamed the accident mainly on the vehicle's steering and the three-wheel design in general. Although an investigation exonerated the Dymaxion, the car received a bad reputation and the British group cancelled its order for Dymaxion car two. It was after Fuller's second daughter was injured in another crash involving a Dymaxion that both he and investors lost interest in the project. The third Dymaxion toured the USA during World War 2 promoting the Allied cause and was eventually sold for scrap in Kansas.

The design of the Dymaxion cars was one of the biggest breakthroughs in automobile design since the car had originated some 50 years earlier. Only one car — number two — now remains and is kept at the National Auto Museum, Reno, Nevada, USA. After borrowing the surviving example from the National Auto Museum and by using the original plans, racing car restorers Crosthwaite and Gardiner built an exact replica of the Dymaxion car number three in 2011 following a commssion from Norman Foster.

Commissioned by Norman Foster and completed in 2011 this Dymaxion is an exact replica of the third Dymaxion made in 1933.
Daniel Blow

Eagle Engineering & Motor Co

1899 — Century Tandem

Ralph Jackson started by building Ralpho bicycles in 1895 in Altringham, Cheshire, UK. He then went on to form the Century Engineering & Motor Co in 1899 and created a three-wheeler called the Century Tandem. First manufactured in 1899, the vehicle was quite refined for its time with the driver sitting at the rear on an upholstered seat above the single rear wheel. The passenger sat at the front on a large padded seat positioned between the front wheels. The Tandem had a tubular steel chassis and, whilst adopting a similar format to other vehicles of the era, had no cross bar and so did not resemble a modified motorcycle. The standard version was fitted with a 5bhp Aster engine that was positioned at the driver's feet. The Tandem had no handlebars and no steering wheel, instead the driver would steer the vehicle by use of a large lever on the right-hand side, which was moved forwards and backwards to determine the direction needed to travel in. A sportier version was also advertised; this was fitted with a 6.5bhp Aster engine and Begbie-Audin radiator. This model was able to travel a mile in one minute 44sec and was recorded at completing a 100-mile journey in three hours, six minutes and 23sec.

1902 — Eagle Tandem

In 1902 the company was sold to Sydney Begbie and changed its name to the Eagle Engineering & Motor Co Ltd. The Century Tandem then became the Eagle Tandem. The vehicle also had its engines

Built from 1902 the Eagle Tandem was available with a choice of engines ranging from 3.5 to 9bhp in 1904. Des Ferguson

changed with three models being introduced. A De Dion 3.5bhp was used to power the standard Eagle Tandem, whilst a 5bhp and 6.6bhp engine were used on the Aster and MMC models respectively. By 1904 the variety of engines available was increased to water-cooled, 4.5bhp, 6bhp and 9bhp units. A year later the Eagle Tandem was updated and now featured a conventional steering wheel. In 1907 the Eagle Engineering Co was wound up and the vehicles were thereafter assembled at Broadheath Generating Station and sold through St Georges Motor Car Co in Leeds, Yorkshire, UK. As a result Jackson started to call these vehicles 'New Eagle' but few cars were sold and production of the Eagle ceased in 1908.

East London Rubber Co

1902 — Kerry Tri-Kar

Having produced motorcycles since 1902, the East London Rubber Co manufactured the Kerry Tri-Kar between 1904 and 1907 in London,

At the dawn of motoring it seemed everyone wanted to produce a motor vehicle as shown in this 1904 advert for the Kerry Tri-Kar from the East London Rubber Co. Grace's Guide

ECC

1897 — Bushbury Electric Cart

Founded by Thomas Parker, the Electric Construction Co (ECC) of Wolverhampton, UK, originally began making horseshoes and then, in 1882, moved on to electrical equipment and then electric vehicles. Parker claimed to have had an electric car running in 1884 and went on to produce electric omnibuses. In 1897 EEC built its first three-wheeler. The Bushbury Electric cart was a two-seat vehicle that was steered by reins attached to a handlebar above the single front wheel. It was powered by two large three-speed electric motors that were placed under the seat along with the batteries. A four-wheel version was also made. However, the vehicles had very limited range and production ceased in 1897 due to development cost. The company itself in one form or another was to survive until 1986.

UK. The Tri-Kar was powered by a 5bhp V-twin engine that provided power to the single rear wheel by a chain. The vehicle had a tubular frame with the driver sitting at the rear on a saddle whilst the passenger sat in a wicker seat mounted between the front two wheels.

Eastman

1899 — Eastman Electro-Cycle

Created by Henry Eastman, the Eastman Electro-Cycle was first built in 1899 in Cleveland, Ohio, USA. It had a single-seat body that is believed to be the first all-steel body produced in the USA. This body was attached to a tubular frame and had two large bicycle wheels to the rear and one at the front; the latter was controlled by a very long tiller. An electric motor powered the rear two wheels. The company ceased making the Electro-Cycle in 1902 but continued to make steel bodies for other manufacturers.

Another early electric vehicle was the Bushbury Electric Cart built in 1897 that used two three-speed electric motors and was also produced in a four-wheel version. Author's Collection

Electric vehicles are not something new, the Eastman Electro-Cycle was first built in 1899 and had an electric motor that powered the rear wheels. Helena Belden

Eco-Fueler Corporation

Powered by Compressed Natural Gas (CNG) the American Roadster is able to achieve 70mpg. Eco-Fueler Corporation

2006 — American Roadster

Manufactured by the Eco-Fueler Corporation from October 2006 in Oregon, USA, the American Roadster is an alternative fuel vehicle powered by Compressed Natural Gas (CNG). The chief designer was John S Green who, from 1976, sold kits to convert petrol vehicles to run on CNG. The Eco-Fueler is powered by a 100bhp, in-line three-cylinder, CNG engine specifically designed for the vehicle. It is able to achieve 70mpg (4-litre/100km) whilst providing a top speed of 120mph (193km/h) and 0-60mph (0-96km/h) in seven seconds with a range of around 450 miles (724km). There is a choice of either a manual five-speed gearbox or a three-speed automatic. The three-seat body is made from plastic and fibreglass attached to a tubular steel frame; this was designed by Pat Blair, a designer of NASCAR Race Cars, and thus meets NASCAR safety and handling design requirements. It also has a removable hardtop. At the time of writing the vehicle remains in production.

With a body designed by Pat Blair, the American Roadster meets NASCAR safety and handling design requirements. Eco-Fueler Corporation

drive to the single rear wheel. Drive was by means of several belts that went from the engine to a countershaft mounted on a swivelling pivot that, through a double pulley mechanism, sent the drive via a belt to the rear wheel. Using a tubular steel chassis the vehicle had a two-seat body that was made from wicker and resembled a large basket. It was advertised as having a steering wheel and a 'free' engine, meaning an engine that could be started at rest with the gears being engaged via the clutch. This also helped to prevent the vehicle stalling when it came to a halt. The Autotrix Cycle Car was one of the contenders in the first cycle car race at Brooklands in 1911.

Economic Motors

1921 — Economic

The Economic first appeared in Wells Street, London, UK, in 1921 and was one of the lightest three-wheelers of the early 20th century. Costing under £60, the Economic was manufactured by Economic Motors and featured a simple two-seat body. It was fitted with seats made of cane and offered very little protection from the natural elements. The body was made of aluminium and fastened to an Ash frame and chassis. The vehicle had no springs or shock absorbers as it was believed the wooden frame would soak up all the shocks from the road. Power came from a two-stroke, air-cooled, horizontally-opposed, twin-cylinder engine that was under 200cc. The final drive was by chain to the rear offside wheel. The vehicle had two coils: one to produce a high-tension current for creating a spark and the other for the purpose of providing a current to illuminate the lights. Empty this three-wheeler weighed just 150lb with a maximum speed of 30mph (48km/h) and was able to carry two 'average-sized persons' up a gradient of 1 in 9. Production ceased in 1922.

Edmunds & Wadden & Co Ltd

1911 — Autotrix Cycle Car (Model No 1)

The Autotrix Cycle Car was manufactured in Weybridge, Surrey, UK, from 1911 and built by Edmunds & Wadden & Co Ltd, a company that built racing cycles. It was equipped with a 3.5bhp, single-cylinder JAP engine that was mounted between the front wheels and provided

1912 — Autotrix Cycle Car (Model No 2)

In 1912 the Autotrix Cycle Car No 2 was introduced; this was again a two-seater but had a more conventional metal body. Using the same mechanics as the first model, the No 2 was powered by a larger 8- or 9bhp air-cooled, V-twin JAP engine and a Charter-Lea gearbox that provided drive to the rear wheel by chains. In addition to this, a 6bhp water-cooled Fafnir engine was also available. Optional extras for the No 2 included a windscreen, canvas hood and a lamp set. Around 30 vehicles were made before production ceased in 1914 with the outbreak of World War 1.

EEC

1952 — Workers Playtime

EEC started as a boatbuilding company in Totnes, Devon, UK, during World War 2 and, in 1952, produced a three-wheeler. EEC planned to build six prototypes; however, only one vehicle was ever constructed. The Workers Playtime model was named after a BBC radio programme. It was constructed with an aluminium body attached to a steel framework. Inside the vehicle a single bench seat was said to seat three adults. Power came from a 250cc Excelsior twin-cylinder two-stroke motorcycle engine that drove the single rear wheel. The first vehicle was used by EEC but the project came to an end when the parts for the other five prototypes were destroyed in a fire in 1954.

Egan

1952 — Egan

The Egan differed from most three-wheelers of its era in that it featured a single front headlamp moulded into a fibreglass body. The air-cooled engine sat at the back of the vehicle, driving the rear wheels. The engine was cooled by louvres in the body work that would pull in cool air. Introduced in the UK in 1952 production was short-lived and ceased in the same year.

Eichler & Bachmann GmbH

1921 — Eibach

From 1921, Eichler & Bachmann GmbH in Berlin, Germany, manufactured a trivan that was powered by a 200cc, single-cylinder, air-cooled, two-stroke DKW engine. The vehicle had a motorcycle-type rear end with a box at the front of the vehicle in between the two steerable front wheels. A passenger version, called the Eibach, was introduced in 1924 and used the same 200cc engine, driving the single rear wheel. Whilst the driver sat at the back of the vehicle, the passengers sat in an open body that resembled a motorcycle sidecar positioned between the front two wheels. This version had two seats and low sides with a windscreen. Production of both models ceased in 1925.

Elektromaschinenbau Fulda GmbH

1951 — Fuldamobil N/N-1/N-2

Originally designed by Norbert Stevenson, the Fuldamobil first appeared in 1950 in Germany. The initial prototype was a two-seater and featured a steel body attached to a wooden frame. Power came from a rear-mounted air-cooled, 198cc Zundapp engine. With the introduction of the first production model — the Fuldamobil N — in 1951 the engine was changed to an 8bhp, air-cooled, 248cc Baker & Pölling whilst the two-seat body still featured an angled front end and a flat sided body with steel panels attached to a wooden frame. In the same year the vehicle became the Fuldamobil N-1 with a revised front end; whilst initial vehicles were made with a steel body, this was then changed to an unpainted hammered aluminium sheet body that led to the N-1 being nicknamed the Silver Flea. Two versions were available: an enclosed Sedan version and an open topped Roadster. The model was modified again in 1952 to become the Fuldamobil N-2; it was now powered by a more powerful air- or fan-cooled Fichtel & Sachs 359cc engine that again sat in front of the single rear wheel that it drove. Whilst the Roadster version remained a two-seater, the enclosed Sedan version now also had room for two children in the back. The N2 was manufactured until 1955.

The original Fuldamobil — the N1 and N2 — had a flat-sided aluminium panelled body that was attached to a wooden frame. RUMCar News

The Eibach passenger version had a sidecar type body mounted between the front wheels whilst the driver sat in a bucket seat at the back. Kerry Croxton

1954 — Fuldamobil S-1/S-2/S-3

Introduced in 1954 the Fuldamobil S-1 — also known as NWF200 — was added to the range to complement the Fuldamobil N-2. The S-1 had a redesigned and fully-enclosed two-door steel body that was a lot more rounded. It was powered by a 9.5bhp ILO 197cc engine that drove the single rear wheel with a chain via a three-speed gearbox. In the same year the engine was uprated to an air- or fan-cooled Fichtel & Sachs 359cc engine and the model then became the Fuldamobil S-2. The body was able to seat two adults and two children, and at the rear featured a tailgate the provided access to a luggage compartment above the rear wheel. The S-2 was built until 1955 and, whilst a Fuldamobil S-3 version was created in 1956, this remained a prototype and never reached production.

With the arrival of the Fuldamobil S-1 (NWF200) in 1954 a fully enclosed steel body was introduced. Hans Bodewes

1955 — Fuldamobil S-4/S-5/S-6/S-7

Though the 1955 Fuldamobil S-4 had acquired an extra wheel to become a four-wheeler, a three-wheel version with a single rear wheel was also available on request. Fitted with a smaller air- or fan-cooled Fichtel & Sachs 191cc engine further variants including the 1955 Fuldamobil S-5 and 1956 Fuldamobil S-6, which were also four-wheelers that could be built as three-wheelers if requested. The last Fuldamobil was the S-7 in 1957; this was again a four-wheeler that now featured a fibreglass body with a dummy grille at the front. This was fitted with Fichtel & Sachs 191cc engine until 1965 when it was replaced with a 10bhp single-cylinder, four-stroke 198cc Heinkel engine. The S-7 was also available as a three-wheeler upon request and was manufactured until 1969.

1955 — Nobeletta

Manufactured in 1955 in Germany, the Nobeletta was designed as a two-seat beach car. The vehicle was built at the Fulda factory and made for the South African market though only a few vehicles were produced throughout 1955. Using the Fuldamobil chassis, the vehicle had an open fibreglass body that had a single headlight at the front.

A hood was erected at the rear of the vehicle , which could be rolled out and attached to the windscreen to offer some weather protection.

1950s — Alta A200, Attica 200, Bambi, Bambino, Fram King Fulda, Hans Vahaar

The Fuldamobil was also built under licence in many countries; each had similar body styles with side doors that opened from the left-hand side and able to carry four people with bench seats in the front and rear. In each country it was manufactured under a different name and was known as the Nobel 200 (UK/Chile), the Alta A200 and Attica 200 (Greece), the Bambi (India; also included a pick-up model), the Bambino (The Netherlands), the Fram King Fulda (Sweden) and the Hans Vahaar (India).

The Elio prototype that was announced in 2013 is a two-seater fitted with a 1,000cc engine. Elio Motors

Destined for manufacture in 2014, this is a rendering of how the production model of the Elio will look. Elio Motors

Elio Motors

2014 — Elio

Founded in 2008 by Paul Elio, Elio Motors of Arizona, USA, announced the Elio in 2013. This is a two-seat vehicle with the passenger sitting behind the driver. Fitted with an inline, 70bhp, three-cylinder, fuel-injected, liquid-cooled, 1,000cc engine that drives the two front wheels via a five-speed with reverse manual or automatic gearbox, the vehicle has a top speed in excess of 100mph (161km/h) with a 0-60mph (0-96km/h) time of just over nine seconds, with an estimated 84mpg (3.4-litre/100km) on the highway and 49mpg (5.8-litre/100km) in the city. Its lightweight composite body that also includes a reinforced roll-cage frame; the vehicle also features amongst other things tempered glass, three airbags, an anti-lock braking system with disc brakes on all three wheels, and electric windows and lock as standard. At the time of writing production is scheduled to start at the company's Shreveport, Louisiana, plant in mid-2014.

ElTrans A/S/Eltrans1 A/S

1987 — CityEl

The CityEl was first manufactured in Denmark 1987 (see CityCom A/S on page 59 for more information) under the name of 'Mini-el' until 1992. The company — El Trans A/S — went bankrupt in 1988, but came back in 1991 under the name of Eltrans1 A/S. At this point it started manufacturing the Mini-el City, which is more or less identical to the present City-el. The company went bankrupt again and the machines were sold to a company in Sweden. They were sold again a couple of years later to a company in Germany, which then recommenced production in 1995. The CityEl is a single-seat electric three-wheeler powered by a 2.5kW electric engine that has a range of 70-90km. The body of the vehicle is made of plastic, whilst the whole top half is hinged to allow access to both the front and back seats. At present, there are two models: the Town Centre L Basic and the Town Centre L TargaFun, which features a detachable top. A Cabrio model was also produced but is no longer manufactured.

Eric

1911 — Sociable

With a weight of 8cwt, the Eric Sociable was one of the heavier three-wheelers of its era. Introduced in the UK in 1911, the vehicle was fitted with a 10bhp, horizontal twin-cylinder, water-cooled engine that provided drive by a cardan shaft to a bevel-driven back axle. It had a three-speed plus reverse gearbox, whilst the chassis and frame were made from steel tubes with a metal body. The body also incorporated a vertical windscreen and a hood. From 1913 a Salmons four-cylinder engine was also available in a version with a closed coupé body.

Fitted with a short body the Eric Sociable was available as an open soft-top version and also with a fully enclosed coupé body.
Author's Collection

Ernst Bauermeister & Sohne

1924 — EBS

The EBS was first manufactured in 1924 in Berlin, Germany, by Ernst Bauermeister & Sohne. The vehicle had been created from a basic motorcycle, which kept the front end more or less intact with the rear end rebuilt as a two-seat cabin that sat over the rear axle. The driver sat at the front of the vehicle in motorcycle style, exposed to the elements, whilst the passengers enjoyed the comfort of the cabin. The EBS was powered by a number of air-cooled engines, with 200cc, 250cc and 350cc being used. The transmission of the EBS was by chain to the gearbox and then by a shaft to the rear axle. Production ceased in 1927.

Fabrica Nacional de Cyclecars David

1951 — David

The Fabrica Nacional de Cyclecars David — David for short — was founded in 1913 in Barcelona, Spain, and manufactured four-wheel cyclecars until 1922 when it then

moved on to taxis and hire cars. In 1951 the first David three-wheeler was made. The vehicle was equipped with a 10bhp, air-cooled, single-cylinder, two-stroke, 345cc engine that provided a top speed of 42mph (68km/h). The engine sat at the front of the vehicle and drove the single front wheel, turning with it as the vehicle was steered. The chassis was nothing more than a longitudinal central tube that ran down the length of the vehicle with the front wheel and engine at one end and the rear axle at the other. The body was made from steel and available with or without a hood. Whilst essentially the David was a two-seater there were also two smaller dickey seats at the rear that were suitable for children.

1951 — Rubia

The Rubia was an enclosed version of the David that had a hard top, which dropped down almost vertically on to the back of the vehicle maximising interior load space. The doors were the rear panels of the vehicle that were extended upwards with wooden side panels to create higher sides.

The David was powered by an air-cooled 345cc engine that not only drove the front wheel but was also mounted to the same frame and so turned with it. RUMCar News

1957 — Torpedo 2 series

Introduced in 1957, the Torpedo 2 series was an updated version of the David that saw a number of changes, including a redesigned grille area. The David was produced until 1959, with around 60 vehicles being built.

Falcon Design

1986 — Falcon LX-3

The Falcon LX-3 was first built in 1986 by Peter Bird of Falcon Design in the UK and was available as a kit — a basic kit cost £400 — or as a set of plans for £10. The vehicle was a Lotus lookalike and used the floor pan of a Citroën 2CV along with its 602cc engine. The suspension was also from a Citroën 2CV, with stubs of both rear swinging arms joined by a beam with one arm repositioned to place the wheel in the centre. The body tub was plywood with a fibreglass bonnet, wings and boot. A number of Falcons also had stainless steel or aluminium panels attached over the plywood. In 1991 Falcon

Design offered a replacement chassis that was the same style as the Citroën floor pan though was less likely to rust as quickly. Following Bird's death the project was passed on to a company in Stratford ; it was passed on again in 1993 when it was sold to Mike Cooper in Somerset. The company was then renamed as Falcon Cars, based in Lincolnshire, in 2001 with kits still being available until 2002.

FAR

1920 — Poney Mécanique

In 1920 FAR formed a partnership with the car manufacturers Chenard & Walcker to build road trains using the Lagache coupling system patented by André Lagache a year earlier. The name FAR comes from the company founders: Fritz Glaszmann, André Lagache and Raymond Glaszmann. Under the new name — Trains Chenard et Walcker FAR — it also manufactured the Scammell Mechanical Horse in France under licence from Scammell from 1937. Known as the 'Poney Mécanique', a number of body variants were produced, including trucks, articulated vehicles and road sweepers. The vehicles were powered by either a Citroën Traction Avant or Walcker engine. From 1952 the vehicles were powered by either Renault petrol or Perkins diesel engines with the carrying capacity increased to six tons in an articulated version. Production of the three-wheelers ceased in 1970 when the range was replaced by a new four-wheeled version.

FAR created a number of tractor units that were fitted with a Lagache coupling system for connection to commercial trailers. Dave Stretton

Felber & Co

1952 — Autoroller T400

Starting as a motorcycle sidecar manufacturer, Felber & Co of Vienna, Austria, first manufactured a three-wheeler in 1952. The Autoroller T400 almost had a 'bubble'-shaped steel body that was to become popular just a few years later. Designed by Ernst Marold, two versions of the model were made with later ones having fixed wings rather than motorcycle-type mudguards. All vehicles were painted in light green paint as standard, the paint originally being designed for machinery. Power came from a two-stroke, 398cc, opposed twin Rotax engine that powered the rear wheel. Around 400 Felbers were produced with production stopping in 1954 when the company turned to manufacturing industrial washing machines.

1953 — Möve

Between 1953 and 1954 a Felber Möve was also built by a company called Hofmann & Moldrich in Vienna that received 12 rolling Autoroller chassis and fitted them with its own curved body made from aluminium that enclosed the front wheels.

Fend

1948 — Fend Flitzer

In Roseheim, Germany 1948, Fritz Fend — a former aircraft designer — introduced the Fend Flitzer. The small single-seat three-wheeler was initially introduced as an invalid car for those disabled as a result of World War 2. The vehicle was steered via a mechanism that was actuated by pushing the handlebars backwards and forwards. The Flitzer was available either in a manually-driven version or powered by either a 38cc Victoria or 98cc Fichtel & Sachs engine, which powered the front wheel. The chassis was made from steel tubing whilst the body was made from steel sheet. At first the vehicles were fitted with small bicycle wheels but these were replaced by small scooter wheels. The engine was also later uprated to a 100cc Riedel engine. Production stopped in 1951 with 252 vehicles being produced.

In 1953, after Fend was approached by Professor Willy Messerschmitt with his idea for a two-seat version, the Fend Flitzer was taken over by Messerschmitt (see page 156) and Fend used the Flitzer to form the basis of a two-seat version: the Fend

Kabinenroller also called the FK 150. In 2000 Fend created a new prototype vehicle; this was a four-wheeler, though the rear wheels were positioned very close to each other giving the illusion of a three-wheeler. The vehicle was to have been powered by a 650cc BMW engine. Fend died on 22 November 2000 at the age of 80, bringing an end to the car's development.

Feora

1981 — Feora

The Feora was created in Los Angeles, USA, in 1981 by Chuck Ophorst. The vehicle had a 1020 steel frame and was powered by a 175cc Honda engine. The suspension was by a trailing arm and the vehicle was fitted with disc brakes on each wheel. The fibreglass body resembled that of an aircraft from the 1950s with access to the vehicle via a lift-up canopy. With a top speed of 93mph (150km/h) and a fuel consumption of 85mpg (3.3-litre/100km) it is believed that the Feora never went into production as a result of its high costs, though Ophorst did agree to sell plans and kits.

Ferdinando Innocenti Co

1949 — Lambretta FA/FB/FC

Founded in 1931, the Ferdinando Innocenti Co in Milan, Italy, produced steel tubes. In 1948, following the end of World War 2, the company started to produce motor scooters; these soon included sidecars that evolved further into three-wheel vehicles in 1949. Early vehicles were advertised as Lambrettas though, as the machines evolved, they were sold under the name of Innocenti Lambro and now had a fully enclosed fibreglass two-seat cabin.

In 1949 the first three-wheel Lambrettas were essentially three-wheel scooters with the back end of the vehicle remaining as a scooter with the front end being modified to have two wheels and either a wooden box or an aluminium cargo compartment set between the front two wheels. The first model, the FA, was never manufactured and remained a prototype, though the Lambretta FB model from the same year was powered by a 125cc engine with a three-speed gearbox with no reverse, which drove

A 1955 Lambretta FD with its open scooter front end that would develop over the coming years into a cabin. KKM Deliveries

the single rear wheel. This model was able to carry 200kg. In 1950 it was replaced by the Lambretta FC model, which had a number of improvements that included a new hydraulic braking system whilst still using a 125cc engine with a top speed of 30mph (48km/h).

1953 — Lambretta FD/FDC/FLi

In 1953 the Lambretta FD model brought along a new vehicle using the same principles, though now the single wheel had been moved to the front and the cargo area sat behind the driver between the two rear wheels. The front end was from the Lambretta D model scooter, whilst a new tubular frame had been made for the back. Still fitted with a 125cc engine, transmission now used a shaft, differential and two axles. In 1955 a larger 150cc engine was available, which increased the top speed to 37mph (60km/h). Amongst the options for the FD model was a pull-over canvas top with a windscreen built into it. Along with the FD model, there was also a Lambretta FDC version that had been introduced in 1957. The C in FDC stood for 'Cab', denoting that the FDC was fitted with a canvas roof as standard with side doors also available as an option for an extra £12 a pair. The FDC also featured a dual seat that would seat two people and the three-speed gearbox now had a reverse. Both the FD and FDC modes were replaced by the Lambretta FLi 175 in 1959. Again, following the trend of continual improvements, the FLi 175 model was now fitted with a larger 175cc engine, providing a top speed of 38mph (61km/h). The FLi had an improved larger cabin, 12V electrics — that permitted an electric windscreen wiper rather than a mechanical one — and a greater range of commercial boxes available at the rear. The FLi 175 was the most popular of Lambretta three-wheelers, with over 82,000 vehicles being manufactured before production stopped in 1965.

1963 — Lambro 200/450/550

The Lambro 200 was introduced in 1963 and, to move the vehicles away from their Scooter image, the name was changed to Lambro and, on promotional material, the maker's name was shown as Innocenti rather than Lambretta. As the name suggests, the Lambro 200 was powered by an 8.9bhp 200cc engine that powered the rear wheels via a four-speed with reverse gearbox. The vehicle featured a new chassis that meant the cargo area had been enlarged, giving the Lambro 200 a payload of 500kg. In 1965 the Lambro 450 and Lambro 550 arrived; the 450 was a replacement for the FLi 175 model and was powered by a 175cc engine whilst the 550 model replaced the Lambro 200. The 550 featured a number of changes, including hydraulic brakes on all three wheels and twin headlights and was built until 1967.

1967 — Lambro 550A/550N/ 550L/550M//550V/550ML/ 600M/600V

Whilst the 1967 Lambro N and the 1968 Lambro resembled the 550 version and still used a 200cc engine, a number of changes were made to improve driver comfort; these included moving the engine from under the seat to outside the cab and deflectors being fitted to the doors to cut wind noise. The 550A had a longer loading area, which was designed to carry larger lighter items rather than increase the payload. The Lambro 550V, 550M and 550ML were all introduced in 1969. The vehicles now had a redesigned cabin that came from the Italian design house Bertone and, on the Lambro 550V model, a conventional steering wheel was introduced instead of handlebars that featured on all other models. In 1970 the Lambro ML model also included a low-sided pick-up version. Improvements continued to be made with the Lambro 600M and Lambro 600V models until production ceased in 1972.

Fiberfab Inc

1975 — Scarab STM

Fiberfab Inc of Pennsylvania, USA, is one of the world's oldest and largest manufacturers of fibreglass sports car bodies. In 1975 the company introduced what could possibly be the first kit form three-wheeler: the Fiberfab Scarab STM (Sports Transport Module). The model was powered by a number of motorcycle engines that were 450cc or larger, which all drove the single rear wheel. The front suspension, which was attached to a steel frame, came from a Volkswagen Beetle. The two-seat body was made in three-sections from fibreglass and was bolted to the chassis. The front of the Scarab featured a collapsible/replaceable bumper and the body had a 'flip top' roof with 'pop-out' windows. It was claimed that Scarab kits could be assembled by one man in about 20 hours. All body parts, hardware and frame were provided with the kits, though owners had to source their own front suspension, which took a further four hours to convert. A few kits were sold in the 1970s, though the car did receive renewed popularity in the early 1990s.

Right: *The Fiberfab Scarab was introduced in 1975 and was possibly the first three-wheel kit car. It was sold in a kit form that was said to take one man 20 hours to build.* Alden Jewell

Left: *Proving to be extremely popular the Innocenti Lambro was built in numerous versions as the model constantly evolved through throughout its life.* Maurizo Bol

Filatov

1915 — Armoured Car: Single/Dual Machine Guns

Designed by General-Major Filatov in 1915, the Filatov was a three-wheeler armoured car that was built in Russia and was one of the few designs — amongst hundreds that were said to have been developed — to see service with the Imperial Army during Word World 1. With large wheels (the single wheel being at the front), a mechanised chassis and a narrow body, the vehicle was designed to travel across rough terrain whilst being narrow enough to tackle hilly or mountainous regions and manoeuvre around obstacles. The Filtatov was also protected by 4-6mm of riveted armour plating around the body along with an armoured shield on the wheels to protect the spokes and was fitted with either a 16- or a 25bhp Case, Gupmobile or Maskwill engine. In 1916, the initial vehicle, designed to carry a crew of three to four people, was armed with dual 7.62mm machine guns fired from the rear of the vehicle. Around 10 vehicles were built with dual machine guns though, with a total weight of 2.6 tons, the vehicles were found to be overloaded and so, on later models, only one 7.62mm machine gun was fitted with around 20 vehicles being made. A third model was also built; this carried a 25mm gun. However, this was not successful and was ruled unsafe with the result that only the machine gun models were deployed. The Filatov not only saw action during World War 1 but was also used during the Russian Civil War and remained in the Soviet inventory until 1922.

1915 — Pick-up

In addition to the armoured cars, the Filatov was also built as an open pick-up type vehicle that had no armour plating and no shields on the wheels. The steering column, stretching across the top of the vehicle above the front wheel, was also completely exposed. As with the armoured vehicles the pick-up type is believed to have been used up until 1922.

FN (Fabrique Nationale d'Armes de Guerre)

1939 — Tricar (AA/Ammunition/MG/Personnel/Repair/Utility)

Manufactured by the firearms company Fabrique Nationale d'Armes de Guerre (FN) in Belgium, the FN Tricar was introduced in 1939. With a motorcycle front end, the vehicle had a modified rear end built in a number of versions that were able to carry a payload of 500kg or five people. It found favour with the Belgian Army who ordered 331 vehicles in a range of models: the AA that had a FN-Hotchkiss anti-aircraft gun mounted to it; the Ammunition version designed for carrying ammunition; the MG designed for carrying a Maxim medium machine gun and crew; a Personnel version that was fitted with a large front windscreen and a canvas roof for carrying up to five people; a Repair model designed to carry spare parts for vehicles; and, a Utility version that had a standard pick-up type rear end. With the exception of the Personnel carrier, all models had the driver sitting on a saddle and controlling the vehicle with handlebars. All versions were built until 1945; however, in 1947 a Tricar was introduced. This was a truck version equipped with a fully enclosed cabin and a van rear end.

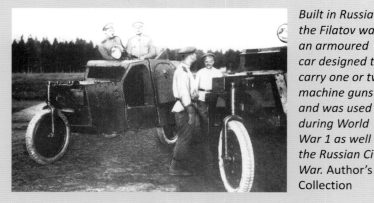

Built in Russia the Filatov was an armoured car designed to carry one or two machine guns and was used during World War 1 as well as the Russian Civil War. Author's Collection

The fully enclosed FN Tricar from 1947 fitted with a van body. Wikipedia — Kelp

Mainly used by the Belgian parachute troops, the FN AS 24 was a lightweight three-wheeler that was designed to be dropped from an aircraft by parachute. Olivier Houllier

1960 — AS 24

Introduced for the military in 1960, the AS 24 was a low-riding three-wheeler that was capable of carrying four people and equipment up to a total cargo weight of 770lb (350kg) when used with a trailer. With 460 vehicles being manufactured, many were used by the Belgian parachute troops when dropped by parachute into operational zones. Powered by a 245cc, two-cylinder, air-cooled, type FN 24 engine, the AS 24 was capable of 60mph (96.5km/h). The steering wheel was easily removable and attached to the rear of the vehicle. This meant a person could walk behind and steer at the same time.

Ford Motor Co

Whilst the Ford Motor Co of the USA was founded in 1903 and has produced many four-wheelers since the Ford Model T, which brought motoring to the masses, the company has also three-wheelers tucked away in its archives.

1935 — Tug (Dorset)

The Ford Tug used parts from Ford Model Y series, including body parts, ancillaries and engines, whilst the chassis was a modified from the Ford BB truck. Designed in 1935 as a mechanical horse, the Tug — also called Dorset by Ford — was available as a tractor with or without either a two- or four-wheel trailer and was able to carry a payload of two tons. The vehicle was equipped with a quick release coupling and had a top speed of 18mph (29km/h). The single front wheel was tucked under the radiator

with an 18in wheel at the front and 23in wheels at the back. In 1936 the Tug chassis was converted by County Commercial Cars Ltd to create a van-based model called the Devon Distributor (see page 64). Production of the Tug ceased in 1938 with 111 vehicles made.

1954 — Maxima

The Maxima was a concept vehicle from 1954 though it never got any further than a 3/8th scale model. With a dart-like shape, with two wheels at the rear and a single front wheel protruding through the body, it was intended that it would be powered by twin jet engines with a top speed of 500mph (805km/h). It was initially designed to commemorate the 50th anniversary of Henry Ford's land speed record. It is claimed that the design of the vehicle was to influence Craig Breedlove's Spirit of America land speed vehicle. (See page 233 for more details.)

1981 — Ghia Cockpit

First shown at the 1981 Geneva Motor Show, the Ford Ghia Cockpit was a concept vehicle powered by a 12bhp, air-cooled, single-cylinder 200cc Piaggio Vespa engine that sat at the back of the vehicle and powered the single rear wheel. The gearbox had four gears whilst reverse gear was achieved by driving the electric starter motor backwards. The body was created mainly from aluminium and housed two seats in a tandem-style layout. It also featured a sophisticated hydraulic suspension system and a canopy section that lifted forward to give access to and from the vehicle.

Produced as a concept vehicle, the Ford Ghia Cockpit featured a large lift up canopy to gain access to the vehicle and was powered by a 200cc Piaggio engine. Ford Motor Co

Framo-Werke

1932 — Delivery Truck

Framo-Werke of Germany had been manufacturing motorcycles since the 1920s and introduced its first three-wheeler in 1932. It was powered by a two-stroke, single-cylinder, 300cc DKW engine with compressed air cooling. Drive was sent to the single front wheel, which had the engine mounted directly above it. The front of the vehicle was completely open and the driver steered with a tiller. The rear van section provided some weather protection with a roof that extended from the box behind the driver over the driver's seat. The vehicle was replaced in 1933 with the Piccolo.

1933 — Piccolo

The Framo Piccolo was an industrial vehicle that featured a fully-enclosed cabin and either an open pick-up or enclosed rear body that had a carrying capacity of 500kg. The vehicle used a 300cc DKW engine that provided drive to the front wheel via a chain. In 1935 the Piccolo was converted into a four-wheeler with a 300cc rear-mounted DKW power unit driving the rear axle; as such it was built until 1943.

1933 — Stromer

In 1933 the Framo Stromer was created; unlike earlier vehicles, it had two front wheels with the single wheel at the back. It was powered by a single-cylinder, two-stroke, 200cc DKW engine. This meant at the time in Germany it did not require a driving licence and was tax free. With a top speed of 40mph (64km/h) fully loaded with two adults, the vehicle had a single tubular chassis onto which sub-frames were attached with a streamlined steel body that tapered off at the rear. Manufacture of the Stromer ceased in 1938.

Frank Tippen & Sons

1955 — Tippen Delta (Mk 1-8)

Frank Tippen first started a company in 1935 making variable speed gears for machine drives under the name of Heterospeed in Coventry, UK. In 1948 the National Health Service was introduced to the UK, and Tippen became interested in invalid tricycles that then became available for the physically impaired. Having worked on motorising a chair with a small motorcycle engine, further development led to a

For its time the Framo Stromer had an extremely stylish streamlined body that tapered off at the rear end. Maximilian Busch

Powered by a 200cc engine the Framo Stromer at its introduction could be driven without the need of a driving licence. Maximilian Busch

The Tippen Delta was the first invalid carriage to feature a sliding door and also had room for a folded wheelchair. RUMCar News

new vehicle in 1955 — the Tippen Delta. It not only offered full weather protection but was also the first invalid carriage to feature a sliding door. It was also capable of accommodating a folding wheelchair next to the driver. Constructed on a steel chassis, the vehicle had a fibreglass single-seat body with a removable soft top and a single headlight at the front. The Tippen Delta had tiller steering, which incorporated a twist grip automatic transmission, and was powered by an air-cooled, single-cylinder, two-stroke, 197cc Villiers Mk 8E engine. This was later changed to the Villiers Mk 9E engine in the Tippen Delta Mk 2 announced in 1958. In 1965 the Tippen Delta was also available in an electric version powered by a 36V electric motor. With the introduction of the Tippen Delta Mk 8 in 1968, the body received further changes with the front of the vehicle now supporting twin headlights, thus making it look much more car like. The petrol version of the Tippen Delta was manufactured until 1970 whilst the electric version continued to be built until 1976.

Frisky Cars Ltd/Frisky Cars (1959) Ltd

With a history that dates back to 1919, Henry Meadows Ltd of Wolverhampton, UK, started as a manufacturer of three-speed gearboxes, later going on to produce the engines that powered such cars as Lagonda, Fraser Nash, HRG, Lea Francis and Invicta. In 1955 President Nasser expelled the British from Egypt; amongst them was businessman and racing driver Capt Raymond Flower, who subsequently approached the company with his concept of a small lightweight peoples' car. Meadows allocated funds and the facilities, and work commenced in the 'back room' at the factory. The first Frisky was a the four-wheel gull-wing prototype displayed at the 1957

Geneva Motor show as 'The Meadows Frisky', which was received with great acclaim. The car was designed and built by Gordon Bedson and Keith Peckmore at Meadows with its fibreglass body styled by the Italian stylist, Giovanni Michelotti, and constructed by Vignale of Turin. Unfortunately it was too expensive to produce and so it was entirely redesigned in time for its re-launch at the 1957 Earl's Court Motor Show as an open-top 'Meadows FriskySport'. In 1958 production of the Frisky was taken over by the Marston Group and the company name was changed to Frisky Cars Ltd, although all production remained at Meadows. The greater sales potential for a three-wheel car with its tax and licence advantages was recognised and the development of a three wheel version was put in hand.

1958 — Family Three Mk 1

At the 1958 Earl's Court Motor show, the new Frisky Family Three was launched. This was a three-wheel version and was so called because it had three wheels and could seat three people on its bench seat (at a pinch). This carried the same in house styling as the FriskySport but in a saloon format. The vehicle's fibreglass body had the same rear hung doors, which were wider than average to allow easy access. It used the same tubular chassis, with MacPherson strut front suspension, and was powered by the smaller two-stroke,

A 1959 Frisky Family Three, so called as it had three wheels and could just about seat three people. John Meadows

Very few Frisky Princes were built, with this particular vehicle being the only known completed example. John Meadows

197cc, single Villiers 9E engine that was located at the rear of the vehicle and which drove the rear single wheel. The paintwork on the Frisky always created a big impression as, after removing the fibreglass body from the mould, it was weathered and any tiny flaws were filled and rubbed down and an undercoat would then be applied. This layer was heat dried and after more rubbing down the topcoat was applied resulting in a very high gloss finish. Production commenced in January 1959.

1959 — Family Three Mk 2

It had been recognised for some time that the Family Three Mk 1 was underpowered and that the MacPherson front struts were not satisfactory and so, in February 1959, development began on the Mk 2 version. The front suspension was changed to the original Dubonnet type used in the FriskySport and the Villiers 9E was replaced with an Excelsior TT-250 twin that had the advantage of a real reverse gear. To accommodate the extra power, the chassis was extended to the rear; this enabled the engine to be moved out of the cabin and into the tail section. An attempt was made to use the resulting space for two small children's seats in the rear but there was not really enough room for this and the idea was dropped early on in production. This was a very different car to drive compared to the Mk1 as it had improved performance and handling. Externally the only noticeable change was the large rear hatch above the engine/fuel tank.

The first Family Three Mk 2s were registered in May 1959 but, shortly afterwards, Frisky Cars Ltd ran into financial difficulties and was put into receivership in June 1959. In August 1959, a Wolverhampton businessman bought the stock, jigs, tools, fixtures and fittings, along with the rights to manufacture and the trade name of Frisky from the Official Receiver and formed a new company Frisky Cars (1959) Ltd. Production of the Family Three Mk 2 commenced in January 1960 with the Excelsior TT-250 engine. Later on the Excelsior TT1-328 or the Villiers 3T engine were offered as options.

1960 — Frisky Prince

Announced in October 1960 at the Earl's Court Show, the Frisky Prince was basically a rebodied Family Three Mk 2. Its new body was 12in longer and now had doors that were front-hinged. In addition, the fibreglass body was colour pigmented with a range of eight colours available. Due to the problems that were then faced by the company, very few Frisky Princes were built and sales were poor. For a short period in 1960 Middlesbrough Motorcraft offered the Frisky in a kit form; it, however, found few takers.

At the same time, the sale of Frisky Cars (1959) Ltd was being negotiated with Petbow Ltd and, in January 1961, Frisky production moved from Meadows to Sandwich in Kent.

Production problems beset the company from the start and production only lasted a short while. In 1962 Frisky Spares & Service Ltd, Queenborough, Kent, was set up and remaining stocks of Frisky parts were moved there from Petbow's works. This company, based in a boat yard, mainly supplied spares for existing car owners. No real production took place; it would assemble a car for a customer if required, but preferred to provide a kit so customers could construct their own. The company ceased trading around 1966 and the remaining bodies were taken down to Queenborough Creek and burnt.

The FRS, a one-off racing machine designed and built purely for hill climbing trials. FRS Motorsport

FRS Motorsport

1995 — FRS

Having raced sidecars in the early 1990s, father and son Fred and Jason Reeve then went on to build the FRS in 1995. The vehicle was designed purely for hill climbing and was powered initially by a Kawasaki 900cc engine. This was then replaced with a Kawasaki 1,100cc engine and finally a Suzuki GXR 1,216cc engine that gave the vehicle 170bhp. All engines provided drive to the two front wheels. At first the FRS used a steering wheel and a foot throttle, though as the rules of hill climbing changed, the FRS was banned and so had to be modified so that it used handlebars with a twist grip throttle. The rules were again altered back to the original specifications. The FRS still holds class records at the majority of the major hill climbs in England and Wales. It was then suggested to the Reeves that a road version of the FRS should be created and so this resulted in the FRS2.

2011 — FRS2

Introduced in 2011 and built by FRS Motorsport in West Yorkshire, UK, the FRS2 is an open two-seater that is available in either a kit form or as a 'turnkey' product. The vehicle has a powder coated tubular steel spaceframe with a fibreglass body that has separate cockpits for the driver and passenger with the passenger sitting behind the driver. It is fitted with a 98bhp, water-cooled, four-cylinder, inline 1,200cc Suzuki Bandit engine that drives the two front wheels via a five-speed sequential transmission and fitted with mono-shock suspension. In July 2013 the FRS3 was introduced; this featured restyled bodywork and a redesigned rear swinging arm and brake unit. A reversing unit, incorporated in the rear swinging arm as an optional extra, was also available.

With dual cockpits the FRS2 is a road legal vehicle derived from the original FRS racer. Steve Hole

Instead of running on liquid fuel, the Alé is fitted with a fuel vapour system that lets the engine run on fuel vapours, which is said to provide up to 92mpg. Fuel Vapor Technologies

Fuel Vapor Technologies

2006 — Alé

Created by George Parker in 2006, the Alé (alay) is a concept car that has been in development since 1995. Built by Fuel Vapor Technologies of Vancouver, BC, Canada, the vehicle has an innovative fuel vapour system that allows the engine to run on fuel vapours rather than liquid fuel resulting in 92 miles per US gallon (2.56-litre/100km). Whilst fuel efficiency is increased by 10 to 20%, CO_2 emissions are reduced by up to 30% meaning that the vehicle does not require a catalytic converter to meet global emissions standards.

The engine is a turbo-charged 180bhp, 1,500cc, Honda VTEC D15B engine that gives the Alé a 0-60mph (0-96km/h) time of under five seconds with a top speed electronically limited to 140mph (225km/h). Transmission is provided by either a five-speed standard or four-speed overdrive automatic gearbox. The Alé uses Porsche 911 rack and pinion for steering and during cornering the vehicle can pull 1.7g. The body is a hand-laid fibreglass composite mounted onto a full tube frame with a roll cage. Seating is tandem style with the passenger sitting behind the driver. From 2012 the Alé was produced in limited quantities though the company is, at the time of writing, currently seeking investors to take it into mass production.

Fuji Toshuda Motors

1955 — Fuji Cabin

Intended as a fully-enclosed scooter the Fuji Cabin first appeared at the Tokyo Motor Show in 1955. Built by Fuji Toshuda Motors, Tokyo, Japan, the vehicle had a 5.5bhp, air-cooled, 121.7cc Gasuden engine. Fitted with a plastic two-seat body it had a top speed of 37mph (59km/h). Engineered by Ryuichi Tomiya, the Fuji Cabin also had rubber suspension, a three-speed gearbox with reverse and a cooling duct that ran down the centre of the car. Production stopped a year later in 1956 after just 85 vehicles had been manufactured.

Designed as a fully enclosed scooter, the Fuji Cabin was a two-seater built in Japan in 1955 though production was shortlived and ceased a year later. Joel Bradshaw

A 1904 Garrard Suspended Tri-car fitted with a 500cc engine.
Author's Collection

Gaillardet

1899 — 5 CV

The Gaillardet 5 CV was designed in 1899 by Frédéric Gaillardet in Paris, France. It was built by the Société Française d'Automobile and had a single seat and tiller steering to the front wheel. Power came from an 800cc, single-cylinder engine. Production ceased in 1902.

Gaitán Constructions SL

1953 — Auto-Tri

Starting as a bicycle rental and repair shop, Gaitán Constructions SL was founded in 1936 by Francisco Gaitán Sanchez in Seville, Spain. The company then moved on to manufacture a pedal-powered delivery tricycle that had a large storage area between the front two wheels. The vehicle had an air-cooled, 76cc Motovelox engine attached directly to the top of the rear wheel and mounted behind the driver's saddle. In 1953 the Gaitán Auto-Tri was introduced. Powered by an air-cooled, 125cc engine, drive was provided either to the two front wheels or the single rear wheel depending on the model as one had the two wheels at the front whilst the other had two wheels at the back. The vehicle had a tubular steel chassis and an egg-shaped aluminium body with a large fin at the rear. Various versions of the vehicle were made, including an ambulance and a prototype developed for the Army though the vehicles were never marketed.

Garrard Co

1904 — Suspended Tri-car

Manufactured for one year, the Garrard Suspended Tri-car was built in 1904 by the Garrard Co in Birmingham, UK. Founded by Charles Garrard in 1900, the company also built the Clement-Garrard motorcycle. The tri-car was fitted with a 4bhp, 500cc engine with drive being passed through to the single rear wheel by a shaft drive via a three-speed gearbox. The suspension was leaf springs at the front and a pivoted fork at the rear. The passenger sat in a large seat between the front two wheels, whilst the driver sat at the rear in a saddle with handlebars for steering. It is understood that few of these machines were built and that production ceased in 1904 with the company closing a year later.

Gasi-Motorradwagen GmbH

1921 — Gasi

The name Gasi comes from the surnames of the company's founders: Fritz Gary and Edmund Sielaff. Manufactured in 1921 by Gasi-Motorradwagen GmbH of Berlin, Germany, the Gasi was powered by an air-cooled, two-cylinder engine. This provided transmission by a chain to an intermediate shaft and then by two belts at each side of the vehicle without differential to the rear wheels. The two-seat metal body saw the passenger sit behind the driver with each seat having what essentially was its own cockpit similar to an old aircraft. The company also produced four-wheelers, with production of all vehicles ceasing in 1924.

Gebhardt & Harhorn

1910 — Geha

With a name that was derived from its makers, Gebhardt & Harhorn, the Geha was an electric vehicle manufactured in Berlin, Germany, from 1910. The electric motor was mounted in the hub of the single

front wheel. The axle of the wheel around which the motor rotated was fixed solidly to the wheel bracket with an intermediate gear causing the wheel to revolve. The motor was powered by batteries that sat under the floor and provided a top speed of 17 to 19mph (25-30km/h) with a range of 50 miles (80km). The Geha was available with many different bodies ranging from passenger versions to commercial vans; all types were made until 1917.

General Developing Co

1947 — Comet

Manufactured by the General Developing Co in New York, USA, in 1947 the Comet was powered by a 4.5bhp, air-cooled engine that drove the two rear wheels by using a split pulley drive. The Comet was quite rare for its time as it had a fibreglass body fitted onto a tubular frame. This lightweight structure — 290cm long and 122cm wide — helped give the vehicle a fuel consumption of up to 100mpg (2.8-litre/100km) with a maximum speed of 50mph (80km/h). Despite being advertised as 'the world's handiest run-around-in-car', production of the vehicle ceased in the same year.

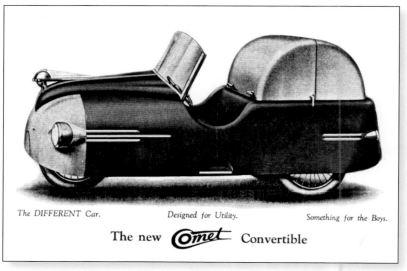

The DIFFERENT Car. Designed for Utility. Something for the Boys.

The new *Comet* Convertible

Above: *Promoted in 1947 as 'Something for the boys', the Comet had one unusual feature for its time and that was that it had a fibreglass body.* Author's Collection

Left: *The Geha was an electric vehicle in which the actual motor was mounted into the hub on the front wheel and caused the wheel to rotate around it.* Author's Collection

General Motors

Whilst around the world General Motors (GM) is well known for its four-wheelers, it has created a number of concept three-wheelers over the years in the USA.

1964 — Runabout

Created in 1964, the Runabout was a concept vehicle that had a front wheel that could turn 180° to allow parking in the tightest of spots. The rear end of the car contained two detachable shopping trolleys with wheels that would fold away when the trolley was parked in the vehicle. The interior had no steering wheel; instead steering was managed by rotating two electronic dials. The Runabout had space for two adults in the front and three children in the rear. It was first presented at the General Motors' Futurama Exhibit in 1964 at the New York World's Fair.

1966 — Maier

In 1966, Peter Maier, one of the youngest designers hired by GM, along with a group of young designers set about creating a concept for a new three-wheeler. Maier's sketch was chosen and, in 1967, was turned into a three-dimensional clay model though the design proceeded no further.

Presented at the General Motors' Futurama Exhibit in 1964, the Runabout would be superb for the author's wife in that it contained two detachable shopping trolleys that would save standing in the rain and unloading the monthly shopping into the car. General Motors

Designed by Peter Maier this concept three-wheeler was created for GM though proceeded no further than a three-dimensional model. General Motors

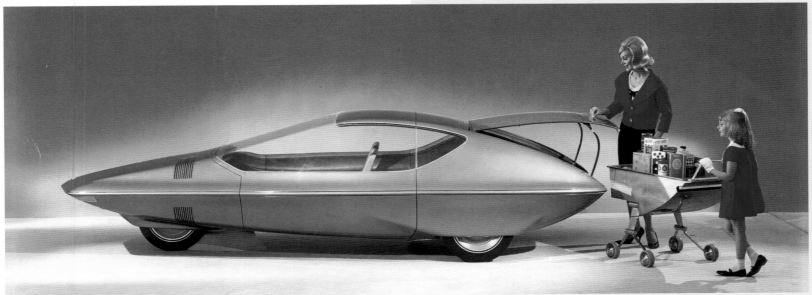

The XP 511 was another concept vehicle by GM that was powered by an Opel 1,100cc engine and featured a lift up canopy to gain access to the vehicle. General Motors

1980s — Lean Machine

The GM Lean Machine was developed by Frank Winchell in the early 1980s as a concept car. The single-seat vehicle was a lean machine in the true sense of the word as it leans into corners like a motorcycle, whilst keeping the stability of a normal car. The controls for the vehicle are also similar to that of a motorcycle as they are mounted into the handlebars. The original model was powered by a 15bhp, two-cylinder, 185cc, Honda engine that produced a maximum speed of 80mph (129km/h) with a fuel economy of 80mpg (3.5-litre/100km) at 40mph (64km/h). Shortly afterwards a second model was produced that was powered by a larger 38bhp engine. With a total bodyweight of 159kg, this gave the vehicle outstanding performance and the Lean Machine was able to reach 60mph (96km/h) in just 6.8sec with a fuel economy of over 200mpg (1.4-litre/100km).

For the futuristic 1993 movie *Demolition Man*, starring Sylvester Stallone and Wesley Snipes, the GM Lean Machine was one of 17 concept cars, with an insurance value of $69 million, produced by GM to be featured in the film.

1969 — XP 511

The XP 511 Commuter car was a concept vehicle designed in 1969 for short urban journeys. It had an Opel 1,100cc, 67bhp, four-cylinder engine and a three-speed gearbox and was said to have a top speed of 80mph (129km/h). The vehicle had two seats and handlebar steering, whilst the body featured a canopy that opened up and forward to allow access to the vehicle.

Living up to its name the Lean Machine was a tilting three-wheeler that had handlebar controls and would lean into corners like a motorcycle. General Motors

Gillet

1937 — Gillet

The Gillet car was built in 1937 by Pierre Thibeau and Corneille Dasoul in Belgium. The vehicle was powered by a 1928 air-cooled, 500cc Gillet Herstal motorcycle engine that was started by a kickstarter. The Gillet had a three-speed gearbox but no reverse. The front assembly of the vehicle is believed to have come either from a Renault or a Peugeot from the 1920s.

Girling Motor Manufacturing Co

Built with a number of bodies to compete with the AC Autocarrier, the Girling three-wheeler was manufactured by the Girling Motor Manufacturing Co in Woolwich, UK, from 1911. It was later manufactured in Bedford and then London. There were two standard models:

1911 — Model A

Power on all Girlings came from an air-cooled, single-cylinder, 6bhp JAP engine that drove the single rear wheel through a gearbox that had seven forward speeds and a reverse. The Model A was for carrying loads up to 5cwt. The front of the Girling was completely open and so both the driver and passenger sat exposed to the elements.

1911 — Model B

Whilst having the same engine and general specifications as the Model A, the Model B had a slightly larger load space and was able to carry up to 7cwt. The vehicles had wheels that were all interchangeable with each other and a number of bodies were offered; these included a trade carrier with box at the rear with various compartments and a double-decker that had two flat beds, one above the other, designed for dairy and poultry farming. Production of both models ceased in 1914.

In 1912 a Girling Model B was used as a fire engine when The British Fire Prevention Committee was conducting tests for vehicles to use to attend fires and invited tenders. Soon afterwards a Girling was stationed at Wood Green Station in London equipped with a 30ft ladder, hose and chemical extinguishers. Author's Collection

Goliath-Werke Borgward & Co

1925 — Blitzkarren

Prior to Goliath-Werke Borgward & Co being formed, its founder, Carl F W Borgward created a three-wheel vehicle in 1925 called the Blitzkarren ('Flash cart'). Powered by a 2.2bhp engine with tiller steering, the open-top vehicle was able to carry a payload of 25kg and was built until 1927. A year later the Goliath company was formed and work started on a new three-wheeler.

1931 — Pioneer

The first Goliath three-wheeler appeared in Bremen, Germany, in 1931. Designed and built by Borgward, the Goliath Pioneer was powered by a choice of two engines: a single-cylinder, two-stroke, 198cc ILO engine or a larger 247cc engine. Both engines drove both rear wheels of the car through a three-speed gearbox. The Pioneer was a two-seat vehicle, with a body that was made from a wooden frame and then covered in synthetic leather. It was manufactured until 1934 with around 4,350 vehicles made.

1933 — F200/F400

The Goliath F200 and F400 were introduced in 1933 and were, in essence, commercial versions of the Goliath Pioneer. Whilst the F200 was fitted with a single-cylinder, 198cc, ILO engine, the F400 had a two-cylinder, 398cc engine of Goliath's own design that was then replaced in 1935 with an ILO 398cc engine. Both variations were made until 1938. During World War 2, Goliath made a number of

The Goliath GD750 that, despite the 750 name, was powered by a 396cc engine that was later uprated to 465cc. Georg Schwalbach

Like many other three-wheel trucks the Goliath came with numerous body types with this particular vehicle built as a mobile fruit and vegetable shop. Maurice de Boer

armoured trucks and tracked vehicles. When the war ended, Goliath went on to produce a number of four-wheel vehicles and alongside them built three-wheel trucks.

1949 — GD750

Built from 1949 to 1955, the Goliath GD750 was a developed version of the F200 and F400. With a larger carrying capacity, the GD750 was powered by either a water-cooled, two-stroke, 396cc engine or a 465cc version. The vehicle was very adaptable with almost 30 different body combinations available and, as a result, over 29,000 vehicles were built.

1955 — Dreirad

The 1955 Goliath Dreirad was a follow up to the GD750 and again was available with numerous body variants. Initially it was fitted with a newly designed air-cooled, two-stroke, 493.5cc engine though this struggled under heavy loads and would overheat. As a result, in 1956 it was replaced in by the water-cooled, two-stroke, 461cc engine. From 1957, as a good will gesture, Goliath replaced all the air-cooled engines in vehicles already sold for the water-cooled version free of charge. Production of the Dreirad ceased in 1961 with just under 10,000 vehicles constructed.

Good Earth Energy Conservation Inc

2009 — Firefly ESV

With the aim of maximising the utilisation of electric vehicles with an increased range and speed, Good Earth Energy Conservation Inc was founded in 2006 in Fort Worth, Texas, USA. In 2009 the company introduced the Firefly ESV. The Firefly is an electric vehicle with zero-emissions using a Lithium Iron Phosphate battery and has a range of 60 to 100 miles (97-161km) per charge with speeds of up to 45mph (72km/h). With a frame made from steel, the vehicle has a modular bed design that is available in many forms including a flat bed, sectional bed, dump bed, refuse bed, lockable storage, or van box. At the time of writing the Firefly is in production.

Gordon

1824 — Gordon

The 1824 Gordon is perhaps the only three-wheeler not only to have wheels but feet as well. Its designer, David Gordon, then went on to obtain a patent for steam carriages to run on common roads. His vehicle had three wheels, one at the front to steer the vehicle and the rear two to take the main weight. Each had a separate axle though these were not powered. Instead the steam engine was designed to power a number of feet that pushed the vehicle forward. The following is a description on how the vehicle worked:

'The steam engines consisted of two brass cylinders, in a horizontal position, but vibrating upon trunnions the piston rods of these engines gave motion to an eight-throw crank, two in the middle for the cylinders, and three on each side, to which were attached the propellers; by the revolution of the crank, these propellers or legs were successively forced outwards, with the feet of each against the ground in a backward direction, and were immediately afterwards lifted from the ground by the revolution of another crank, parallel to the former, and situated at a proper distance from it on the same frame. If the carriage was proceeding upon a level, the lifting of the propellers was equivalent to the subtraction of the power, and soon brought it to a stoppage; and in making turns in a road, the guide had only to lift the propellers on one side of the carriage, and allow the others to operate alone, until the curve was traversed.' (*The Engineer's and Mechanics Encyclopaedia of The Machinery 1836* [Vol 2; Page 460])

Göricke-Werke Nippel & Co

1954 — Lasten roller

Founded in 1903 in Bielefeld, Germany, Göricke-Werke Nippel & Co manufactured bicycles, motorcycles and tricycles. From 1954 it produced the Göricke Lasten roller — motorised trade bike — that was powered by either an air-cooled, 48cc or 97cc Fichtel & Sachs engine and drove the single rear wheel by a chain through a three-speed gearbox. With a tubular steel frame, the vehicles were essentially a motorised tricycle with the driver sitting on a saddle and steering via handlebars. The cargo area had a payload of 150kg and was positioned between the two front wheels and came in a number of forms with either a cage or a box. Production ceased in 1959.

GRECAV

1991 — Nuova Amica

Having specialised in agricultural engineering and the production of body panels since 1964, in 1991 GRECAV from Gonsaga in Italy acquired BMA (see page 29) and took over production of the Amica, renaming it as the Nuova Amica. Powered by a choice of air-cooled, two-stroke petrol — 49cc and 125cc — or two-cylinder, three-stroke 250cc engines, with a fibreglass body, it was whilst building this that the company then designed the EKE, a small four-wheel vehicle that then replaced the Nuova Amica in 2000.

Greenheart Millennium Transport Ltd

1999 — GMT Microcab

The GMT Microcab was a hybrid vehicle manufactured by Greenheart Millennium Transport Ltd, London, UK. Plans for the vehicle were first drawn up in October 1996 with the idea of building a hybrid human powered/electric taxi. By September 1997 a 1/5th scale model was built, which resulted in the first full-scale vehicle in August 1999. More modifications were made to the design and a new lighter version of the Microcab appeared in April 2000. The vehicle had an E-glass, carbon-epoxy foam sandwich-moulded floor pan with GRP and ABS moulded body panels attached to it. The roof and side panels were removable to correspond to weather conditions. The body housed two passenger seats in the rear and a bicycle type seat for the driver with handlebar controls.

When not being propelled under pedal power, the vehicle was powered by a 600W Honda electric motor with a differential drive shaft. The 48V batteries in the vehicle were charged when the vehicle braked and trickle charged via a solar panel on the roof. The Microcab weighed just 125kg and was almost silent in operation. In 2007 the project appeared to end and no further reference to the vehicle appears to have been made.

Grenville

1875 — Steam Carriage

Believed to have taken 15 years to build from 1875, the Grenville Steam Carriage is possibly the oldest self-propelled passenger-carrying road vehicle that is still on the road today. Built in Glastonbury, Somerset, UK, it was initially powered by a single-cylinder engine that was then replaced by a side-valve twin-cylinder engine fitted to a rear-mounted boiler with drive going to the rear two solid wood wheels. With a top speed of around 18mph (29km/h) the Steam Carriage consumed five gallons of water and 6lb of coal per mile. It was designed by Robert Grenville, with assistance from George Jackson Churchward (who later became the Chief Mechanical Engineer of the Great Western Railway in 1902). Weighing around 4,500lb, the vehicle had space for four passengers, though it also

The Grenville Steam Carriage is possibly the oldest self-propelled passenger-carrying road vehicle that is still on the road today. John Napper

needed two people to control it: a fireman, who stood on a platform at the back of the vehicle, and a driver, who sat over the front wheel. The carriage was used in Glastonbury until 1898 when Grenville then modified it to be a stationary engine driving a cider mill. It was after Grenville died in 1936 that the carriage was then completely restored and at the time of writing is owned by Bristol City Museum.

Grey & Harper Ltd

1953 — Edith Mini-Car

In 1953 Grey & Harper Ltd of Victoria, Australia, manufactured the two-seat Edith Mini-Car. It was powered by a rear-mounted 197cc Villiers two-stroke engine that drove the single rear wheel by chain via a four-speed gearbox. With a top speed of 58mph (93km/h), the vehicle also had independent suspension on each wheel. The body was made from fibreglass and was somewhat square in shape with straight sides and a slightly sloping front. Very few vehicles were sold and so, as a result, a four-wheel version was made. In 1957 it appeared at the Melbourne Motor Show and was the cheapest car on display with a price tag of £350 plus tax and two weeks' delivery. In total, around 12 three- and four four-wheelers were made, with production ending in 1957.

Grinnall Specialist Cars

1991 — Scorpion III

Grinnall Specialist Cars of Worcestershire, UK, was already well-known for its refined conversions of vehicles; these included the Triumph TR7 and the Grinnall TR8 four-wheeler. In 1991 the company's founder, Mark Grinnall, set about creating a three-wheeler; this was introduced in 1992 as the Grinnall Scorpion III. The body of the Scorpion III was designed by Steve Harper, whilst Mark Grinnall and Neil Williams designed and developed the chassis and mechanics; these were then refined and tested in collaboration with leading engineering analysts, Mecal Engineering of Holland. The car is a two-seat sports three-wheeler and was initially powered by a range of engines from BMW motorcycles from the K100 1,000cc eight-valve engine up to the K1200 1,200cc 16-valve engine giving an average top speed of 130mph (209km/h) and a 0-60mph (0-60km/h) time of around six seconds. In 2008 the Scorpion III was offered with the BMW K40 of either 1,200cc, 170bhp or 1,300cc, 180bhp. Grinnall Specialist Cars are BMW Partners with an Original Equipment Manufacturer supply

The Grinnall Scopion III, which, as the graphics suggest, is powered by a variety of BMW engines up to 1,200cc. Grinnall Specialist Cars

status and so all BMW parts are supplied to them directly from BMW. Early 1,000cc vehicles used a five-speed gearbox whereas the 1,200cc and 1,300cc vehicles are six-speed with an electric reverse gear. The front suspension is provided by double wishbones in oval tubing with inboard concentric coil springs and dampers whilst the rear uses a standard BMW rear swinging arm suspension system with K40 models featuring a race developed 'Rising Rate' linked rear suspension. All models have disc brakes on the front and rear.

The body of the Scorpion III is made of a reinforced fibreglass construction that is mounted onto a steel tube space frame that has an epoxy powder coating and houses two orthopaedically designed seats that feature fire resistant upholstery. From 2009 the vehicles also featured a steering column that was adjustable for height and reach. The vehicles are sold either as completed vehicles or as a kit that contains all the parts required to build the machine. A four-wheel version, the Grinnall Scorpion IV, was introduced in October 2000. Grinnall also manufactures a range of motorcycle trikes including the Grinnall R3T, BMW 1150R, 1200c, 1150R and the 1200CL. At the time of writing all vehicles remain in production.

Grünhut & Co

1955 — Belcar

Manufactured in 1955 In Switzerland by Grünhut & Co under licence from the German manufacturer Egon Brütsch, the Belcar was a two-seat three-wheeler that was built in limited numbers before production stopped a year later. Powered by a 14bhp, 197cc, one-cylinder, two-stroke Fichtel & Sachs engine at the rear of the vehicle the Belcar was able to reach 53mph (85km/h).

Gurgel Motors

2003 — Gurgel TA-01

Sold by Gurgel Motors in Brazil since 2003, the Gurgel TA-01 is a commercial two-seater that is imported from China. Weighing 1,000kg and powered by a water-cooled, single-cylinder, 20bhp, 1,194cc diesel engine, the vehicle can reach speeds of 37mph (60km/h). The TA-01 has a 1,200kg loading capacity in addition to a 600kg towing capacity. The standard model features a hydraulic metal tipping platform at the rear, though other body variations can also be fitted. In addition it comes with no roof or side doors and a half-length front windscreen. With a four forward and reverse gearbox, transmission to the rear wheels is through belts. Initially the TA-01 could be only used in rural areas though, in 2006, it got approval from the DENATRAN — the National Traffic Department in Brazil — and so was then allowed to run on public roads. The Gurgel TA-01 remains in production at the time of writing.

GWK Ltd

1927 – Grice

Founded by A Grice, J T Wood and C M Kellor in 1910, GWK was based in Maidenhead, Berkshire, UK, before moving to Datchet, Berkshire, in 1912. The company manufactured both four-wheeled cars and delivery vans. However, in 1927 it stopped making four-wheelers and introduced a three-wheeler called the Grice. The two-seat vehicle was essentially a prototype with only a handful of cars being made. It was powered by an air-cooled 680cc JAP V-twin engine that drove the two rear wheels and had a sheet steel body with a hood for protection against the weather. The company closed in 1931.

Whilst a number of two-seat prototypes were built, the Grice was mainly a single-seat vehicle built from 1927. Kerry Croxton

Hawk Vehicles Inc

1982 — Trihawk

The Trihawk was originally envisaged by Lou Richards, and further design and development was accomplished by a core group including Bob McKee, David Stollery, Dick Kleber and Bill Molzon. The Trihawk was first manufactured in 1982 by Design Lab Inc at a facility in Mokena, Illinois, USA. After completing a preproduction run of 10 to 12 units, manufacturing and sales were moved to a new facility in Dana Point, California, under the new moniker of Hawk Vehicles Inc with full production beginning in 1983. The vehicle was powered by a four-cylinder, air-cooled, 1,299cc boxer engine that drove the front wheels. The engine and transmission came from the Citroën GSA. Suspension components were utilised from the Renault R5 (Le Car) whereas Honda was the choice for the dashboard instrumentation. Due to its extremely low centre of gravity and wide front track, the Trihawk was capable of attaining upwards of 1G force during skid pad testing, matching the Corvette and Countach of the day. Production ceased at the end of 1985, after the company was purchased by Harley Davidson. Between 90 and 100 units were produced.

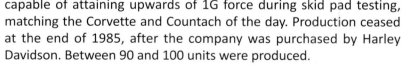

Above: *An early mechanical prototype of the Trihawk with lift up gull-wing doors and an angular metal body that would give way to a more aerodynamic fibreglass body.* Dave Stollery

Left: *With its low centre of gravity and 70% of the vehicle's total weight over the front anti-roll system, the Trihawk had superb handling abilities.* Dave Stollery

Heinkel Flugzeugwerke

1956 — 175 Type 153

The Heinkel was introduced in Germany in 1956 by Heinkel Flugzeugwerke and was designed by Prof Ernst Heinkel. Heinkel had been to the Geneva Motor Show and had seen the ISO Isetta (see page 124) on display. Being the builder of the first rocket-powered aircraft, his company was experiencing financial problems as, after World War 2, the need for aircraft dramatically declined. Heinkel was, at the time, already producing two-stroke engines for SAAB and, in 1952, also produced a scooter. Inspired by the Isetta, Heinkel then set about building his own vehicle. He believed the Isetta was too heavy a vehicle and so did not apply to ISO for a patent as his vehicle would be completely different internally though externally it would look similar. As he was building his vehicle, BMW took out the ISO patent for the Isetta and had started to manufacture it. In 1955 BMW discovered that the Heinkel looked like the former's Isetta and so a meeting was arranged for Ernst Heinkel to meet the head of BMW, Kurt Donath. During the meeting Heinkel stated that his vehicle was in no way similar to the Isetta and that it would not start full production until 1956. Grasping the sales advantage BMW started production of the Isetta one month after the meeting in April 1955.

The Heinkel was available in both a three- and four-wheel version. The three-wheel version, being a 175 Type 153, was powered by an air-cooled, one-cylinder, 174cc engine with a top speed of around 54mph (87km/h). It went into mass production as planned in 1956 and was around 100kg lighter than the Isetta. The Heinkel featured an opening front that led to a bench type seat and, unlike the Isetta, the steering column remained static when the door was opened. However, despite this, the Heinkel was said to be a lot roomier inside than the Isetta. As the vehicle had no reverse, in order to prevent drivers being trapped in vehicles when access to the front door was impeded, a fabric sunroof provided an emergency escape. The last German-built Heinkel was made in June 1958 — the year that Ernst Heinkel died — when the Irish Government started negotiations for a takeover. The bid was successful and production of the Heinkel was moved from Speyer to Dundalk in Ireland where it was built under licence by the Dundalk Engineering Co. In 1961 Trojan of Croydon, UK, took over the plant and production was switched to Croydon where it made the Heinkel under the name of Trojan (see page 258). Heinkel continued to supply engines until 1967 when it ceased production.

As the Heinkel was not equipped with a reverse gear, it was fitted with a fabric sunroof that also acted as an emergency exit. Rik Borgman

Introduced in 1932 the Hercules passenger vehicle was made for just one year from 1932 to 1933. Author's Collection

Hercules Werke AG

1932 — Coupé

Hercules Werke AG was founded in 1904 as a bicycle manufacturer in Nuremberg, Germany. The company also produced a number of commercial vehicles from 1905 until 1928 but it was not until 1932 that Hercules produced a three-wheel passenger vehicle: the Hercules Coupé. The Coupé was powered by an ILO 200cc proprietary engine at the rear, which drove a single rear wheel, whilst the body was made of steel housing two seats. Production of the vehicle ceased in 1933.

Highway Aircraft Corp

1962 — Fascination

After designing the Airomobile in 1937 (see page 16), Paul Lewis went on to form the Highway Aircraft Corporation of Colorado, USA, in 1962. The company then produced a concept vehicle called the Fascination that was a large three-wheeler capable of 130mph (209km/h). It was stated at the time that the Fascination would be powered by a new type of thermonuclear energy that operated a Nobel Plasma engine. The company stated in its literature: 'This engine is a closed two cycle reciprocating engine that has no intake, uses no air, emitting no exhaust at all. A hermetic gas chamber is created by the telescopic fitting of two cylindrical units each open at one end, fitting one over the other to permit extension end retraction on the unit under the cycling pulses of a varying gas pressure confined within the chamber.' *(Highway Aircraft Corporation promotional literature)*

The fuel was to have been self-contained within the unit, with each cylinder pre-charged; this was said to provide enough fuel for 60,000-75,000 miles (96,561-120,700km) before it needed recharging. The unit, however, never came to be and the prototype Fascination was powered with a four-cylinder Renault engine. It had a single front wheel that was driven by a propeller shaft with recirculating ball steering that meant the wheel could turn through 180°, thus allowing the vehicle to turn within its own length. It was whilst the vehicle was being demonstrated that the prop failed, bringing with it a number of lawsuits. As a result, the Fascination

Advertised as the car of tomorrow the Fascination was set to be built at a rate of 10 vehicles per eight-hour shift though only five were ever made. Alden Jewell

was redesigned and instead used a Volkswagen engine. It now had two wheels at the front that were set closely together resembling the original three-wheel layout. The last car was fitted with a V6 Chevrolet engine. The Fascination had a steel chassis with a fibreglass body that seated four adults and featured steel roll bars along with a curved shock absorbing front bumper. In total five vehicles were made, with the last one being completed in 1974; all five survive at the time of writing.

Hino

1961 — Humbee

Originally called Tokyo Gasu Denki from 1917 in Tokyo, Japan, the company went through several names before it became Hino in 1959. Hino specialised in heavy four-wheel trucks and buses; it was also contracted to manufacture the Humbee range of three-wheelers from 1961. With a single front wheel, most vehicles had a cab with two seats and an open pick-up rear end. Vehicles were made up into the 1970s.

HM Vehicles

1979 — Freeway

The first Freeway to be manufactured by HM Vehicles — HM meaning High Mileage — in Burnsville, Minnesota, USA, was in 1979 and designed by Dave Edmonson. Each car was handmade and it was guaranteed that each Freeway would achieve 100mpg (2.8-litre/100km) at 55mph (88.5km/h) on a freeway. The Freeway was also sold as an Electric vehicle that would travel 20 miles (32km) at 40mph (64km/h) though, due to the short range between charges, this version was not a great success. The petrol version was powered by a 345cc or a 453cc air-cooled, Tecumseh engine. A diesel version was also offered though no vehicles are believed to have been ordered with it. The engine was mounted at the rear of the vehicle and drove the single rear wheel by a belt drive. The chassis was a welded tubular steel frame with the body being moulded from fibreglass in to which the colour was injected. The Freeway was available in red, yellow and orange. Whilst being a single-seat car, it was stated that a passenger could 'squeeze' into the back for shorter trips. The back window of the Freeway was a hatch that opened to allow access to a storage area. HM Vehicles built approximately 700 Freeways from 1979 until 1982, but the company halted manufacture in 1983 as a result of financial problems. In the same year, D & A Vehicles of Minnesota acquired the rights to the Freeway and built a two-seat version called the Minikin (see page 72).

With each vehicle being handmade, every Freeway was guaranteed to travel 100mpg at 55mph (88.5km/h). Danny Higgins

Designed for the narrow streets of Japan, the Hino Humbee was a small commercial pick-up with a three-seat cab. John Cleve Graham

With a 320kg (700lb) payload the Hopestar was built until 1968 when the company was purchased by Suzuki.
John Cleve Graham

Hope Jidosha Co

1959 — Hopestar SM

In 1959 the Hope Jidosha Co of Tokyo, Japan, built a three-wheeler called the Hopestar SM. The vehicle was powered by a twin-piston, two-stroke, 350cc engine that provided power to the rear wheels. With a carrying capacity of 320kg (700lb) the Hopestar SM came with a number of body variations. The company also produced four-wheel trucks up until 1968 when the company was purchased by Suzuki.

Horlacher AG

1988 — GL-88 (Egg)

Specialising in the manufacture and development of products made from fibre-reinforced plastics and composite materials, Horlacher AG of Switzerland was founded in 1962 and supplied custom-made components and manufactured models, moulds and prototypes. In 1988 the company produced the Horlacher GL-88 (also called the Egg). It was designed by Max Horlacher and was built to enter Solar Races in Europe during the 1980s and early 1990s. It entered the Tour-de-Sol (world championship), the ASEM in Switzerland, the Solar Cup Denmark, the Tour de Ruhr in Germany and the Austria Solar Cup and

many more, winning all of them in its category. Fuelled by 11 Levo GT55 12V lead acid batteries that powered a Brusa AMC 200ac motor, it could reach 49mph (79km/h) and travel approximately 62 miles (100km) between charges. The GT-88 had a fibre-reinforced composite material body with the single wheel to the rear and weighed 300kg with batteries. Approximately 32 vehicles were made for private Swiss consumers and it is believed around 20 of these are being used on the roads at the time of writing. Production of the Horlacher ceased in 1990.

Howecette

1968 — Howecette

The Howecette was built by Bob Howard in 1968. It won the special of the year award at the BMF Rally in 1978. The original engine was a water-cooled, 500cc Velocette MAC engine but Howard fitted a 500cc Venom engine later. The front-end mechanics were from an early 1950s Ford Popular. The steering was such that one half turn of the steering wheel took it from lock to lock. The single-seat body had no doors or roof, and was made from aluminium. The vehicle remained a one-off.

Hudson Component Cars

1989 — Free Spirit

Initially built by Roy Webb for his own use, the first Hudson was created in 1989. The vehicle generated so much interest that, after a number of orders, Hudson Component Cars in Norwich, UK, was set up. Sold in kit form, the Free Spirit was a single-seat vehicle that used a Renault R-5 Le Car as a donor vehicle for all its mechanical parts, including the transmission, front suspension and complete steering assembly; Hudson then provided the chassis and fibreglass body parts.

1990s — Kindred Spirit

Due to the success of the Free Spirit, the chassis was lengthened by 12in (300mm) to accommodate either a second seat or storage space behind the driver's seat; the vehicle then became the Kindred Spirit. Hudson three-wheelers in the UK were powered by a number of different engines, though the choice was limited to only the 1,397cc Renault engine in the USA. In 1998 the manufacturing licence and remaining inventory were sold and, to date, no further kits have been produced. As well as three-wheelers, Hudson also developed a prototype four-wheeler called the Mystic Spirit.

Humber

1896 — Tricar

Humber was founded in 1868 by Thomas Humber as a bicycle manufacturer though, in 1896, the company started to build powered tricycles in Coventry, UK, that used a 2.5bhp single-cylinder engine. The rear end resembled a bicycle with a tubular steel frame and had a saddle for the driver along with handlebars for steering. The passenger sat in a padded chair positioned in between the front two wheels with a foot well extending forward from under the seat.

1904 — Olympia Tri-car

By 1904 the Humber Tri-car had evolved into the Humber Olympia Tri-car that had numerous improvements over its predecessor. The vehicle was now fitted with a fully enclosed 5bhp, single-cylinder, 611cc engine and creature comforts had been extended to the driver, who now also got a padded seat at the rear of the vehicle and a steering wheel. At this time the company was experimenting with four-wheel vehicles and these eventually took over from the three-wheelers in 1909.

Initially built as a one-off the Hudson Free Spirit created so much interest that it was then sold in a kit form. Robert Knight

As a follow up to the Free Spirit the Hudson Kindred Spirit was introduced; the vehicle was now lengthened and included a passenger seat behind the driver's seat. Philippe

Below: *The Humber Olympia Tri-car; this particular vehicle was built in 1904 and, following the usual configuration for its time, the driver sat on a saddle at the back.* Author's Collection

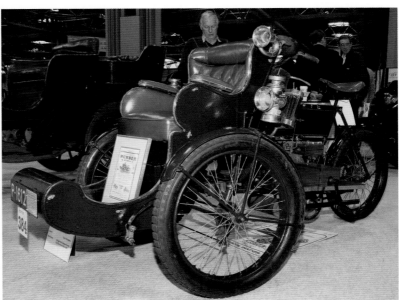

Hunslet Engine Co/ Scootacars Ltd

1958 – Scootacar

Dating back to 1854 when the Hunslet Engine Co of Leeds, UK, started making steam locomotives, the company introduced the Scootacar in 1958, using a new division of the company called Scootacars Ltd. The vehicle was created by Henry Brown, who had designed the Scootacar around the body of an occupant sitting astride the engine. The 60in (152cm) high body was made from fibreglass and attached to a steel chassis; the latter included a steel floor pan. The vehicle was advertised as having a 'Car-sized door' and so access in and out of the Scootacar involved no crouching as was needed in other three-wheelers of the period. In the original model the driver sat astride the air-cooled, 197cc, Villiers 9E engine, as on a motorcycle, with handlebars for steering. With the engine driving the single rear wheel through a four-speed gearbox, the top speed was 50mph (80km/h). Around 750 vehicles were made.

1960 – Scootacar De Luxe

The Scootacar De Luxe (or Mk 2) was introduced in 1960. It had been completely redesigned with a new body offering more car-like seating with enough room for three people. The top speed had also been increased to 55mph (88.5km/h) and around 200 vehicles were built.

Opposite top: *A 1962 advertisement for the Scootacar De-Luxe Twin that is detailed as being Longer, Lower and Lovelier and able to carry two adults and a child.* Author's Collection

Opposite bottom: *Advertised as having a 'Car sized door' with a higher that average body the Scootacar was much easier to get in and out of compared with some other three-wheelers at the time.* Oliver Hartmann

Below: *The shape of the Scootacar derived from originally being designed around a person sitting astride an engine.* Oliver Hartmann

1962 — Scootacar De Luxe Twin

Arriving in 1962, the Scootacar De Luxe Twin (or Mk 3) was powered by a larger twin-cylinder, 324cc Villiers engine that boosted the top speed up to 68mph (109km/h). Around 20 vehicles were made in this form before production ceased in 1965

Hydromobile

1942 — Hydromobile

The Hydromobile was an amphibious three-wheeler built in 1942 and manufactured in the USA. The vehicle had the ability to drive straight from land into water, whereupon the rear and front wheels would retract through a complex system of transmission channels. It was powered by a V8, 4,700cc, Ford engine that was positioned mid-section and appeared in the cabin as a large bulk between the front two seats. With its wheels retracted, the Hydromobile was capable of 28mph (24.30kt; 45km/h) in the water; alternatively, it could achieve 87mph (140km/h) on land. The body was made entirely from wood and had five seats with three being in the back. It also had a wraparound windscreen and headlights that were integrated into the body. A vehicle with the same name was also built in France in 1926 though there is no connection between the two.

Built in 1942 the Hydromobile was an amphibious vehicle powered by a 4,700cc V8 engine that is able to reach 24kt on the water. Olivier Houllier

Above: *Introduced in 2012 the Fire Aero ACX is also sold in a kit form and is powered by a 1,200cc Honda Goldwing engine.* Dave Stollery

Inset: *An advertisement for the Fire Aero that was a kit based vehicle and initially fitted with an air-cooled motorcycle engine but redesigned to use a water-cooled engine.* Dave Stollery

Industrial Design Research Co

1984 — Fire Aero

Sold in a kit form, the Fire Aero was introduced in 1984 at Laguna Beach, California, USA, by the Industrial Design Research Co. Designed by its owner Dave Stollery, two variations of the Fire Aero were available. The first type was a Fire Aero kit to be powered by air-cooled motorcycles (mostly 750cc four-cylinder Hondas). It is estimated that 53 of these kits were sold. However, due to issues with cooling, a second type of Fire Aero was then designed for water-cooled bikes (mostly the Honda Goldwing). This new version also had a larger cockpit along with a few other style changes. Approximately 50 of these kits were sold. Both types of Fire Aeros were two-seat vehicles with a fibreglass body and gull-wing doors. The vehicle used a Volkswagen Beetle torsion bar front suspension at the front whilst the back end remained the rear end of the donor motorcycle. In 1988 the company was sold and it then belonged to California Alternative Vehicles (CAV) who sold Fire Aeros complete and ready to drive away.

2012 — Fire Aero ACX

After obtaining the company back from CAV, in 2012 Dave Stollery introduced an updated version of the Fire Aero with the Fire Aero ACX that is sold in a kit form and powered by a 1,200cc Honda Goldwing engine.

IndyCycle

1999 — IndyCycle

The IndyCycle was created by Jamieson G Durette in the late 1990s. The vehicle was initially created as a prototype vehicle simply named 'Vehicle' to test a theory Durette had for a vehicle with two wheels at the front and one to the rear. Durette, who at the time was a teacher at Pittsylvania County Schools in the USA, spent several years designing the prototype and drove it around for two years before the vehicle entered its final phase shortly after Durette moved to Baltimore. The 'Vehicle' was rebuilt and modified closely to match Durette's original plan to build an IndyCycle. After many modifications the 'Vehicle' became the IndyCycle in late 1999. The body of the IndyCycle was a custom-made fibreglass upper unit that was hand-laid over a front shell made of laminated wood strips with a rear shell formed from Polyisocyanurate panels with additional aluminium side panels. The frame was a safety cage bolted to a 1987 Suzuki GSXR aluminium engine cradle at five points. Power came from the Suzuki GSXR's 750cc motorcycle engine complete with six-speed gearbox that, combined with the ultra-light body, gave the IndyCycle exceptional performance with a top speed in excess of 150mph (241km/h) and a 0-60mph (0-96km/h) time of just 4.2sec. At the time of writing, plans for the vehicle are still available.

Initially called the 'Vehicle' in the late 1990s, numerous modifications were made which resulted in the IndyCycle in 1999 that has a top speed in excess of 150mph (241km/h).
Jaimieson Durette

Invacar Ltd

1946 — Invacar (Model 12D)

The UK-based Invacar Ltd was established in 1946 by Oscar Greeves after he had built a three-wheeler for his paralysed cousin, Derry Preston-Cobb. As a result of the many casualties from World War 2, Greeves realised the need for such transport to be available. After contacting the government, the latter agreed to pay for the vehicles to be made. The model sold in great numbers and technologically was viewed as being the industry's greatest leap forward since the powered vehicles of the 1920s, with each vehicle being built to suit a specific need. The first vehicles had an open body built on to a tubular steel chassis with a single seat. They were powered by an air-cooled, 122cc, Villiers Mk 9D engine, which was followed by a 197cc Villiers Mk 6E engine from 1948. Both versions powered the right-hand side rear wheel.

1952 — Invacar (Mk 8/8A)

The Invacar Mk 8 was introduced in 1952 and, whilst using the same chassis as its predecessor, now offered full weather protection with a windscreen, fixed hood and a canvas body, which was stretched over a welded steel tubular frame that was attached to the chassis. In 1955 the Mk 8A version replaced the Mk 8; this had a larger hood and was fitted with rubber-in-torsion rear suspension. The vehicles were fitted with a 197cc Villiers Mk 8E engine that was again side-mounted, though a small number of Mk 8A models were fitted with a 242cc British Anzani engine. Production ceased in 1956.

This particular Invacar Model 12D built in 1947 is the oldest Invacar known to exist with the chassis number being No 2. Stuart Cyphus

1957 — Invacar Mk 10

The Invacar Mk 10 was introduced in 1957 as a result of the Ministry of Health standardising its requirements in the same year. These now stated that the vehicle was to be powered by an air-cooled, 197cc Villiers Mk 9E engine, have a single seat and have steel pressed wheels with the single front wheel powered. The vehicles were then leased to disabled drivers as part of their disability benefit. The Invacar Mk 10 had a pressed steel body with a 197cc Villiers Mk 9E engine, now being rear mounted and fitted with SIBA Dynastart. The Mk 10 was made until 1959.

1960 — Invacar Mk 12 (Mk 12A/12B/12C/12D/12E)

The last Invacar to be made by Invacar Ltd — as opposed to the last Invacar made — was the Invacar Mk 12 that appeared in 1960. The vehicle now had a full fibreglass body with all vehicles being finished in Peacock blue. It was powered by the 197cc Villiers Mk 9E engine with a Villiers Mk 11E engine being used in the Mk 12A model onwards from 1962. The Mk 12A also featured glass side windows. Produced until 1971, the vehicle went through numerous other changes with a Mk 12B in 1966, Mk 12C in 1967 (which incorporated hydraulic braking), Mk 12D in 1968 and finally the Mk 12E in 1969, which was fitted with parallelogram front suspension. This was replaced by the AC Model 70 (see page 10) in 1971.

As well as Invacar, other manufacturers also received a contract from the Ministry of Health to produce three-wheelers. These included Harding Ltd, Dingwall & Son, AC Cars Ltd, Barrett, Frank Tippen & Son, Thundersley and Coventry Climax. It was the Thundersley Invacar that perhaps became the most memorable of Invacars as it remained in production until the end of the final Department of Health & Social Security contact in 1977. It is estimated there were approximately 1,300 Invacars in use around the UK in 2002 but on 31 March 2003 the vehicles became illegal to drive on British roads*. Government service centres were then extremely busy crushing around 50 Invacars per month with the last vehicle being collected in October 2004. A few privately-owned examples escaped, with a few finding their way into museums. The vehicle was replaced by a government-approved four-wheeler powered by a 340cc engine.

* It is worth noting that Invacars appear to have been classed under two categories: Invalid Carriages and Tricycles. Invacars taxed as invalid carriages can no longer be used though those that were classed as tricycles are technically still legal.

Iso Autoveicoli SpA

1951 — Isocarro Titan/ Isocarro 150c

Iso Autoveicoli SpA — originally called Isothermos — was founded in Milan, Italy, by Renzo Rivolta and manufactured refrigerators and scooters before, in 1951, producing a commercial three-wheeler. The Isocarro Titan was an open motorcycle-type with a motorcycle front end and a modified rear end that had a cargo area between the rear two wheels. It was powered by a 7.5bhp engine that drove the rear wheels via a four-speed with reverse gearbox. The Isocarro 150c followed the same design, though it now featured a partial cab fitted to the front of the vehicle with open sides and a bench seat inside that would seat two adults. It was powered by a 6.5bhp, single-cylinder, two-stroke, 148.7cc engine that powered the rear wheels via a four-speed with reverse gearbox. The model was replaced by a four-wheel Isocarro in 1955.

1952 — Isetta

In 1952 Rivolta looked into the possibility of producing a small car and as a result the Isetta prototype was created, going into production in 1953. The Iso Isetta — also known as Bubblecar due to its egg shape and curved bubble like windows — was designed by Ermenegildo Preti and Pierluigi Raggi and was powered by a 9.6bhp, two-stroke, twin cylinder 236cc engine that drove the rear wheels through a four-speed with reverse gearbox. Although the prototype was a three-wheeler, it was prone to rolling over and so production vehicles were four-wheelers with the back two wheels being set 10in (25cm) apart. The Isetta had a steel chassis and a metal body that featured a single door at the front of the vehicle that hinged outwards; all vehicles also had a large roll-back canvas roof that acted as an emergency exit should the front door become obstructed and was not able to open. Inside the vehicle there was a bench seat for two adults with a large parcel shelf behind the seat. The steering wheel and dashboard were attached to the front door and would swing out of the way when the door was opened to facilitate access to the vehicle. In 1954 Rivolta was contacted by BMW asking if the German company could manufacture the Isetta under the BMW name in Germany. Although the Isetta had been well received and had a respectable top speed of 53mph (85km/h), increased competition from small four-wheelers like the Fiat 500 was starting to affect sales. As a result Rivolta sold both the design and manufacturing rights to BMW in 1955 (see page 35) with the last Iso Isetta being built in 1956.

Issi SpA

1953 — Microbo

The Instituto Scientifico Sperimentale Industriale SpA (or Issi SpA; 'Experimental Industrial Scientific Institute') of Milan, Italy, first exhibited the Issi Microbo in 1953 at the Turin Motor Show. The Microbo was a two-seater with the passenger sitting in tandem-style behind the driver. The vehicle had a tubular steel chassis with an aluminium body and a Plexiglas roof. It used a single-cylinder, two-stroke, 125cc Idroflex engine that powered the rear wheel by chain through a three-speed with reverse gearbox. With a total weight of 349.8lb (159kg), the Microbo had a top speed of 45mph (72km/h). Production models differed from the original prototype in that they had a number of modifications, including a slightly squarer body with a solid roof. The Microbo was built until 1954.

Itar

1928 — Delivery Tricycle

Itar (Itar J. Janatka & Spol) of Prague-míchov (and later Holubovsky & Spol, Prague-Radlice) in Czechoslovakia had been manufacturing motorcycles since 1921 when, in 1928, it introduced a delivery tricycle. The vehicle was powered by a 350cc, air-cooled JAP engine of the same type that was used in its motorcycles. With a single rear wheel at the back, the tricycle had a small loading area between the front two wheels that had a capacity of 100kg. A number of machines were sold both in Czechoslovakia and its neighbouring countries before the company switched back to motorcycles only in 1929.

This 1958 advertisement shows both the three-wheeled and four-wheeled Isetta with the three-wheeler having the benefit of less road tax, something that made this flavour more popular in the UK.
Author's Collection

J

J A Prestwich

2011 — Japster

Legendary for its engines, J A Prestwich (or JAP) was founded in 1895 and made thousands of engines at its works in Tottenham, UK, until 1963 when the company was closed down. Whilst the buildings and completed engines were all acquired by Norton Motorcycles, the name itself remained unclaimed until it was purchased by Alec Card, who was then able to set up as J A Prestwich Industries Ltd and develop engines using the JAP name with his sons Dave and Les. In 2011 the Card family built a brand-new air-cooled, V-twin 1,272cc JAP engine and, following collaboration between themselves and Planet Engineering Ltd (see page 192), the engines were made available for the Planet Ellipse. The Planet Ellipse was designed by Alan Pitcairn and Dave Kennell though following Pitcairn's death in 2012 the whole project was then passed over to J A Prestwich with the Ellipse renamed as the Japster. The Japster retains the original specification of the Ellipse with a tubular steel spaceframe and a fibreglass body with power, as detailed, coming from a new air-cooled, V-twin 1,272cc JAP engine that drives the single rear wheel through a Ford Mk 9 five-speed with reverse gearbox via a BMW bevel box. The Japster remains available at the time of writing.

Above: Planet's production version of the Ellipse not only features the S&S engine though also has a JAP variant made from 2011 that is powered by a brand-new 1,272cc JAP engine. Arthur Rayner

J J Calver Industrial Engineers

1991 — Skip

Based on a Mini, the Skip was designed and built in 1991 by Jeffrey Calver in Durham, UK, in 1991. Designed for trail racing, the vehicle used a Mini 1,098cc engine along with the Mini floor pan and several other Mini components. It had a metal body with fibreglass top panels that seated two people, whilst the engine at the front was left completely exposed. The Skip was built by J J Calver Industrial Engineers with three or four vehicles being completed in the early 1990s.

Designed for trail racing the Skip was based around a Mini using its engine and floor pan. Mike Bennett

The last surviving JMB Mustang known to exist, this is a 1935 model with an OHV 500cc JAP engine. Matthew & Tony Cox

J M B Motors Ltd

1933 — Gazelle

The JMB was first manufactured in Ringwood, Hampshire, UK, in 1933 by J M B Motors Ltd and was designed by G H Jones. The car got its JMB initials from the partners involved with the project, who included R W Mason and C Barrow. The standard Gazelle model was powered by a side-valve, single-cylinder, 497cc JAP engine that was mounted at the rear of the vehicle and drove the back wheel via a chain through a three-speed with reverse gearbox. This meant that the front area behind the dummy radiator grille was free for storing luggage. With a top speed of 55mph (88.5km/h) the Gazelle was able to achieve around 62-68mpg (3.8-3.4-litre/100km) though a speedometer was not fitted as standard. The engine was started by a motorcycle-like kick-starter that was mounted towards the rear at the side of the vehicle. The first production vehicles of 1933/34 had a main chassis consisting of two eight-inch deep Ash planks, to which a small tubular steel sub-frame was attached at the rear, through rubber pivots. The latter frame carried the engine, gearbox and rear wheel. The bodywork was of timber framing with plywood panels finished in two-colour fabric. The 1935 models replaced the timber chassis with tubular steel, and the body panels were changed to steel. Both variations were also equipped with a fold down hood and were able to seat two adults and, it was claimed, two children in the back though in reality this was not actually possible.

1935 — Mustang

Introduced in 1935 the sports Mustang model was a two-seater that was essentially the same specification as the 1935 Gazelle though now powered by a OHV, 497cc JAP engine. The model featured a close ratio three-speed with reverse gearbox that provided a top speed of 68-70mph (109-113km/h). The Mustang also featured a speedometer covering speeds up to 80mph, a spare wheel and various trims. JMB three-wheelers were manufactured until 1936 with four (and a half) JMB vehicles still known to survive.

Starting life as a JMB Gazelle, this particular vehicle has had a special body fitted during its lifetime. Joel Loiseau

James Cycle Co

1929 — 5cwt Handyvan

Having built bicycles and tricycles since 1897 and then motorcycles from 1902, the James Cycle Co Ltd of Greet in Birmingham, UK, launched the James Handyvan in 1929. With a 5cwt carrying capacity, the van was based around the James motorcycle using the latter's 247cc engine.

1932 — Samson Handyvan (8cwt/12cwt)

The Handyvan was continually updated and, in 1932, the James Samson Handyvan was introduced. This was fitted with a more powerful air-cooled, V-twin, 1,096cc, JAP engine with a three-speed plus reverse gearbox that drove the rear wheels through a belt drive. The Samson had a welded steel frame chassis along with steel body panels. The rear

Left: With an eight- to 12cwt loading capacity the James Samson Handyvan featured dual petrol tanks with one acting as a reserve. John Napper

Below: Aimed at factories and farm use the James Industrial truck was an open vehicle able of carrying 15cwt. Author's Collection

body gave a cargo loading area of 8cwt; this was increased with a 12cwt version in 1934. This model also had angled front end and was longer. Another feature was the dual petrol tanks with one acting as a reserve tank whilst the other was in use. The Samson Handyvan was also available as just a chassis and front assembly option, which was aimed at specialist coachbuilders. This variant included the chassis with all running gear and the scuttle around the engine.

1932 — Samson Handyvan Truck (8cwt/12cwt)

Introduced at the same time as the Samson Handyvan models and with the same specification, the Truck version also had a 8cwt (later 12cwt) carrying capacity. It had an open-pick-up back with a drop down tail gate.

1932 — Samson Handyvan 8cwt/12cwt Open-side van

The Samson Handyvan also came in an Open-side version with a choice of 8cwt or 12cwt loading capacity. The rear of the vehicle was similar to the Truck version, with a drop down tail gate, though it had a framework built above it with drop down canvas sides and roof.

1938 — 15cwt Industrial Truck

In 1938 the company introduced a 15cwt Industrial truck that was designed for heavier loads over shorter distances or more specifically as an internal transport solution for companies that relied on moving things by man power or hand trucks. The vehicle was fitted with the

same V-twin, 1,096cc engine, though the rear end used a more robust channel-section steel chassis supported by a pair of strong half-elliptic leaf springs. The body was completely open with a bare chassis, though a single-seat standard version that was termed 'simple lorry' was also available. This had a large pick-up truck type rear end with additional wooden sides that could be increased to improve the load capacity. Although the vehicle was aimed at factory and farm use, it was also legal for use on the public highway. The company ceased production of all three-wheelers in 1939.

James Robertson

1915 — Cyclecar

Detailed as a 'non-skidder' as a result of its stability on the road, the Robertson Cyclecar was manufactured by James Robertson of Cross Street, Sale in Manchester, UK. The vehicle was an exceptionally sturdy machine that used a girder-type frame with the suspension being semi-elliptic springs throughout, with two being used for the single front wheel. The body was made from pressed steel and tilted upwards to provide access to the transmission. The Cyclecar was powered by a choice of two engines: either an air-cooled, 965cc, JAP or an air-cooled, V-twin Precision. The engine provided drive by chain, through a two-speed gearbox, to the back axle. Offering 70mpg (4-litre/100km) and tyres that would last for 14,000 miles (22,531km), the Robertson cost £95 complete with lamps, horn and tool kit or, for an extra £7 10s, with a hood and windscreen. Both a passenger and commercial version were built, with the latter having a large storage box in place of passenger seats. Production of the vehicle ceased in 1916.

With initial plans to sell the JBF Boxer as a kit car, it remained a one-off that was built using numerous components from a Citroën 2CV. John Fernley

John Fernley's original sketch of the JBF Boxer showing how it was first conceived. John Fernley

Amongst the features of the James Robertson Cyclecar were tyres that would last 14,000 miles, the version shown here is the commercial model. Author's Collection

JBF Boxer

1992 — JBF Boxer

The JBF Boxer was created in 1992 by John Fernley in Manchester, UK. Fernley owned a motorcycle business at the time and, after seeing a Lomax, he wanted to make a kit car. The idea was to sell a set of plans for a plywood and aluminium body to drop onto a Citroën 2CV chassis. The car could be either three- or four-wheeled. The prototype had a rigid body made from marine ply with fibreglass seams. This was then clad in thin aluminium. Fernley wanted to use as much of the donor car as possible, including the instruments and running gear. Even the Citroën's side windows were used as a kind of Brooklands aero screen. Unfortunately the motorcycle business had to be wound up and, as a result, the car was sold to an enthusiast in Devon. At the time of writing, another JBF is on the drawing board; this will again resemble the Morgan three-wheeler but will be a two-thirds scale child's car powered by an electric bike motor.

Jitsuyo Jidosha Seizo Co

1919 — Gorham

In 1918 an American, William R Gorham, went to Japan to manufacture aircraft and engines, but the recession after World War 1 caused the venture to fail. Undeterred and as a result of his interest in vehicles, Gorham built an experimental truck in a factory at Kawasaki City in 1919. He also built a special three-wheel vehicle for his disabled plant manager, Mr Kusibiki. As a result of the three-wheeler the Jitsuyo Jidosha Seizo Co was established and, by 1920, had started to produce the Gorham three-wheeler. With handlebar controls, the Gorham was effectively a three-wheel motorcycle with a semi-enclosed cab that had seating for three people. The driver sat centrally at the front with space for two passengers at the rear. Power came from an air-cooled, two-cylinder, 8bhp engine that had chain drive to the right rear wheel giving a speed of 30mph (48km/h). This vehicle is said to be an important design historically as it influenced the fledgling Japanese car industry and many similar machines were built as commercial vehicles. By 1921 the Gorham was replaced with a four-wheel version with the engine increased to 10bhp. Production ceased in 1926.

Based on the traditional Morgan, the JZR is a kit-based vehicle powered by a variety of motorcycle engines. Steve Maguire

The Jones Tourer was a one-off vehicle that used parts from numerous vehicles including the Morris Minor, Standard Vanguard and Reliant Regal. Kerry Croxton

John Ziemba Restorations/JZR Trikes

1989 — JZR

Created in 1989, the JZR was an idea conceived by John Ziemba Restorations (JZR) in Lancashire.UK. Having an avid interest in the Morgan three-wheeler, John Ziemba created a kit form for a Morgan replica. This was initially powered by a Honda CX500 (50bhp) or CX650 (64bhp) water-cooled, V-twin engine. This became the first trike to use these engines. The JZR's chassis was made from steel square tube that was mated to the rear end of the Honda frame including the rear wheel and swinging arm. The body was made from galvanised metal sheets with a fibreglass bonnet and rear section with a 'Beetle Back' rear end that tapered off. In 1992 the JZR received a longer cockpit and a 'Barrel Back' version also became available; this allowed a spare wheel to be carried at the rear of the vehicle. A year later, in addition to the Honda CX version, a JZR that used either the air-cooled Moto-Guzzi 850cc or 1,000cc V-twin engine was introduced. This had a modified chassis to accommodate the Moto-Guzzi's rear swinging arm. At the same time JZR also manufactured a vehicle fitted with an 1,100cc Honda Pan European V4 engine; this provided 105bhp with the vehicle's wheelbase being extended by three inches to accommodate the larger engine. An option of the 1,340cc Harley Davidson Evolution engine was also introduced, which provided 65bhp. As with most kit-based vehicles, each JZR is unique to its owner's taste with many featuring either a machined alloy or walnut dashboard and leather trim. Approximately 320 JZRs were produced up until 1998 when JZR temporarily ceased production in the UK. Production started up again in 2000 with a new JZR being powered by a Triumph Daytona three-cylinder engine. Kits are still available at the time of writing.

Jones

1958 — Jones

The Jones Tourer was built between 1958 and 1960 in the UK. It was designed and built by a Mr Jones. Mounted on a tubular steel space frame chassis, the car was of fibreglass and aluminium construction. Externally the vehicle had Morris Minor front wings and grille surround, with the remainder of the body fabricated from aluminium sheet or moulded in fibreglass from a mould produced by its designer. The rear engine cover had Reliant Regal rear lights and air vents from a Standard Vanguard. The cover hinged just behind the seated area to expose the drive train. Originally the rear wheel was suspended from the tubular cross members by 12 yards of catapult elastic, but this was replaced by bungee elastic. The front suspension was taken from a Morris Minor. Internally the seats were handmade and sprung with rubber from an industrial tyre inner tube. The instruments were from various vehicles, including the Wolseley, whilst the fabric top was made by Jones' wife. The engine was a Ford Classic 1,340cc with twin SU carbs, mounted transversely, with a sprocket on the end of the gearbox to a counter shaft to get the ratios correct, with final drive by chain to the single rear wheel. It was originally intended to fit a 997cc Ford Anglia engine; however, it was not until the short motor was obtained that it was found to be 1,340cc. This gave the car performance beyond what was considered safe as it could happily cruise all day at 70mph (113km/h), but was expected to be capable of exceeding 90mph (145km/h). The car was built for performance rather than fuel economy, though it still returned approximately 40mpg (7-litre/100km) with the front-mounted petrol tank. The vehicle remains a one-off.

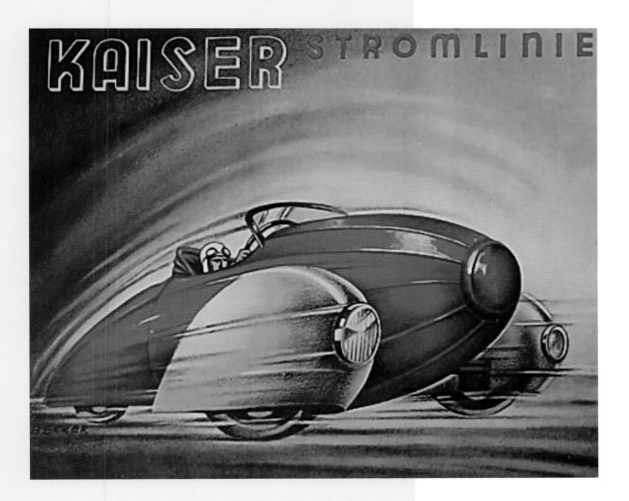

K

Period artist impressions of vehicles often have various attributes stretched as is the case for this image of the 1935 Kaiser that wasn't quite as big as the tiny driver suggest. Author's Collection

Kaiser Fahrzeugbau

1931 — Kaiser

Founded by aircraft engineer, Theodor Kaiser in Saxony-Anhalt, Germany, Kaiser Fahrzeugbau built its first three-wheel prototype in 1931. It had tandem seating and a 200cc engine that powered the rear wheel. Following a second prototype in 1932, the model went into production in 1935. Now with two seats that were side-by-side, the Kaiser was powered with a number of air-cooled, single-cylinder engines from 200-600cc supplied by NSU, DKW or Columbus. The engine was placed over, and provided power to, the single rear wheel with a maximum speed of 65-70mph (105-113km/h). The body was made from wood and artificial leather with front wheels that stuck out each side. In 1936 a new model was introduced; this had a steel body and a flattened front and was produced until 1939.

The Kapi Platillo Volante was started by a kick-starter at the back of the vehicle so it wasn't an ideal vehicle to stall in a busy street. RUMCar News

Kapi

1950 — Kapi/Platillo Volante

The Kapi was first manufactured in 1950 in Barcelona, Spain. In 1955 the vehicle was completely restyled with the introduction of a new model called Platillo Volante ('flying saucer'). Although the vehicle was made in Spain, it was powered by an English 8.5bhp Villiers motorcycle engine that enabled the Platillo Volante to do 60mph (96.5km/h) and over 100mpg (2.8-litre/100km). The vehicle was started by a kickstart pedal at the rear of the car. The body featured plastic doors and a light frame that meant it only weighed 397lb and stood 49in high. It came in various forms and was available as a roadster, combined station wagon and family car, and as a cargo model. The cargo model was able to carry around 650lb at 48mph (77km/h). Production ceased in 1958.

Karrier Motors Ltd

1929 — Colt

Initially founded as Clayton & Co (Huddersfield) Ltd in 1908, Karrier Motors Ltd of Huddersfield, Yorkshire, UK, built heavy commercial trucks. In 1929 it started to manufacture the Karrier Colt as a dustcart chassis for Huddersfield Corporation. Fitted with a 14bhp, four-cylinder engine that drove the rear wheels, which had dual-tyres for extra traction, the Colt had a payload of 2.5 tons (50cwt). It was built on a heavy steel chassis with fully enclosed two-seat passenger cab at the front and an open drop-side body at the rear.

A 1929 advertisement for the Karrier Colt that suggests it will do a full day's work carrying up to 2.5 tons on just two to three gallons of petrol. Author's Collection

A Karrier Cob owned by the City of Birmingham Gas Dept and fully loaded with coal. The sign behind the driver states the vehicle is limited to 16mph (26km/h). Colin Pickett

1930 — Cob (three-ton)/ Cob Major

Introduced in 1930, the Karrier Cob was a tractor unit (mechanical horse) developed to transport road trailers for the London, Midland & Scottish Railway. The Cob had a fully enclosed cabin with a large steering wheel connected to the single front wheel, which allowed the vehicle to turn virtually in its own length. With a payload of three tons, the vehicle had a variety of bodies from a drop-side tray body to an articulated trailer. It was powered by a flat-twin, 7bhp Jowett engine. In 1934 Karrier failed and was taken over by the Rootes Group; production ceased in Huddersfield with all work being transferred to Luton. In 1934 a new range of vehicles was introduced, which included a Cob Major that was similar to the three-ton Cob though had an increased payload of four tons. The three-ton Cob then became the Cob Junior. Production continued until the 1960s but eventually ceased as a result of increasing regulations affecting heavy-duty three-wheelers. Thereafter the company concentrated on four-wheelers with the name ultimately disappearing following the take-over of the Rootes Group by Chrysler.

Kenda Technology (International)

1993 — Trio

Kenda Technology (International) Ltd of Hong Kong was first incorporated in 1993 with an intention of selling Italian automotive technology to Far East countries and producing a high-performance three-wheel utility vehicle for transporting passengers and cargo. Whilst the vehicles were manufactured in Hong Kong, the Trio was developed by Kenda's associated company, AD Engineering, in Italy as a low cost vehicle for, but not exclusively, developing countries. As a result the Trio was able to negotiate unpaved roads and trails with heavy loads. The standard Trio was powered by a two-cylinder, four-stroke, water-cooled, 546cc engine with 25bhp, which was manufactured in China and attached to a car-type gearbox with four forward gears and reverse. The body was made from reinforced fibreglass panels that were supported by a tubular steel roll bar that complied with European regulations. The fibreglass panels could be easily removed and replaced if they should become damaged. The Trio came in three versions: the Trio Pick-up, this was an open back vehicle that had a load capacity of one ton or up to seven people; the Trio Delivery Van had an enclosed 3cu m cargo area; and, the Trio Passengers vehicle that had a passenger section that could carry up to 11 people. It is believed the company ceased making three-wheelers in 2010.

KillaJoule

2010 — KillaJoule

Designed and built in 2010 by Eva Håkansson with help from friends and family, the KillaJoule is a three-wheel electric sidecar motorcycle that, at the time of writing, is rated as the fourth fastest electric motorcycle in the world and the fastest electric sidecar motorcycle. Piloted by Håkansson herself in 2012 the vehicle was recorded at 214.050mph (344.480km/h) in the flying mile and 216.504mph (348.429km/h) in the flying kilometre at the BUB Motorcycle Speed Trials at Bonneville Salt Flats in Utah, USA. As the American Motorcycle Association require an average time from two runs, the official speed stood at 191.488mph (308.170km/h), which set a new world record for electric sidecar motorcycles. Additionally Håkansson was also handed the prestigious Female Rider award for her achievements and the Fastest Sidecar Award of the event. The KillaJoule is fitted with a 500bhp permanent magnet ac motor made by EVO Electric Ltd. This provides drive to the rear wheel and is powered by a 375V, 1,800 amp battery pack that is constructed from 1,210 cordless tool cells manufactured by A123 Systems. The battery pack was previously used in KillaJoule's 'sister' – the dragbike KillaCycle, which is the world's quickest electric motorcycle and does 0-60mph (0-96km/h) in 0.97sec.

To date the KillaJoule is rated as the fourth fastest electric motorcycle in the world and the fastest electric sidecar motorcycle. Anthony Olway/TTxGP

Knight

1895 — Trusty

Both an inventor and a pioneer, John Henry Knight of Farnham, Surrey, UK, built, amongst many other things, a four-wheel steam-powered vehicle in 1868. He then went on to build one of Britain's first petrol-driven motor vehicles in July 1895. Known as Trusty, Knight's vehicle was a two-seater with tiller steering and was controlled via several levers positioned in front of the driver. Said to be 'almost silent' when running it had two speeds: a low speed of 4mph (6km/h) and a top speed of 9mph (14km/h). It was powered by a 1,565cc Trusty engine; this was a further development of the 'Trusty' oil engine Knight had designed in 1884. In his 1902 book *Light Motor Cars and Voiturettes*, Knight details that, after fitting a vaporiser, the engine at first ran with heavy oil-lamp oil or paraffin but it was not possible to prevent the smoke and smell that the vehicle emitted. After experimenting, he then removed the vaporiser and ran the car on benzoline.

Suspension was provided by coil springs on all three wheels. Knight was prosecuted whilst driving the vehicle in his hometown on 17 October 1895 whilst accompanied by his assistant, James Pullinger. Knight and Pullinger were both fined half-a-crown (2s 6d) plus 10 shillings costs for not having a traction engine licence, for not having a man walking in front of the car with a red flag and for driving at 9mph (14km/h). (In towns the speed limit was 2mph [3km/h] and 4mph [6km/h] on country roads.) Knight was then restricted to using the vehicle on farm roads only until the Locomotive Act was replaced with the Locomotives on the Highway Act on 14 November 1896. The vehicle then went into very limited production, though manufacture of the three-wheel model soon ceased in favour of a four-wheel version. This was partly because Knight did not feel the three-wheel vehicle was safe as it had such a high centre of gravity. The original car, converted to a four-wheeler, was exhibited at the 1896 Motor Car show at Crystal Palace in London; it was the only British car there with the three other carriages being of French or German manufacture. The original vehicle still exists and is in the National Motor Museum in Beaulieu, UK.

John Henry Knight and wife aboard his 1895 three-wheeler nicknamed Trusty. *In the same year Knight was fined for speeding at 9mph (14km/h).* National Motor Museum, Beaulieu

Knox Automobile Co

1900 — Waterless Knox

Produced by the Knox Automobile Co and designed by Harry A Knox in Springfield, Massachusetts, USA, the Waterless Knox was introduced in 1900. The vehicle was called a 'Waterless' as, instead of being powered by a water-cooled engine, it used an air-cooled, 4bhp, single-cylinder, 1,500cc engine that had two-inch studs screwed into the cylinder barrel and head. This also earned it the name 'Old Porcupine' and meant that Knox was the first car manufacturer to use air-cooled engines. With drive passing through a two-speed gearbox to the rear axle by a single chain, the Knox was controlled via a tiller that steered the single front wheel. Compared with most other vehicles at the time, the Knox was an exceptionally high vehicle, which enabled its passengers to stay dry and clean when driving through mud and puddles. With over 100 vehicles built, manufacture ceased in 1903 when the company turned to making four-wheel vehicles only.

Korf Co
1974 — Duo Delta

Created by the Korf Co, the Duo Delta was designed by Walter Korff. It was available in either a kit form or as a set of plans and was first announced in California, USA, in 1974. The rear half of the vehicle used a 750cc motorcycle that was mated into a car-type front end. The owner simply removed the front fork and wheel assembly of the motorcycle and, using a Korff-patented coupler, plugged it into the car front end. The two-seat car section had standard car-like controls and consisted of a steel frame that incorporated a roll cage and a body that was made from fibreglass and had side opening doors. With a top speed of 98mph (158km/h) the Duo Delta was capable of 56mpg (5-litre/100km). Production is believed to have ceased in the early 1980s.

Krejbich
1949 — VK48

Designed by Vaclav Krejbich in Czechoslovakia during 1949, the Krejbich VK48 was an experimental three-seat vehicle. The engine, which sat at the rear of the vehicle, was an air-cooled, two-cylinder, two-stroke Jawa engine that ranged from 250-350cc. The engine provided power to the single rear wheel by chain and with a four-speed plus reverse gearbox and offered a top speed of around 50mph (80km/h). Around 72 vehicles were produced in total.

Kroboth
1954 — Allwetter Roller 200

The Kroboth Allwetter Roller 200 was designed and built in 1954 by Gustav Kroboth in Bavaria, Germany. The vehicle was a two-seater with an open body that had low cut doors and a foldaway pram-type hood. The first five prototypes were powered by a two-stroke, air-cooled, ILO 197cc engine. Production cars from September 1954 were fitted at the rear with single-cylinder, two-stroke 174cc Fichtel & Sachs engines with a three-speed with reverse gearbox that powered the single rear wheel. A few vehicles were also fitted with 191cc ILO engines in late 1955. Optional extras included an electric starter and a heater. The vehicle was not commercially successful and production ceased in 1955 with 50 vehicles having been made.

KTM
2011 — E3W

KTM are internationally known for manufacturing motorcycles. In 2011 the company announced the E3W (Electric three-wheeler). It was created by KTM along with the Austrian Institute of Technology and, at the time of writing, was a two-seat electric vehicle planned for 2013. The vehicle is primarily built of plastic and powered by a 15kW 20bhp motor and lithium-ion battery giving the vehicle a range of 62 miles (100km). The E3W also features lift-up doors that allow it to park in confined spaces. If production had gone ahead, KTM had planned to build at least 50,000 vehicles in 2013, although there has been no further news about the vehicle.

Kurier
1948 — Kurier

The Kurier was designed by Karel Strejc and built in Czechoslovakia in 1948. Powered by an air-cooled, two-stroke, 250cc Jawa engine, the Kurier had a tiny single rear back wheel that almost looked like a castor. The open body had two seats in tandem and was made from aluminium with no side doors and swooped down towards the rear of the vehicle.

The Kroboth Allwetter Roller 200 was built from 1954 to 1955 though was not a commercial success. Terry Parkin

A 1907 Lagonda Tricar in its final form before production ceased that same year in favour of a four-wheeled version. *Ken Baker*

Lagonda Engineering Co

1901 — Tricar

Named after Lagonda Creek — Lagonda being the Shawnee Indian name for what is now Buck Creek near Springfield, Ohio, USA — the Lagonda Engineering Co of Staines, Middlesex, UK, was founded in 1899 by Wilbur Gunn who had immigrated to the UK in 1890, having previously lived in the village of Lagonda. In 1901 the Lagonda Tricar was introduced; this was powered by a 5bhp engine that drove the single rear wheel. Whilst the driver sat at the back and controlled the vehicle with handlebars, the passenger sat in a padded chair positioned between the front two wheels. The vehicle went through a number of changes and, by 1905, it used a two-cylinder, air cooled 12bhp engine. It also had bucket seats for both the passenger and driver, with the handlebars now being replaced with a steering wheel. Production of the Tricar continued until 1907 with around 74 vehicles being built; Lagonda then concentrated on four-wheelers.

Larroumet & Lagarde

1904 — La Va Bon Train

Manufactured by Larroumet & Lagarde, which was founded in 1891 as a bicycle maker in Lot-et-Garonne, France, the La Va Bon Train ('goes like blazes') was introduced in 1904. It was fitted with a 6bhp, single-cylinder engine that was either the company's own design or a De-Dion engine at extra cost with the final drive being by belt or chain. With a chassis made from iron, the La Va Bon Train was a two-seater with a retractable hood and had a steering wheel. Production ceased in 1910, with fewer than 100 vehicles being built, though the vehicles remained on sale up to 1914.

Land Shark

In development — Land Shark

Although this book does not generally cover vehicles still in their development stages the Land Shark is perhaps an interesting exception. The Land Shark was a prototype designed in the UK that hoped to go into production in 2003. Based on an idea in the mid-1980s by David Baker, the vehicle was conceived as an amphibious three-wheeler that hoped to beat the world record for a vehicle of this type with estimated speeds of 200mph (321km/h) on land and 50mph (80km/h) on water. The three-seater was to have been constructed from lightweight, non-corrosive, recycled materials and to have featured a range of engines from 400cc up to 1,100cc with a semi-automatic gear change. The larger engine was capable of producing 180bhp.

On land the Land Shark was to travel as a conventional three-wheeler. When in water, the front mud guards were to have rotated under the wheels whilst the back wheel powered the vehicle through an inbuilt propulsion system acting as a turbine pump and thus propelling the vehicle forward hydroplaning on its lowered front mud guards. Both Lotus Engineering Ltd and Defence Evaluation Research Agency (DERA) were involved with the Land Shark, agreeing to handle the Research & Development stage as well as constructing the speed prototype. The Land Shark Project achieved its first two objectives by completing the basic design and being granted a full US patent; at the time of writing the project continues to seek full funding in order to continue.

Le Patron

1998 — Le Patron 3

The Le Patron 3 was created in The Netherlands in 1998 and is very similar to the Lomax in its design. The vehicle is provided in both a kit form and as a turn-key product and is built using the chassis and running gear of the Citroën 2CV. It also uses the Citroën's air-cooled 602cc or 652cc engine and four-speed with reverse gearbox. Available in both left- and right-hand drive versions, the Le Patron is a two-seater with a fibreglass body and the single wheel at the rear. The Le Patron kits are also supplied with a locally tested and officially approved rear wheel arm and, whilst most kits have been sold in The Netherlands, a few have also reached Germany, Belgium, UK, Spain and the Maldives. Kits for the Le Patron 3, along with a four-wheel version, are available at the time of writing.

L

Léon Bollée Automobiles

1895 — Voiturette

The Léon Bollée Voiturette first appeared in France in 1895. The vehicle was created by Léon Bollée, who was a son of Amédée Bollée (a pioneer of steam road vehicles in France). The Voiturette was a two-seater powered by a 3bhp air-cooled, single-cylinder, 650cc engine. It used a hot-tube ignition and three forward gears with drive going to the single rear wheel by a belt. At the time the vehicle was the fastest petrol-engined vehicle on the road with a top speed of 22mph (35km/h). It had a tubular frame with a steel foot well at the front to protect passenger's feet from puddles whilst the driver sat on a padded seat at the rear. In 1899, the vehicle was superseded by a four-wheel vehicle and, in 1901, the design rights were sold to Darracq. Even though the Léon Bollée name temporarily disappeared — although re-emerging between 1903 and 1933 — the name Voiturette (derived from the French word for automobile: *voiture*) lived on. Léon Bollée was the first person in France to create a small petrol car; he used the Voiturette to differentiate it from steam-powered vehicles. The name, however, was taken up by both the trade and the public in France to refer in general to a small light car and so it continued to be used.

Lepoix

1974 — Urbanix

Created in 1974 the Urbanix was a two-seat vehicle designed by Loius Lepoix in Germany purely as a commuter car. It was fitted with a Volkswagen 1,600cc engine and transmission. The vehicle also had interchangeable body parts so that could easily be changed into a van if required. It is not believed to have entered production.

1975 — Ding

One of the more unusual designs of three-wheeler that appeared at the 1975 Frankfurt Show was the Lepoix Ding designed by Louis Lepoix. Powered by two 1.5kW 24V electric motors that provided power to the back wheels, the vehicle had a large tubular chassis that was welded into a 'T' formation looped from the front wheel, over the seats, connecting to each rear wheel. Beneath it, the fibreglass

An 1897 Léon Bollée Voiturette that at the time was the fastest petrol-engined vehicle on the road with a top speed of 22mph (35km/h). Ron Will

Designed as a commuter car the Lepoix Urbanix had interchangeable body parts so that it could be easily converted into a van. Author's Collection

Powered by a large wooden propeller at the front of the vehicle, the Leyat Helicycle may not have been the safest machine on three-wheels. Author's Collection

body was suspended from the frame, which had two seats moulded into it. The Ding was said to have a top speed of around 16mph (26km/h). No vehicles are believed to have been sold as the vehicle never reached production although this had been planned for 1977.

Lewis

1921 — Electric Sedan

Designed as an 'invalid carriage' or a town shopper, the Lewis Electric Sedan was announced in the UK in 1921 and, as the name suggests, was powered by an electric motor. Looking almost like a telephone booth on wheels, the vehicle had no pedals at all and was operated with a single lever to control the current — and thus the speed. The lever also acted as a brake on the rear wheel. The second brake was worked by a Bowden control. Weighing 6.5cwt without passengers, the Electric Sedan had a range of 50 miles (80km) on a single charge, with the electric motor driving the single rear wheel and providing a top speed of around 10mph (16km/h). At the time, the running cost worked at one half penny per mile. The tall body of the vehicle had two doors at the front. The vehicle had exceptional all round weather protection and was manufactured until 1922.

Leyat

1914 — Hélica

The Leyat Helicycle (Hélica; 'The plane without wings') was a prototype vehicle created in Paris, France, in 1914. Designed and built by Marcel Leyat, it was powered by a large wooden propeller attached to a radial engine at the front. The body of the vehicle was made from plywood and weighed less than 550lb (250kg). Even though the vehicle could accelerate rapidly, with two wheels at the front the vehicle became very unstable and was involved in many accidents before the three-wheel version was scrapped. In 1919 Marcel founded a company, Marcel Leyat Ingénieur ECP, and production started of a four-wheel version with 30 vehicles being constructed.

Serving as both an invalid carriage or a town shopper the Lewis Electric Sedan cost just one half penny a mile to run. Author's Collection

Built in 1895 the Leyland was fitted with a steam powered lawnmower engine. Kerry Croxton

The LDV Tri-van was an open vehicle that had a 168cc engine mounted directly above the front wheel. Author's Collection

Leyland

1895 — Steam Tricar

Built by James Sumner, who had always been fascinated by steam power, the first Leyland Steam Tricar was constructed in 1895 in Leyland, Lancashire, UK, for the biscuit manufacturer Theodore Cart. The vehicle was powered by a Leyland steam lawnmower engine, which was mounted at the centre of the vehicle behind the passengers and in front of the driver. Production of the tricycle ceased in the same year. The business that Sumner created, however, was ultimately to become one of the key parts of British Leyland, following a series of mergers and take-overs that created one of the largest motor manufacturers in the world.

Light Delivery Vehicles Ltd

1949 — Tri-van

The LDV Tri-van was manufactured in Wolverhampton, UK, in 1949 by Light Delivery Vehicles Ltd. The business was a subsidiary of the Turner

Manufacturing Co and so the vehicle was equipped with a two-stroke, 168cc Turner-Tiger engine. The engine was mounted directly above, and provided power to, the single front wheel and provided a top speed of 30mph (48km/h). With a chassis made of metal channel, the vehicle had a large motorcycle-style single seat, handlebars for steering and a rear carrier that had a loading capacity of 3cwt.

1951 — Rixi

In 1951 a taxi version, called the Rixi, was announced that was intended for sale in the Far East. This had two additional seats at the rear for passengers with a windscreen behind the driver to protect the passengers. It was also fitted with a collapsible hood. The Rixi was powered by a 168cc Turner-Tiger engine mounted above the front wheel. Production of all vehicles ceased in 1952 due to very low sales.

Libelle Fahrzeugbau

1952 — Libelle

The Libelle was first manufactured in Austria in 1952 by Libelle Fahrzeugbau & Vertriebsgesellschaft. The Libelle had a rear-mounted, single-cylinder, two-stroke, 199cc Rotax engine that drove the rear wheel through a four-speed gearbox. The whole rear-end drive arrangement closely resembled that of a motorcycle. The vehicle had

With a covered motorcycle type rear end the Libelle was two-seater with a roll back fabric roof and side flaps. Author's Collection

no doors, though it did have side-flaps that were made of the same material as the rollback roof. The tubular handles at the side were raised to allow entry; they also acted as arm rests to hold you in whilst the car was moving. The interior contained an upholstered bench that accommodated two people. The Libelle was made the opposite side of Austria from the Felber, and had no connection with the Felber but, as a sheer coincidence, was painted in exactly the same shade of green as the Felber. Production ceased in 1954.

Liberty Motors

2005 — ACE Cycle Car

Manufactured by Liberty Motors in Seattle, USA, the ACE Cycle Car was conceived in 2001 and first driven in 2005. The inspiration for the model came from the Morgan Super Sport three-wheelers of the 1930s. After another year of testing and further improvements, the vehicle was ready for production. Designed by Pete Larsen, who decided to make his own vehicle after failed attempts to import a British-made Moto-Guzzi into the USA, the ACE — so called after the project name: American Cycle-car Endeavor — is built as a full turnkey vehicle. It has a TIG welded tubular steel space frame and a fibreglass body. Power comes from a 45°, V-twin Harley-Davidson, in twin-cam B-motor form, that is available either as a 75bhp, 1,450cc or a 98bhp, 1,690cc engine. Drive is sent by a shaft to the single rear wheel through a five-speed with reverse gearbox, with the 1,450cc engine providing the ACE with a top speed of 120+mph (193km/h). The ACE is available at the time of writing with each vehicle being hand-built to order,

Lion Cycle Co

1900 — Convertible Motor Cycle

Created by the company's founder, Thomas Pinnell, the Lion Convertible Motor Cycle was manufactured from 1900 by the Lion Cycle Co, 267 London Road, South Lowestoft, Suffolk, UK. One of the main features of the vehicle was that it could be transformed from a motorcycle to a three-wheeler and back again. Converting the front wheel from a single to a double required the single front wheel to be detached and then the replacement two front wheels and fore-carriage were coupled to the frame with six bolts. When these were secured and the steering connections made good, it could then be used with no further modifications. The makers gave the assurance there was no inconvenience from the siting of the 2.75bhp De Dion engine between the legs of the rear passenger. The transmission was provided by a belt drive to the rear wheel via an intermediate countershaft to provide a reduction ratio.

The Lion Convertible also featured a seat in front for a young child complete with a dummy steering wheel to keep the infant amused. The vehicle included a spare accumulator that was said to provide enough electricity for 700 miles (1,126km) whilst the petrol tank had a capacity of 100 miles (161km). The speed was described as 'marvellous' with a cautionary note detailing that, after descending a steep hill with two riders, the power should be reduced or else the speed would increase to 30mph (48km/h). Another of the vehicles attributes was that it could be stored in a very small space and fitted through a doorway less than three feet wide. The Lion Convertible model cost £85 whilst a non-convertible tandem tricycle was also available at £75. In 1904 Thomas Pinnell moved to Canada and, it is believed, that production of the Lion tricycle ceased shortly after. It did, however, reappear on 10 February 1933 when an advertisement in the *Radio Times* showed Thomas Pinnell, Anne Maria Pinnell and Cyril Harvey Pinnell in a Lion Convertible. Advertising Mullard valve radios, the photograph has been altered to give Thomas a moustache and glasses. Anne Maria complained to the magazine and the advert was withdrawn.

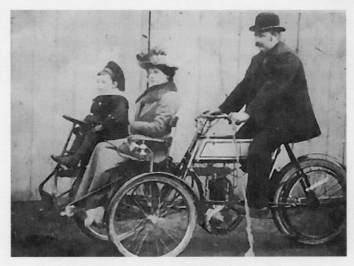

Whilst following the standard layout of most vehicles of its time, the Lion convertible motor cycle could not only be converted back to a motorcycle but also had a child seat up front with a dummy steering wheel. Alan Pinnell

four-wheel vehicle in 1983; this was called the Lomax 224 (224 signifying two cylinders, two seats and four wheels). The 224 was based on a Citroën Ami engine and floor pan though, when given the opportunity to exhibit vehicles at the Lincoln kit car show, Whall only had the one car and as a result built a Lomax that had two real wheels close together with a six-inch gap between them. Believing that this would be classed as a three-wheeler, Whall, however, discovered that it was still classed as a four-wheeler and so set about creating a true three-wheeler — the Lomax 223 — to take advantage of the three-wheel licensing and tax laws in the UK. Lomax was initially based in Lincolnshire; in 1984 it moved to Snow Hill in Birmingham. From 1986 it traded in Worcestershire, followed by Halesowen from 1992. In 1994 Nigel Whall passed over full control of the company to David Low. The company continued to grow and the vehicles continued to be improved upon, with around 180-200 vehicles being made annually. 2003 saw the company being briefly passed to Bob Turnock at RS Jigtec; this company, however, ceased trading in spring 2005. The Lomax was then acquired by Bob Bousell of Cradley Motor Works in East Sussex; at the time of writing kits are available for both the 223 and the 224.

Lomax Motor Co

Next to the products of the Reliant Motor Co, the Lomax three-wheeler at its peak was one of the most popular three-wheelers in the UK. The Lomax Motor Co was founded by Nigel Whall. He initially created a

1986 — 223

The Lomax 223 — 223 signifying two cylinders, two seats and three wheels — was first created in 1986 and, whilst being designed by Whall, was also improved upon by Peter Bird of Falcon Automotive

One of the most popular kit based vehicles is the Lomax 223 that uses a Citroën 2CV engine and floor pan. John Robson

and Brian Mumford, the creator of the Mumford Musketeer (see page 173). The first Lomax 223s were powered by a Citroën 2CV air-cooled, 602cc engine, which was bolted directly to a Citroën floor pan. The vehicle was fitted with a body made of fibreglass and a bonded in wooden floor. The Lomax was sold in kit form and as a result many variations of the vehicle appeared, including the option of using the Citroën Ami Super chassis with a 1,015cc engine. One of the biggest changes to the Lomax was the introduction of a 'ladder frame chassis', provided by Lomax, and a new front anti-roll bar. By 1993 the vehicle was using a lightweight round tube space frame chassis and improved

suspension whilst keeping a fibreglass body. Between 1983 and the time of writing around 3,500 Lomax 223 vehicles have been built.

1992 — Supa V

The Lomax Super V was announced in 1992; this was fitted with an air-cooled, V-twin, 100bhp, 1,543cc engine that was developed from a Chevrolet V8 and had been purchased from the USA. Fitted with a Citroën GS gearbox, the vehicle was built around a lightweight space frame chassis and used aluminium and fibreglass body panels. It also

The Lomax 223 uses the shape of the Citroën engine to its advantage with the cooling fins protruding out from each side of the body. Harry Kraemer

Despite quite a large rear end the Lomax 223 had no opening boot and the storage area contained within was accessed from behind the seat. Harry Kraemer

featured a unique double wishbone system with horizontal coil spring damper units. Despite the sporty performance and the handling abilities of the Supa V, the engine was found to be completely unreliable and so the project was shelved with the vehicle remaining a one-off and being used as a publicity vehicle.

1993 — Lambda 3

The Lambda 3 was launched at the 1993 London Motor Show and, whilst it could be built using the floor pan from a Citroën 2CV, a custom-made ladder frame chassis was also available. The body on the Lambda was completely restyled compared with that on the 223 and hosted a number of new features, including new suspension, new bonnet and front wings as well as a new interior. Carbon fibre was also used to strengthen the body. Whilst still using the Citroën 2CV engine, the Lambda cost significantly more than the 223, with the standard kit with body panels costing £898 plus tax compared with a similar kit for the 223 costing £698. Around 80 vehicles were built before the kit ceased to be manufactured in 2003.

Lovson Auto Division

2005 — CL1-RE175/CL2-RE175/CT2-RE175

The Lovson Auto Division is part of the Lovson Group based in Maharashtra, India, and manufactures a wide range of engineering products. Founded in 1968 by Shri Bharatlal G Shah, Lovson started out as a trading firm and began the manufacture of petrol and diesel engines in the 1980s. In 2005 the Lovson Auto Division was set up to manufacture a wide range of three-wheelers; these are currently being exported to more than 16 countries.

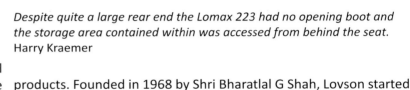

Fitted with a 173.5cc engine the Lovson CL-RE175 is a three- or four-seat passenger vehicle. Lovson Auto Division

The CL1, CL2 and CT2 are passenger vehicles that feature a tubular steel chassis and have an open body with a fabric roof. All are three- or four-seaters and, whilst the CL1 has a single front headlamp, the CL2 and CT2 have twin headlamps. All vehicles are powered by a 7.6bhp, air-cooled, four-stroke, single-cylinder, 173.5cc petrol engine that drives the rear wheels via a four-speed with reverse gearbox.

2005 — Auto Rickshaw Five-Seater/Six-Seater/Eight-Seater

The Auto Rickshaw range uses a tubular steel ladder chassis with helical coil spring and hydraulic double acting shock absorbers both front and back. It also has an extended wheelbase that offers five-, six- or eight-seat variants. All models are fitted with either a 7.6bhp, air-cooled, four-stroke 395cc, diesel engine or a 436cc version, which drive the rear wheels via a four-speed with reverse gearbox.

2005 — Utility Vehicles

The Lovson utility vehicles come in a number of guises that all use either a 7.6bhp, air-cooled, four-stroke, 395cc diesel engine or a 436cc version, which drive the rear wheels via a four-speed with reverse gearbox. The range includes a pick-up with low sides or a high cage, an enclosed delivery van with double doors at the back, a soft drink carrier that has an open van body full of pigeon holes for crates, a tipper truck with a hydraulic rear tipping body, and a water tank that contains a large tank for liquids attached to the rear. All vehicles have a maximum payload of 500kg and at the time of writing all Lovson three-wheelers remain available.

Lurquin-Coudert

1907 — Forecar

The Lurquin-Coudert was manufactured in Paris, France, from 1907. It had a unique feature compared with many other forecars of the same era in that the front seat tilted forward to create space for a 3cwt luggage area. It was powered by a 4.5bhp engine with chain drive to the single rear wheel.

1907 — Sociable

The company also built a Sociable three-wheeler; this was powered by a 9bhp, water-cooled, twin-cylinder engine. Production of the three-wheelers ceased in 1907 though the company continued to make motorcycles until 1914.

Built with numerous body types, the Lovson takes on many forms; this particular example shows a customised kiosk body. Lovson Auto Division

The Mahindra Champion was available both as a four- or five-seat passenger version and, as shown here, a commercial version.
RUMCar News

Mahindra Rise

1947 — Champion Cargo/ Passenger

Founded in 1945 by brothers J C and K C Mahindra, Mahindra Rise of Mumbai, India has been producing numerous vehicles including commercial three-wheelers since 1947. Whilst the three-wheelers have been modified numerous times, each incorporating the latest technology, each series consisted of two staple variants: a Passenger version, with four or five seats, and a Cargo version. The latter was a commercial vehicle — often called Champion — fitted with a variety of bodies from a flatbed pick-up to a van. The Mahindra Champion series was powered by a number of engines, both petrol and diesel, and had a steel chassis with a metal body that had no doors.

2008 — Alfa (Champion/Plus)

The Alfa series was introduced in 2008. The Alfa Champion is fitted with an air-cooled, four-stroke, 10bhp, 395cc diesel engine driving the rear wheels through a four-speed gearbox. The vehicle has a steel chassis and an aluminium body with a two-seat cab that has doors and a 24.5cu ft cargo box. An Alfa Plus model is also available; this has a longer wheel base with a tubular ladder type steel chassis and a cargo area that offers 20% more space with thicker metal panels. A Champion model is also available that runs on compressed natural gas (CNG).

2008 — Alfa Passenger

With the same standard specification as the commercial variants, the Alfa Passenger model has an open back with a canvas top that offers additional padded passenger seats and increased headroom. The Alfa series of vehicles remain available at the time of writing.

Malone Car Co

1992 — Skunk Mk 1

The Malone Car Co is a small family business that was started in 1992 in Devon, UK, by Jon Malone. The Skunk 1 was the first road legal prototype from Malone. With power coming from either a Yamaha XJ 650 or 900 engine that provided drive to the single rear wheel, the vehicle had a steel space frame with an aluminium body.

1998 — Skunk Sports Special

In 1998 the company launched the Skunk Sports Special at the Stoneleigh Kit Car show. The vehicle was powered from a range of motorbike engines from 650 to 1,300cc, including the Suzuki GSX 1100G, the Yamaha 1200V-Max and the Yamaha XJ 900F. The last-named, when combined with the vehicle's average weight of 290kg, gave the Skunk Sports Special a power-to-weight ratio of around 385bhp/ton, leading to a top speed of 132mph (212km/h) and a 0-60mph (0-96km/h) time

Fitted with a Suzuki GSX 1,100cc engine the Malone Skunk Sports had a top speed of 132mph (212km/h). Brian Snelson

of approx 4.9sec. The body consisted of a fully triangulated space-frame chassis that had an aluminium floor pan and was covered with a GRP body shell. The cavities between the chassis and body were injected with rigid closed-cell polyurethane foam that strengthened the whole body and enhanced side impact protection.

1999 — Skunk Sports GSX1100

With similar mechanics to the Sports Special, the GSX1100 was introduced in 1999 and, as the name suggests, was powered by a Suzuki GSX 1100 engine. This gave it a top speed of 138mph (221km/h) and a 0-60mph (0-96km/h) time of 4.3sec.

2002 — Skunk MAX

Arriving in 2002 the Skunk Max was a prototype developed for the American market. It was powered by a V4 Yamaha V-Max 1,200cc engine.

2006 — ST F1000

Powered by a Yamaha R1/Frazer 1,000cc engine that drove the single rear wheel via a six-speed gearbox, the 'Super Trike' ST F1000 was announced in 2006. Featuring a chassis built from round and square steel tubing and then covered in aluminium or dural

sheeting, the vehicle also has a GRP/Kevlar reinforced body shell that is riveted and bonded to the chassis.

2010 — TAZR

Arriving in 2010, the TAZR is an electric sports trike that has a similar construction to other Malone three-wheelers though is fitted with a lightweight, high-power, liquid-cooled, three-phase electric motor. Two variants of the engine are available: a 36bhp/27.5kW engine in the TAZR E, offering 70+mph (113km/h); and, a 72bhp/55kW with a top speed of 110mph (177km/h). The engine is mounted just in front of the rear wheels and provides drive to them using a toothed belt. Fuelled by high capacity Lithium batteries the vehicle is able to cruise for around 100+ miles (160km+).

At the time of writing the ST F1000 and TAZR — plus variants — are available as either complete vehicles built by the company or partially constructed up to a certain point so that the purchaser can compete the build customising it as they wish.

Malvern Autocraft

1992 — Triad Sport/ Triad Warrior

Based on the Mosquito (see page 169), the Triad was first manufactured in 1992 by Malvern Autocraft, UK. It was a three-wheel kit car based around the front end of an Austin Mini. The Triad featured the front sub frame of a Mini and was powered by a Mini engine. The body was made from fibreglass and, unlike the Mosquito, was now made in one piece rather than several parts. Two versions of the Triad were available: the Triad Sport, which was a modified version of the Mosquito, and the Triad Warrior, which was built for hill climbing events and so its weight was reduced to 375kg. Production ceased in 1993 with around 13 vehicles built.

Marotti Automotive

2009 — Marotti

With an initial concept that was designed in 2008, the first Marotti prototype was built in 2009 by Marotti Automotive in Poland. The single-seat vehicle has a unique body design that features twin stabilisers rising from the body at the rear of the vehicle combined with a low spoiler at the front. The fibreglass body has a steel, high resistant frame and is fitted with a 100bhp, V4, 750cc Honda engine and six-speed sequential gearbox with electronic reverse. Power is provided to the single rear wheel by a chain whilst the suspension consists of a double rocker arm at the front and a roller rocker and shock absorption system at the rear. Disc brakes are fitted to all three wheels.

Marotti announced in 2012 that the vehicle would be going into production, though the production version would be fitted with either a 1,300cc or 1,400cc engine providing 160-190bhp. At the time of writing no production details have been released.

The Marotti has distinctive styling with its twin stabilisers at the rear and low front spoiler. Marotti Automotive

Powered by a 750cc Honda engine the Marotti has disc brakes all around and an electronic reverse. Marotti Automotive

Martin Development Laboratories/Martin Stationette Associates

1932 — Martin Martinette

Capt James Vernon Martin was a pioneer aviator, engineer, and inventor who built numerous three- and four-wheel concept and prototype vehicles in the USA, hoping he would find someone willing to produce them. In 1932 Martin Development Laboratories of Rochelle Park, New Jersey, USA, created a prototype called the Martin Martinette, Initially known as the Martin Aerodynamic Autoette, this was a two-seat vehicle that had rubber suspension. It was fitted with a 7bhp, water-cooled, four-cylinder, 750cc American Austin engine that was mounted at the back of the vehicle and drove the single rear wheel through a three-speed with reverse gearbox. The top speed was claimed as 70mph (113km/h) whilst fuel consumption was around 45mpg (6.3-litre/100km). With a body made from aluminium and attached to a wooden frame, access to the Martinette was gained by a door at the front of the body, a design usually associated with bubblecars of the 1950s.

The location of the Martinette was unknown until 4 October 1987 when it appeared for sale in the *Newsday* classified adverts for $2,500. The vehicle was then rescued from a chicken coop in the Hamptons, Long Island, New York, and donated to the Cradle of Aviation Museum in Garden City, New York, USA, which subsequently restored it. It is now owned by the Lane Motor Museum in Nashville, Tennessee, USA, where it is on display.

1950 — Martin Stationette

Designed by James V Martin, the Martin Stationette was built by Martin Stationette Associates of New York, USA, in 1950 and 'engineered for production' by the Commonwealth Research Corporation of New York. In 1954 it appeared at the World Motor Sports Show in Madison Square Garden where it was awarded the Grand Prix award. The Stationette was a two-seater that featured a tear-drop shaped wooden body built by George W Biehl Auto Body of Reading, Pennsylvania, with side doors that were typical of the wooden-bodied station wagons of the era. It

Initially called the Martin Aerodynamic Autoette, the Martin Martinette remained a one-off prototype. Lane Motor Museum

Almost 25 years before the Isetta bubblecar the Martin Martinette featured a front opening door that invited its occupants to a bench like seat. Lane Motor Museum

was fitted with a four-cylinder, water cooled, 20bhp Hercules engine that was rear-mounted and powered the single back wheel. With a top speed of 60mph (96km/h) fuel consumption was around 60mpg (4.7-litre/100km).

The vehicle also used a number of parts from Harley Davidson motorcycles as well as from Studebaker and Chevrolet cars, and had a suspension that involved the entire vehicle being suspended on rubber cords. The Stationette was said to have had a Martin Magnetic fluid transmission, though there is no evidence to suggest that this was ever made. Despite much interest and a proposed price tag of $995, the vehicle remained a one-off prototype and its location was unknown until it appeared for auction on eBay in July 2005. The vehicle was purchased and then fully restored in 2008. It was found to use a Harley Davidson three-speed with reverse gearbox with no apparent modifications suggesting that the Martin Magnetic fluid transmission was never used. The Martin Stationette is now on display in the Lane Motor Museum in Nashville, Tennessee, USA. (See Tri Car Corporation of America on page 250 for information on the TRI-CAR that is also associated with Martin.)

Fitted with large wheels and steel chassis the body of the Scootmobile almost looks as though it was added as an afterthought and not actually quite following the contours of the chassis. Author's Collection

Martin Motor Co

1921 — Scootmobile

The Martin Scootmobile was introduced in 1921. It was made by the Martin Motor Co, Springfield, USA, and priced at $250. Designed by Charles Martin, it was powered by an air-cooled, V-twin, 616cc engine. The body was made from pressed steel fixed to a steel frame. Weighing 150lb, the vehicle had, the manufacturers claimed, a top speed of 40mph (64km/h) and a fuel consumption of 75mpg (3.7-litre/100km). Production ceased in 1922.

The Mathis 333 was so called as it had three wheels, three seats and a 3-litre/100km engine. Author's Collection

Despite being made from aluminium, the Mathis 333 had a surprisingly futuristic body with vehicles of similar designs appearing over 60 years later. Author's Collection

Matchless

1904 — Forecar

Well known for its bicycles and motorcycles, Matchless was founded in 1878 in Plumstead, Kent, UK, by Harry and Charlie Collier. It initially started by building bicycles before moving on to motorcycles before manufacturing a three-wheeler in 1904. The 1904 Matchless Forecar was fitted with either a De Dion or MMC engine. It was on display at the Stanley Cycle Show in 1906; however, despite interest, very few orders were taken and so no further Forecars were produced.

1913 — Cyclecar

In 1913 the Matchless Cyclecar was introduced; this was powered by a 9bhp, two-cylinder, 90° JAP engine that provided drive to the single rear wheel by cardan shaft through a two-speed gearbox. The vehicle was a two-seater with a pressed channel steel chassis and frame with a steel body and pram-type hood. The vehicles were built until 1929, alongside a four-wheel version that was introduced in 1923.

Mathis

1946 — Mathis 333

The designs for the Mathis 333 started in 1940 in the factory of Ste Mathis, Gennevilliers, France, in total secrecy during the period Paris was under German occupation. The vehicle was codenamed VEL 333, which meant Light Economical Car with three wheels, three seats

and three litres to 100km. Under the guidance of Emile Mathis, the Mathis 333 was designed by Jean Andreau. It was powered by a 707cc, flat-twin, water-cooled engine that featured separate radiators for each cylinder. Externally, the vehicle was very futuristic in appearance. With its aluminium body, the car weighed 840lb (381kg). It was presented at the 1946 Paris Motor Show but never went into production as, it is believed, the French Government would not authorise production of the vehicle. As a result only 10 vehicles were made. In 1948 a new design was drawn up for a vehicle that was powered by a front-wheel drive 80bhp, 2,800cc engine. This was again a futuristic saloon that featured a panoramic windscreen but once more the vehicle never went into production. Mathis closed as a company in 1950.

Using a pressed channel steel chassis, the Matchless Cyclecar was built both as a three- and four-wheel version. Author's Collection

Above: *Even Maserati is no stranger when it comes to three-wheelers as this Maserati Elettrocarro EC10 van manufactured from 1942 demonstrates.* Author's Collection

Right: *With a payload of 500kg the Mazda T600 was built from 1959 to 1971 and received numerous changes throughout its life span.* Don Dennes

Maserati

1942 — Elettrocarro EC10

Widely known for its exotic sports cars, Maserati is amongst a number of car makers that are no strangers to three-wheelers. In 1941, during World War 2 Maserati started to manufacture milling machines and electric grinders under the Maserati name. As fuel was restricted at that time, Maserati also started to build electric trucks and, in 1942, introduced the Elettrocarro EC10 van. Powered by a 4bhp electric motor that drove the rear wheels, the EC10 had a maximum speed of 16mph (25km/h). With a payload of 1,000kg, the vehicle was built upon a steel chassis, which had a metal two-seat cab fitted. This had a rear section that could be built either as an open or enclosed truck, the latter having an additional metal frame covered in canvas. Around 321 vehicles were manufactured before production of the EC10 stopped in 1950. Alongside the EC10 Maserati also created four-wheel versions, with the EC15, EC20 and EC35, each having an improved payload of 1,500kg, 2,000kg and 3,500kg respectively.

Mazda Motor Corp

1931 — Mazda-Go Type DA/ Type KC/Type-CA/Type CT01/ Type GL

Well known for their four-wheelers, Mazda has also manufactured thousands of three-wheelers for the Japanese market. Originally founded in 1921 as Toyo Cork Kogyo Co Ltd. in Hiroshima, Japan, the company initially manufactured machines. The name Mazda came from the name of its first three-wheel vehicle that it was associated with — the Ahura Mazda (God of Light) — and was used to help brighten the image of the vehicles. It was not until 1984 that the company formally adopted the Mazda name although every automobile sold from 1936 bore that name. In 1923 the company started to build motorcycles and, in 1931, produced its first vehicle in the form of a three-wheel truck; this was known as the Mazda-Go Type DA. Fitted with an engine that was built in-house, drive was sent to the rear wheels. The Type DA was an open vehicle with a motorcycle front end and a modified rear end that had a storage box positioned between the rear wheels. This was closely followed by the Mazda-Go Type KC and then, in 1950, the

1959 — K360

The Mazda K360 was built from 1959 to 1971. It was visually almost identical to the T600, though it was fitted with a smaller 11bhp, 356cc engine and a shorter cargo bed that provided a loading capacity of 300kg. In Japan the K360 qualified as a 'Kei car', meaning that it complied with Japanese government tax and insurance regulations so, in most rural areas, it was exempt from the need to certify that there was adequate parking available for it.

1959 — T1100/ T1500/T2000

Introduced in 1959, the Mazda T1100 and T1500 were large commercial vehicles with a steel chassis and a two-seat steel cab. As

Type CA that was a one-ton truck powered by an 1,157cc engine. In 1950 the Type CT01 appeared, which, whilst following the same structure, now included a partial single-seat cabin that consisted of a fairing around the engine, a windscreen and a fabric roof that pulled over the driver's seat on to a frame and then also formed a cabin back behind the driver. This was replaced in 1954 by the Type GL, which now featured a larger semi-enclosed cab that had two headlights at the front. The Type GL was built until 1959, when it was replaced with the T series of three-wheelers.

1959 — T600

The Mazda T600 was a small pick-up truck with a payload of 500kg that was introduced in 1959. The first models had a steel chassis and a two-seat steel cabin that had a canvas roof. They were fitted with a 20bhp air-cooled, V-twin, 566cc engine, which was positioned directly behind the cabin and which provided drive to the rear wheels through a three-speed gearbox. In 1962 a number of changes were made to the vehicle; these included fully opening windows on the doors. The model was amended again in 1964 and now featured a steel roof. The T600 was manufactured until 1971.

their names suggest, each was fitted with a different engine with a 46bhp, 1,139cc engine in the T1100, which came in two versions providing a payload of 1,000kg and 1,500kg, whilst a 60bhp, 1,484cc engine was used in the T1500; this had a payload of 2,000kg. All versions had a variety of cargo beds, from a low-level flatbed to a high deck bed with folding sides. The T1100 and T1500 were also the first Mazda three-wheelers to have brakes on the front wheel as well, with all three wheels now having brakes. In 1962 the models were uprated and the T1100 was replaced by a new T1500 to cater for payloads of 1,000-1,500kg and the old T1500 model was replaced with a new T2000 model, which was powered by an 81bhp, four-cylinder, water cooled, 1,985cc engine that provided a payload of 2,000kg. Whilst the 1500 received minor changes to update it, the T2000 had a new chassis, new brakes and a fully floating rear axle. The T2000 was upgraded further in 1965 with power brakes and both versions became available with a longer flat bed at the rear. Whilst full-scale production ceased in 1970, vehicles were still being built to order until 1974.

Fitted with Active Tilt Control the Mercedes F300 Life Jet was a tilting three-wheeler that cornered like a motorcycle. Andreas Kukuljan

Mercedes Benz

1997 — F300 Life Jet

The Mercedes F300 Life Jet was first unveiled at the 1997 Frankfurt Motor Show in Germany. It was a two-seat 'tilting' three-wheeler that used 'Active Tilt Control' (ATC). The technology assessed the driving situation and a computer then used a hydraulic system to control the F300's cornering angles. At a greater speed the angle would be far less than moderate speeds in which the vehicle could tilt at an angle of up to 30°. It was powered by the same 1,600cc petrol engine that was used in the Mercedes A160 series, giving the vehicle a top speed of around 130mph (209km/h) with a 0-60mph (0-96km/h) time of 7.7sec. The vehicle had an alloy space frame with aluminium panels attached to it. The panels were double-skinned and filled with aluminium foam that increased body strength and provided added sound insulation. Inside the vehicle, the interior had been designed like a jet aircraft with a central cockpit-style dashboard. The passenger sat behind the driver as this helped balance the weight when only one person was in the car. The vehicle never reached production though, if it had, according to the 2000 *Guinness Book of Records*, it would have been the most expensive three-wheeler in production. The total weight of the F300 was 800kg though, if it had reached production, there were plans to reduce that to just 600kg.

Messerschmitt

1953 — FK150

Messerschmitt AG was established in 1938 from an earlier aircraft manufacturer by Wilhelm Emil 'Willy' Messerschmitt, who was both the chairman and managing director. The company built numerous types of aircraft up to and during World War 2 though, after the war, it was no longer permitted to build aircraft and so looked into an alternative. In 1952 Willy Messerschmitt approached Fritz Fend (see page 95) who had created a three-wheel invalid carriage called the Fend Flitzer. Messerschmitt proposed the idea to turn Fend's vehicle into a two-seat version. Messerschmitt offered the facilities of his factory in Regensburg, Germany, and it was there that the first Kabinenrollers ('scooter with cabin') were made in 1953. The initial vehicles kept Fend's name and were sold as the Fend Kabinenroller; also known as the FK150, it used a 148cc Fichtel & Sachs engine.

1953 — KR175

By March 1953, Messerschmitt decided to market the vehicle under its own name and it was renamed the Messerschmitt KR175. It was now fitted with a more powerful 174cc Fichtel & Sachs engine. The Messerschmitt was just over four feet tall and had a monocoque construction that incorporated two seats with the passenger sitting behind the driver. The top of the vehicle had a large Plexiglas canopy

that was hinged to allow access. It was claimed that the narrow body of the KR175 was to improve the aerodynamics of the car rather than having the wider twin seats at the front combination. The two front wheels were controlled by handlebars; these had a twist grip throttle with power going to the single rear wheel. When Messerschmitt was asked to summarise his design in one word he replied 'weglassen' ('leave off'), denoting that only the essential parts were used leaving off everything that was not required. There is a legend that Messerschmitt Kabinenrollers were built from modified surplus cockpits for Messerschmitt Me109 fighter aircraft, but this is false. Weighing 460lb, the KR175 had a top speed of 50mph (80km/h) and was manufactured until 1955 when it was superseded by the KR200. The KR175 was also made under licence in Italy as the Mivalino during the same period (see page 158).

1955 — KR200

Whilst the Messerschmitt KR200, introduced in 1955, in principle looked the same as the KR175, there were a number of improvements. These included better suspension and a slightly different body as the front wings had cut outs in them so that the wheels could steer better. This in turn also gave the KR200 a better turning circle. As the name suggests it was now powered by a larger 191cc Fichtel & Sachs engine that gave the car a top speed of 56mph (90km/h) and a fuel consumption of 87mpg (3.2-litre/100km). In 1955, Messerschmitt prepared a KR200 to break the 24-hour speed record for three-wheel vehicles under 250cc. The vehicle had a single seat, highly modified

Recognised by its covered front wheels, this particular photo of a Messerschmitt KR175 was taken in Paris in 1955. Allan Hailstone

Advertisers were forever encouraging people to buy their vehicles though claims such as this stating 'Limousine comfort' for the Messerschmitt KR200 meant that some claims were harder to swallow than others. Dave Starr

engine and a low drag body with everything else being standard. The vehicle was run at the Hockenheimring for 24 hours during which it broke 22 international speed records in its class, including the 24-hour speed record, which it set at 64mph (102km/h). Around 40,000 KR200s were built and sold worldwide until production stopped in 1964. It is estimated that about 6,800 were imported into the UK of which about 1,000 remain. In 1956 Messerschmitt sold the factory to Fend, who incorporated Fahrzeug & Maschinenbau GmbH, Regensburg, to continue production of the KR200 although the cars retained the Messerschmitt brand until the end of the production run in the 1964.

1957 — KR201 Sports Roadster

Although the KR201 Sports Roadster had the same specifications as the KR200, this was a Cabriolet version with no canopy and was fitted with a small windscreen attached to the body. In 1958 a four-wheel version was also introduced; this was the FMR Tg500 (nicknamed 'The Tiger') with a 500cc engine and a top speed of 89mph (143km/h). Production of the KR201 ceased at the same time as the KR200 in 1964.

Meyra

1936 — Invalid Carriage (Model 55/various models)

Meyra manufactured motorised wheelchairs for the handicapped from 1936 in Germany. The Meyra Model 55 version was the first car-like version and had the single wheel at the front. It was an open single-seater with a windscreen and side doors. It was powered

With a slightly different body the Messerschmitt KR200 now had cut outs in the front wings to allow the wheels to turn better. Chris Van Rooy

Fitted with a modified engine and sleek body the Super Messerschmitt 200 (of which this is a replica pictured) broke 22 international speed records in its class. Wilfried Dibbets

by a 150cc Fichtel & Sachs engine that drove the rear wheels via a three-speed gearbox, which had very low gears. The gearing enabled the vehicle to climb the steepest of hills with heavier passengers. After World War 2 various versions of the vehicles became very popular and were manufactured until the early 1970s.

Designed as an Invalid Carriage, the Meyra Model 55 was produced in various versions with its popularity increasing after World War 2. Wikipedia — Buch-t

With a door at the front of the vehicle, the Meyra 200 had its engine positioned at the rear. Author's Collection

1955 — 200

Deciding to enter the Microcar market, Meyra announced the Meyra 200 in 1955. The vehicle was the complete opposite of the Invalid Carriage having two wheels at the front and one at the back. It had a fully-enclosed fibreglass body and was powered by a single-cylinder, two-stroke, 199cc ILO engine that drove the single rear wheel by a chain. Entrance to the 200 was via a door at the front of the vehicle. Production ceased in 1956.

Metalmeccanica Italiana Valtrompia (Mi-Val)

1953 — Motocarro 150/170

Mi-Val — originally Minganti Valtrompia and then Metalmeccanica Italiana Valtrompia — was founded by Ettore Minganti in 1950 and produced motorcycles at its factory in Sarezzo, Italy. The Motocarro 150 and Motocarro 170 were built from 1953 to 1956 and were pick-up based three-wheelers. The front half was essentially a motorcycle powered by either a 147cc or 171cc engine whilst the rear section had a steel-box frame chassis between the rear wheels that allowed various types of body to be attached, offering a cargo payload up to 350kg.

1954 — Mivalino

In 1954, after an agreement with Messerschmitt (see page 156), the company started to build the Messerschmitt KR175 under licence; this was known as the Mivalino. Using a 172cc engine, power was sent to the single rear wheel through a four-speed gearbox. Like the Messerschmitt KR175, it was built with a tubular steel chassis and had a two-seat pressed steel body with a Plexiglas canopy in which the passenger sat behind the driver. Production ended in 1956.

Miari & Giusti

1896 — Miari & Giusti

La Società Miari & Giusti was established in Padova in 1896 to build the Miari & Giusti. The vehicle was originally invented in 1894 by Professor Enrico Bernardi and was possibly the first vehicle to run on the roads of Italy. Powered by a 624cc, single-cylinder, four-stroke engine with overhead valve, the throttle control was a bulb-mounted on the handlebars. This had to be squeezed to control the speed of the vehicle. The drive to the rear single wheel was by chain. Patents to sell the vehicle were obtained in several countries including Britain. Bernardi formed his own company — Società Italiana Bernardi — to take-over from Miari & Giusti and continued to produce the Bernardi (see page 34) until 1901.

(see page 34)

Michael Krauser GmbH

1989 — Krauser Domani

Developed in 1989 by Michael Krauser GmbH from the racing world, the Krauser Domani is built in Germany and produced for the Japanese and European markets. In Japan only a standard car licence is required to drive it. The vehicle is a blend of motorcycle, sidecar and three-wheeler and, whilst appearing to be a motorcycle and sidecar, the vehicle has a torsionally rigid tubular steel chassis in which the sidecar is integral to the whole construction. It is fitted with a 150bhp BMW K1200 motorcycle engine and a five-speed gearbox that, combined with an aerodynamic fibreglass body, provides a top speed in excess of 124mph (200km/h). A Dopo Domani version was also introduced that, whilst being the same construction, has a more traditional looking motorcycle and sidecar look. Both models are available to date.

Michelotti

1974 — Lem

Giovanni Michelotti is a name well known in the sports car world and, during his life, Michelotti designed sports cars for numerous manufacturers including Triumph, BMW, Alfa Romeo and Reliant. In 1960 Michelotti began to build cars in Turin, Italy, and, whilst all vehicles were standard four-wheelers, in 1974 the Michelotti Lem concept vehicle was unveiled at the Geneva Motor Show. At first glance the vehicle appeared to be a three-wheeler, with the single wheel at the front, though it was actually a four-wheeler with its wheels positioned in a rhomboidal layout. The fourth wheel is hidden and positioned at the centre of the car just behind the rear axle giving the Lem three back wheels. Designed by Michelotti and engineered by Gianni Rogliatti, the Michelotti Lem (Laboratorio Elettrico Mobile) was a two-seater with a luggage area behind the seats. It had an aluminium body

Announced in 1974 the Michelotti Lem was an electric two-seat vehicle that was perhaps ahead of its time. Damiano Garro

that featured two large gull-wing doors. It was an electric car powered by a rear-mounted 48V electric motor that used lead batteries. The vehicle was intended for use in urban cities in order to reduce both noise and air pollution, though it never reached production.

Milde & Mondos

1900 — Milde & Mondos

The Milde & Mondos was first created around 1900 in Seine, France, by Charles Milde who was joined by Robert Mondos. Alongside other items, like telephones, Charles Milde created some of the best-known electric cars in France. His first vehicle in 1898 was powered by a 3bhp electric motor that, with the drive system, could be fitted to any carriage. The Milde & Mondos was a light three-wheeler that used two electric motors on the rear axle. It was built until 1903 when it was discontinued; Milde then created a range of four-wheel vehicles that were suitable for urban use. Commercial vehicles were made until about 1914. Milde and Mondos also worked on plans for an 'Electric House', which consisted not only of a garage where the car could be charged but also featured electric lighting, electric heating and a lift, along with electric charging stations around the richer districts of Paris. It has also been documented that the plans also meant that their electric car was meant for Parisians who owned a horse and carriage worth between 3,000 and 5,000 francs. Anyone, owning a horse worth 1,200 francs or less and attempting to buy a vehicle, was politely referred to the 'gasoline horse'. The plans, however, remained on paper.

Miller Technology

1980 — Mine Kart

The Mine Kart was a heavy-duty common personnel carrier for underground mines introduced in 1980. Designed by Ron Miller of Miller Technology in Ontario, Canada, the vehicle was able to carry eight adults, including the driver, over rough terrain to and from mine faces. Whilst the rear seats were static, both the driver's seat and passenger seat had their own suspension and were waterproof and fully padded. The chassis and frame was made from heavy-duty steel tube with metal covers, whilst the flooring was made from checker plate. Under the body a reinforced belly and skid guards protected the engine, transmission, disc brakes and rear axle from rock damage.

A choice of three engines was fitted to the Mine Kart: an air-cooled, 28bhp, 1,600c Deutz Diesel F2L-511W engine; a water-cooled, 29bhp, 1,184cc Isuzu Diesel QD27 engine; and, a water-cooled, 40bhp, 1,777cc Isuzu Diesel. These provided power to a spiral-bevel Dana ¾-ton truck rear axle via a heavy duty three-speed with reverse gearbox. Weighing 2,700lb empty, the top speed was 15mph (24km/h). The last three-wheeler was built in 1996 when it was replaced by a four-wheel version — the Miller Truck 8200 series — that remains in production at the time of writing.

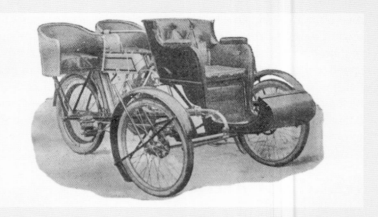

Bucking the trend for the usual layout of a single saddle at the back, the Millford Social Car was equipped with twin bucket seats at the rear. Author's Collection

Mills & Fulford

1903 — Millford Social Car

Mills & Fulford initially manufactured trailers and sidecars for bicycles from 1901. Based in Coventry, UK, the company started to build motorcycles in 1903 and introduced the Millford Social Car the same year. This was different to many other forecars/tri-cars of the era in that it was a three-seater. Rather than the usual saddle to the rear and a passenger seat between the front two wheels, the Social Car had two bucket seats at the back that sat either side of the frame. This meant that the front two wheels were wider apart than usual. Both rear seats were furnished with pedals that allowed either or both of the riders to start or assist the engine. The vehicle had a single horizontal tiller, pointed towards the right-hand seat, for steering. Whilst images of the Millford Social Car show an engine fitted, this was not included and it was up to purchasers to source their own engine. Production ceased in 1904.

Able to carry eight adults the Mine Kart is a heavy duty vehicle designed for taking people over rough terrain to and from mine faces. Miller Technology

1955 — Go (TM1 8BH)

Introduced in 1955 the Mitsubishi Go was a heavy-duty pick-up truck with an extended floor pan, providing an overall length of 5,120mm, that had a carrying capacity of two tons. With a strong steel chassis and a fully enclosed two-seat cab with a heater, the vehicle was fitted with a 47bhp, four-stroke, two-cylinder, 1,489cc ME18 engine that drove the rear wheels by shaft through a four-speed with reverse gearbox. To cope with the extra payload, it was equipped with dependable front suspension and a special RBA rear-spring suspension with hydraulic shock absorbers. The Go was produced until the mid-1970s.

1959 — Leo (LT10/LT11)

The Mitsubishi Leo first appeared in 1959. Built as a small commercial vehicle with a payload of 660lb (300kg), the Leo was available in a standard version as a truck — Model LT10 — that also had the option of a canvas van body at the rear as well as a van (Model LT11). The vehicle had a two-seat cabin with side doors made from steel and a steel chassis. It was powered by a 12.5bhp, air-cooled, four-stroke, single-cylinder, 309cc ME20 engine that provided drive to the rear wheels via a three-speed with reverse gearbox. Around 28,000 vehicles were built before production ceased in 1962 with five vehicles known to survive at the time of writing.

Never reaching production, the Mink was a three-wheeler planned to be made in Bermuda. Author's Collection

Mink

1968 — Mink

Built in the UK and appearing as a one-off prototype in 1968, the Mink was a vehicle that was planned to be manufactured in Bermuda and thus offered minimal weather protection. Fitted with an air-cooled, 198cc Lambretta engine it offered a top speed of 55mph (88km/h) with a fuel consumption of 70mpg (4-litre/100km). The vehicle had an open rounded fibreglass body with an exceptionally long overhang over the front two wheels and a bench seat inside for two people.

Mitsubishi Motors

1946 — Mizushima/TM3D

Built by Mitsubishi Motors in Japan, the Mitsubishi Mizushima was manufactured from 1946 to 1962. It was a lightweight commercial vehicle with a payload of 400kg. Built upon a rugged steel chassis the vehicle had an open two-seat cab that featured a single headlight and was equipped with a folding canvas roof to pull over the frame of the cab. By 1948 a hard top was introduced with the TM3D model.

Powered by a 309cc engine, the Mitsubishi Leo was available with a number of commercial bodies. Author's Collection

1960s — TM15F

Manufactured in the 1960s, the Mitsubishi TM15F was designed to provide a payload of 1,000kg. It was powered by a 36bhp, four-stroke, two-cylinder, 1,145cc engine that had a four-speed with reverse gearbox that drove the rear wheels. Built upon a steel chassis, the vehicle had a fully enclosed two-seat cab, with a range of bodies at the rear.

Monet-Goyon

1921 — Auto Mouche

Monet-Goyon of Saone-et-Loire in France was founded in 1917 by Joseph Monet and Adrien Goyon and manufactured motorised tricycles for those who had been physically impaired during the war. These vehicles evolved to become the Auto Mouche that was announced in 1921. The vehicle was powered by an air-cooled, single-cylinder engine that was mounted directly over, and provided power to, the single front wheel. A number of versions were available, including passenger and light truck versions. These were built until 1923 and, in later versions, the Auto Mouche was redesigned with the engine being moved to the back of the vehicle providing power to the rear wheels. It remained very motorcycle like with two bucket seats.

1922 — Cyclecarette (Type CY)

Monet-Goyon reversed the layout in 1922 with the Cyclecarette, which had the single wheel at the rear of the vehicle. With car-like controls that used a wheel for steering, the Cyclecarette was available in a number of models. Manufactured from 1922 to 1923, the Cyclecarette CY was powered by a single-cylinder, 250cc Villiers Mk VI-A engine that provided power to the single rear wheel. The CY was a two-seat passenger version that had a steel chassis and a plywood body.

1922 — Cyclecarette (Type VT1/VT2/VT3)

A commercial variant of the Cyclecarette was the VT series, which had virtually no body work when compared with the CY. The VT1, VT2 and VT3 were all powered by a 270cc Villiers Mark V engine that drove the single rear wheel through a single-speed gearbox. They were again manufactured between 1922 and 1923. Whilst all models had the same chassis and engine, with a driver's seat made from wicker, the VT1 was an open two-seat vehicle with a flat space between the front wheels, whilst the VT2 had a large storage box positioned between the wheels. The VT3 was an open passenger version that had a large seat and footrest in the same style as older forecars from the turn of the century.

Morford Motor Co

1993 — Morford Flyer/Morford Flyer Mk 2

Designed and created in Cambridgeshire, UK, by Peter Morley and Peter Crawford — Morford being a combination of their names — the Morford Flyer was first built in 1993. The vehicle was an open two-seater with an aluminium body that was attached to a tubular steel frame. Most of the mechanics for the vehicle came from a Renault 5 using the Gordini engine. The suspension was provided by a double wishbone at the front and a Jaguar spring and shock absorber at the rear. In 1995 the Mk 2 version was introduced; this featured a redesigned body and a number of mechanical improvements. The Morford Flyer was available until 1999.

The Monet-Goyon Cyclecarette (Type CY) had a body made from plywood that was attached to a steel chassis. Author's Collection

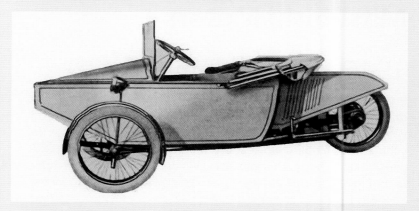

Harry Morgan with the first Morgan three-wheeler that had virtually no bodywork. Morgan Motor Co

Morgan Motor Co

To date the Morgan three-wheeler is one of the most emulated in the world with many three-wheelers being based on the Morgan design. During the 1920s and 1930s the Morgan did more than any other three-wheeler to dispel the myths about three-wheelers being slow and unstable, and became an instant success, especially amongst those who wanted to use them for racing. The Morgan three-wheeler was classed by the British Automobile Racing Club as a 'cyclecar' and, in competitions, it pretty much won everything, often resulting in the only cars on the leader boards being Morgans. It was not just the three-wheelers that the Morgan was beating but also its four-wheel counterparts. So successful was Morgan that organisers would look at ways of banning the cars and indeed penalise them with severe handicaps. So much so that, as the result of a Morgan crashing at over 85mph (137km/h) at the Junior Car Club International 200 mile Light Car Race in 1924, all three-wheel vehicles were banned from competing. This, however, was lifted in 1928 and Morgan again went on to set world records, achieving numerous successes and wins. In 1925 a Blackburne-powered Morgan was recorded at 103.37mph (166.35km/h), making it the fastest unsupercharged car in the world at that point in time. All this was down to one man — Henry Frederick Stanley Morgan (or H F S as he was to become known) — who, in 1901, purchased an Eagle Tandem three-wheeler fitted with an 8bhp, water-cooled De Dion engine.

In 1906 H F S Morgan opened a garage and motor works in Malvern, UK. At the time Morgan was a district agent for Wolseley and Darracq and he also started one of the first bus services in the country, running a 15-seat Wolseley from Malvern Link to Malvern Wells and, later, from Malvern to Gloucester. The Morgan Co became The Morgan Motor Co Ltd in 1912.

1909 — Prototype Runabout

Due to his experiences of owning his Eagle Tandem and a 7bhp, two-cylinder car called *The Little Star*, Morgan created his first prototype three-wheeler in 1909; this he called the Morgan Runabout. Morgan had intended to build a motorcycle but changed his mind and built a single-seater three-wheeler powered by an 8bhp, twin-cylinder Peugeot engine. The chassis — made from tubular steel — was built at the Malvern College workshop by William John Stephenson-Peach, then engineering master at Malvern and Repton. All Morgan three-wheelers that followed (until 1952) had a single rear wheel suspended by a swinging arm with a ¼ elliptic leaf spring on each side with the single rear wheel being driven by a chain and had independent pillar coil sprung, sliding axle, front suspension. With slight variations, all also had a tubular chassis until 1935 when they were replaced with a steel ladder type in the F Types.

1910 — Runabout

In 1910 Morgan obtained his first patent for his design and, after exhibiting two Morgan Runabouts at the Olympia Motorcycle and Cycle Show, these went into production, powered by either a single-cylinder, 4bhp, 482cc, air-cooled, side-valve JAP or a twin-cylinder, 8bhp, 964cc, air-cooled JAP engine. The initial Runabout was a single-seater with a minimal body made from sheet steel and had tiller steering. By 1911 a two-seat Runabout was introduced; other improvements were the addition of a large steering wheel and an extra leaf in the rear springs. Using the same engines, the two-seat Runabout received a number of major body changes; these saw a new bonnet covering the engine at the front of the vehicle with a

The 1910 Morgan Runabout was a single-seater with tiller steering via a lever on the right-hand side of the vehicle. Morgan Motor Co

suitable cut out to allow cool air through onto the engine. A hood was also added to offer some kind of protection against the elements. With its lightweight and good performance, the Runabout became very popular and continued in its single-seat form until 1911 and as a two-seater until 1915.

1911 — Sporting

Morgan successfully collected numerous gold medals, first-class awards and trophies in trials, hill climbs and races, and the Morgan became advertised as 'The Fastest three-wheeler in the World'. Morgan's first attempt at Brooklands was in the International Cyclecar Race, when a Morgan driven by Harry Martin easily came first. H F S Morgan then broke the 1,100cc Hour Record at a speed of 57mph (92km/h) and, as a result, became the first holder of *The Light Car & Cyclecar* Challenge Trophy. The Sporting model, introduced in 1911, was essentially the same as the two-seat Runabout, though there was no hood, no windscreen and many of the body panels were more rounded. It was made until 1921. In 1926 a Sporting four-seat model was introduced; this was driven by a Blackburne or JAP engine and was built until 1932.

1911 – De-luxe

The De-luxe version was also introduced in 1911 and again, whilst being similar to the two-seat Runabout, there were a number of subtle changes. The most obvious change was that the body had higher sides, which, as a result, now included a door to gain access to the vehicle. The rear wheel also had deeper skirts each side to reduce the amount of road dirt being thrown up.

1913 — Grand Prix

Morgan went on to produce a racing car with a longer chassis in 1913; this won the 1913 Cycle Car Grand Prix in France with ease. As a result Morgan then introduced a two-seat replica of the racing model; this became known as the Grand Prix and was manufactured until 1926. It was powered by a water-cooled, OHC, V-twin, JAP competition engine. The successes of the Morgan Motor Co were demonstrated by the fact that, as the World War 1 broke out in 1914, sales had never been higher. Despite the fact that part of the factory had to be converted to producing shells and other munitions for the war effort, limited production of the Morgan to order was able to continue throughout the war. H F S Morgan also submitted a prototype to the War Office for a 'Mobile Machine Gun Carrier' though it was not developed.

World War 1 flying ace Capt Albert Ball, whose vehicle inspired the new sporting Aero model in 1920, with a special-bodied Morgan Grand Prix. Morgan Motor Co

single door on the passenger side. Other changes included a full windscreen and a high-sided body that, with the hood, offered a well-designed family vehicle. In 1932 the Family model had its body revamped; changes included a more rounded bonnet, raked windscreen and a rounded barrel back. It was fitted with a new three-speed gearbox, replacing the old two-speed one that had been used in all models previously, and, from 1934, was only available with a Matchless water-cooled engine. This model continued in production until 1937.

Morgan frequently referred to its racing successes in adverts and, in 1925 when a Morgan became the fastest three-wheeler in the world at 104.6mph (168.3km/h), this was indeed something to broadcast. Morgan Motor Co

1920 — Family Runabout

Morgan was aware that the sooner he could get his factory back into full production after the war, the sooner he could sell many cars in the post-war rush. This he managed to do, as at the end of the war, most manufacturers were unable to switch to full production for nearly a year due to the lack of materials. It was in the two years after the war that then record sales and profits were achieved by the Morgan Motor Co. Morgan had built a four-seat model for his personal use in 1915. This later became successfully marketed as the Family Runabout in 1920. The standard model was fitted with an 8bhp, side-valve, V-twin, water-cooled JAP engine, though Anzani, Blackburne and MAG engines were also used. The Family model used the same chassis as the Aero as this was eight inches longer than the Standard Runabout; two small seats, which were only really suitable for children, were added behind the front seats. The latter were now changed so that the folded forward to allow access to the rear seats via a

Designed for the family, the Morgan Family Runabout was able to seat four adults or two adults and three children. Morgan Motor Co

1922 — Aero/Super Sports
Aero/Super Sports

Initially, from 1917 until 1921, the Aero was only available to special order and it was not officially listed in Morgan's catalogue until late 1922. With its sporty styled body and a range of engines that could be ordered, including Anzani, Blackburne, JAP and MAG — all offering in excess of 70mph (113km/h) — the Aero became a very popular model and was manufactured until 1932. From 1927, a Super Sports Aero was also available; this was powered by a tuned water-cooled, OHV, V-twin JAP engine and was the first Morgan to have shock absorbers as standard. It remained in production until 1932. In 1933 the Super Sports arrived; this was powered by a Matchless MX2 engine. The MX2 was subsequently replaced with a MX4 engine and the model was built until 1939.

1920 — Standard/Popular

1920 also saw the reintroduction of the Standard version; this had been improved from the original Standard Runabout. The vehicle now had a fully integrated body with curved panels and a door. There was also a better hood for increased weather protection and an improved chassis.

A 1928 British Anzani-powered Morgan Aero at Old Rhinebeck Aerodrome in New York, USA. James Nichol

The Morgan F Type F4 that featured a new chassis and used a Ford 'Y' type side-valve engine. Morgan Motor Co

1923 — Darmont

The Morgan three-wheeler became so successful that, in 1923, they were built under licence in France by R Darmont.

1928 — Commercials

Morgan offered commercial vehicles between 1928 and 1935 with a van-like body attached to the rear of the vehicle that had twin doors at the rear. Both the Standard Runabout and the Family versions have been used to create commercials, though the single rear wheel did hamper the load area giving it a load capacity of 1-3cwt.

Towards the end of the 1920s and early 1930s, it was the General Strike of 1926 and Depression, after the Wall Street Crash of 1929, that changed Morgan's advertising to emphasis 'tax, economy, comfort and cost'. However, Morgan realised that, to beat the slump and to prevent the business from going into liquidation (as many other companies had done), he had to introduce a four-wheel car. This the company did in 1936, continuing to produce three- and four-wheel cars up until the outbreak of World War 2.

Although built in small numbers, the Morgan was also available as a commercial van though the single rear wheel did intrude into the interior load space. Author's Collection

1934 — F-Type F4

In 1934 Morgan produced the F series; these were much quieter and smoother than their twin-engined predecessors and were now powered by a Ford Y-type, 933cc, side-valve, four-cylinder engine that drove the single rear wheel by chain via a three-speed with reverse gearbox. The F4 had a new ladder-type pressed steel chassis and the four-seat body was refined further with a restyled front end to incorporate the new radiator and sweeping mudguards. The F4 was built until 1952.

1936 — F-Type F2

The F2 was a two-seater powered by either the Ford Y-type engine or the Ford C-type 10bhp, 1,172cc engine for an additional seven guineas. Whilst the front was the same as the F4, it had a rear section that housed a luggage area behind the front seats. The F2 was built for just two years, between 1936 and 1938, when it then became the F Super.

1938 — F-Type F Super

Replacing the F2 in 1938, the F Super was offered with either the Ford 8bhp or the 10bhp engine along with a slightly wider and shorter chassis. There were also a few discreet changes to the body to provide more of a sports image; these included a slightly lower bonnet with more louvres, a luggage carrier and recessed spare wheel. Morgan continued to produce three-wheelers until 1952, when the last three-wheeler, an F Super, left the Works. One reason for this was that, due to post-war export policies, steel was only available for manufactured goods that were to be exported. Few three-wheelers were exported at that time, though the four-wheeler models were popular in the USA and so they continued to be built. As a result Morgan was then to concentrate solely on four-wheeler models for the next 58 years.

The 2011 Morgan SuperDry Edition that was limited to 200 vehicles and included SuperDry branding, orange wall tyres and quilted leather seats. Morgan Motor Co

In 2011, 58 years after the Morgan F series ceased production, Morgan reintroduced a new three-wheeler that, whilst styled on its predecessors, is equipped with the latest mechanics and technology. Morgan Motor Co

2011 — Three-wheeler

In October 2010 Morgan announced that it was going to reintroduce the famous three-wheeler; this was launched at the Geneva Motor Show in March 2011. The 2011 Morgan three-wheeler follows the classic design of the original but is updated with modern technology. It is powered by a 1,990cc, V-twin, S&S engine that powers the rear wheel by chain via a Mazda MX5 five-speed (and reverse) gearbox. Unlike Morgan three-wheelers from the past that required several tweaks and checks before each journey, the 2011 model is to offer 'get in and drive' simplicity and reliability. With a padded leather interior, the 2011 Morgan has a tubular frame with two roller bars that surround the passenger compartment. An aerodynamic superformed 'bullet' hull, made from aluminium, protects the occupants from the weather. The overall weight is estimated at 500kg with 80bhp giving the vehicle a top speed of an estimated 115mph (185km/h) and a 0-60mph (0-96km/h) time of 4.5sec. To retain the vintage look the Morgan also has wire spoke wheels and costs £25,000 + VAT for the standard specification.

The Morgan Three-Wheeler is in production at the time of writing with a Brooklands limited edition model introduced in September 2013. The company remains a family-owned business, which was taken over by H F S Morgan's son, Peter, in 1959 and then by Peter's son, Charles, in 2003.

The Mosquito was a Mini based vehicle that used the engine, gearbox suspension and trailing arm from a Mini. David Buckley

Moss of Kidlington

1971 — Mosquito

The Mosquito was manufactured by Moss of Kidlington, Oxford, UK, and was designed by Robert Moss. A Mosquito prototype was created in 1971 though it was not until 1974 that it went into production. A total of seven vehicles were made; these were based on a Mini engine, gearbox suspension and single trailing arm rear. Of the seven vehicles built, all had a fibreglass body whilst two were powered by 850cc Mini engines, two with a 998cc engine, two with 1,275cc engines and one powered by a 1275 GT engine. It is believed that the company needed to submit several cars to the government at the time for crash testing and that this stopped further vehicles being produced. Around 1985 the body moulds, along with various production items for the Mosquito, were sold to Mead & Tomkins, a Hereford motorcycle shop, and new modified moulds were created to receive later style Mini lights and a rear window from a Mini to serve as a windscreen. The project, however, was halted in the early 1990s. The moulds were then sold again and later reappeared in a modified form as the Triad (see page 148).

Whilst the Moto-Guzzi Ercole featured side doors they were often taken off to reduce the noise inside the vehicle. Maurizo Bo

Moto-Guzzi

1928 — Tipo 107 Motocarro/ Motocarro S/ ER Motocarro

Moto-Guzzi was founded in Italy in 1921 by Carlo Guzzi and Giorgio Parodi, who had met in the Italian Air Force in 1917. Moto-Guzzi started to produce three-wheelers in 1928 with the Tipo 107 Motocarro. With a motorcycle front end, the rear was modified with a tubular steel frame that had a cargo box positioned between the two rear wheels. The first vehicle was powered by a four-stroke, single-cylinder, horizontally-mounted, 498cc engine that had been used in the Sport 14 motorcycle. This enabled the vehicle to carry 350kg of cargo whilst being able to achieve 31mph (50km/h). Drive was sent to the rear wheels by a chain through a three-speed gearbox. The Tipo 107 was built until 1930.

Introduced in 1934 the Motocarro S was again a motorcycle front end with a cargo area built between the back wheels. It had a rear axle with a differential whilst the payload was increased to 800kg. This was followed in 1938 by the ER Motocarro; this was also equipped with the 498.4cc engine though it now used a four-speed with reverse gearbox. It also had a number of changes to improve the design, including drum brakes on all three wheels. Production ceased in 1942.

1946 — Ercole

Introduced in 1946, the Moto-Guzzi Ercole ('Hercules') had a steel chassis and, initially, was only built as an open version though, from 1960, was also available with a fully-enclosed metal cab that was bolted on top. The single-seat cab was built by a company called Ariasi, and featured side doors and a roll back canvas roof. The vehicle had a hydraulic flatbed with sides at the rear and had a payload capacity of 1,500kg. It was powered by a single-cylinder, 500cc engine with forced air-cooling that drove the rear wheels through a five-speed gearbox. Production ceased in 1980.

1956 — Motocarro Ercolino

The Moto-Guzzi Motocarro Ercolino was introduced in 1956; this was a lightweight commercial vehicle powered by a single-cylinder, 192cc scooter engine. It was available as an open vehicle or with a cab and had a payload of 350kg (772lb), though this was increased in later versions to 590kg (1,300lb). The model was built until 1970.

1959 — Mullo Mechanico

At the request of the Italian Ministry of Defence, Moto-Guzzi manufactured a 3x3 vehicle called the Mullo Mechanico ('Mechanical Mule') powered by a 700cc, 90°, transverse V-twin engine. Steering was to the front wheel, whilst the rear wheels featured track-like wheels that enabled the vehicle to climb brick walls. 220 vehicles were built between 1959 and 1963.

1962 — Aiace Motocarro

The Aiace Motocarro was introduced in 1962 and again was aimed as a lightweight goods transporter. It had a cab with no doors. With a single seat and controlled by handlebars, the Aiace was powered by a Zigolo 110 engine. Production ceased a year later, in 1963.

1965 — Dingotre/ Ciclocarro Furghino

The 1965 Dingotre was another lightweight goods vehicle and was powered by a 50cc engine that drove the rear wheels by chain through a three-speed gearbox. As the engine was 50cc, owners in Italy did not require a driving licence to drive it. The vehicle had an open body that was built on to a tubular chassis and large leg shields at the front to help protect the driver from the elements. The Dingotre was replaced by the Ciclocarro Furghino in 1968. Whilst this was similar to the Dingotre and used the same engine, a number of changes had been made to the body and to the transmission. The latter now provided power to the rear wheels by a shaft drive. In addition, the engine was now outside the cab rather than under the seat, which meant the vehicle was much quieter to drive. Production ceased in 1971.

Motom SpA

1952 — Motocarro

Manufactured by the Motom SpA motorcycle factory in Milan, Italy, from 1952, the Motom Motocarro was powered by a four-stroke, 48cc engine that drove the rear wheels by chain through a three-speed gearbox. The 3cwt vehicle had a motorcycle front end with an enclosed cab built around it and had a van-type storage box at the rear built upon a tubular steel chassis. Fitted with fully interchangeable wheels and suspension that consisted of oscillating front forks and longitudinal leaf springs at the rear, the vehicle did not require a driving licence in Italy. Early vehicles were also sold under the Gavonis name, with all versions being built until 1966.

Motor Development International (MDI)

2009 — AirPod

Powered by compressed air and manufactured by Motor Development International in France the AirPod is a prototype vehicle with zero pollution that was originally conceived in 2000. The first prototypes emerged in 2009 and were initially defined as a three-wheeler though they actually had four-wheels with the front having two wheels set close together. The standard AirPod is a passenger version with three or four — three adult and one child — seats with space for luggage and measures 2.07m in length, 1.60m in width and 1.74m in height. It is aimed at both the private and public sectors for markets such as airports, municipalities and railway stations where a cheap non-polluting vehicle is required. Prototypes have been tested by KLM/Air France at airports. With a steel chassis, the body is made from a composite sandwich of fibreglass and polyurethane foam, and features gull-wing-type doors at the front and back for the driver and passengers. The AirPod is fitted with a 44P06 à chambre active motor and has a top speed of 50mph (80km/h) whilst offering a range of 125 miles (201km) on a tank of air (a full tank holding 175 litres of compressed air). The vehicle does not have a steering wheel and is controlled with a joystick that utilises pneumatic motors; these use pressurised air to drive the car's pistons. The AirPod was said to be a three-wheeler out of 'technical necessity' though, in November 2011, a new version of the AirPod was introduced that was a distinct four-wheeler, with the front wheels being moved further apart into each corner. At the time of writing, the AirPod has not been put into production.

2009 — AirPod Cargo

In addition to the passenger version, an AirPod Cargo version has been made; this is a single-seater with a load space of just over 1cu m. It is planned as a low-cost zero-pollution vehicle for towns.

2009 — AirPod Baby

The AirPod Baby has two front seats and a rear load space of 500 litres and is planned to be a small versatile vehicle that can either carry a passenger and or be used for deliveries.

Motores y Motos SA

1954 — Mymsa Rana 3R

Along with manufacturing motorcycles and sidecars, in 1954 Motores y Motos SA of Barcelona, Spain, introduced the Mymsa Rana 3R. This was a fully-enclosed van that had a steel chassis and body. It was initially fitted with a 125cc engine that drove the rear wheels via a three-speed gearbox, though this was replaced with a larger 175cc engine in 1956; this allowed for an increase in the payload from 200kg to 400kg. In 1957 a Rana 3R four-door passenger vehicle was created, though it remained a prototype and never went into production. The Rana 3R was built alongside a four-wheel variant called the Rana 4R with vehicles being manufactured until 1961.

1958 — T-650 12 GA

In addition a 650 version called the T-650 GA was also made from 1958. This was powered by a 15bhp two-cylinder, four-stroke, 650cc engine and had a payload of 750kg. The T-650 was available either as a base vehicle with a two-seat cab and bare chassis to the rear or as a pallet or container van. This was built until 1961.

Powered by compressed air, the AirPod was unveiled at the Geneva Motor Show in 2009. Wikipedia — El monty

A 1956 Mymsa Rana 3R van powered by a 175cc engine. RUMCar News

Motorette Corp

1946 — Motorette (Model 20/Model 30)

Introduced in 1946, the Motorette was manufactured by the Motorette Corporation of Buffalo, New York. USA. With an open body with no doors or roof, the vehicles were primarily designed for use in a mile-long aircraft plant but, due to their practicality, found many other useful roles. The Motorette was powered by a one-cylinder, air-cooled, 4.1bhp, 293cc engine that drove the left rear wheel via an automatic two-speed gearbox and had a top speed of 39mph (63km/h) (though it did not have a speedometer). The body of the Motorette was all aluminium with a channel construction 'X' frame chassis with steering achieved by what can only be described as oval handlebars. A windscreen was an optional extra. The Motorette came in a number of forms; these included the Model 20, which was an all-round two-seat vehicle that with 6cu ft of luggage space, and the Model 30, which was also a two-seater but with luggage capacity increased to 10cu ft. Famous owners of the Motorette include the American comedian Bob Hope who wanted an extra 'get-about car' where no car could go. Production of the Motorette ceased in 1948.

Motoscoot Co Ltd

2010 — Velor-X-Trike

Announced in 2010 the Velor-X-Trike was designed by Pavel Brida in the Czech Republic and manufactured by Motoscoot Co Ltd. The Velor-X-Trike is a modern interpretation of the Velorex (see page 267), which was built by Stránský in 1950. It was driving his 60-year-old Velorex in 2008 that Brida came up with the idea to build a modern Velorex, which, whilst having the same shape as the old one, used the latest components. Intially called the New Velorex, the prototype Velor-X-Trike (No 00) is powered by a 1,300cc Honda CB motorcycle engine that drives the single rear wheel with a chain and provides a top speed in excess of 124mph (200km/h). The vehicle has a steel space frame chassis along with a laminate and carbon body, with the interior providing seating for two with four-point seatbelts, radio and DVD player. Access to the vehicle is by side doors that swing upwards. Each Velor-X-Trike is unique and handmade to the individual customer's specification and choice of motorcycle engine. Each vehicle contains a silver plaque with the serial number on it, along with the customer's name to celebrate the 60th anniversary of the Velorex. At the time of writing production of around six to 10 vehicles a year is planned with several versions being available: the S (Standard); LS (Luxury); GLS (Grand Luxury); and, R (Racing) version for racetracks with an engine that produces over 200bhp.

Designed as a modern interpretation of the Velorex the Velor-X-Trike uses the same shape whilst using the latest components. Pavel Brida

The Velor-X-Trike contains a host of features that includes lift up gull-wing doors and a hatch back. Pavel Brida

Designed as a single-seater, the MT was actually a four-wheeler with two rear wheels at the back that were set very close together. RUMCar News

MT

1955 — MT

Although the MT looked like, and was classed as, a three-wheeler, it actually had twin rear wheels set very close to each other. The MT was first manufactured in Spain in 1955. The open body was exceedingly narrow and, although a two-seater, was ideally suited for just one person if the driver was on the large size. The vehicle was powered by a single-cylinder, 125cc engine that was mounted behind the seats and provided drive to the rear wheels. Air louvres at the side of the body pulled in air to cool the engine. Production ceased in 1962.

Mumford Engineering

1971 — Musketeer

The first prototype Mumford Musketeer was built in 1971 in Gloucestershire, UK. The vehicle was designed and built by Brian Mumford of Mumford Engineering and production started in 1973. Sold as a complete kit costing £887 and based around a Vauxhall Viva, the Musketeer used a Viva engine, gearbox, front hubs and brakes. The Viva prop shaft drove the single rear wheel via a specially made final drive system. The aerodynamic fibreglass body was attached to a riveted aluminium monocoque chassis and featured fold down headlight covers and a detachable hood. Made until 1978, around four vehicles were built, when Mumford then concentrated on its trailer and sheet metal business.

1983 — Musketeer (Series 2)

In 1983 a Series 2 was introduced with minor modifications to the body with a complete kit costing £1,270 plus tax. In production until 1999, around six Series 2 models were made.

Below left: *Sold as a kit the Mumford Musketeer used Vauxhall Viva mechanics.* Robert Kermode

Below: *The Mumford Musketeer had an aerodynamic fibreglass body attached to an aluminium chassis.* Richard Robinson

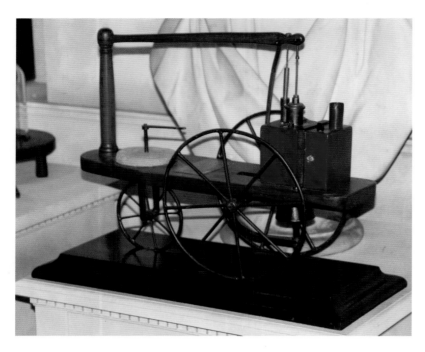

William Murdock's working scale model of a three-wheel steam vehicle in 1784 is the first recorded machine that could move under its own power in the UK. The model is now at the Thinktank Birmingham Science Museum. Author's Collection

Murdock

1784 — Model

In 1784, after designing a steam-powered carriage, William Murdock, working as an assistant for James Watt, built a working scale model of it that ran around his home in Redruth, Cornwall, UK. The model became the first recorded example of a man-made machine that could move under its own power in the UK. The model was a three-wheeler about 12in (30cm) high that had an engine and boiler placed between the two rear wheels and used a spirit lamp to heat the water. It had a small 20mm piston inside a small cylinder that provided drive to the rear wheels. The smaller front wheel was steered by a tiller. As the vehicle was not successful though, James Watt discouraged further development, dismissing high-pressure steam as impractical and dangerous. The principles were later used by Richard Trevithick (see page 250) for his steam coaches.

Myers Motors

2004 — NmG

Myers Motors (MM) was formed in August 2004 by Dana S Myers in Ohio, USA, after acquiring 70 partly built three-wheel vehicles following the closure of Corbin Motors (see page 62). Initially a number of obstacles prevented the company from building the vehicles, with problems of wiring and fusing, dc/ac conversion, braking, swing arm and alignment to name but a few. With the expert help of Robert Q Riley as full time Chief Engineer, all of these issues were addressed and fixed. The consequence of the work was that the first vehicles were initially referred to as MM 1.0 but as a result of the number of changes they were renamed MM NmG (No more Gas). In October 2005 the company announced that it was to start delivery of the NmG at a rate of four per month from the stock of vehicles. It also stated that: 'The MM NmG is a vehicle that will be the official beginning of the transformation of gasoline powered/assisted transportation to the transportation vehicle of the future ... the all-electric, 200 mile, 4 passenger, domestic or solar energy content only, car.' (*Myers Motors Newsletter* October 2005)

The NmG is an all-electric, fully-enclosed, single-passenger vehicle. Chargeable from a 110V outlet, it has 13 sealed Lithium-Ion batteries that power a 156V dc motor. The vehicle has an approximate range of 45 miles (72km) and is governed to a maximum speed of 75mph (121km/h). This is assisted by its spherical body design of a layered composite construction that gives the vehicle an overall weight of 1,350lb, of which the total battery weight is 598lb. The vehicle is reported to capable of travelling for 1,000 miles (1,609km) on $20 worth of electricity working out at $0.10/kWh. The NmG is in production at the time of writing.

2009 — Duo

In 2009 the Duo was announced as a two-seat electric vehicle. With a base model range of 60 miles (97km) the Duo (Doesn't Use Oil) was planned to enter production in 2012. In 2012, when asked about the vehicle, the company announced that it was behind schedule for putting the car onto the road, stating that it had all the technology but unfortunately not the funds. At the time of writing, no further announcements have been made though the company remains optimistic about the Duo.

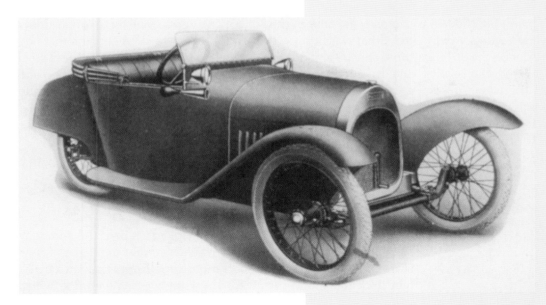

Initially a four-wheeler that lost a wheel, the New Hudson Light Car did not feature a door on the driver's side for the first two years of production. Kerry Croxton

Nederlandsche Moterrijtuigfabriek

1948 — Nemo (Musketier)

Built by the Nederlandsche Moterrijtuigfabriek at Utrecht in The Netherlands from 1948 to 1950, the Nemo was a commercial three-wheeler that was available as a pick-up type truck and as a van. The vehicles had a steel chassis and a load capacity of 15.5cwt. Also known as the Musketier ('Musketeer'), it used a two-cylinder, 688cc Coventry Victor engine that was mounted over, and drove, the single front wheel by chain.

Nelco Industries England

1929 — Auto-Electric Carriage

The Auto-Electric Carriage was an electric vehicle designed for the disabled and was first introduced in 1929. Designed by Leonard Murphy, it had a single seat with tiller steering and an open body built upon a tubular steel chassis with steel body parts. It was powered by a 36V electric motor — fed from six 6V batteries under the seat — that drove directly onto the transaxle at the rear of the car, giving the vehicle a maximum speed of 12mph (19km/h). The engine was accessible through a boot at the rear.

1947 — Nelco Solocar

In 1947 the Auto-Electric Carriage went through a major body restyle at the back of the vehicle and was renamed the Nelco Solocar. Like its predecessor, the Solocar featured tiller steering, handbrake, horn and lights as well as full-sized car brakes. The tiller device also controlled the speed; three speeds were obtained by rotating it clockwise with an anti-clockwise motion providing regenerative control when descending a hill. In 1952 the production rights for the vehicle were sold to Reselco Invalid Carriages in London, though it continued to be sold as the Nelco Solocar until production ceased in 1967.

New Hudson Cycle Co

1919 — Light Car

The evolution of the New Hudson Light Car was different to many three-wheelers. Whilst vehicle development for early manufacturers tended to result in a three-wheeler evolving to a four-wheeler, the New Hudson actually started life as a four-wheeler — the New Hudson Cyclecar — in 1913 and then lost a wheel to become a three-wheeler in 1919. Manufactured by New Hudson Cycle Co Ltd, which also built motorcycles, of Icknield Street, Birmingham, UK, the New Hudson was a two-seat vehicle that was initially fitted with a V-twin, air-cooled, MAG engine. The first vehicles had no door on the driver's side of the vehicle and so, once the hood was erected, the vehicle became extremely difficult to get into. In 1921 the New Hudson received numerous updates; the most notable was a side door to ease entry into the vehicle. The engine was also updated with a water-cooled, 1,100cc MAG engine that provided drive to the single rear wheel through a three-speed and reverse gearbox with a fully enclosed chain. The vehicle also had a permanent rear wheel jack, which was spring loaded and deployed by winding down by a handle included with the tool kit. It also featured fully interchangeable wheels, which were quickly detachable, and it was claimed that, with the rear jack deployed, the back wheel could be changed in just three minutes. The New Hudson was said to have a 'very smart appearance', with black wings and a royal blue body along with a mahogany dashboard, and aluminium bonnet. It cost £250, a price that included the hood, windscreen, horn, Lucas Magdyno lighting set and a spare wheel (with the Dunlop tyre for it costing extra). Production of the Light Car ended in 1924.

New Map

1950s — Solyto

Dating back to 1920, New Map was a company that originally manufactured motorcycles and then small four-wheel microcars from 1938. Based in Lyon-Chassieu, France, during the 1950s the

company introduced the Solyto. This was a small three-wheel utility truck that was fitted with a Ydral 125cc, two-stroke engine that had three speeds and no reverse. The body was made from sheet steel and came in three body styles, including a soft-top van version and a 'camper'-style body. The latter featured a steel top at the back and a canvas top at the front. Production of the Solyto ceased in 1963.

Nippon Jidosha Co

1928 — New Era/Kurogane

Built by Nippon Jidosha Co, Ohmort (Tokyo), Japan, the company first started manufacturing three-wheelers under the name of New Era in 1928. These vehicles had a motorcycle front end with a truck-type back end and were powered by a single-cylinder engine, which was changed to a V-twin in 1936. In 1937 the name was changed from New Era to Kurogane and the model was built up until World War 2 when production of three-wheelers was halted in favour of a 4x4 military scout car.

1949 — Kurogane KW8/Kurogane KY10

In 1949 production of the three-wheeler resumed with two new vehicles; these were available as an 8cwt version with the Kurogane KW8, which was powered by a 42bhp, four-cylinder, 1,046cc engine, and a 10cwt version in the shape of the Kurogane KY10, which had a longer wheelbase and was powered by a 62bhp, four-cylinder, 1,488cc engine. At the time, the KY10 was one of the most powerful machines of this type. Both versions had a four-speed with reverse gearbox that powered the rear wheels via a propeller shaft to the back axle. Using a robust steel chassis and equipped with a fully enclosed two-seat steel cab with side doors, the vehicles were fitted with a number of rear body styles. Production of the Kurogane ceased in 1962 when the firm went bankrupt.

Said to have been designed as a basic truck for farmers to take a pig to market, the New Map Solyto featured either a soft top or one made from steel. Donald Le Bihan

Nitta Sangyo Co

1950 — Sun

Manufactured in 1950 by the Nitta Sangyo Co in Japan, the Sun was a two-seat electric vehicle. With a convertible top and fibreglass body, the vehicle weighed 960kg with its batteries in place. Power was provided to the single rear wheel by chain and the vehicle had a maximum speed of *circa* 30mph (48km/h) and could do 60-70 miles (97-113km) on a single charge.

The Norton Shrike with its semi-exposed tubular steel space frame.
Dave Norton

Norton

1983 — Shrike

Designed and built by Dave Norton, the Shrike was first built in 1983 in California, USA. Initially the vehicle used a Yamaha 650cc engine though, after 78,000 miles (125,530km), now uses a four-cylinder, BMW K1200RS engine with a six-speed gearbox providing drive to the single rear wheel. With a top speed estimated to be more than 120mph (193km/h) the vehicle is said to accelerate at over .2G at 80mph (129km/h) and average around 30-40mpg (7-9.4-litre/100km). The Shrike is a two-seater with the passenger sitting behind the driver and has a semi-exposed tubular steel space frame with composite aluminium/polypropylene body panels called Alucobond (also

Dibond), which are fitted flush to the chassis. It also has Triumph Spitfire front suspension and Porsche steering. At the time of writing, an information pack is available on the Shrike; it is not a step-by-step guide on how to build a Shrike though it does contain all the relevant information about the Shrike to do so.

Nouveau Developments

1976 — Stimson Scorcher

The Stimson Scorcher was first produced in the UK in 1976. Designed by Barry Stimson, it was powered by an Austin Mini engine and also used a Mini sub-frame and gearbox. It was claimed that, using the 850cc Mini engine, the Scorcher had a top speed of 100mph (161km/h). The body was made from fibreglass and was, in most cases completely open, offering the driver no weather protection at all. The vehicle could seat three and, as it was classed as a motorcycle-sidecar combination under UK law, the driver and passenger had to wear a crash helmet though the third person did not. The Scorcher was available preassembled and as a kit, sold by Nouveau Developments of Brighton, UK. Around 30 Scorchers were made before production ceased in 1980. In 1981 the Scorcher project was sold to Gerald Pickford in Clanfield, who redesigned the lower front end with three vehicles understood to have been made by the end of 1982.

Almost a vehicle that you sit on rather than in, the Stimson Scorcher used a Mini engine to move it along at up to 100mph (161km/h). Steve Hole

NSU

1905 — Tricar

NSU was founded in 1873 and in 1880 it relocated to Neckarsulm, Germany. The company did not actually get its NSU name until 1882. The company first produced motorcycles in 1901 and, as was the trend at the time, developed a Tricar from a motorcycle in 1904. Whilst the driver sat at the rear of the vehicle on a motorcycle-type saddle and steered with a steering wheel — something very unusual for this type of vehicle at the time — the passenger sat in a padded seat that was positioned between the front two wheels. In addition to the Tricar, a commercial version was also manufactured; this saw the passenger seat replaced with a cargo area positioned between the front two wheels. Powered by an air-cooled, 6bhp, twin-cylinder engine that drove the rear wheel, the Tricar was practically the last car of this kind by 1910. Companies like Riley and Singer, which both produced similar designs, were all ceasing manufacture of such vehicles in favour of four-wheel designs. NSU stopped producing the Tricar in the early 1920s and concentrated on motorcycles. By 1955 the company was the world's largest motorcycle manufacturer.

Although based on a similar design to other three-wheelers of its era, the NSU was different in that it featured a steering wheel rather than handlebars. Wikipedia — Butch T

Luke Skywalker's Landspeeder X-34 from the film Star Wars *is perhaps the last vehicle you would expect to find in this book though in reality it was a three-wheeler based around the chassis of a Bond Bug.*
Scott Merrill

Officine Meccaniche Daldo e Matteucci

1952 — Demm

Manufactured in Milan, Italy, from 1952 until 1962 Officine Meccaniche Daldo e Matteucci usually built motorcycles, though its also built a number of three-wheelers using engines varying from 50cc up to 172cc. The single-cylinder, two-stroke engines powered the rear two wheels via a shaft from a four-speed gearbox. The vehicles had a number of various body types, from a passenger-carrying vehicle to trucks.

Ogle Design

1977 — Landspeeder X-34

Manufactured by SoroSuub Corporation, the Landspeeder X-34 was powered by three turbine engines and had a number of repulsor counter balances that used a repulsorlift allowing it to cruise at about 10cm above the ground at speeds of up to 155mph (250km/h). In reality the Landspeeder was a fictional anti-gravity craft used by Luke Skywalker (Mark Hamill) in the 1977 film *Star Wars* (Episode IV: *A New Hope*) and was actually designed and built by Ogle Design in Hertfordshire, UK. The vehicle was fully driveable and based upon the chassis of a Bond Bug (see Reliant Motor Co Ltd on pages 210-211 for more information on this and other Ogle-designed three-wheelers) though, during filming the wheels were masked, to give the illusion that the vehicle was hovering. Reflective material, gelatin placed on the camera lens and mirrors angled at 45° to the ground under the vehicle were used to help hide the wheels. A broom handle was also attached to the underside of the body to help kick up dust as it travelled along.

Omega Motors

1979 — TriStar

The Omega TriStar was one of numerous electric vehicles that were being built by Omega Motors — the Electric Car Co — in both three- and four-wheel designs. Manufactured in 1979 in Huntington Beach, California, USA, the TriStar was designed as a utility vehicle with a detachable back that allowed it to be used as a covered truck type vehicle or open pick-up. Weighing in at 840lb, the TriStar had a top speed of 30mph (48km/h) and a range of 40 miles (64 km) on a single charge. To charge the vehicle took six to eight hours (if using 110V) or four to five hours if using 220V. Production is believed to have ceased in the mid-1980s.

OTI

1957 — OTI 125

Manufactured by Office Technique International (OTI) in France, the OTI 125 was built in 1957. Designed by Roland Pilain, it was an open two-seat vehicle with no doors powered by a two-stroke, 125cc Gnome et Rhône engine that drove the single front wheel and provided a top speed of 28mph (45km/h). In 1959 a second model was built; this featured a number of changes, including the use of a Bugatti horseshoe grille at the front as it was intended the vehicle would be manufactured at the old Bugatti works in Molsheim, France. The new model featured side doors and, unlike its predecessor, the headlights had been moved from the top of the body into the side. Production was planned to start in 1960 though it never went ahead.

Featuring a Bugatti horseshoe grille, it was planned that the OTI 125 would be built at the old Bugatti Works in Molsheim. Hans van Scharrenburg

Featuring a detachable back that Omega TriStar was an electric vehicle that could be converted from an open pick-up to a covered truck. Author's Collection

PAL-V Europe NV

2012 — PAL-V ONE

Announced in 2012, the PAL-V ONE (Personal Air & Land Vehicle) is a two-seat hybrid car and gyroplane. It is not only a three-wheel sports car on the road but also a patented vehicle, which is able to fly like a gyrocopter through lift generated by an auto-rotating rotor with forward speed generated by a foldable push propeller on the back. PAL-V Europe NV was founded in The Netherlands in 2001 with the aim of building a 'roadable aircraft'; the work has involved a number of institutes, including the Dutch National Aerospace Laboratory and Delft University. In 2012 the PAL-V's proof-of-concept prototype made its first flight at Breda Gilze-Rijen Airport in the Netherlands.

On land the rotors on the PAL-V ONE fold into the body to produce a road legal sporty vehicle with a DVC™ tilting system so that it tilts into corners like a motorcycle. PAL-V Europe NV

On the road the PAL-V One uses a patented DVC™ tilting system that was developed for the Carver (see page 265) and enables the vehicle to tilt like a motorcycle when cornering. It is fitted with a 230bhp engine providing a top speed of 112mph (180km/h) with a 0-60mph (0-96km/h) time of eight seconds. At present, vehicles run on petrol with a range of approximately 750 miles (1,200 km), although bio-diesel and bio-ethanol versions are also planned

Whilst flying, the PAL-V ONE is quieter than a helicopter as the main rotor is slower and so it is able to take off at low speed on either a concrete or grass runway of 540ft (165m). The vehicle is designed to fly below 4,000ft (1,200m), which is the airspace available for uncontrolled Visual Flight Rules (VFR) traffic so that it does not interfere with commercial air traffic. The engine used for driving is also used to power the propeller and provides a maximum flying speed of 97kt (112mph/180km/h) with a minimum speed of 27kt (31mph/50km/h) required for flight. It has a flying range of between 220 and 315 miles (350-500 km) depending on load and wind conditions. The gyroplane technology is such that, even if the engine fails, the PAL-V ONE can be steered and landed safely as the main rotor continues to auto-rotate. Once landed, the conversion

In the air the PAL-V ONE becomes a gyrocopter with a flying range of up to 315 miles (500km). PAL-V Europe NV

from aircraft to car takes around 10min with the rear propeller folding automatically into the driving position once the engine stops. Then, pressing a button lowers the rotor mast into a horizontal position above the car roof with the outside of the rotor blades folding over the inside. The telescopic tail section then slides forward to shorten the overall length and cover the propeller.

The PAL-V ONE complies with existing regulations in all major markets, which means it is allowed both on the road and in the air. At the time of writing, the company is inviting new investors to fund the development of a commercial product to launch on the market. It is stated that governments are already preparing for increasing traffic with Personal Air Vehicles with governments in the United States and Europe developing programmes that determine an infrastructure of 'digital freeways' that provide a safe highway using GPS technology.

Paolo Pasquini

1978 — Valentine 125/250

Built as both a three- and a four-wheeler, the Valentine was manufactured by Paolo Pasquini of Bologna, Italy, in 1978. It was powered by either a two-cylinder 125cc or a 251cc engine, which was positioned between the front two wheels and provided drive directly to them. The vehicle was a two-seater that had a light tubular steel spaceframe and a fibreglass body. Production ceased in the same year.

Panther Motors Inc

2003 — Scoot Coupe P49/P50/P150

Following the creation of a prototype Scoot Coupe in 2003, Panther Motors Inc of Florida, USA, was founded in 2004 by Dominick Livoti Jr and Jerry Liu. Prior to this, Livoti had set up a company in 1991 called Fun Rentals that rented Scooters. He then wanted to create a reliable three-wheeler that could carry two passengers. The first generation of the Scoot Coupe — the P49 — was released in 2005. In 2008 the Scoot Coupe was completely redesigned with a number of improvements including better steering and front suspension. The vehicle is powered either by a 1.9bhp, air-cooled, four-stroke, 49.3cc engine — the Scoot Coupe P50 — or a larger 9.28bhp 147.5cc version — the Scoot Coupe P150 — with both engines having automatic transmission. The vehicle has a tubular steel chassis with stainless steel roll bars and a fibreglass body that offers seating for two and has a locking boot and glove box. A GPS Coupe version is also available, which, when being hired, allows customers to locate historic sites, restaurants, etc, in addition to providing warnings for speed and instructions on how to return to base. The vehicles remain available at the time of writing and the company is currently working on a 500cc commuter vehicle.

Built as both a three- and a four-wheeler, the Valentine was available with either a 125cc or 251cc engine. Author's Collection

Popular as a rental scooter in many resorts in the USA the Scoot Coupe also comes in a talking GPS version that amongst other things locates historic sites to visit. Jim Nichol

Below: *Available as both a single- and a two-seater, the Pasquali Riscio featured an electric motor that was fuelled by four 6V batteries.* Jez Hildred

Pasquali

1990 — Risciò Elettrico (Type 105.10/Type 105.20)

The Pasquali Risciò Elettrico was an electric vehicle available in two versions: a single-seater that in Italy did not require a driving licence (Type 105.10); and, a two-seat version (Type 105.20) that did require a licence. Manufactured in Florence, Italy, by Pasquali from around 1990, the vehicle used an electric motor that was fuelled by four 6V Pb-gel batteries. With a maximum speed of 25mph (40km/h) and a range of 50km in city centres, the Risciò had a tubular steel frame with a fibreglass body. Pasquali is believed to have ceased making vehicles in the early years of the 21st century.

Peel Engineering Co

1955 — Manxcar

Based in the Isle of Man, the Peel Engineering Co initially built fibreglass hulls for boats and motorcycle fairings through its subsidiary company, West Marine Ltd. In 1955 the company produced the Peel Manxman though, as a result of an Excelsior motorcycle having the same name, the name was changed to the Peel Manxcar. The vehicle had a tubular steel chassis with a fibreglass body. It was initially fitted with a 350cc Anzani engine but this was soon replaced by a 250cc version. The engine drove the single rear wheel. The Manxcar was originally designed to be sold as a kit though never went into production.

1962 — P50

At the London Motor Show in 1962, the Peel stand exhibited a new Peel three-wheeler — the Peel P50 — that was designed by Cyril Cannell. At just 52.8in (1.34m) in length and 39in (99cm) in width, the Peel P50 was classed as the world's smallest production car, a record that it held until 2009. The initial prototype of the P50 had the single wheel at the front though, on production models, this was reversed with the single wheel being at the rear. With a top speed of 38mph (61km/h) and fitted with a fan-cooled, 49cc DKW engine and three-speed gearbox, it was designed purely as a single-seat town car to carry one adult and a shopping bag. The Peel 50 had no reverse gear. With a light tubular steel chassis and a fibreglass body, which had just one door on the left hand side, it weighed just 59kg (130lb) and so it was light enough to pick-up and park manually using the handle provided at the rear of the vehicle. When new, all P50s were shipped in a wooden box that also doubled up as a garage. Production ceased in 1966 with around 75 vehicles built.

1965 — Trident

Introduced in 1965 the Peel Trident featured a clear 'bubble top' and used the same 49cc engine as the P50, though some vehicles were also made with a 98cc Triumph Tina engine. Again designed by Cannell, the vehicle was a two-seater (with an option of a single-seater with a shopping basket at the side), though at 72in (1.82m) in length and 42in (1.06m) in width, it was only marginally wider the P50. Access to the Trident was through the bubble glass top, which ratcheted upwards along with the front section of the body. Around 45 vehicles were made before production stopped in 1966.

A Peel P50 on the left whilst on the right the Peel P50 prototype that features a completely different layout with the single wheel at the front. Andy Carter

The two-seat Peel Trident that features a bubble glass top that hinges forward with the body to allow access in and out. Andy Carter

The 2010 Peel P50 available in two versions with power coming from either a 49cc engine or a 2.5kW electric motor. Peel Engineering Ltd

Peel Engineering Ltd

2010 — P50

The Peel Engineering name reappeared in 2010 when two businessmen, Gary Hillman and Faizal Khan, acquired Peel and went onto the British TV series *Dragons' Den* asking for £80,000 to set up a business to start remanufacturing the Peel P50 and the Peel Trident in the UK. James Caan, one of the most successful entrepreneurs in the UK, agreed to invest the amount required for 30% of the company. Manufactured from 2010, the new Peel P50 differs from its predecessors in that there is an option for either a petrol or an electric version. Whilst the petrol version uses a 49cc, four-stroke CVT engine that offers a top speed of 28mph (45km/h) and 118mpg (2.4-litre/100km), the electric version uses a 2.5kW dc Brushless CVT motor that provides a top speed of 31mph (50km/h) with a range of 15 miles (24km). In addition, it has brakes on all wheels with a Kinetic Energy Recovery System. With a fractionally larger fibreglass body 54in (1.37m) long and 41in (1.04m) wide, the vehicles are in production at the time of writing.

2010 — Trident

The 2010 Trident is also offered with two power units, both of which are the same as in the P50. Using a fibreglass clamshell body, the Trident remains the same size as the original at 72in (1.82m) in length and 42in (1.06m) in width. The Trident also has all-wheel braking with a Kinetic Energy Recovery System. It also remains in production at the time of writing

Pembleton

1999 — Super Sport

Founded in Worcestershire, UK, in 1999, the Pembleton is a kit-based car in both three-wheel — Super Sport — and four-wheel — Brooklands — versions that utilise many parts from a Citroën 2CV. The Pembleton Super Sport — also referred to as Grasshopper — is styled on sports three-wheelers from the interwar years. It has a square/tubular steel space frame with a stressed aluminium skin and copper cowling. Suspension, rack and pinion, gearbox, braking system and the horizontally-opposed, air -cooled — either 602cc or 652cc — engine are all taken from a Citroën 2CV, though some models are fitted with BMW 7 series or Moto-Guzzi V-twin engines. With a possible build weight of around 300kg most vehicles are able to achieve around 60mpg (4.7-litre/100km). Kits remain available at the time of writing.

Using many parts from a Citroën 2CV, the Pembleton is a kit-based vehicle. RUMCar News

Penguin Speed Shop

2010 — Buckland B3 Mk2

In 2010 Penguin Speed Shop based in Sarn, North Wales, UK, acquired the rights from Dick Buckland to produce the 1985 Buckland B3 (see page 50), which was developed as the Buckland B3 Mk 2 and went into production in April 2011. Based, where possible, upon the original, the B3 Mk 2 is 30% lighter with a hand-built chassis made from Zintec steel with a fibreglass two-seat body and wings. A number of updated upgrades, including all-round disc brakes, drivetrain, new suspension and a revised rear bulkhead, have also been incorporated into the vehicle. The B3 Mk 2 is powered by a front-mounted, four-cylinder, 95bhp, 1,300cc Ford Escort engine that drives the rear wheel via a four-speed gearbox. At the time of writing, the vehicle is available as either a kit or a full turnkey product.

Updated for 2010 the Buckland B3 Mk 2 retains the styling of the original with updated mechanics. Steve Hole

Persu Ventures

In Development — V3 (Gen I: Internal Combustion Engine)

Following the bankruptcy of Carver Europe in 2009, which manufactured the Carver One tilting vehicle (see page 265), the business behind the Carver's innovative leaning technology — the Advanced Technology Licensing Co — remained in business and, in 2010, the technology was licensed by Persu Ventures in the USA. Called the Persu V3 (or the 'Vehicle') a new model is being designed with a body that produces a lower drag coefficient and has a chassis that incorporates the patented Dynamic Vehicle Control system that allows the vehicle to tilt up to 45° when cornering. The V3 retains a fully enclosed two-seat cabin in which the passenger sits behind the driver, with standard features including a steering wheel, automatic transmission, driver's airbag, seatbelts and air conditioning. Using an 80bhp, two-cylinder, turbocharged engine the vehicle is estimated to have a top speed of around 100mph (161km/h) with a 0-60mph (0-96km/h) time of approximately six seconds and achieve around 55mpg. Manufacture is expected to start in 2014.

In Development — V3 (Gen II: Plug-in Hybrid)

Also planned is a hybrid version. Whilst featuring similar specifications to the Gen 1 V3, the hybrid vehicle will use an internal combustion engine that is combined with an electric propulsion system and is expected to achieve around 100mpg (2.8-litre/100km) based on 75mpg+ (3.8-litre/100km+) on fuel and an electric range of around 25 miles (40km). Planned production dates are at the time of writing not known.

Peugeot

1889 — Peugeot Type 1

Peugeot Frères was founded in 1810 when Jean-Pierre Peugeot along with his two sons, Jean-Pierre II and Jean-Frédéric, turned their father's old grain mill into a steel foundry and started to manufacture a vast assortment of steel items including springs, saws, coffee grinders and umbrella frames. The first vehicle was to arrive 79 years later when, in 1889, Armand Peugeot (great-grandson of the original Jean-Pierre) approached the Serpollet brothers (see page 226) with a view to building tricycles fitted with their instant steam generator. The resulted in the Peugeot Type 1; this was a five-seat vehicle that was powered by twin-cylinder steam engines of 4-6bhp, giving the vehicle a maximum speed of 16mph (26km/h). The boiler was placed at the back of the vehicle, between the wheels, and was automatically fed with coke, whilst a much smaller single wheel at the front was steered with a tiller. By 1889 production of the model ceased in favour of vehicles built with an internal combustion engine.

1941 — VLV

Although it is often referred to as a three-wheeler, the Peugeot VLV (Voiture Légère de Ville or 'Light City Car') actually had four wheels with the two wheels at the back closely set together. Announced in 1941 and built from 1942, the VLV was a two-seat, electric vehicle that was powered by 12V batteries located under the bonnet. With a reported top speed of 22mph (35km/h) the VLV had a range of 50 miles (80km). It was built during World War 2 as a means of escaping the fuel restrictions that were imposed on non-military users by the occupying German forces. However, it was banned in 1945 after 377 vehicles were made. Most of the vehicles built were used for distributing post or for medical assistance.

With an open body that has no doors the Peugeot 20Cup is built around a one-piece carbon chassis. Peugeot

2005 — 20Cup

The Peugeot 20Cup Concept Car was a sports three-wheeler unveiled at the 2005 Frankfurt Motor Show and was a co-operation between Peugeot Citroën and BMW. Powered by a turbo-charged, four-cylinder, 1,600cc petrol engine with direct injection, it had 16 valves and two overhead camshafts that developed a maximum power of 125kW — more than 170bhp — with 0-60mph (0-96km/h) possible in less than five seconds. Drive was sent to the single rear wheel through a sequential six-speed manual gearbox. The body was open, with no doors, and built around a one-piece carbon chassis that incorporated a separate two-seat cockpit located at road level. It had rack-and-pinion steering and a multifunction steering wheel that had control paddles for the piloted gearbox and, at the centre, a touch screen that displayed a virtual image that remained horizontal irrespective of the position of the steering wheel. This screen image was computed according to the steering wheel angle. It also contained all of the car's operating indicators and, in addition, allowed the driver to switch on the headlamps and provided assistance during sporty use by showing transverse as well as longitudinal acceleration. Two Peugeot 20Cup vehicles are known to have been built.

Built by Peugeot the 20Cup is a concept vehicle that used a turbo-charged 1,600cc engine. Peugeot

187

A 1925 Phanomobil with its engine positioned directly above the front wheel. This shot taken in Assen in The Netherlands in 1927 shows the father of the photo contributor, who worked for a Phanomobil dealer as a mechanic, in the front driver's seat. Harry Kalsbeek

Phantom Vehicle Co

1978 — Phantom

It was whilst working as a designer at General Motors (GM) for the Corvette Studio in the USA that Ron Will started to develop the Phantom. A ³/8th scale model was produced and tested at GM's Tech Center's Harrison Wind Tunnel. This showed that the wing-shaped body did not lift and had a drag coefficient of .31. Will then left GM and moved to California to build the car with his brother Lee, establishing the Phantom Vehicle Co. After creating a full-size clay model, work then began on the Phantom; the vehicle was first shown at the Los Angeles Auto Expo in April 1978.

For maximum stability, the Phantom — also known as Turbo Phantom — had an exceptionally wide body (6.5ft) that was built like a large surfboard with an upper and lower fibreglass shell filled with lightweight Urethane foam. There was no metal frame and so the body also formed the chassis with the suspension and engine mounting attached to flat plates on the inner fibreglass surface. The vehicle also featured a sandwich steel firewall panel between the rear engine compartment and the front passenger compartment; this also acted as a roll bar. Access to the passenger compartment was via a lift-up canopy;

Phanomen Co

1907 — Phanomobil

Up until 1907 the Phanomen Co of Zittan, Germany, had been building just bicycles and motorcycles. In 1907 it produced its first three-wheeler — the Phanomobil — which was designed by Franz Louis Huttel, who also designed the very similar Cyklonette. The Phanomobile was powered by an 880cc, V-twin engine, which was used until 1912 when it was upgraded to a four-cylinder, 1,536cc engine. The engine sat directly above, and powered, the single front wheel whilst also turning with it; steering was achieved by a tiller. The Phanomobil was very economical and so, as a result, became very popular. It was available in both two- and four-seat passenger versions; in addition commercial bodies were also fitted. It was produced up until 1927 when the company concentrated on the four-wheelers that it had also been manufacturing since 1911.

With a width of 6.5ft the Phantom was exceptionally wide. It is show here with its creator Ron Will. Ron Will

Also called the Turbo Phantom, the Phantom's sleek body shape was tested at GM's Tech Center's Harrison Wind Tunnel. Ron Will

this also raised the steering column and digital instrument panel. The Phantom used a turbocharged, 1,000cc Honda Goldwing motorcycle engine that gave the car a top speed of over 125mph (201km/h) with a 0-60mph (0-96km/h) time of six seconds. The front suspension was taken from a Volkswagen Beetle whilst the rack-and-pinion steering came from a MG Midget. The US government tested the Phantom on a skid pad and it was able to generate about .8Gs. As a result, the examiners were very impressed as many of the other contemporary three-wheelers were deemed to be dangerous on the skid pad. Whilst several miscellaneous parts were made in advance for the second and third models, as a result of lack of funds, only one Phantom was built; this is still owned at the time of writing by Will. A full-size mould was later sold, from which one body was made. However, this was believed to have been lost or destroyed in a fibreglass shop that went out of business. A further body is in Ann Arbor, Michigan, USA where another enthusiast is building his own Phantom.

1981 — Jet Fighter Commuter

Announced in 1981, the Jet Fighter Commuter was to be a special kit that could be built from any mid-size street motorcycle. Will was working on plans for a much simpler tandem design vehicle. This had a tubular frame and thus would be easier for a kit-car builder to make at home. It was called the Jet Fighter Commuter because of its appearance. Unfortunately there were not enough funds at the time to complete the vehicle or the plans. The plans were advertised with a drawing of the design; as a result thousands of letters from not only the USA but countries around the world were received. Will believed that, had the simpler Jet Fighter construction been built before the very complex Phantom, they would have succeeded in building a small, unique three-wheel car business. Subsequently, Ron Will went on to work for Subaru as a designer and the Subaru Outback was largely his concept and design.

Phiaro Corporation Inc

2005 — three-wheeler

Unveiled in October 2005 in Tokyo, Japan, the Phiaro three-wheeler is simply called 'three-wheeler'. The vehicle was a full working prototype with no plans to put it into production. It was based on the Vandenbrink Carver One, and Phiaro worked in conjunction with Brink Dynamics to create a new styling concept for the exterior and interior of the Carver One. The vehicle was to tilt with the main body having a swivel joint that allowed the main body to lean up to 45° whilst the two rear wheels stayed firmly on the road. Below 6mph (10km/h) the three-wheeler had a hinge lock that kept the vehicle upright. Power came from a 659cc, liquid-cooled, four-stroke transverse, turbocharged, four-cylinder engine with an intercooler. The vehicle remained a one-off (see Vandenbrink on page 265 and Persu on page 186 for more information on the Carver).

Phoenix Motors Ltd

1903 — Trimo

Introduced in 1903, the Phoenix Trimo won a gold medal in the 1,000-Mile Autocycle Club's Trial as a result of its reliability the same year. Built by Phoenix Motors Ltd in London, UK, and designed by J Van Hooydonk, who was originally from Belgium, the Trimo was like many three-wheelers of its era in that it was essentially a motorcycle at the rear with the driver sitting on a saddle and controlling the vehicle via handlebars with the passenger sitting in a detachable — on this

Known for its reliability the Phoenix Trimo was powered by various engines with the final drive being either by chain or belt drive. Author's Collection

Although never completed the initial design for the Jet Fighter Commuter aroused much interest. Ron Will

particular model — padded seat positioned between the front two wheels. The initial 1903 model was available with a 3bhp Minerva engine that drove the single rear wheel through an optional chain or belt drive. In a modified form it used a Singer motor-wheel in place of its engine and usual rear wheel. A choice of alternative 2.5bhp and 4.5bhp engines was available from 1905 and, in the same year, an advertisement for the vehicle featured a 'Doctor's experience' with the machine; he concluded that, due to its reliability, the vehicle did the work of three horses. The Trimo was built until 1906 when it acquired an extra wheel to become the Quadcar.

Piaggio

Piaggio was established in September 1882 in Sestri Ponente, Genoa, Italy, as a timber stockyard, by Enrico Piaggio with his son Rinaldo. In 1884 Rinaldo left to set up his own business — the Società Piaggio — in which he intended to develop an activity in ship outfitting. This, however, changed in the early 20th century when Rinaldo went into railway coach construction. Around 1916, Piaggio developed an interest in aeronautics and built aircraft engines. After World War 2 his interest turned to transport to satisfy a demand for private vehicles. The result was a prototype scooter, which was nicknamed Paperino (or 'Donald Duck'), but Enrico, the son of Rinaldo, was not happy with it and handed the project over to Corradino D'Ascanio for a complete overhaul. In 1946, as a result, the first Vespa scooter appeared. Following the Vespa, 1948 saw the introduction of a new three-wheel vehicle — the Ape (pronounced 'ah-pay') — which helped commercial activity pick-up in Italy after the war. The Ape continued to be made in basically the same form thereafter on Piaggio's range of two-wheel scooters. The Ape range is built around a semi-monocoque frame that uses a single load-bearing chassis in sheet-steel and a steel body that houses either one — in some older models — or two seats. Many versions of the Ape have been built since 1948.

1948 — Ape A

The first Ape was introduced in 1948 and was powered by a 125cc engine. It had a wooden pick-up bed behind the driver's cabin, whilst inside it had a column-mounted gear lever. The front fork was mounted to the left of the wheel hub. This model was made until 1952.

1952 — Ape B

Introduced in 1952, the Ape B was similar to the A model but was now powered with a larger 150cc engine. It also now had a pressed steel cargo bed, cable-operated gear change and the front fork was mounted to the right of the wheel hub. This model was made until 1956.

1956 — Ape C

The Ape C followed in 1956. It was still fitted with a 150cc engine but was totally redesigned. This was the first Ape to have an enclosed cab. The engine was under the driver's seat and, running on a 5% oil mix, had to be manually started as with previous versions though an electric starter was optional. It was built until 1964.

1964 — Ape D

With the arrival of the Ape D in 1964 the vehicle was now powered by a 175cc engine. It also featured a trapezoidal headlight fitted on the bulkhead rather than fixed to the mudguard. The engine now had an intake valve that allowed the engine to run with a 2% oil mix. It was also the first Ape to offer the driver warmth with the introduction of a cab heater. This model was made until 1967.

1965 — Ape E

The 1965 Ape E was made until 1973 and was identical to the Ape D model but with a smaller 150cc engine.

1968 — Ape MP

With the Ape MP — Motore Posteriore or 'Rear Engine' — in 1968, the engine was moved from the cab to the rear of the vehicle to improve overall comfort. The Ape MP was made until 1978.

1970 — Ape E/400R

In 1970 the Ape was again fitted with a 175cc engine and, following a few other minor changes, became the Ape E/400R, which was built until 1978.

1979 — Ape P

Introduced in 1979, the Ape P kept the 175cc though it received a number of minor changes. Production of the model ceased in 1981.

1981 — Ape 500

The 1981 Ape was called the Ape 500 and, still fitted with the 175cc, received a new bulkhead with two headlights. It remained in production until 1993.

1993 — Ape 50/Ape Web/ Ape Cross 50

In 1993 the Ape was fitted with a much smaller 49.8cc engine to become the Ape 50. It also had redesigned headlights that now

At the time of writing Piaggio still manufacture various versions of the Ape. It also manufacture a trike-based three-wheeler called the MP3 with a range of engines from 125-500cc. The company also builds two- and four-wheel vehicles.

Pip Car Engineering

1988 — Modulo GT 1100

Designed and built in 1988 by Carlo Lamattina in Milan, Italy, the Modulo GT 1100 is powered by a either a 100bhp BMW K100 1,100cc or a Moto-Guzzi 1,100cc Sport engine, which provides drive to the single rear wheel via a five-speed gearbox with electric reverse offering a top speed of 125mph. The vehicle has a tubular steel and aluminium sheet spaceframe with a fibreglass body that incorporates pop-up headlights and curved windscreen. The Modulo is available as either a single- or a two-seater with the passenger sitting behind the driver. A closed body version is also available as an option, though aesthetically this causes the vehicle to lose its sporty looks completely. Perhaps testimony to the vehicle's handling, Nigel Mansell, the former Formula 1 and Indy champion, was once an owner of the Modulo GT 1100. The vehicle is still available at the time of writing and is built to order.

Available as either a single- or two-seater, the Modulo GT 1100 is powered by either a BMW or Moto-Guzzi engine. Carlo Lamattina

incorporated sidelights. In 1994, a second 49.8cc model was introduced; this was called the Ape Web, which featured redesigned lights. This was then replaced in 2000 with the Ape Cross 50, which was restyled to offer a sporty look. In 2000, Reliant Cars Ltd sold the Ape 50 that used a 50cc catalysed engine with four-speed transmission in the UK. Like many other Apes, the Ape 50 also comes in different body forms and featured a number of additional specifications; these includes ice cream vending equipment, urban refuse collection vehicle, insulated van, plumbers'/electricians' equipment, and fish counter. These models remain in production at the time of writing.

1993 — Ape TM

Also introduced in 1993 was the Ape TM, which was powered with either a 218cc petrol or a 412cc diesel engine. This model is available at the time of writing.

2006 — Ape Classic

The Ape Classic introduced in 2006 and built in Pune, India, the Ape Classic is powered by a Lombardini 422cc diesel engine and remains in production at the time of writing.

2007 — Ape Calessino

Announced in 2007, the Ape Calessino was a limited edition version with only 999 vehicles being made. With a 1960s' look that was originally designed by Corradino d'Ascanio, the Calessino is a passenger-based version with a collapsible hood and powered by a 422cc engine. In 2012 Piaggio manufactured 100 of the vehicle fitted with an electric motor powered by a Lithium-ion battery. The electric version also features wooden panelling at the sides.

Planet Engineering Ltd

2007 — Ellipse

Planet Engineering in Salisbury, Wiltshire, UK, was formed in February 2007 with the aim of developing a vehicle that could provide the driving experience of the original Morgan three-wheeler. Designed by Alan Pitcairn and Dave Kennell, the Ellipse was an open two-seater powered by a V-twin, 1,575cc S&S engine with a Ford Type 9 five-speed gearbox, giving the vehicle a top speed in excess of 125mph (201km/h) and a 0-60mph (0-96km/h) time of approximately 6.5sec. An automatic version was also available. The chassis at the front of the vehicle was constructed from round DOM (Drawn Over Mandrel) mechanical tubing with unequal-length front wishbones whilst the rear was constructed from square tubing with a mono swinging arm and a BMW R90 bevel box. The body was self-coloured fibreglass and fully bonded to the chassis for increased strength. This helped to provide the vehicle with a weight of less than 850lb. It also featured removable front and rear sections to allow maintenance. It was sold as a turnkey vehicle that featured all new parts and so did not rely on a donor vehicle. In 2011 collaboration was established between Planet Engineering and J A Prestwich Ltd, which provided a brand-new air-cooled, V-twin 1,272cc JAP engine for the Ellipse. Following Pitcairn's death in 2012 the whole project was passed over to J A Prestwich Ltd (see page 126).

The Planet Ellipse prototype fitted with a 1,575cc S&S engine and built in 2007. Planet Engineering

Powerdrive Ltd

1956 — Powerdrive

Compared with other three-wheelers, the Powerdrive was wider than most and able to seat three people abreast. Manufactured from 1956 by Powerdrive Ltd in Wood Green, North London, UK, the Powerdrive had a steel chassis with a sporty aluminium body, which had a fabric hood and side curtains. It was powered by a rear-mounted, 16bhp, fan-cooled, two-stroke, 322cc Anzani engine that drove the single rear wheel via a three-speed gearbox. Despite weighing 895lb, it was claimed to have a top speed of 65mph (105km/h) and average 65mpg (4.3-litre/100km) although 40mph (64km/h) and 55mpg (5.1-litre/100km) appear to be more realistic figures. The Powerdrive, sold mainly through Blue Star Garages Ltd at a cost of £330 plus Purchase Tax, was built until 1958. The design of the vehicle was reused with a number of modifications to produce the Coronet (see page 62).

The **POWERDRIVE**
The most elegant 3-WHEELER ever produced in Britain.
YOURS FOR **£83** DEPOSIT.
Price £412-7-0 incl. Purchase Tax.
65 M.P.G. — 65 M.P.H.
322c.c. Twin Engine.
Road Fund Tax only £5.
3-Speed and Reverse Gearbox.
J. SODERGREN
29-31 PASTURE ST., GRIMSBY. Tel. 3194.

This 1957 advert for the Powerdrive details it as the most elegant three-wheeler ever produced in Britain; a wild claim perhaps, though it certainly was one of the better looking ones of its time. Author's Collection

Below: *Able to seat three people abreast the Powerdrive was a wide and low vehicle fitted with a sporty styled aluminium body.* RUMCar News

Poirier

1928 — M2/M3/F3/F4

The Poirier was first manufactured in France in 1928. The company primarily manufactured single-seat invalid carriages powered by an air-cooled, 47cc Saxonette engine with either a single-speed or two-/three-speed gearbox. The vehicles featured a wide range of adaptations based upon the individual's need. It appeared as models M2 and M3, which had a hand-crank operation, along with the F3 and F4, which had a steering wheel and a two-speed gearbox.

1935 — Monoto

In 1935 the Monoto was introduced; this was available either as a single- or tandem-seater where the passenger sat behind the driver. These vehicles were built on a tubular steel frame with sheet steel body work. Prior to World War 2, the Poirier was powered by either a 175cc Train or a Fichtel & Sachs engine with Peugeot and Gnome-et-Rhône as alternatives. Along with a 'Cardaflex' shaft transmission, the engines were replaced after the war with either the 98cc Fichtel & Sachs or the 125cc Ydral engines. With handlebar steering, there were two hand levers next to the driver — the one on the right for acceleration and the one on the left for gear changes. Production of all vehicles ceased in 1958.

Powers Motor Corporation (PMC)

1974 — PMC AEV

The PMC AEV (Alternative Energy Vehicle) was designed and built in 1974 by Ronald H Powers, the President and founder of Powers Design International (PDI), a design-consultancy company of Newport Beach, California, USA. PDI has grown to become the largest, privately-owned, vehicle design/development company in the USA and has been designing, engineering and building different kinds of prototype vehicles for over 35 years. Powers designed the PMC AEV to be the most 'energy efficient vehicle possible' utilising current technology and to be a testing/proving ground for all new drive train technologies in the future. Powers realised the importance of not only the vehicle itself but also the power-train to meet the owner's driving needs as different owners have different vehicle needs. These include:

The concept drawings for the PMC AEV that was made out of just three major parts. Ronald Powers

Built for the sole purpose of exploring different fuel-efficient technologies, the PMC AEV utilised four different drive trains. Ronald Powers

- Daily short range commuting within the city centre;
- Daily long range commuting 30-50+ miles (48-80km) away;
- High-performance Sports Vehicle;
- Most frugal/efficient use of energy possible.

In the interest of maximum efficiency, the fourth wheel was eliminated, as it was not deemed necessary for stability. The primary design feature was its ability to accept different power-trains with different vehicle architecture. PDI was contracted to engineer, produce the chassis, body tooling, composite body and construct the AEV running prototype. There are plans to mass-produce these AEVs internationally, offering different power-trains for different driving needs.

Planned vehicles are:

- Mid-engine/rear wheel drive, high-mileage turbo diesel with CVT automatic transmission tested at over 80mpg (3-litre/100km);
- Front engine/front-wheel drive, high mileage petrol — over 65mpg (3.6-litre/100km) or 100mpg+ (2.4-litre/100km) with hydrogen system;
- Front engine/rear-wheel drive, high-performance six-cylinder double-overhead cam, 120bhp stock, 160bhp turbocharged;
- Electric power-train, all-wheel drive/three-wheel motors, different price/range battery packages available, offering 110-200-mile+ (177-354km) range.
- External combustion power-train, closed loop system, allowing for most any liquid, gaseous or solid fuels available with no harmful emissions. (This is still under development by SWEEP, Powers' energy development company.)

At the time of writing, Powers is seeking funding for mass production and has no plans to offer individual vehicles or low volume production.

Praga

1952 — Praga Diesel

Founded in 1907, Praga is one of the oldest automobile factories in Prague, Czechoslovakia, building motorcycles, cars and vans. In 1952, the Praga Diesel was introduced; this was designed by Baron von Thyssen. With a top speed of around 28mph (45km/h), it was fitted with an air-cooled, 9bhp diesel engine that powered the single rear wheel and had a two-seat body with a fabric top that could be rolled open. At the time, the company was also building four-wheelers and the three-wheel model was dropped in 1953.

Built to order, the Predator is said have a top speed of 160mph (227km/h). Allan Daniels

Predator Trikes

2008 — Predator

Based in Queensland, Australia, Allan Daniels started work on the Predator trike in 2003 with a desire to build a fuel-efficient high-performance vehicle. Completed in 2008, the first Predator was powered with a Kawasaki 1,000cc motorcycle engine that provided power to the single rear wheel through a six-speed sequential gearbox, though any motorcycle engine can be specified. The vehicle has a lightweight space frame chassis with a roll bar and side

Praga was one of few early three-wheelers that were fitted with a diesel engine. Hans van Scharrenburg

Covered with a fibreglass body, the Predator uses a lightweight space frame chassis that includes a roll bar and side intrusion bars. Allan Daniels

The PMC Motorette in 1913 was not a vehicle to test an emergency stop in as only the single rear wheel was fitted with brakes. Author's Collection

intrusion bars along with a fibreglass body, providing an overall weight of 500kg. It also has a steering and braking system specifically designed for it to counteract the three-wheel characteristics of under steer, braking balance and anti-squat. With a top speed of 160mph (257km/h), the Predator will do 0-60mph (0-96km/h) in 3.62sec and a quarter-mile in 10.35sec at 141mph (227km/h). At the time of writing, the Predator is only built to order with only three vehicles built per annum, each one being unique.

Premier Motor Co (PMC)

1913 — PMC Motorette

Initially called the Premier Motor Co Ltd and based in Birmingham, UK, the company produced four-wheel cars in Belgium under the Premier name and motorcycles in the UK called the Premo. The Premo name was used until 1909 when an injunction was taken out against the company by the Premier Cycle Co of Coventry and so the vehicles then became PMC. In 1913 the company introduced the PMC Motorette; this was an open two-seat vehicle built on a steel tubular frame. It showed strong hints of being based on earlier forecars with a large front seat and a foot well, though the driver sat inside and had the additional protection of a vertical windscreen and a hood. The vehicle was powered by a water-cooled, single-cylinder,

7bhp, 723cc, JAP engine positioned behind the seats. This drove the single rear wheel via an epicyclic two-speed gearbox. A brake was only fitted on the rear wheel though, for an extra £3, brakes could also be fitted to the front wheels as well.

1913 — PMC Motorette Commercial/Omnium

A commercial version of the Motorette was also produced; this used the same chassis and running gear as the standard version. Also sold under the name of Omnium, the vehicle had a single seat at the back and a 5cwt loading area, either a box or a flatbed, positioned between the front wheels. All versions of the Motorette were produced until 1917.

Premier Motor Engineering Co

1919 — Merrall Brown

Located in Bolton, Lancashire, UK, the Premier Motor Engineering Co introduced the Merrall Brown Cyclecar in 1919. Initially powered by an 8bhp, water-cooled JAP engine, later models were fitted with a water-cooled, four-cylinder, 1,500cc Precision engine. The transmission was unique for a three-wheeler in that there were two drive shafts that provided two speeds and a reverse with power going to the single rear wheel by a chain. Although the vehicle was classed as a three-wheeler, the rear wheel consisted of two wheels that were fixed together just a fraction apart from each other, thus

Although classed as a three-wheeler. The Merrall Brown had two wheels at the rear that were fixed together to form a wider wheel. Author's Collection

The Tourette was available with an open body or an enclosed body that had a removable flip-up hard top. Bob Purton

acting as a single wide wheel. All wheels were interchangeable and fitted with polished aluminium disc as standard. The vehicle had a steel chassis with an aluminium body that housed two seats and also had a pram type hood. Production ceased in 1921.

Progress

1930 — Progress

Using Seal commercial vehicles as a base (see page 226), the Progress was built in Percy Street in Hulme, Manchester, UK, from 1930. Like the Seal, the vehicle looked like a motorcycle and sidecar though, with the Progress, the driver sat beside the load in a bucket seat. The Progress used a number of engines, including a 343cc Villiers, a 680cc JAP and a 980cc JAP engine.

1932 — New Progress

In 1932 a new variant of the Progress was introduced; this was called the New Progress, which had a central front wheel. This was fitted with a 680cc JAP engine that sat above the front wheel, driving it via a chain and three-speed with reverse gearbox. Production ceased in 1934.

Progress Supreme Co Ltd

1956 — Tourette

Manufactured in 1956 the Tourette was a three-seat vehicle manufactured in London, UK, by the Carr brothers, who then formed the Progress Supreme Company Ltd. The vehicle was fitted with a two-

stroke, air-cooled, 197cc Villiers engine, which drove the single rear wheel through a four-speed gearbox that had a Dynastart reverse. The vehicle was available with either an aluminium or a fibreglass body that was attached to an Ash frame. The body featured a flip-up hard top that could be removed. Seating was provided for two adults via a single bench seat, with space for a small child behind the seat. Costing £386 10s 5d, the top speed of the vehicle was 55mph (88km/h) with around 35 vehicles being made before production ceased in 1958.

Publix Motor Car Co

1947 — Publix

The Publix was manufactured by the Publix Motor Car Co in Buffalo, New York, USA, between 1947 and 1948. The vehicle had an open six-foot aerodynamic body that was made from aluminium, with no doors or roof, and an aluminium chassis. Power came from an air-cooled, single-cylinder, 1,75bhp Cauffiel engine. This was attached to an unique shock-absorbing rig, which was connected to the drive mechanism and finally to the rear wheels. Another unique feature of the Publix was that the steering wheel could be removed from the left-hand side to the right at will. To save space the vehicle could also be flipped onto its rear end and parked upright.

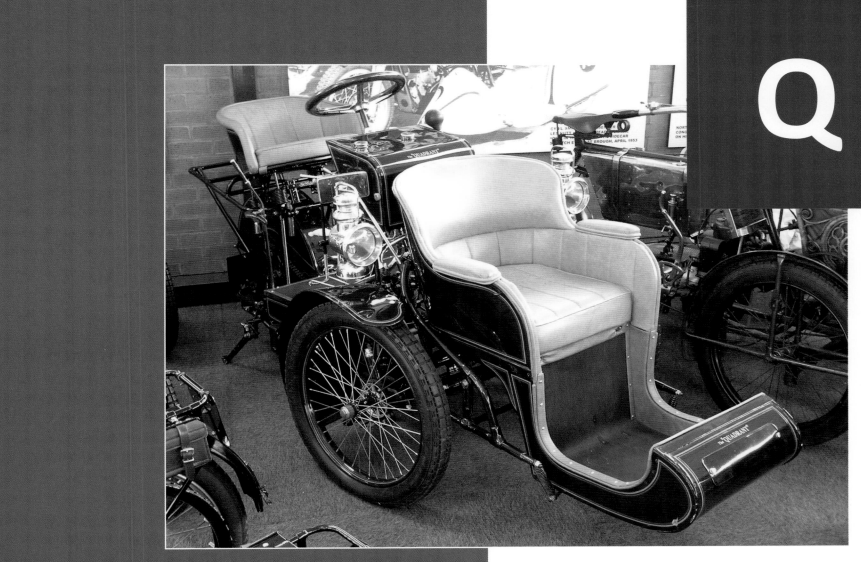

Initially fitted with a single-speed gear the Quadrant Forecar was built from 1903 to 1907. Author's Collection

Quadrant Cycle Co

1903 — Forecar

Founded in 1883 by brothers Walter and William Young, the Quadrant Cycle Co manufactured bicycles and tricycles in Birmingham, UK, before moving on to motorcycles in 1900. In 1903 the Quadrant Forecar was introduced as a single-speed machine that was fitted with either a 2bhp or 3bhp engine that drove the single rear wheel by a chain. A year later a two-speed model arrived. The vehicle had a single padded passenger seat, which was situated just ahead of the two front wheels, whilst the driver sat in motorcycle style at the rear of the vehicle on a saddle with handlebars for steering. The Forecar was built until 1907.

Introduced in 1980, the Trimuter used a new technique in which the body was made from a GRP /foam composite. Robert Q. Riley Enterprises

Quincy-Lynn Enterprises Inc

Although Quincy-Lynn operated from 1974 in the USA, it was in 1978 that a company was formed to create Quincy-Lynn Enterprises Inc. Founded by Robert Quincy Riley and David Lynn Carey, the company developed, amongst other things, a multi-function home gym under the name of 'Lean Machine' along with DIY plans for a vast assortment of vehicles that included cars, campervans, single-track vehicles, hovercraft, boats and, of course, three-wheelers.

1980 — Trimuter

Available as a set of plans, the Trimuter first appeared on the cover of the magazine *Mechanix Illustrated* in February 1980 and went on to become the magazine's most popular project in its 75-year history. Due to the vehicle's futuristic looks, it was also used as a background vehicle in the Arnold Schwarzenegger film *Total Recall* in 1990. Mounted on a steel box chassis, the two-seat body was made from a GRP/foam composite that was a technique pioneered by Quincy-Lynn Enterprises Inc. The original composite comprised polyester resin and glass cloth laminations over a core of rigid urethane foam board stock — fibreglass over a foam core — whilst modern variations sometimes used an epoxy resin or vinyl-ester resin and carbon-fibre-cloth over urethane foam. With this process, the vehicle's creator directly built upon the body itself rather than used a mould. Another unusual feature of the Trimuter for its time was that it was powered by a choice of an electric engine that offered a top speed of 60mph (96.5km/h) with a range of 60 miles (97km) or a 16bhp, two-cylinder, industrial petrol engine that had a top speed of 63mph (101km/h) and a range of 850 miles (1,368km) when fitted with a 17gall fuel tank.

With eight to 10 6V batteries the electric version weighed around 1,400-1,550lb compared with the petrol version at 850lb. The average build time for the vehicle was quoted at 400 to 600 hours.

1983 — Tri-Magnum

The Tri-Magnum, which was designed as a high performance three-wheel sports car, was first featured in *Mechanix Illustrated* in February 1983. The chassis of the Tri-Magnum was a stripped motorcycle chassis minus the fork and front wheel, whilst power came from a Kawasaki KZ900 motorcycle engine. This was then attached to a Volkswagen Beetle front suspension assembly using a simple framework. The aerodynamically shaped body was a sandwich of urethane foam and fibreglass bonded together. The body housed a two-seat cabin with seats side-by-side. In addition, it also featured a lift-up canopy, which had a steel framework embedded into it. Steering was via a conventional automobile steering wheel, whilst gear change was by a 'jet-fighter-style control stick' that emerged from the floor.

Quincy-Lynn Enterprises Inc ceased trading at the beginning of 1986, with all assets being liquidated. However, Riley and Carey both held the rights to publish plans or manufacture the patented products on their own. In 1987, Riley operated as Robert Q Riley Enterprises although plans for all vehicles remained out of print until 1996 when they were all updated/upgraded, becoming available once more through Robert Q Riley Enterprises (see page 217).

Using a stripped motorcycle chassis, the Tri-Magnum incorporates the front suspension assembly from a Volkswagen Beetle. Robert Q Riley Enterprises

A 1927 advert that shows Harding's invalid vehicles being both hand powered and motor driven.
Grace's Guide

Introducing a full body with doors, windscreen and hood the Harding Consort ceased production after 12 vehicles were made. Robert Knight

R A Harding (Bath) Ltd

1926 — Harding Deluxe

From 1921, R A Harding Ltd of Bath, UK, manufactured hand-propelled three-wheelers that came in a form that had a single rear wheel steered by moving side-to-side in the seat. This adjusted the seat's backrest, which, in turn, steered the wheel. Alternatively, a single front wheel was hand powered and steered. In 1926 Harding introduced the Harding Deluxe; this was a motorised version powered by an air-cooled, 122cc Villiers engine. Electric versions were also made; these shared the same foundation as the petrol models but were powered by a 24V or 36V motor. A four-wheel version, called the Pultney, was made alongside the three-wheeler, fitted with a 200cc or 300cc JAP engine. In 1945 the company changed its name to R A Harding (Bath) Ltd.

1948 — New Harding Deluxe

Late 1948 saw the announcement of the New Harding Deluxe models, which were now powered by a larger, fan-cooled, 147cc Villiers engine. They also featured larger wheels along with a new petrol tank.

Consort

In 1956 the Consort model — also known as Harding Mk IV — was introduced. This had a full metal body with open sides and a hood. The vehicle had a single seat. In total 12 vehicles were made. Production of all motorised Harding vehicles ceased in 1966 with the hand-propelled vehicles continuing until 1973.

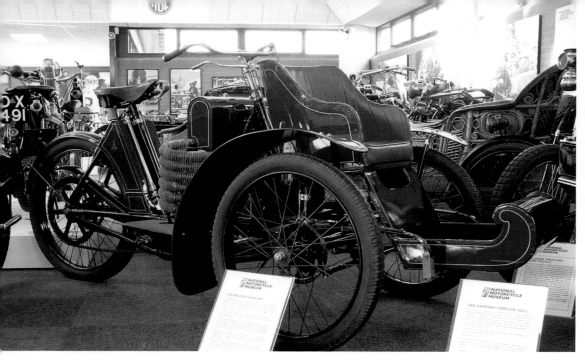

1929 — Karryall

In 1929, in response to the economic climate of the late 1920s, Raleigh again turned its hand to manufacturing three-wheelers. The first of these was the Karryall parcel van, which was based on the Ivy Karryall van, the rights to which Raleigh had acquired. The van was more or less a 500cc motorcycle enclosed into a 5cwt van body with the addition of a third wheel. The front wheel of the van was exposed, giving away its motorcycle construction, and steering was via a steering wheel inside the van. In 1931 the engine was up rated to 600cc and in 1933 a two-seat version became available.

Raleigh

1903 — Raleighette

World renowned for its bicycles, Raleigh was founded in 1887 by Frank Bowden in Nottingham, UK. At the time Raleigh made Safety Bicycles and in 1899 manufactured its first motorcycle. This was basically a bicycle with a 2bhp German Schwan engine which drove the rear wheel by a belt, mounted to the frame. Raleigh modified its motorcycle several times, moving the engine into a sturdier framework.

In 1903 Raleigh created its first tri-car — the Raleighette. This had a 3.5bhp, water-cooled engine and a chain drive to the single rear wheel through a two-speed gear, the control of which was on the handlebars. In addition to the Brooks' special motorcycle saddle for the driver, the vehicle had a large leather upholstered seat, finished in Panhard Red, in between the front wheels for a passenger. In 1906 a 6.5bhp version was made but the company soon began to make a loss and so, from 1908, the model was dropped and Raleigh reverted back to the manufacture of only bicycles and motorcycles.

A 1933 Raleigh Karryall 5cwt van in suitable period livery. Helen Sanders

Raleigh's first and only passenger car, the Safety Seven fitted with four seats and able to achieve around 60mpg. Martin Strange

1933 — Safety Seven

In 1933 Raleigh also introduced its first three-wheel car — the Raleigh Safety Seven. Powered by a twin-cylinder, 742cc engine the Safety Seven was a four-seat vehicle, with an aluminium body fastened onto an Ash framework. With a top speed of around 55mph (88.5km/h) and a fuel consumption of 60mpg (4.7-litre/100km), the Safety Seven sold very well. In 1935, a saloon version of the Safety Seven was introduced though very few were produced as, in the same year, the Motor Department at Raleigh was closed down. The Works Manager (and Chief Designer) of that department, Tom L Williams, then purchased all the equipment and stock and moved to Tamworth, Staffordshire, to carry on building the van in a slightly modified form under a new name — Reliant (see page 204).

Based on the full front sub frame of a Mini, the Ranger Cub was a two-seat kit car. Steve Hole

Designed as a single-seat performance vehicle, the Rayvolution Evo is said to take 10 weeks to build from a kit. Olivier Houllier

Ranger Automotive

1974 — Ranger Cub

Designed by Alan White, the Ranger Cub was a kit-car that was based on the Austin Mini and was available from 1974 until 1976. Produced by Ranger Automotive in Essex, UK, the two-seat Cub had a square tubular frame and a self-coloured fibreglass body, with power coming from the 850cc Mini engine. The full front subframe, including the radiator and suspension, came from the Mini, with the rear of the vehicle using one half of the Mini rear sub frame. A Mk II version was available in 1975; this had a number of enhancements to the design. There was also a four-wheel version called the Ranger Cub 4.

Rayvolution Cars

2008 — Evo

Tony Lafaye used to work for Sivax Inc — a Japanese car design supplier — and, whilst there, designed the X-tile concept car that was exhibited on the Mondial de l'Automobile show in 2004. In 2008 he founded Rayvolution Cars in France and then designed the Evo. The Evo is a kit car that is available in three forms: a starter kit, intermediate kit and a full kit. The full kit provides everything apart from the engine and transmission. Built around a steel tube space frame chassis, the vehicle has a single bucket seat and a fibreglass body, with suspension at the front coming from a Mazda MX-5. Driven by a Suzuki GSX-R 750cc engine, power is sent to the single rear wheel by chain. Build time of the kits is estimated at 10 weeks without the need for mechanical skills. At the time of writing all kits are available.

The Razor is built upon a stainless steel backbone chassis and has seats that are moulded into the main body. Razor Cars

Made from self-coloured fibreglass the body of the Razor features a forward lifting canopy. Razor Cars

Razor Cars

2012 — Razor

Razor Cars was founded by John Barlow and David Chapman, who had been producing kit cars since the 1980s. Based in Lancashire, UK, the company runs alongside the Imperial Motor Co, which is also owned by Barlow and Chapman. Launched in 2012, the Razor is available in kit form only, with kits costing around £4-5,000 and an estimated build cost of around £9,000 and an estimated build time of 100 hours. The body of the Razor is made from self-coloured lightweight GRP, which helps to give the vehicle an overall weight of 500kg. The body is bonded by the factory to a stainless steel backbone chassis to ensure perfect alignment. Access to the Razor is gained by lifting the whole roof canopy, which hinges up and forward assisted by a gas ram. Internally, the seats are moulded into the main body. Power comes from a Hayabusa 1,300cc engine — or any suitable bike engine — that provides power to the single rear wheel. The rear swing arm, wheel and fuel tank are all fitted to a separate subframe, which is assembled off the vehicle and then attached to the body via four bolts. At the time of writing the kits are available.

Reaction Dynamics Inc

1970 — Blue Flame

Driven by Gary Gabelich, Blue Flame — the first vehicle to exceed 1,000km/h — set a new land speed record of 622.407mph (1,001.667km/h) for the flying mile and 630.389mph (1,014.513km/h) for the flying kilometre at the Bonneville Salt Flats in Utah, USA, on 23 October 1970. Designed and built by Reaction Dynamics Inc in Milwaukee, Wisconsin, USA, and sponsored by the American Gas Association, Blue Flame was a rocket-powered vehicle that was 37ft 4.6in (11.394m) long. It consisted of an aluminium semi-monocoque with a nose made from a welded tubular steel frame and was covered in an aluminium skin. It was fitted with a liquid-propellant engine of the variable thrust type that provided 22,500lb of thrust the equivalent to 58,000bhp. It was fuelled by a combination of high-test peroxide and liquefied natural gas (LNG), pressurised by helium gas. Although the vehicle was a three-wheel design, it had two wheels at the front that sat directly opposite each other. After breaking the land speed record, Blue Flame went on a promotional tour and was not used for any further record attempts. Blue Flame's mile record stood until 1983, whilst its kilometre record was not broken until 1997. At the time of writing, Blue Flame is a permanent exhibit in the Sinsheim Auto & Technik Museum, near Heidelberg in Germany.

In 1970, the Blue Flame set a new land speed record of 622.407mph (1,001.667km/h) for the flying mile and 630.389mph (1,014.513km/h) for the flying kilometre. Author's Collection

Reliant Motor Co

The Reliant three-wheeler is perhaps the most familiar three-wheeler in the UK, with almost everyone at least aware of the Reliant Robin model (though often misnaming it as 'Robin Reliant'). Less well known is the sheer number of three-wheel models that Reliant actually produced. In the UK especially, the Reliant is often a vehicle used by the media as a joke usually overemphasising the perceived instability of the Reliant; however, in reality, Reliant was one of the most successful manufacturers of three-wheelers and its vehicles were much more stable than the media would have you believe. Reliant also made four-wheelers alongside its three-wheeler range over the years, with both an economy and sports range of vehicles. The Reliant 850cc engine has found its way into many items, including fire pumps, lawn mowers, boats and, in the 1980s, there was even the Quasar Motorcycle that was a revolutionary covered motorbike capable of 100mph+ (161+km/h). All Reliant three-wheelers had the single wheel at the front.

Originally formed as the Reliant Engineering Co Ltd in 1935, the first Reliant prototype was built by Tom Lawrence Williams in his garden at Kettlebrook, Tamworth, UK, with the assistance of E S Thompson. Williams, a former Works Manager at Raleigh, had worked on the Raleigh Safety Seven and, when that company made the decision to cease production of three-wheelers, Williams then left Raleigh to build his own three-wheeler. He completed and licensed the vehicle as 'The Reliant' on 1 January 1935. It is believed Williams called the company Reliant as some of the old Raleigh parts he used had the initial 'R' on them and so he needed a company name starting with the same letter; Reliant was the first name he found in the dictionary that suited his needs

One of the oldest Reliants known to survive is this 1935 model powered by a single-cylinder JAP engine and restored to resemble the original 1934 prototype. Author's Collection

1935 — 7cwt

The first production Reliant was delivered on 4 June 1935; this was a three-wheel 7cwt van powered by an air-cooled, single-cylinder, 600cc JAP engine with a chain drive to the back axle. The chassis was box steel with motorcycle-type girder forks at the front. The body was made from aluminium panels attached to a wooden coach-built frame. The vehicle had a single seat set in the centre of the vehicle along with a central steering wheel and was manufactured until January 1938, with 171 vehicles being made. At the time of writing there are three known survivors.

1938 — 10cwt

Reliant soon realised that it needed something that was more car like and had more power. Therefore, in March 1936, a new 10cwt van was introduced. This used a 747cc, V-twin, water-cooled JAP engine with shaft drive and spiral bevel rear axle. Whilst visually appearing the same as the 7cwt, the 10cwt had a longer wheelbase and inside two front seats that were side-by-side. The 10cwt also remained in production until January 1938 with 528 vehicles made.

1938 — 8cwt/12cwt

Reliant was forever looking to improve its vehicles and it was during a visit to the 1937 Commercial Vehicle Show that Reliant acquired

From 1938 to mid-1939 the Reliant 8cwt and 12cwt van were fitted with an Austin 7 engine. Author's Collection

the supply of the 7bhp Austin 7 engine and gearbox units for its vehicles. The first Austin 7-powered Reliant, the 8cwt van, was delivered on 12 March 1938. This not only used the Austin 7 engine and gearbox but also carburettor, petrol pump, starter motor and dynamo amongst other parts. In July 1938 a slightly larger 12cwt van was added to the line-up; this was also powered by the Austin 7 engine. These models were, however, short-lived as late in 1938 it was announced that Austin was to discontinue production of the unit

1939 — 6cwt/8cwt/12cwt

With news that the Austin 7 engine was to be discontinued, Reliant, not wanting to return to a motorcycle engine, decided to produce its own engine and Williams with Thompson produced an almost carbon copy of the Austin 7 engine. However, with several internal differences, parts were not interchangeable. The new Reliant was a 747cc, four-cylinder, side-valve, water-cooled engine that produced 14bhp at 3,500rpm and again drove the rear axle by a prop shaft. In September 1939 the Reliant-powered Reliant was delivered; it was installed in both the 8cwt and 12cwt van models. Production, however, only continued until 1940 when, following the start of World War 2, Reliant turned its attention to machining parts for the war effort. During the war over one and a half million parts were machined. At the end of hostilities, Reliant was able to revive the manufacture of the 8cwt, with the first one being delivered on 13 March 1946. The 12cwt model followed in February 1947. In 1949, in an attempt to modernise the vehicles, small windows were added behind the doors. The 12cwt continued in production until March 1950, when it was replaced with the Regent 10cwt. The 8cwt remained in production until September 1954 although its quoted payload was reduced from 6cwt to 5cwt in 1950.

1950 — Regent 10cwt

Although the 1950 Regent used the same chassis and 747cc Reliant engine as its predecessor, its body had been totally redesigned, becoming much more 'square-rigged' in appearance. The Regent 10cwt also featured steel pressed wheels, replacing the earlier spoked wheels, and was fitted with 12V electrics. Production ceased in September 1956.

1952 — Prince Regent 6cwt

With an unladen weight of 953lb, the 1952 Prince Regent 6cwt van was too heavy to be classed as a tricycle for UK licensing laws and so, it is believed, that this was an export model. It was manufactured alongside the standard 1950 6cwt model until September 1954. No survivors of this model are believed to exist.

1952 — Regal Mk I

In 1952 T L Williams decided to modify the body of the Reliant van to accommodate four people and so, in 1952, the Regal Mk I was exhibited at Earl's Court. The model entered full production in January 1953. The Mk I had a complete new chassis made of 18-gauge box section steel upswept at the rear to clear the rear axle. The single front wheel was attached to a stub axle on a single forged arm linked to a traverse torsion bar suspension system bolted across the front of the chassis. The open body had two doors and was made from aluminium

Below Left: *A 1949 Reliant 8cwt van; this one still in use as a daily workhorse at the Black Country Living Museum in Dudley.* Geoff Payne

Below: *Right from the start Reliant found great success in exporting its vehicles around the globe. This particular vehicle was a Reliant Rickshaw built upon an early Reliant van chassis.* Author's Collection

panels fixed to an Ash frame along with a convertible hood for protection against the elements. Power was provided by the same 747cc Reliant side-valve engine used in the girder fork Reliants. This drove the rear axle via a four-speed (plus reverse) non-synchromesh gearbox. With a top speed of 65mph (105km/h) and being capable of 50mpg (5.6-litre/100km), the Mk I was very well received.

1954 — Regent Mk II 10cwt

In September 1954, in an attempt to update the Regent, Reliant introduced the Regent II 10cwt van. This had the nose cone off the Regal Mk II coupé hiding the exposed girder forks.

1954 — Regal Mk II

The Regal Mk II, released in May 1954, looked almost identical to the Mk I, though a number of alterations had been made. These included a smaller radiator grille, which no longer had an additional magnesium cast grille attached, and an integral windscreen surround that replaced the separate frame on the Mk I. By November 1955, Reliant was starting to experiment with fibreglass and the Mk II saloon appeared with not only a hard top made from the material but also a fibreglass bonnet and rear wings. Reliant also created a Mk II based 'Utility' vehicle; this was a 5cwt van with two rear opening doors that remained in production until May 1958. The saloon and coupé versions were replaced with the Mk III.

In an attempt to update the girder-forked Reliant van, the 1954 Regent Mk II 10cwt version featured the nose cone from the Reliant Regal Mk II passenger car. Kerry Croxton

Reliant produced its first all fibreglass vehicle with the Regal Mk III in 1956 pictured here with Reliant employee Marlene Gaskin. Marlene Gaskin

1956 — Regal Mk III

By October 1956, Reliant's skills in fibreglass had developed so much that its first all fibreglass saloon vehicle was introduced in the form of the Regal Mk III. This model can lay claim to the first mass produced full-fibreglass-bodied car. In a bid to strengthen the car, the Mk III was very curvaceous with not a straight edge anywhere. To make the vehicle more car-like, the body also incorporated dummy wings either side at the front. Whilst the chassis remained the same as the Mk II the body attached to it was now five inches longer and six inches wider. In addition, whilst still being powered by Reliant's side-valve engine, the Mk III now had a synchromesh gearbox.

1958 — Regal Mk IV

Continuous improvements resulted in the Regal Mk IV being announced in September 1958. With the Mk IV the original front torsion bar suspension system and the overly complicated double-cranked steering arrangement were replaced with a simplified suspension system using a box section radius arm with an Armstrong combined coil-spring and hydraulic damper. The steering system was also simplified with a drop arm from the steering box with a single-track rod to the stub axle. With the exception of drop-down windows in the doors and a few other subtle changes, the Mk IV looked similar to the Mk III. The new version did not remain in production long before it was replaced with the Mk V. There was also an equivalent Mk IV 5cwt van.

1959 — Regal Mk V

The Regal Mk V, whilst remaining the same under the body, was introduced in June 1959 with a totally revamped body. This was longer and wider and also included separate chrome bumpers. The Mk V saloon was also the first Reliant to have external boot access at the rear of the vehicle. In addition, both the 5cwt van and saloon models had twin windscreen wipers. All window glass was now safety glass, except for the sliding door windows that were Perspex.

1960 — Regal Mk VI/ Mk VI-A

The Mk VI was Reliant's last side-valve model and the last model to feature a coachwork built body built with an Ash frame on a steel box chassis with a fibreglass body. The Mk VI was very similar to the

Mk V, though now it had a much deeper windscreen and, at the front, the separate indicator and sidelights were built into one unit — resulting in white indicator light rather than amber — whilst at the back of the saloon all the lights were merged into one combined unit. The van retained separate rear lights as on the Mk V. The saloon also had improved passenger space, which resulted in an overhang over the top of the rear window, whilst the interior now had a large central speedometer on the dashboard.

When the Regal 3/25 replaced the saloon model there was, at that time, no van version and so the Mk VI van continued to be made until 1963 — when the 3/25 van was released — though now powered by the new 598cc, OHV engine; this became known as the Mk VI-A. The Mk VI van was the only vehicle in Reliant's history that could be purchased new with either a side- or an overhead-valve engine. A total of 500 Mk VI-A vans were built.

1962 — Regal 3/25/Regal 3/25 Super

In 1962 a major step forward was taken with the introduction of the Regal 3/25; '3' indicated the number of wheels and '25' signified 25bhp. Instead of an internal wooden frame, the 3/25 had a unitary construction body of reinforced glass fibre. Polyester was moulded in two major units — outer and inner; these were then bonded together and bolted to a steel chassis. The vehicle was also powered by Reliant's new 598cc OHV engine; this was Britain's first flowline production light alloy motor engine. The Regal 3/25 had a new box section steel chassis and a more refined interior compared with the side-valve Regals. The 3/25 was tremendously successful, breaking all previous production and sales records. In 1964 the company was renamed from the Reliant Engineering Co Ltd to the Reliant Motor Co Ltd.

By 1965 it was thought that the model was starting to look dated and so Reliant called in Ogle Designs Ltd, which redesigned the body. The redesign included giving the front end a much neater appearance, which was much more aerodynamic compared with the previous large rectangular grille. As a result, the restyled 3/25 was sold as the 3/25 Super whilst the old 3/25 became the standard model with its price reduced. The standard

The Regal Mk VI saloon was the last Reliant passenger car to use the 747cc side-valve engine and a hardwood frame. Caroline Payne

Following a face-lift the Regal 3/25 became the Regal 3/25 Super with a more streamlined front end. Thomas Touw

3/25 5cwt van remained as the standard, whilst the 3/25 Super based van, announced in March 1966, became the Supervan. The names changed again in September 1967, when various changes to the cylinder head, exhaust manifold and a new carburettor increased the power from 24.5bhp to 26bhp. This resulted in the 3/25 Super saloon becoming the 3/25 De-Luxe saloon and the 5cwt Supervan becoming the 5cwt Supervan II.

1966 — 10cwt Pick-up

Reliant sales were not only booming in the UK but also worldwide as its new Managing Director Ray Wiggin — appointed following Williams' death in 1964 — ignited Reliant's profitability, exporting vehicles around the world. As a result a 7cwt capacity 3/25 was introduced in May 1966 aimed purely at the export market. This was powered by the same 598cc Reliant engine and had the rear part of the bodywork removed to leave just the Supervan based cab. The chassis was cut and had a 14in extension welded in to give the vehicle a longer wheelbase and allow a specialist body to be mounted.

Although it was rated at 7cwt, it was soon found that it could easily manage 10cwt and so became the 10cwt. This model was superseded a year later by the TW9.

1967 — TW9

Reliant had been exporting the 10cwt Regal as a pick-up model to markets overseas and its success was such that, in 1967, the company created a new pick-up type vehicle — the TW9 — with a 16cwt carrying capacity. The TW9 was much larger than other Reliant three-wheelers and had a fibreglass cab attached to a ladder frame chassis that was easily adapted to be any kind of vehicle such as a pick-up truck or a road sweeper. Initially, it was powered by Reliant's 598cc and then the 701cc engine; however, it was soon discovered that these could not cope with the extremely mountainous terrain in some provinces and, from 1968, a much larger 1,200cc engine from a Triumph Herald was sourced and fitted to all vehicles purchased by Mediterranean Engine Brand Enterprises Association (MEBEA).

Originally designed for export to the Mediterranean and the Middle East, the vehicle also found a good market in the UK from 1972. In 1977 the production rights were sold off to BTB Engineering Ltd (see page 48), which renamed the vehicle the BTB Ant.

The Reliant Supervan III fitted with a 700cc OHV engine and capable of a 5cwt payload. Author's Collection

1970 — Bond Bug/Sprint

In 1969 Reliant took over Bond Cars Ltd, its biggest rival at the time. In August 1970, Reliant ceased the production of all Bond models but, prior to this, it had commissioned Ogle Design Ltd to produce a sports three-wheeler for the 'young' generation. This was to be sold under the Bond name as the Bond Bug. Introduced in June 1970, the early Bond Bugs were manufactured at the Bond factory in Preston, but shortly afterwards, when the factory closed, Bug production was transferred to Reliant at Tamworth. The Bond Bug used all the mechanics of a Reliant Regal, including the 701cc water-cooled engine and an early modified Reliant Robin box steel chassis. The only non-Regal part was the coil spring suspension at the rear of the car; this was used instead of the Regal's telescopic damper. The Bug featured a complete glassfibre body in a futuristic wedge shape. It had a lift-up front canopy, which incorporated the side windows and allowed access to the vehicle. Every Bug made was painted bright tangerine with black seats and trim, though a handful of lime green and white Bond Bugs were also produced for advertising purposes. There were three models: the 700, which was a stripped out

1968 — Regal 3/30

Reliant's production was such that, in 1968, the 50,000th 3/25 was delivered. In the same year, the 701cc engine was introduced and so, remaining essentially the same vehicle visually, the Regal 3/25 now became the Regal 3/30 — the '30' now signified 30bhp — and the 5cwt Supervan II became the 5cwt Supervan III. Like the 3/25, the 3/30 was extremely popular, especially the 21E version that offered an additional 21 extra items, including extra dials and cosmetic additions. The 3/30 received several minor changes; these included, in 1971, a 'luxury black' interior to give the vehicle the same sort of look as the company's four-wheel Scimitar sports car range. Production was such that, in December, 1972 Reliant produced its 100,000th OHV Regal and, when the model finally ceased production on 31 October 1973, over 110,000 OHV Regals had been built.

Although using the Bond name, the Bond Bug was a Reliant product that used Reliant Regal mechanics and an early modified Robin chassis. Author's Collection

economy version; the 700E, which included side panels, styling refinements and 29bhp engine; and, the 700ES, similar to the 700E but with a high compression 701cc engine delivering 31bhp. However, the Bond Bug was not as successful as Reliant had hoped and so, after some 2,268 vehicles were built, production ceased in 1974 to provide more space to manufacture the Reliant Robin.

In 1995 an attempt was made to revive the Bond Bug in a modernised form; this resulted in the Sprint. With looks that had more than a passing resemblance to the original Bond Bug, the Sprint was given a launch date but the company went into receivership and so the project was abandoned.

1973 — Robin (750-850)

The Reliant Robin is perhaps the most iconic of all Reliant's three-wheelers. Introduced in October 1973, the Robin was a totally new vehicle from the ground up with a new fibreglass body, which was designed by Ogle Designs Ltd, along with a box steel chassis and a new engine. The OHV Reliant engine was now uprated to 748cc, offering 32bhp and a top speed of around 80mph (129km/h). Available as a saloon or a van, the former had a lift-up hatch window at the rear, whilst the van had a single rear door. The creature comforts in the Robin moved on considerably, with the Super model having numerous dials and switches on the dashboard, including, for the first time in a Reliant three-wheeler, a built-in radio. The standard model was less well appointed. The four-speed with reverse gearbox now had synchromesh on all gears. The first Robins were produced until 1975 when it received minor changes and a larger 40bhp, 848cc engine with a SU carburettor replacing the Zenith downdraught used previously. By 1976 an estate version was added to the line-up; this used a van body with windows in the rear. Originally it was to be a limited edition model; however, the demand for it was so great that it remained in production until January 1982 when the Robin model ceased production.

Perhaps the most iconic of Reliant three-wheelers is the Reliant Robin, this particular one being a later Mk 1 version fitted with an 850cc engine.
Author's Collection

1982 — Rialto/Rialto 2

In January 1982, Reliant introduced the Rialto, which, whilst still using the 850cc engine, now featured a galvanised chassis. Whilst the interior was essentially the same as the Robin, albeit with different dials and switches on the dashboard, the body was sharper and more streamlined, resembling the Austin Mini Metro from the same era. Available as a saloon, estate and a van, the Rialto actually managed to use the same side and rear doors as the previous Robin. The saloon, however, was to receive a drop-down tailgate below the rear window; this severely hampered loading the vehicle from the back.

By 1984 the Rialto 2 was announced; this was almost identical apart from a few different cosmetic differences. It was now powered by a new version of the 848cc known as the HT — High-Torque-Economy — engine. This had its torque increased by 7.3% to 49.5lb that, with various changes, gave a 14.3% reduction in engine speed and thus greater fuel economy. It had a top speed that was said to exceed 100mph (161km/h). The Rialto 2 was also available in saloon, van and estate versions. In 1986, the Rialto saloon became a hatchback, with the rear hatch and window lifting as one. In the same year, the van model was discontinued although it reappeared again in 1990. Production of all Rialto models ceased in September 1993.

1989 — Robin (Mk II)

Such was the fame of the previous Reliant Robin that the name was reintroduced in 1989 with the Reliant Robin LX, This is often referred to as the Robin Mk II. The new Robin closely followed the styling of the Rialto, though it was given a new nose incorporating Ford Fiesta Mk II headlights and a much smaller radiator grille. Initially, only the hatchback model was available but this was supplemented by the arrival of the Supervan — now based on the Robin Mk II — in 1996.

The 1990s were a turbulent time for Reliant. The company called in the receivers on 25 October 1990. The company was then brought by Beans Engineering for an estimated figure of £1.5 million. However, Beans itself was to call in the receivers in November 1994. Reliant was acquired by the Avonex Group on 16 January 1995; in December 1995, this company also had to call in the receivers. Reliant was then purchased in April 1996 by 'a consortium of Businessmen'. From this point onwards business, for Reliant, had returned to normal and, by the end of August 1996, production of the Reliant Robin had resumed.

1999 — Robin (Mk III)

Reliant production ceased in Tamworth in late 1998 and, in January 1999, the company moved to a new purpose-built factory at Burntwood. Its name also changed to Reliant Cars Ltd. In late February, the company introduced a new Reliant Robin Hatchback for the new Millennium. This had a completely fresh design and represented the first major change made to the Reliant Robin for 10 years. This model became known as the Robin Mk III. The new design, whilst still having an interior similar to the original 1973 Robin, now featured a curved front end that utilised Vauxhall Corsa headlights.

After an announcement on 26 September 2000, Reliant ceased making three-wheelers in February 2001 although original plans had been to stop production in December 2000. To mark 65 years of three-wheel production — though it was actually 66 years by the time the last Reliant was made — Reliant built 65 Special Edition Robins — the Robin 65 — that were individually numbered with a plaque on the dashboard. The last Reliant Robin was collected by its owner on 14 February 2001. Two months afterwards, Reliant moved its premises to Cannock, and at the time of writing still exists as Reliant Partsworld Ltd selling spare parts.

2001 — Robin BN-1/BN-2

B & N Plastics began production on 30 April 2001 in Suffolk, UK, under licence to the Reliant Motor Co Ltd (see page 26).

Replicar

1985 — Cursor Microcar

In 1985 Replicar Ltd in Kent, UK, produced the Cursor Microcar. The car was designed by Alan Hatswell and created to allow 16-year-olds the chance to drive a car on the UK roads using only a moped licence. This meant that most buyers would potentially only keep the car for one year as they could then drive a full size car when they turned 17 years old.

The body of the Cursor was constructed from reinforced fibreglass that was mounted onto a tubular steel chassis. As the fibreglass body was made, pigment was added to produce a self-coloured body shell. The vehicle was powered by an air-cooled, 49cc, Suzuki CS50 engine that drove the single rear wheel through a three-speed gearbox. As the Cursor was in effect a moped, its design speed was 26mph (42km/h) with a fuel consumption of around 90mpg (3.1-litre/100km). In 1985 the Cursor cost £2,200; in comparison a standard two-wheel moped cost around £1,000. A two-seat version was also built though production of both types ceased in 1987 with just over 100 single-seat and fewer than 10 two-seat Cursors being built.

Introduced as a limited edition of 65 vehicles, the Robin 65 was the last Reliant to be made by Reliant with the last vehicle leaving the factory on 14 February 2001. Reliant Motors Ltd

Repton Engineering Works

1904 — Repton

The Repton was built in 1904 by the Repton Engineering Works, Repton, Derbyshire, UK. The vehicle was a very small open single-seater that was powered by a 4bhp, water-cooled, single-cylinder engine. This was attached to a two-speed epicyclic gearbox in which top gear was direct. As a result, a maximum speed of 25mph (40km/h) was possible.

Rex Motor Manufacturing Co

1901 — Rex Tri-Car

The Rex Motor Manufacturing Co was established in Coventry, UK, in 1901 as a merger between the Birmingham Motor Manufacturing & Supply Co and Allard & Co. In the same year it introduced the Rex Tri-Car; this was powered by a 550cc engine that drove the single rear wheel. The driver sat at the back of the vehicle with handlebar controls, whilst the passenger sat in a seat positioned between the front two wheels. On some models the seat also doubled up as a storage box when the seat was not in use. A Rex was advertised by the company in 1904 as having run for 886 miles (1,426 km) from Land's End to John O'Groats in 48 hours and 36min.

1904 — Rexette

In 1904 the Rexette was introduced; this featured a conventional steering wheel in place of the handlebars. In addition, the driver now had a padded bucket seat whilst the front seat was now equipped with a wrap-around canvas cover to protect the passenger from the weather. Powered by a 5bhp engine that drove the single rear wheel via a two-speed gearbox, the Rexette was made until 1908.

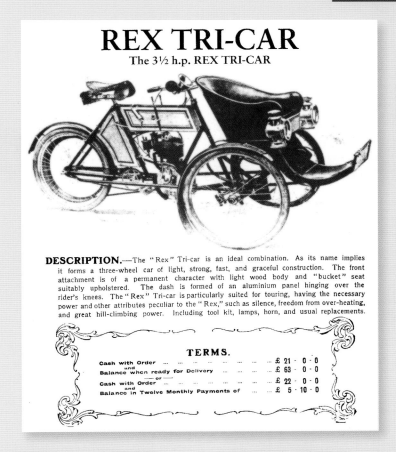

A 1903 brochure for the Rex Tri-Car that notes its attributes as silent and offering freedom from over-heating. Author's Collection

Reynold Jackson & Co Ltd

1899 — Doctors' carriage/ Miscellaneous

Founded in 1899 Reynold Jackson & Co Ltd of London, UK, produced its first three-wheeler — a Doctors' carriage. This was a two-seater powered by a 3.5bhp De Dion engine. The company went on to build a number of three-wheelers powered by De Dion engines. The engine was replaced in 1913 by a JAP 12bhp, V-twin. The vehicles used a Lacost & Battmann chassis, in which the single rear wheel was driven by a chain. Later versions were available in both car and parcel van models, with the latter using a heavier car chassis as the company was also manufacturing four-wheelers as well. Production of all vehicles ceased in 1917.

With virtually no bodywork, the Ribble Tricar was designed for just one person. John Rothwell

Ribble Motors

1900 — Tricar/ Tandem

Ribble Motors was established in 1900 in Eastbank Street, Southport, Lancashire, UK, by Messrs Jackson & Kinnings, who appear to have traded as both Ribble Motors and Jackson & Kinnings. The Ribble 4.5bhp Tandem and the 8bhp single-seat Tricar were both fitted with water-cooled engines, which provided power to the single rear wheel by chains. Both models were built on a tubular steel frame with forks of forged steel. More unusual for this period is the inclined steering wheel and the deep bucket driver's seat with the body built up around it. Below the leather seat was a large drawer for tools and a cupboard for accumulator and coil. A 1905 catalogue for the vehicles states that 'no pains have been spared to bring this popular and handy type of vehicle to perfection'. Manufacture ceased three years later, in 1908.

Rickett

1858 — Steam Carriage

As a manufacturer of agricultural implements, Thomas Rickett started to make steam engines in Buckingham, UK, in 1857 and, a year later, produced a steam plough. As a result of witnessing this in action, the Marquess of Stafford then ordered a steam carriage; this was completed in 1858. With a claimed top speed of 19mph (30.5km/h), the carriage was driven by a large steam engine, which had pistons either side of the boiler that drove the huge right-hand side rear wheel. All three wheels had brakes and iron tyres. A padded bench sat ahead of the boiler; this could seat three people side-by-side, with the person on the right operating the regulator and steering the smaller single front wheel by a tiller. A boilerman was also required to sit at the back of the vehicle. In 1860 Rickett completed a 150-mile journey at an average speed of 12mph (19km/h) in a second vehicle produced for the Earl of Caithness. The Earl himself drove the vehicle, which differed slightly to the original, with Rickett acting as engineman. Although advertised as being available for £180-200, it is believed that no further examples were completed.

Ricketts

1972 — Gilcolt

Ricketts was a Reliant dealer in Streatham, UK. In 1972 it created the Gilcolt; this was based on a Reliant Regal chassis and running gear. It had a fibreglass body enhanced by gull-wing doors either side an extended nose. The Gilcolt was sold in both kit form and as a complete car, though no more than four vehicles are believed to have been made.

With its sleek shape and gull-wing doors the Gilcolt was built around a Reliant Regal chassis and running gear. Author's Collection

Riley Cycle Co Ltd

1900 — Royal Riley

Riley was originally based around a family of weavers that manufactured weaving machines. William Riley Junior took over the family business in 1870. Riley then acquired the Coventry-based cycle company Bonnick & Co Ltd in 1890, with both companies eventually merging in 1896 to form the Riley Cycle Co Ltd in Coventry. Up until 1900 the company mainly produced bicycles although it had produced a prototype four-wheel car in 1899; this, however, was never put into production. It was at the 1900 National Cycle Show that a Royal Riley motor tricycle, with a 2.5bhp De Dion engine, was exhibited. The Royal Riley was essentially a motorised version of the pedal tricycle that was also manufactured by the company; there were, however, problems in converting it.

1902 — Tricar

Riley experimented with a three-wheel car from 1902; this was planned to be light and carry two passengers and resulted in its first Tricar in 1904. This showed strong signs of being based around a motorcycle with the driver sitting at the rear astride a saddle. It used a 4.5bhp, single-cylinder, water-cooled engine designed and built by the Riley Engine Co. This company had been founded in 1903 by William Riley's son, Percy, who was working on a design for an 8bhp, water-cooled engine. The engine was built into the frame and used a two-speed gearbox driven by a primary chain with a secondary chain drive from the outer side of the box to the hub of the rear road wheel.

Fitted with an electric motor the 1896 Riker was fuelled by lead-sulphuric acid batteries. Author's Collection

Riker Electric Motor Co

1896 — Riker

The Riker was first manufactured by the Riker Electric Motor Co in New York, USA, in 1896. Designed by Andrew Riker, the vehicle was to prove a success at racing. His first electric vehicle was a two-seat phaeton that had a range of 25 miles (40km) using a series of lead/sulphuric acid batteries. The vehicle itself had a tubular steel frame and a Riker electric motor fitted at the rear with drive going to the single rear wheel. With three forward and two reverse speeds, the vehicles proved to be very fast — compared with other vehicles at that time — and, despite competing against petrol engined cars, won a race at Providence. The vehicles continued to be sporty and, in 1900, a special low-slung torpedo racer was manufactured. This instantly established a number of records for electric cars, including achieving a mile in one minute 46sec. From 1899 Riker also produced a four-seat vehicle and a truck. In 1900, the company merged with the Electric Vehicle Co with only the trucks continuing to be made under the Riker name until production ceased later in the same year. Andrew Riker joined the Overman Automobile Co in 1902 and designed cars and trucks for Locomobile.

A 1904 Riley Tricar with this particular vehicle reputed to be the oldest Riley in the world still running. John Cleve Graham

Unlike most three-wheelers of the time, the Riley Tricar also featured a starting handle that fitted into the rear end of the engine shaft. With the 1905 version of the Tricar, the appearance became much more car-like with changes that included swapping the saddle for a bucket seat. In addition, the handlebars were replaced by a steering wheel and it now had a choice of either the air cooled 4bhp engine for 70 guineas or three water-cooled engines — the 4.5bhp for 85 guineas, the 6bhp for 120 guineas and the 9bhp for 130 guineas. The 9bhp Riley Tricar often swept the board in competitions. Its only real rival was the Singer Tricar, which was similar in design and was fitted with the Riley engine. Amongst other trophies the Tricar received a gold medal for making a 125-mile non-stop journey on just 2¾gall of petrol. In 1905 and 1906 the Tricar appeared regularly in published competition results for hill climbs, reliability runs and trials. The Tricar was eventually phased out in 1907 in favour of a new four-wheel vehicle that Riley had been developing since 1905.

With an exo-skeletal fully triangulated steel space, the MEV tR1ke is available in either a kit form or as a turnkey vehicle. Steve Hole

Road Track Race Ltd
2010 — MEV tR1ke

Introduced in 2010 and designed by Stuart Mills, the MEV tR1ke is an open two-seat vehicle that has an exo-skeletal fully-triangulated steel space frame with a fibreglass front end. Manufactured by Road Track Race Ltd in Nottingham, UK, the MEV tR1ke is available in either a kit form or as a turnkey vehicle. In a kit form the vehicle uses a 1998-2006 Yamaha R1 motorcycle as a donor vehicle; this provides engine, gearbox, swinging arm, rear wheel, chain drive, wiring loom, clocks and ignition whilst the kit provides all other components that are required. With fully adjustable suspension to change ride height and damping, the MEV tR1ke uses a 150+bhp, four-cylinder, 998cc Yamaha R1 motorcycle engine that powers the single rear wheel through a six-speed sequential gearbox (with an electric reverse being an optional extra). A turbo kit is also available for the RI to boost the power up to 235bhp. At the time of writing the vehicle is still in production.

The XR3 is a hybrid vehicle that has a diesel engine driving the front wheels and an electric motor that is able to drive the rear wheel. Robert Q Riley Enterprises

Robert Q Riley Enterprises

Based in the USA, Robert Q Riley Enterprises began in 1987 with Robert Q Riley as a design consultancy specialising in product design and development. It became Robert Q Riley Enterprises LLC in 2005. Previously Riley had been the President and half owner of Quincy-Lynn Enterprises Inc (see page 198) and, after that closed in 1986, he retained the rights to publish plans for products that included the Trimuter and the Tri-Magnum. Along with many other innovations Riley also created further vehicles including the Pegasus hovercraft, recumbent bicycles, high-speed boat and the XR3 hybrid three-wheeler that are sold as a set of DIY plans ready for the owner to build themselves completely from scratch.

1980 — Trimuter

Designed by Quincy-Lynn Enterprises Inc, the Trimuter was powered by either an electric engine or a 16bhp, two-cylinder industrial engine. The body was made from a fibreglass/urethane foam composite that housed a two-seat cabin.

1983 — Tri-Magnum

The Tri-Magnum, which was also designed by Quincy-Lynn Enterprises Inc, though the latest plans have been updated. These include a change to the engine, with the preferred unit now being a Honda Gold Wing — GL1800 — as this also has a reverse gear.

2008 — XR3

Over 2,500 advanced order reservations were placed for a set of plans for the XR3 during its two-year development phase. Announced in August 2008, the XR3 Personal Transit Vehicle (PTV) was unveiled as a 'super-fuel-efficient two passenger plug in hybrid' that achieves 125mpg (2.2-litre/100km) when diesel alone and the equivalent of 225mpg (1.2-litre/100km) when diesel and electric power are used in series. Available as a set of DIY plans, the vehicle has a steel chassis with large steel beam crumple zones and a fibreglass/urethane foam composite body, which features a clam-shell type canopy that lifts from the back to allow access to the vehicle. It uses a Volkswagen type 1 transmission and is powered by both a Kubota D902 industrial engine and an advanced DC eight-

Available as a set of plans, the XR3 features a clam shell-type canopy that lifts forward to allow access. Robert Q Riley Enterprises

inch (200mm) motor. It has a three-mode design in which the vehicle can be powered independently by either the diesel or the electric motor or utilise both, using the electric motor as an electric supercharger. The two front wheels are powered by the diesel engine whilst the single rear wheel is driven by the electric motor. The vehicle uses a Lithium-Ion battery pack that, in 1.5 hours, can achieve 80% of its full charge by plugging it into any domestic outlet. With a range of 40-50 miles (64-80km) on battery power alone, the XR3 can achieve 375 miles (603 km) on thee gallons of fuel when switching the car to diesel power.

At the time of writing, a new company is being formed in Atlanta, Georgia, USA, to manufacture a vehicle based on the XR3 design. Several versions are planned with Riley being one of the principals/owners as well as the Director of Vehicle Design. Plans for all vehicles detailed are available when this book was compiled.

Rogers Inter Auto Inc

1985 — Rascal

Designed by Blythe Rogers, the Rogers Rascal was first unveiled at the Auto Expo in Los Angeles in 1980. It went into production in 1985 and was manufactured by Rogers Inter Auto Inc of Vancouver, Washington State, USA. The Rascal was a microvan constructed with parts from 15 countries. The vehicle was powered by an air-cooled, four-stroke, 750cc Fiat engine that drove the rear wheels through a four-speed gearbox. The body was made from fibreglass, whilst the bumpers were made of Surlyn, which is the same plastic compound used for covering golf balls. Weighing 900lb, the Rascal had a top speed of around 75mph (121km/h) at 60mpg (4.7-litre/100km). The interior of the Rascal offered seating for two adults and two children, whilst still offering 50cu ft of luggage space with a maximum payload of 500lb.

Rollfix

1933 — Commercial

The three-wheel Rollfix was built from 1933 in Hamburg-Wandsbek, Germany, and came in two combinations — with the single wheel either at the front or the rear. Initially the company built three-wheel commercial vehicles with a single wheel at the front. The vehicle had a two-seat cab with a number of commercial type bodies at the rear.

1934 — Passenger

In 1934 a passenger car was produced; this had the single wheel at the rear of the vehicle and was powered by a single-cylinder, 200cc ILO engine. A small engine was used as this brought the vehicle into the bracket granted tax exemption for vehicles of 200cc or less that prevailed at that time. In 1936 the company was purchased by Vidal & Söhn also known as Tempo (see page 269).

Roustabout Co

1962 — Trivan

Manufactured in 1962 by the Roustabout Co in Frackville, Pennsylvania, USA, the Trivan was a three-wheel lorry that had a fully-enclosed cab for two people. Designed by C Harry Payne, who is well known amongst Jeep historians for being one of the men credited for designing Bantam's Jeep prototype, the vehicle had seven years of testing. The Trivan's power came from either a 32bhp, two-cylinder, four-cycle, air-cooled Kohler petrol engine or a 30bhp, two-cylinder, two-cycle, air-cooled diesel engine that powered the single rear wheel. Both engines gave the vehicle a maximum speed of around 55mph (88.5km/h). With a load capacity of 1,000lb, the Trivan had a fibreglass body attached to a heavy-duty steel tube chassis and airbag suspension. All models had an open pick-up type rear body with drop down sides. A fully enclosed rear body was designed for a prototype but never manufactured. Production ceased in 1964 after 112 vehicles had been made. A number of them were purchased by affiliates of East Coast Trailways.

Designed by C Harry Payne who is credited for the Bantam Jeep prototype, the Trivan had a payload of 1,000lb. Bill Fidler

The brochure for the Trivan showing the vehicle is in default layout with an open flatbed at the rear with drop down sides. Bill Fidler

Ruhr-Fahrzeug-Bau

1953 — Pinguin

The Pinguin was originally built in 1953 by MEV (Research Association for Automobile Development in Germany) with two prototype vehicles, both fitted with a 10bhp, air-cooled, single-cylinder, 200cc, ILO engine. The vehicles were exhibited at the Motor Cycle show in Frankfurt in the same year. The project was then taken over by Ruhr-Fahrzeug-Bau of Germany and, following further improvements and design changes, an improved version was then developed. It was fitted with a Fichtel & Sachs 200L-AZL-R 200cc engine that drove the single rear wheel through a three-speed with reverse gearbox and had a top speed of 53mph (85km/h). The streamlined alloy body housed two seats and, whilst the prototypes had a steel tube frame, the improved versions had a double-tube frame. Despite plans to go into production, the project ended in 1954 with *circa* 10 vehicles being constructed.

Royal Ruby Cycle Co

1913 — Royal Ruby

Having manufactured motorcycles since 1909, the Royal Ruby Cycle Co of Altrincham, Manchester, UK, produced a four-wheel cyclecar in 1913 initially. The vehicle was, however, short-lived, with production ceasing in 1914 on the outbreak of World War 1. The company continued to make motorcycles and then, in 1922, went into liquidation. After being sold, the business moved to Oldham, Lancashire. In 1927 the Royal Ruby Cyclecar returned; however, this time with three-wheels. The car had an open two-seat body that featured a vertical windscreen and a hood. It was fitted with either a 2.5bhp or a 5bhp single-cylinder JAP engine that drove the single rear wheel via a three-speed with reverse gearbox. Designed by Maurice Edwards, the Royal Ruby is believed to have been sold under the MEB brand from 1928. In the same year a parcel van was also introduced; this was built by the commercial vehicle bodybuilders Bromilow & Edwards in Bolton. The Royal Ruby Cycle Co ceased trading in 1932.

Produced in small numbers the Royal Ruby was also sold under the MEB brand name. Kerry Croxton

S

S E Hamblin

1960 — Hamblin Mk 2

Sid Hamblin of S E Hamblin Ltd, Dorset, UK, ran a panel-beating business when, in 1956, he designed an aluminium body shell that could be used with an Austin 7 chassis; this was known as the Hamblin Deluxe. From there other kits were then produced. Created in 1960, the Hamblin Mk 2 was a sports three-wheel kit car. Using a fibreglass body, the vehicle had an optional hard top and a chassis built by David Buckler of Buckler Cars Ltd. With a windscreen from a Ford saloon, the vehicle was as wide as a standard vehicle and so said to be quite spacious. During the period from 1960 until 1962 one vehicle was made.

Saccomando

1980s — Saccomando

Only three Saccomando Trikes were made, the first being constructed in Walkley, UK, in the mid-1980s by Ed Saccomando. The Trike used an Austin Mini as a donor car and was powered by the Mini's 998cc engine. The body was formed using a tubular steel chassis (four-inch diameter) with a fibreglass shell attached to it. The vehicle also featured detachable wings and bonnet. The second Saccomando was built in Sheffield in 1988 and featured twin carbs and a three-branch manifold. The third and final one was built in 1992. The Saccomando, unlike other trikes of similar design, is a four-seater with two small seats with lap belts in the back suitable for children. The first Saccomando is believed to have been destroyed by fire and so only two exist at the time of writing.

SAMCA

1947 — Atomo

The Società Applicazioni Meccaniche Costruzioni Automobilistiche (SAMCA) Atomo first appeared at the 1947 Milan Auto Show in Italy and was manufactured in Parma, Italy. The vehicle was a two-seater that had a chassis consisting of a central tube frame and an aluminium body with a fabric roof that could be rolled back. It was fitted with an air-cooled, two-cylinder, 246cc engine that, through a three-speed gearbox, provided drive to the front wheels with the rear wheel being used for steering. The top speed was 40mph (65km/h). Sales of the Atomo were very low and ceased production in 1948.

S

Sanchis

1906 — Tricar EST

The Sanchis Tricar EST was first manufactured in Seine, France, in 1906. It was designed and built by Enrique Sanchís Tarazona, who was a civil engineer at the Ministry of Public Works. It was studying the emerging automobile industry in France that prompted him to build his own car; this also included manufacturing his own engine. The vehicle was first shown at the 1906 Paris Salon and was a two-seater with a unit construction of body and chassis. The original vehicles were powered by 4.5bhp engines that drove the single rear wheel; however, this was increased to 10bhp in later models. The Tricar EST was manufactured until 1912 when, in the same year the company was sold to L Pierron (of Automobiles Mass) who continued building the vehicles for the UK market. They were sold in the UK by Mass Cars under the Mass name and production continued until 1923.

Built with larger engines, the Sandford met customer demand by supplying vehicles with more power. Silvano Notaro

Sandford

1922 — Sports/Family/Tourisme/Economy

The Sandford was first introduced in 1922 in Paris, France after the Englishman Malcolm Stuart Sandford had moved to the city and found employment selling Morgan vehicles. Sandford saw a niche in the market for cyclecars that had more powerful engines, something many customers had been requesting. Designed and built by Sandford the vehicles became highly successful at time trials and races, beating most contemporary four-wheelers. Many variations of the Sandford were produced, including numerous racing models such as the Sport, the Super Sport and the Super Charged Sports. In addition, a Family model and Tourisme model were also introduced. With the exception of the Economy model (FT5) that had a 950cc Ruby engine, all Sandfords were powered by 900-1,100cc, water-cooled, four-cylinder Ruby engines. Production of all models halted in 1936 when the Ruby Engine Co was purchased by a competitor and forced out of business.

Sautel et Séchaud

1902 – Nouvelle Voiturette

Introduced in France 1902, the Nouvelle Voiturette was built by Sautel et Séchaud. It was powered by a vertically positioned, single-cylinder, 3.5bhp engine that was mounted behind the rear seat. This drove the rear wheel via a two-speed gearbox. All the controls were mounted on the steering column and so gear changing was achieved by moving the column forwards or backwards. The vehicle was produced until 1904.

Sazgar Engineering Works Ltd

1994 — Deluxe Mini Cab/ Royal Deluxe Mini Cab

Sazgar Engineering Works Ltd is a manufacturer of auto rickshaws and automotive wheel rims based in Lahore, Pakistan. Incorporated as a Private Limited Company in 1991, it was converted to a Public Limited Company in 1994. The Sazgar Deluxe Mini Cab is a passenger vehicle built on a tubular steel frame with a single-seat cab. It has a rear bench seat, with a canvas roof and sides, for three passengers. Powered by a four-stroke, water-cooled, 200cc engine, the vehicle is controlled via handlebars. Perhaps one feature advertised that is necessary in the crowded streets of India is that the horn is 82-85db. A Royal Deluxe version is also available; this includes extras like two-tone paintwork, improved interior and a cover over the spare wheel.

1994 — Tempo

Using the same engine as the Mini Cab, the Sazgar Tempo is a delivery van version fitted with a single-seat cab and a metal pick-up type body at the rear that offers a payload of 450kg.

1994 — Six-seater

The Sazgar Six-seater again uses the 200cc engine and is a modified version of the Deluxe model. The rear of the vehicle provides an additional bench seat placed back-to-back behind the rear seat; the latter faces outwards. A footrest has then been moulded into the back end of the vehicle. The vehicle is also fitted with an extended canvas roof that drops down at the back to shield rear-facing passengers. All vehicles detailed are available at the time of writing.

Scammell Lorries Ltd

1934 — Mechanical Horse (or Trivan)

With a history that dates back to the late 19th century, when the company built steam wagons, Scammell first introduced its Mechanical Horse in the UK in 1934. From the late 1920s railway companies had been searching for a vehicle that they could use to replace the horse-drawn carriage. The London & North Eastern Railway initially approached Napiers and, although that company created a few designs, the project was sold to Scammell Lorries Ltd, where the Mechanical Horse was designed by Oliver Danson North. One of its unique features was that it automatically coupled and uncoupled with trailers. The Mechanical Horse was a large three-wheeler with a steel frame with a wooden cab attached. It came in two sizes with either a three- or six-ton load capacity. Power came from Scammell's own 1,125cc, side-valve, petrol engine in the three-ton model and the 2,043cc engine in the six-ton version. Another unique thing about the Mechanical Horse was that its single front wheel could turn 360°

Built in India the Sazgar Deluxe Mini Cab is just one variation of this vehicle. Mian Muhammad Ali Hameed

thereby producing a highly manoeuvrable vehicle. With a top speed of 20mph (32km/h), the Mechanical Horse had a fuel consumption of *circa* 10-20mpg (28-14-litre/100km). The vehicles achieved great success with railway companies and were also employed by the British armed forces. The latter used them in stores and on aircraft carriers. With around 14,000 Mechanical Horses built, the model remained largely unchanged until 1948 when the tractor section was redesigned, creating the Scammell Scarab. The Mechanical Horse was also made under licence by the French company Chenard-Walcker as the FAR (see page 95), which used the Citroën Traction Avant engine.

1948 — Scarab

The Scammell Scarab featured the same successful automatic coupling from the original but now used the Scammell 2,090cc, side-valve engine in both the three- and six-ton versions. A diesel version was also introduced; this was fitted with a Perkins four-199 engine in the three-ton and a Perkins four-203 engine in the six-ton version. The Scarab's cab was more rounded and made from steel whilst the engine, gearbox and axle — all built as one unit — were mounted lower down, thus making the Scarab more stable. The radiator was also moved and positioned on the back wall of the cab. It pulled in air from a duct behind the driver's door. Production of the Scarab ceased in 1967 and was replaced with the Scammell Townsman.

Designed to replace the horse-drawn carriage for the London & North Eastern Railway the Scammell Trivan (Mechanical Horse) was able to carry three to six tons. Peter Smeaton

The engine, gearbox and axle in the Scammell Scarab were all built as a single unit. Paul

With its futuristic shape the main customers of the Scammell Townsman were British Rail and — as pictured here — the Royal Mail. Colin Pickett

1967 — Townsman

Whilst following the basic design of the Scarab, the Scammell Townsman had a number of differences; of these, the most obvious was a rounded fibreglass cab. The Townsman also utilised many of the developments in large vehicles, including vacuum-assisted hydraulic brakes and, although the same automatic coupling feature was used, this now had a vacuum operated release mechanism rather than a hand lever found in earlier models. Whilst the Townsman replaced the three-ton Scarab, there was not a six-ton version. Being part of the Leyland group since 1955, the vehicle was fitted with a Leyland OE160 engine that provided a top speed of 50mph (80km/h). Despite numerous improvements, the Townsman was mainly only sold to British Rail and the Royal Mail. Production ended in 1968 with over 30,000 Scammell three-wheelers in total having been built.

Sceadu Design

2002 — SD-1

The Sceadu SD-1 was created by Dave Mounce of Sceadu Design in Arizona, USA, based upon a set of questions posted in a user poll on the author's website in 2002. From the results, the first prototype was created. The first SD-1 prototype was constructed from a powder-coated steel perimeter frame with roll bar and an open fibreglass body that seated two people side-by-side. Power came from a 6.5bhp, overhead-valve, four-stroke engine that drove the single rear wheel. This, combined with the low weight of the vehicle (350lb), resulted in a top speed of 50mph (80km/h) through an automatic transmission. The vehicle was controlled by a tiller system with all controls attached to it. This prototype, after completing 2,500 miles (4,023km), was retired and at the time of writing is on permanent display at the Petersen Museum in Los Angeles, California, USA. To date six prototypes have been created, with each following the same design theme although looking continually to improve the vehicle. Planned variants include petrol-, diesel- or electric-powered versions. Initially it was planned that the SD-1 would go into production in 2006; however, due to all of the National Highway Traffic Safety Administration (NHTSA) rules and regulations required in the USA — and potential fines if things are wrong — the plan remains to release the Sceadu in kit form. At time of writing, a release date for the kits has not been announced.

Schmidt & Bensdort GmbH

1925 — Mops

Built by Schmidt & Bensdort GmbH in Mannheim, Germany the Mops three-wheeler was only manufactured in 1925. The two-seat vehicle had an open body with low cut sides. A hood was provided for protection against the elements; however, with no side doors, the hood hampered access to and from the vehicle when up. The vehicle was powered by a 350cc engine that drove the rear single wheel. All three wheels had a decorative disc over the spokes.

Initially based upon a poll from the author's website, the Sceadu SD-1 continues to be developed with one prototype now in the Petersen Museum in Los Angeles. Dave Mounce

Scott Autocar Co

1916 — Sociable

The UK-based Scott Motorcycle Co was founded in 1908 by Alfred Angus Scott. For many years Scott built motorcycles; these enjoyed tremendous success in competitions, so much so that Scotts were deemed to be overly efficient against motorcycles of the same capacity and, as a result, their cubic capacity was multiplied by a factor of 1.32 for competitive purposes. It was during World War 1 that Scott started to make sidecar machine gun carriers and, in 1919, Alfred Scott left the company he had established so that he could pursue the development of a three-wheeler

The Scott Sociable was initially designed in 1916 for military use as a gun carrier. This resulted in an unusual layout when compared with most other three-wheelers as the single front wheel was on the offside and was in line with the rear wheel resulting in a layout similar to a motorcycle and sidecar combination. As orders for the military failed to materialise, Scott converted the vehicle to a civilian version; this was introduced in 1921 by the Scott Autocar Co. The body was made from wood and mounted onto a tubular, triangular steel frame. Fitted with Scott's own water-cooled, two-cylinder, two-stroke, 578cc engine, power was sent to the rear offside wheel by a shaft through a three-speed gearbox. In 1921 the Sociable was priced at £215, though the priced had dropped to £135 by 1923. Around 200 vehicles were manufactured before production ceased in 1925. Alfred Scott did not return to the Scott Motorcycle Co, but the latter continued to make motorcycles until 1979. Its models featured some of the key characteristics of the original models built in 1908.

Initially designed as a gun carrier, the Scott Sociable has an unusual layout in that the single front wheel and the right-hand rear wheel are in line with each other. Robert Iveson

Scorpion Motorsports

2012 —Scorpion P6

Introduced in 2012 by Scorpion Motorsports in Miami, Florida, USA, the Scorpion P6 is a single-seat vehicle that is available as a turnkey product. Fitted with a 126bhp, 600cc Kawasaki ZX6R6 engine that redlines at 16,000rpm, the P6 is able to achieve 0-60mph (0-96km/h) in 3.5sec. Using a steel tube spaceframe with an aluminium semi-monocoque and a Formula 1 style fibreglass body — with the option of a full carbon fibre body with optional carbon fibre wings — the vehicle has an overall weight of 725lb. It also has adjustable shock absorbers at the front and rear as well as an adjustable anti-roll bar. The Scorpion P6 remains available at the time of writing.

Designed as a high performance vehicle, the Scorpion P6 is able to achieve 0-60mph (0-96km/h) in 3.5sec. Scorpion Motorsports

2012 — Scorpion P13

In 2012 a custom one-off Scorpion P13 was built. This, whilst using the same design as the P6, was powered by a 1,300cc Suzuki Hayabusa engine that provided almost 200bhp and a top speed of 202mph (325km/h).

A custom one-off, the Scorpion P13 has a top speed of 202mph (325km/h). Scorpion Motorsports

Seal Motors

1912 — Standard/ Family models

Looking like a motorcycle with a large sidecar, the Seal was at first built by Haynes & Bradshaw between 1912 and 1920, when the company became Seal Motors Ltd of Manchester, UK. The name Seal came from the manufacturer's description of the vehicle — 'Sociable, Economical And Light'.

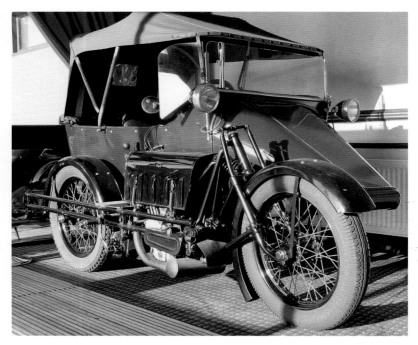

Initially powered in 1912 by a 770cc JAP engine, this was uprated to a V-twin, 980cc JAP engine the following year. The engine provided drive to the rear wheel by chain. The Seal was essentially a motorcycle and sidecar though steering was done inside the body by a tiller in early versions and then by a steering wheel, whilst the gear lever for the three-speed gearbox was outside. The body, containing two seats side-by-side, was made of steel and had a fabric convertible top. During the early 1920s, three- and four-seat family models were also introduced. Weighing around 5cwt, the vehicle managed around 50-60mpg (4.7-litre/100km). These passenger vehicles were made until 1924.

1922 — Commercial models

In 1922 commercial variants of the Seal were introduced; these included a van and pick-up version. These were built to the same specification as the passenger vehicles except that, from 1924, the chain-drive changed to a driveshaft, and the sidecar part had a modified body in order to carry a cargo with the driver sitting at the side of the load. The bodies came in a number of sizes, able to carry 4cwt, 6cwt or 7cwt. In 1930 all Seal commercial models were upgraded and then sold under the name of Progress (see page 196).

Serpollet frères et Cie

1888 — Serpollet Tricycle

Serpollet frères et Cie (Serpollet Brothers & Co) was founded in 1858 by brothers Henri and Léon Serpollet in France. The company manufactured various cutting machines powered by steam but, not having its own engines, it started to make its own. It was whilst doing this that Henri discovered an instant steam generator that used the principle of flash evaporation being able to transform water into steam by using heat to actuate a mechanism. This concept was then patented by the brothers in October 1879 and, following further experiments, a much-improved boiler was made. This resulted in steam becoming a more acceptable power source for vehicles. After seeing a De Dion-Bouton in action, the Serpollet brothers set about building their steam-powered vehicle made from parts that they found in their workshop. This vehicle took the form of a steam tricycle completed in May 1888. Powered by a 1bhp, single-cylinder

Resembling a motorcycle and sidecar, the Seal was operated from inside the body. Author's Collection

engine and boiler, the vehicle had a top speed of 19mph (30.5km/h), which was exceptional for the time. In the same year, Léon Serpollet got the first official authorisation to drive through the streets of Paris with his vehicle. It was also in 1888 that Serpollet was approached by Armand Peugeot — who was an ironmonger and cyclemaker at the time — who wished to build tricycles fitted with the Serpollet steam generator. This resulted in the Peugeot Type 1, which became the first vehicle of the Peugeot motor company (see page 187). By 1891 the metallic wheel rims on Serpollet's vehicles had been replaced by rubber tubes and a new twin-cylinder engine was added. This was followed, in 1892, by a seven-seat tricycle, though Serpollet was also now producing steam-powered four-wheelers. However, with the ever-increasing popularity of trams and railways along with the emergence of the petrol engine, the company finally ceased to produce vehicles in 1898.

Serpuhovsky Motorcikletny Zavod

1952 — S1L

The SMZ S1L was a vehicle made for those who had been disabled as a result of World War 2. Manufactured from 1952 in Serpuhov, USSR, by Serpuhovsky Motorcikletny Zavod (SMZ), it used a 123cc engine that produced 4bhp. The vehicle was a two-seat, two-door cabriolet that had a top speed of 19mph (30km/h). A total of 19,128 vehicles were made when the vehicle was replaced by the more powerful SMZ S3L in 1956.

1956 — S3L

The SMZ S3L was exactly the same vehicle but it was now powered by a larger 8bhp, 346cc engine that permitted a top speed of 37mph. (59.5km/h). A total of 17,053 S3L models were built before manufacture ceased in 1958. Thereafter the company concentrated on four-wheelers.

Fitted with an instant steam generator, the 1888 Serpollet Tricycle was able to achieve 19mph (30.5km/h). Author's Collection

Built in the USSR, the SMZ S3L was designed for the disabled and over 17,000 examples were sold. Arseny Zhdanov

Shanghai Automotive Industry Corporation

1957 — Shanghai SH58-1

Amongst its vast range of four-wheel trucks and cars, the Shanghai Car Decoration Factory in Shanghai, China introduced in 1957 a three-wheel truck — the Shanghai SH58-1 — with a maximum payload of 1,000kg. The importance of such vehicles at the time was that they could fit through narrow alleyways in big cities like Shanghai and Beijing and carry cargo to places where a larger four-wheel vehicle could not get. The SH58-1 was powered by a four-stroke, V-twin, water-cooled, 25bhp engine manufactured by the Shanghai Internal Combustion Engine Parts Plant. At the time, all the Shanghai factories were separate entities but later on merged to form Shanghai Automotive Industry Corporation. With a top speed of 37mph (60km/h), the vehicle had a heavy steel chassis and metal sheet body, which consisted of a two-seat cab, and a range of commercial bodies at the rear. Initially the vehicle went into small-scale production in 1958 but, by 1959, had gone into full production. Manufacture continued until 1969 by which date 18,954 vehicles had been completed with many exported to Tibet and Nepal.

Shell

1999 — Solar Car

Designed and built by Shell Research in 1999 as an experiment, the Shell Solar Car was a hybrid solar electric car. It was driven by a standard brushless 1bhp dc electric motor and was designed and built by Sheffield University, UK. It was capable of a range of about 50 miles (80km) on its two small batteries. Alternatively it could travel as far as you wanted whilst the sun was shining with a top speed of over 50mph (80km/h) on a flat road. The body was made from a one-piece carbon-fibre composite with a glass-encapsulated 250wp 1.6sq m solar panel attached at the top. This, combined with the batteries, gave the vehicle an overall weight of 98kg. With fully independent suspension and disc brakes on all wheels, the vehicle was capable of carrying one small person. During a 1,000-mile run in Australia, it recorded an equivalent fuel consumption of over 7,000mpg (0.04-litre/100km) at an average speed of about 20mph (32km/h) on sunshine.

Shelter

1954 — Shelter

The Shelter was created in Amsterdam in 1954 by Arnold van der Goot. At the time van der Goot was at the University of Delft and was looking for an engineering project. As a result, he decided to build a city pool car. Manufacturing most of the parts himself over a period of two years Van der Goot had enough parts to build 20 vehicles, though only seven were ever completed. The Shelter was a two-seater powered by a 228cc, single-cylinder engine, which was also made by Van der Goot with connecting rods produced from standard gas pipes. The engine was situated at the rear of the car and could be removed in 10min with the rear panel of the Shelter removed. The 6ft 3in-long body was made from sheet steel and the headlamp surrounds came from a local saucepan factory. Unfortunately the Shelter had serious problems, with axles reportedly snapping, and it also had a tendency to catch fire. Despite the early interest from the Dutch government, these problems caused it to lose interest and the project was eventually abandoned.

Although a revolutionary electric vehicle, the Sinclair C5 was not the commercial success that was hoped for. Robert Knight

Sinclair

1985 — C5

Created by the innovator and inventor Sir Clive Sinclair, most famous for his ZX80 and ZX81 personal computers from 1980, the Sinclair C5 was first launched in the UK on 10 January 1985. The C5 was a revolutionary electric vehicle weighing in at just 99lb. The vehicle used a 33lb lead-acid battery that powered a 250W Hoover electric motor similar to those found in washing machines. As the C5 was created to fall in line with the 1983 Electrically Assisted Pedal Cycle Regulations, this determined that the vehicle's engine could not exceed 250W in power. This, therefore, resulted in the C5 having a top speed of 15mph (24km/h) with a claimed 20 miles (32km) battery life in between charges. The vehicle also had pedals for extra assistance up hills. The body of the C5 was made of self-coloured lightweight polypropylene and measured 2ft 6in in width, 2ft 6in height and 5ft 9in in length.

From day one of its launch, the Sinclair C5 came under continuous attack from the media, which criticised it for numerous reasons and argued that it should be banned. The main reason was that, due to its low stance on the road, it could not be seen easily by other road users. This opened up the debate about C5 drivers being at the same level as exhaust pipes from larger vehicles and inhaling the latter's fumes. In addition, the C5's power performance was also criticised as it was stated that, during independent tests, the vehicle could rarely tackle a hill climb without manual assistance. It was also claimed that the vehicle only ever lasted approximately 10 miles (16km) on one battery charge and not the 20 claimed by Sinclair. In some cases, this was reduced to six to seven miles (10-11km) in winter as the cold affected the battery's performance. A high visibility mask was available for the C5 as an optional extra, though many claimed it should have been standard. As a result of these problems, the Sinclair quickly gained a bad reputation and interest in sales plummeted. The vehicle had originally been planned as a mail order item and to be sold on the high street through electrical retailers. As a result of the lack of sales, prices fell to just £199 from the original £399 in a bid to sell surplus stock. On 15 October 1985, Sir Clive Sinclair announced that Sinclair Vehicles had officially been placed in the hands of the Receiver four days earlier and production of the C5 ceased. Later Sinclair unveiled plans to modify the C5 to make a C10 (a two-seat version) and a C15 (a four-seat version) though at the time of writing nothing has been announced.

Singer & Co

1901 — Tricycle

The Singer Cycle Co of Coventry, UK, was first formed in 1875 when George Singer left the Coventry Machinist Co to set up his own business. Singer then produced the world's first safety cycle; in addition, George Singer also patented the curving of the front forks of a bicycle to aid steering. This is an innovation still found on modern bicycles and helped turn the company into the world's largest cycle manufacturer. In 1901 Singer obtained the manufacturing rights of the 2.5bhp Motor Wheel developed by Edwin Perks and Frank Birch, and, from it, made a front-wheel drive tricycle in which the engine was fitted within the single front wheel.

A 1904 advertisement for the Singer Forecar proudly stating amongst its claims the 'Finest system of Piston Rings'. Grace's Guide

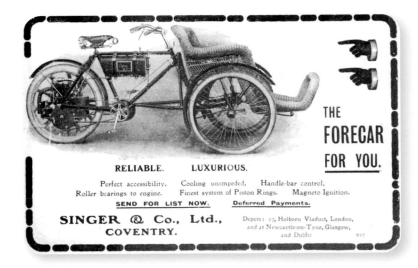

The tricycle itself was virtually unchanged from its pedal power predecessor and so retained pedals that drove the rear wheels by human power. Along with a standard motorised tricycle, a motorised commercial version for carrying cargo was also created; this had a Governess cart body located behind the saddle.

1904 — Forecar

In 1903 a new company, called Singer & Co, was registered to take over from the Singer Cycle Co. George Singer then began to adapt and improve upon the tricycle design, producing a more conventional three-wheeler with the introduction of the Singer Forecar in 1904. This had the single wheel at the back. Still sharing much from its cycle heritage, the vehicle had a tubular steel frame with a Perks and Birch Motor Wheel fitted in the rear wheel. The driver sat at the rear of the vehicle on a saddle, controlling the vehicle through handlebars, whilst a large wicker seat was positioned between the front two wheels for a passenger.

1905 — Tri-Car

Introduced in 1905, the Singer Tri-Car was a development of the Forecar. However, it was now much more car-like with some steel bodywork around the seats. The driver, whilst still sitting at the rear, now did so in a bucket seat that was positioned much higher up than the passenger seat at the front. The handlebars had also been replaced with a conventional steering wheel. The Tri-Car was powered by either a 6bhp or a 9bhp, water-cooled engine that had two speeds. The engine was produced by the Riley Cycle Co and helped the Singer perform well in time trials and competitions. Ironically, using the Riley engine made the Singer three-wheeler one of Riley's main rivals in competitions. In 1905 Singer produced its first four-wheel car and the Tri-Car was manufactured up until 1907, when production turned completely to four-wheelers.

SNCAN

1953 — Inter Torpedo

Whilst a number of bicycle and car manufacturers have turned their hand to making three-wheelers, the transition is not something instantly associated with aircraft builders. In 1953 at the Paris Salon, Société Nationale de Constructions Aéronautiques du Nord (SNCAN) of Lyon, France, introduced the Inter Torpedo microcar. This kept an aeronautical theme with a similar style of cockpit housing two seats in tandem. Powered by a two-stroke, 175cc, Ydral engine that drove the single rear wheel, the Torpedo was started by a Gyro starter device,

Built by the aircraft manufacturer SNCAN, the Inter Torpedo featured front wheels that folded into the body to allow storage in small places. Caroline Payne

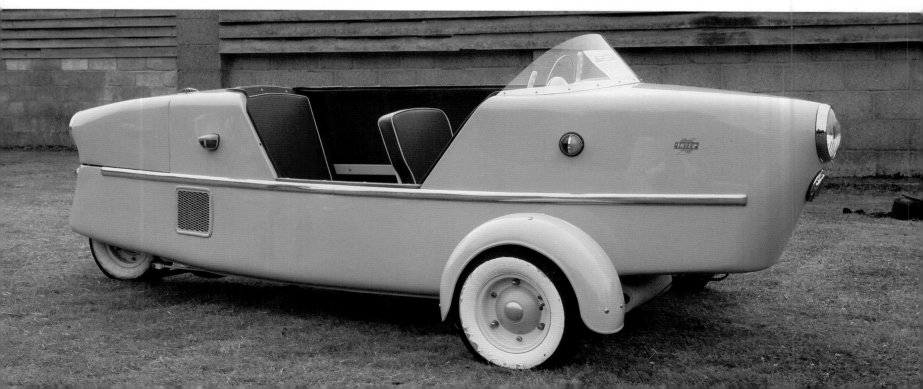

Equipped with a cockpit cover that hinged to the side, the Inter Berline had the same specifications as the Torpedo otherwise. Author's Collection

The La Nef had a chassis that consisted of two longitudinal sections of wood joined at the front. Wikipedia — Butch T

which was essentially an electric kick-starter. On early vehicles the two front wheels folded upwards under the body so that the vehicle could be stored in narrow places; however, this idea was dropped in later models. The suspension was created using large rubber bands.

1953 — Inter Berline

Whilst the Torpedo had an open body, the Berline had the same specifications but was equipped with a cockpit cover that hinged open to the side. Whilst production ceased in 1956, the models were still sold until 1961 with 283 vehicles built.

Société des Automobiles La Nef

1899 — La Nef/ Lacroix-de Laville

The Société des Automobiles La Nef was formed in France in 1899 by Joseph Lacroix. He then produced a three-wheeler called La Nef ('The Ship'). In 1902 he was joined by Colonel de Laville, who financed the company, and so the vehicles were then called Lacroix-de Laville. The main chassis consisted of two longitudinal sections of wood that joined at the front with the single wheel at the front with the engine sitting behind it. Several engines were fitted as the vehicle evolved. These ranged from was a single-cylinder, air-cooled,

2.3-4bhp De Dion-Bouton engine to 4-8bhp water-cooled engines that drove the rear wheels with side belts. No gearbox was fitted, with vehicles only having a single speed. On versions that had rear seats, the seats were enclosed from the side of the car so passengers would climb aboard through a central door built into the rear panel of the body. Steering was by a large tiller to the front wheel. La Nef stopped producing vehicles in 1909.

A Lacroix-de Laville Tricycle fitted with a 4.5bhp engine. Olivier Houllier

231

Sold as the QPOD City 50 in the UK, the Fun Tech 50 was a two-seater with a 49cc engine. Nigel Scarr

The Souriau — also known as the Obus — had an engine that was built on a separate sub-frame with the front wheel and so both turned as a single unit. Kerry Croxton

Société SECMA

1996 — FunTech 50/ QPOD City 50

The FunTech 50 was manufactured by Société d'Étude et de Construction Automobile (SECMA) in Aniche, France. Founded in 1995, the company manufactures a range of lightweight vehicles. These are mostly four-wheelers that do not exceed 550kg. Introduced in 1996, the FunTech 50 was fitted with an air-cooled, single-cylinder, two-stroke, 50cc Morini engine with a top speed of 30mph (48km/h). It was equipped with two seats, padded side protection bars, head restraints, three-point inertia seatbelts, rollover protection (stabilisers) and a safety glass windscreen. The body was made from a high resistance plastic that was moulded as a central cell and attached to an anticorrosion shell. The FunTech was steered by handlebars, via an automatic twist grip, with braking via footbrakes. Roof and door options were also available. The vehicle was discontinued by the company in 2010. In the UK, the vehicle was launched in 2004 as the QPOD City 50 and was sold by the Unique Motor Co; this company was founded by television presenter Noel Edmonds, who imported the vehicles from SECMA in France. Being 50cc, the vehicle was classed as a moped and so aimed at 16-year-olds as a vehicle they could drive legally. It was sold until 2010.

Souriau

1912 — Model 5 CV/Model 8 CV

The Souriau was first created in Loire-et-Cher, France, in 1912 by Albert Souriau although an experimental model had appeared as early as 1907. The vehicle, also known as the Obus, was powered by a number of engines. The Model 5 CV was driven by a 5bhp, single-cylinder, 625cc engine whilst the Model 8 CV used either a much larger two-cylinder, 1,260cc engine or an 8bhp, four-cylinder, 1,460cc engine. The engine turned with the front wheel as both were in a separate sub-frame within the main chassis. The chassis was built from tubular steel and was left exposed. Production ceased in 1914.

Spijkstaal

1955 — Spijkstaal

Although Spijkstaal produced four-wheelers from 1938 in Spijkenisse, Holland, it was not unit 1955 that it produced a three-wheeler. Its first three-wheeler was a milk float powered by an electric motor that drove the single front wheel. With a top speed of 10mph (16km/h), the vehicle was built in many other forms, particularly during the 1970s when it was popular as mobile shops or rubbish trucks and was also used by Netherlands Railways for transporting mail and goods.

At the time of writing the company continues to produce both three and four-wheel vehicles. The majority of the three-wheelers are electric tractors with single seats to be used as workhorses. These are powered by a 48V, 8.7kW motor, giving the vehicles a towing capacity of between two and 10 tons and a top speed of *circa* 6-11mph (10-18km/h).

Spirit of America

1962 — Spirit of America

Spirit of America is officially the world's fastest three-wheeler. Designed by Craig Breedlove and built in 1962, first trials of the vehicle showed that it had issues with handling and, as a result, a stabiliser was added to permit the front wheel to steer. At 38ft 6in in length, 6ft in height and 11ft 4in in width, *Spirit of America* was fitted with an ex-military General Electric turbojet engine from a F-86 Sabre that provided 5,200lb of thrust. On 5 September 1963, Breedlove took the vehicle to the Bonneville Salt Flats in the USA and became the first man to exceed 400mph (644km/h). Just over a year later, in October 1964, his world record was beaten by Art Arfons and so Breedlove and *Spirit of America* returned to the Salt Flats. It was on 15 October 1964 that the jet-powered three-wheeler reached a speed of 526.277mph (846.960km/h), which again broke the Land Speed Record. It was whilst on the second run that the vehicle lost its parachute brakes and skidded for five miles (8km) before crashing through a row of telegraph poles and into a brine pond at approximately 200mph (321km/h). Breedlove amazingly emerged from the crash unscathed and unwittingly broke another record — the world's longest ever skid marks. After the crash the vehicle was dragged out of the pond but was beyond repair. In 1965, it was donated to the Museum of Science and Industry in Chicago, USA where, at the time of writing, it remains. A new *Spirit of America — Sonic 1 —* was built, but this was now a four-wheel design in which Breedlove went on to break further land speed records.

Officially the world's fastest three-wheeler, the Spirit of America achieved 526.277mph (846.960km/h) whilst driven by Craig Breedlove (pictured) in 1964. Sam Hawley

1973 — Screaming Yellow Zonkers

Craig Breedlove also built a three-wheel dragster nicknamed the 'Screaming Yellow Zonkers'. In 1973, a slightly modified version of the vehicle was clocked at 377.754mph (607.936km/h) in a quarter mile from a standing start at the Bonneville Salt Flats. The elapsed time was 4.654sec. On a drag strip in the UK this car is listed in the top 20 cars at 280mph (451km/h) for the quarter mile; however, it could not use full power at a normal drag strip because there is no way to stop it soon enough. The rocket engine in the dragster is from a US lunar lander from the 1960s. This type of engine was used to take off from the moon for the return to earth. It used several liquid fuels that ignited when mixed. For short burst it could generate 15,000bhp. There were two chutes packed above the engine right under the large tail. The car was eventually outlawed from the NHRA drag strips as a result of fuel and oxidiser concerns. Subsequently it was sold to a car collection at Kruse Classic Car Auction for $30,000.

SportCycle Ltd

2002 — SportCycle

The SportCycle was conceived in the late 1980s by Jim Musser in the USA and released in 2002 by SportCycle Ltd. Musser, an automotive and race engineer, wanted to design a car that had racecar handling with superbike performance and so a three-wheeler offered both of these characteristics. The SportCycle was a kit three-wheeler that was offered as a completely assembled vehicle or an unassembled kit. Essentially it was designed around a Kawasaki ZRX/1100/1200 motorcycle although any donor bike could have been used. Once the front forks of the motorcycle were removed, the assembled SportCycle kit bolted on with the SportCycle's levers and hoses being connected to the motorcycle's clutch, rear brake, throttle, gear controls and electrics. The body of the vehicle was made from a glossy white gel coat FRP that did not require painting. It was designed as a single occupant vehicle complete with a

five-point harness. The front suspension was a radius rod-type with inboard springs and shocks along with hydraulic disc brakes front and rear. Plans for the vehicle are believed to have been last sold in 2008.

Stanhope Motors (Leeds) Ltd

1919 — Stanhope

Founded by brothers Harry, Ted and Herbert Stanhope, who had applied for a patent for a type of front-wheel drive in 1914, Stanhope Motors (Leeds) Ltd was based in Burley Road in Leeds, UK. By 1919 the first Stanhope prototypes appeared; these were powered by an air-cooled, 8bhp, JAP engine that was bolted immediately behind the front wheel to two tubular cross-members of the chassis. Two Whittle belts then ran over automatic governor pulleys, with drive being sent to the front wheel by sliding forks that also allowed the wheel to steer. Stanhope Motors had been financed by Rowland Winn, who ran a number of garages; however, as a result of the post-war slump, he withdrew his backing in 1921. In 1922 Walter Bramham agreed to provide finance and take over the company with the result that the name was changed to Bramham Motors (Leeds) Ltd and the vehicles became known as Bramham (see page 43).

The chassis of the Stanhope clearly showing the front-wheel drive arrangement. Peter Stanhope

Powered by either an electric motor or a petrol engine the Stanley Argson Runnymede was designed as an invalid carriage. Jonathan

Stanley Engineering Co Ltd

1930s — Argson Runnymede

Starting as the Argson Engineering Co in 1919, the company initially built hand-propelled tricycles, moving on to motorised versions in 1922. An electric version followed in 1923 in which the tiller was twisted clockwise to go forward and then the opposite direction for reverse. The company was renamed as the Stanley Engineering Co in 1926 and moved from Twickenham, UK, to Egham, Surrey, UK. In 1934 the Argson Runnymede was introduced; that was powered by a 147cc, two-stroke Villiers engine that used a chain drive to the nearside wheel. The vehicle was a single-seat invalid carriage with an armchair-type seat and tiller steering. The Runnymede was replaced by the Argson Victory in 1946; this was built until 1953 when the company was taken over by C B Harper (see page 53).

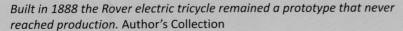

Built in 1888 the Rover electric tricycle remained a prototype that never reached production. Author's Collection

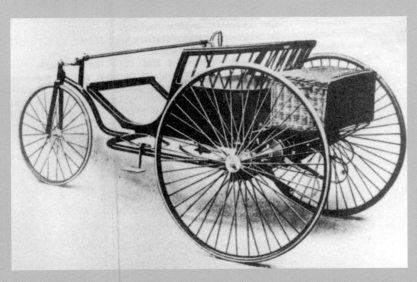

Starley & Sutton

1885 — Rover

Starting out as a bicycle manufacturer, Starley & Sutton Co was founded in 1877 by John Kemp Stanley and William Sutton. In 1882 the company started to manufacture pedal tricycles including the Meteor and the Royal. These were followed by a Rover tricycle a year later. In 1885 Stanley made history with a new Rover Safety bicycle with rear chain drive and two similar sized wheels, which historians record as the first recognisably modern bicycle. Starley & Sutton was one of few companies that also experimented with electric vehicles and, in 1888, built its first electric tricycle. With minimal bodywork and a steel tubular frame, the vehicle was a two-seater with tiller steering to the single front wheel. The tricycle never went into production although the firm continued to develop vehicles. In 1896 the company became the Rover Cycle Co Ltd and, by 1904, was producing four-wheel cars. It later became the Rover car company, which went on to produce numerous vehicles until 2005, when the company went into administration; MG Rover, as the company was then known, used the 'Rover' name under licence from BMW — the brand's then owner — before the name was sold to Ford in 2006. The rights to the brand were sold to Tata Motors in 2008, when the Indian car manufacturer bought Jaguar Land Rover from Ford.

A 1936 Stevens Light Commercial Van; this particular vehicle is often spotted driving around the Black Country Living Museum in Dudley. Geoff Payne

Stevens Brothers

1932 — Stevens

Stevens Brothers (Wolverhampton) Ltd was established in 1932 following the liquidation of the AJS motorcycle company. The Stevens brothers — Harry, George, Jack, Joe and Billie — had owned AJS and, after its closure, decided to start a new company. In 1932 it produced its first light commercial vehicle; this was actually based on a three-wheel prototype van that had been built in 1921 at AJS. The vehicle was based heavily on a motorcycle with a complete motorcycle front end. It was powered by a water-cooled, single-cylinder, 588cc Stevens engine with a three-speed plus reverse gearbox. The wooden framed body housed a single motorcycle type seat with a steering wheel and had a canvas roof. To start with no side doors were fitted although they later became standard. In addition, the first vehicles were chain-driven but this led to a number of problems and, as a result, in 1935 a shaft drive was introduced. Whilst early vehicles had a 5cwt load capacity, this was increased to 8cwt in later shaft driven models. The vehicle was constructed up until late 1936, when the brothers decided to cease production with *circa* 500 vans completed.

Structural Plastics Inc

1975 — SPI-TRI (Mk I)

Structural Plastics Inc of Oklahoma, USA, was founded by William M Gillespie, who designed and developed three prototype vehicles called the SPI-TRI. Gillespie was principally responsible for design and development. The first, or Mk I vehicle, in 1975, was powered by an Electro electric engine that gave the vehicle a top speed of about 50mph (80km/h) and a range of 40 miles (64km) between charges. The Mk I also utilised an Austin-American drive train for a petrol version. There is often a misconception in a number of resources that the Mk I body was an extended version of one made by Reliant for the Bond Bug; this, however, is not the case. Gillespie had once worked on a Bond Bug that had been imported to the USA as the owner was driving from New York to the West Coast. The driver was having mechanical issues and was recommended to contact the Structural Plastics Inc shop in Tulsa because of the company's reputation for developing engineering solutions to an array of unique problems. The Bond Bug was fixed at the shop and Gillespie saw how the design of the Bond Bug could be improved upon. As a result, whilst the Mk I body is heavily influenced by the Bond Bug, it does not use the same body. It is a monocoque construction with the body and frame being one and the same.

The electric powered SPI-TRI Mk I with the skyline of Tulsa, Oklahoma USA in the background. Larry Barker

1980 — SPI-TRI (Mk II)

The Mk II SPI–TRI was larger than the Mk I, enabling it to carry more batteries for an extended range in the electric version and affording more room and comfort in the vehicle's driver/passenger compartment. It also had larger diameter wheels to afford more braking power, which was needed with a heavy battery pack when running electrically. In 1980 this vehicle participated in three-wheel vehicle stability testing at Edwards Air Force base in California. The vehicle was fitted with a custom-made Baldor electric motor that utilised a proprietary design infinite ratio transmission.

1984 — SPI-TRI (Mk III)

The Mk III preproduction prototype vehicle was designed to be a car that could be built anywhere in the world, using a readily available engine from the region of the world where it was to be manufactured. In addition to the larger wheels of the Mk II, it incorporated squat bars for enhanced handling and large bumpers for increased safety as well as other structural refinements such as the addition of carbon cloth and Kevlar at stress points during construction. It also included a leather and oiled walnut interior for the pleasure and comfort of the occupants. This vehicle, tagged and titled in 1984, was powered by a 993cc Daihatsu CB engine and transmission. The Reliant 848cc engine was considered to power the SPI-TRI Mk III; however, the Daihatsu was chosen for a number of reasons. Daihatsu was not importing vehicles or engines to the USA in 1985 and so agreed to provide a sample CB engine and transmission along with many spare parts. It was not until a few years later that Daihatsu started sending cars to the USA; the ones they did send used a different engine to that fitted to the SPI-TRI. A total of three SPI-TRI vehicles have been built. A fourth body is, at the time of writing, in the moulds in order to maintain its integrity until the vehicle is assembled. The tooling and spares along with the Mk I and Mk II are in protective storage. The Mk III remains tagged and titled and is frequently driven to maintain its operational integrity. Its crisp handling, solid performance, extreme reliability, and futuristic styling remain as outstanding today as when it first hit the road in 1984.

Designed as a world car that could be built anywhere, the SPI-TRI Mk III could have used any readily available engine. Harry Kraemer

were no plans to enter production as a result of the cost; however, they would consider building one-off vehicles. At the time of writing, no further vehicles are believed to have been built.

Sub Motorsports

2005 — Sub G1

Sub Motorsports of California, USA, was set up by Niki Smart, Jay Brett and Nick Mynott. It completed the first three Sub G1 vehicles in March 2005. The initial idea for the vehicle was to use a Yamaha R1 engine; however, it was soon discovered that this might cause issues and so a liquid-cooled, V-twin, 996cc Suzuki engine was used with a six-speed gearbox. This was estimated to give a top speed of 140mph (225km/h). Being a single seater, the engine was positioned to the right-hand side of the driver's seat; this helped to split the weight of the vehicle evenly between the front and the back and also provided a shorter wheelbase. With a total weight of 330kg, the Sub G1 uses a tubular mild steel space frame construction with aluminium and composite bulkheads and a fibreglass body. In 2006 the trio reported that there

Subaru

1980 — X-100 Gyronaut

Designed in 1980 by Alex Tremulis, who was a consultant at Subaru of America, the Subaru X-100 Gyronaut was an experimental prototype that had a rocket-shaped fibreglass body. It was based on the 1964 Gyronaut X-1. Powered by two Triumph 650 engines, it achieved 245.667mph (395.362km/h). The X-100 was a single-seater with a steel frame and was tested in Japan by a female Japanese racing driver. In test it achieved 100mpg (2.8-litre/100km). In 1980, it was also tested at the Ontario Motor Speedway in California, USA, where it is reported to have achieved 100.2mpg (2.8-litre/100km) using a twin-cylinder, four-stroke, 544cc engine that drove the rear wheels. The engine was unmodified from a Subaru Rex and provided a top speed of over 100mph (161km/h). The X-100 was able to accelerate 0-60mph (0-96km/h) in 12sec. The vehicle is, at the time of writing, still owned by Subaru.

Viewed from the front the single-seat Subaru X100 is almost shaped like a missile. Peter Tenn/Subaru

Sunrise Auto Industries Ltd/ Sipani Automobiles Ltd

1975 — Badal

Sunrise Auto Industries Ltd was set up in 1974 with assistance from the UK-based Reliant Motor Co. Established in Bangalore, India, the company's first vehicle was the three-wheel Badal. This arrived in 1975 and was very loosely based on the Reliant Robin. That said, it was quite different in that it was fitted with a rear-mounted, single-cylinder, two-stroke, 198cc engine and a four-speed constant-mesh gearbox. Braking was fitted to the rear wheels only, whilst the fibreglass body was made in two versions as either a three- or five-door. In 1978 the company was restructured by S R K Sipani, who was one of the founding shareholders, and renamed as Sipani Automobiles Ltd. It continued to manufacture the Badal until 1981 when the model was replaced with the four-wheel Dolphin; this was in essence a Reliant Kitten, a model that had been initially produced in the UK.

Below: It's been said that the Badal fell out of the ugly tree and hit every branch on the way down; despite this, it was offered as either a three- or five-door version. Willem Alink

Suntera Corporation

1987 — Sunray/C-Mobile/Picket

Suntera was founded in the early 1990s by Jonathan Tennyson, who had created a number of ingenious vehicles. These included the Mana La, which was a hybrid solar/electric vehicle that took part in the 1987 Australian Solar Challenge. In 1987 the Suntera Sunray was introduced; this was an electric vehicle with an enclosed cabin and became the first composite electric vehicle to be produced in Hawaii. Built by the Suntera Corporation, the vehicle had a fibreglass body, with various prototypes built. These consisted of a lightweight pick-up version — the C-Mobile — of which examples were built for both the US Navy and the US Air Force. A variant with a small luggage carrier fitted at the rear — the Picket — was also built, as was the Sunray, a two-seat passenger version. The vehicle's windscreen was made from a glass-coated Polycarbonate of a type that is also used in bullet-proof windscreens. Powered by a 13bhp electric motor that used 10 lead-acid batteries, the vehicle had a range of 100 miles (161km) at 25mph (40km/h) and 65 miles (105km) at 45mph (72km/h). With a top speed of 70mph (113km/h), the vehicle could do 0-60mph (0-96km/h) in 18sec. Eight preproduction prototypes were built under a grant programme from the Defense Advanced Research Projects Agency (DARPA), but it never reached production following Tennyson's death in 1997.

With a range of 100 miles the Suntera Sunray was powered by a 13bhp electric motor. Budd Steinhilber

Suzuki

1981 — CV1

Manufactured initially in 1981 by Suzuki of Japan, the CV1 — CV meaning Commuter Vehicle — was a single-seat vehicle. Fitted with a colour-moulded fibreglass body, the vehicle used a two-stroke, single-cylinder, 50cc engine with automatic transmission. Whilst often classed as a three-wheeler, the CV1 actually had two rear wheels that were close together. With a top speed of 50mph (80km/h), the CV1 was able to achieve around 200mpg (1.4-litre/100km). The interior offered enough space for both the driver and shopping bags. Air conditioning was also provided. Production is believed to have ceased in the mid-1980s.

Although classed as a three-wheeler, the Suzuki CV1 actually had four wheels with the rear two being very close together. John Mulders

The LSD Demonstration Van leaves no doubt as its manufacturer or its purpose. Author's Collection

Sykes & Sugden

1919 — LSD Passenger Models (Popular, Standard and Family)

Produced by Sykes & Sugden Ltd of Huddersfield, Yorkshire, UK, the LSD Cyclecar first appeared in 1919. The name of the three-wheeler is said to come from the British currency at the time and was used to emphasise the pounds, shillings and pence that the owner could save driving the LSD. However, it is also said to arisen from Longbottom (the vehicle's designer), Sykes (the manufacturer) and Dyson (the accountant).

The LSD was powered by a conventional 8bhp, air-cooled, V-twin, 980cc JAP engine with a two-speed with reverse gearbox whilst a 10bhp version was also available powered by either a JAP or a Blackburn engine. The vehicle was underpowered for its weight as it had a welded angle iron chassis with a wooden frame and metal plates attached to them. With large artillery type wheels, suspension was provided by independent coil springs at the front and radius nods and quarter-elliptic springs at the rear. Whilst the Popular and Standard models had two-seats with a dickey seat available in the boot, the Family version had four fixed seats.

1919 — LSD Commercial models

The LSD also came both as a commercial van and a pick-up variant. With similar specifications to the passenger models, these variants were fitted with a JAP engine and a two-speed with reverse gearbox that provided drive to the single rear wheel via a chain. The van had a longer bonnet and a vertical windscreen with a large enclosed rear section. The pick-up version resembled the front of the passenger vehicle though it had a flatbed area behind the driver's seat. All models were manufactured until 1923. In the same year production was moved to Mirfield in Yorkshire with vehicles being manufactured by the LSD Motor Co Ltd until 1924.

T

T3 Motion

2011 — R3

Based in Costa Mesa, California, USA, T3 Motion manufacture three-wheel electric stand-up vehicles (ESV). With vehicles like this, the rider stands on a platform and controls the vehicle via handlebars. The main market for these vehicles is law enforcement and security officers on patrol, as it allows them to travel greater distances at up to 20mph.

Initially announced in June 2010 as the GT3, in 2011 the company unveiled the first prototype of a car now called the R3 — R3 for Revolutionary three-wheel vehicle. Although, at first glance, the vehicle appears to have four wheels with two at the back positioned next to each other, the rear is quite unique in that it is actually a very wide single rear wheel, which has two high performance tyres on it thus improving traction, stability and handling. Designed by Dan Ellis with the direction of Ki Nam, the R3 is a front-wheel drive electric vehicle that has an ac induction motor powered by a lithium-polymer battery, which has a range of 80-100 miles (129-161km) on a single charge and a top speed of 70-120mph (113-193km/h). A hybrid version is also planned; this will have a range of 300 miles (483km) and a top speed of around 100mph (161km/h). The vehicle has two seats and contains the latest electronics, including an integrated 'black box' video and data

recording system. The dashboard contains a mounting point for a Samsung Galaxy tablet, which, when incorporated into the dashboard, allows the driver to control the stereo and navigation system. At the time of writing, a launch date for vehicle production has not yet been announced.

Talleres Metalurgicos Barcino

1960 — Barcino

Powered by a range of engines from 125cc to 197cc, the Barcino was built by Talleres Metalurgicos Barcino in Barcelona, Spain, between 1960 and 1966. The Barcino was a light delivery vehicle in which goods were carried in a tray above the rear engine compartment.

Above Top: Whilst the R3 prototype is an electric vehicle with a range of 100 miles on a single charge, a hybrid version is also planned with a 300-mile range. T3 Motion

Above right: Although the R3 appears to have two wheels at the back, it actually has a very wide single wheel fitted with two high performance tyres. T3 Motion

Tankettes Ltd

1920 — Runabout

Capable of 100mpg (2.8-litre/100km), the Tankette Runabout was a diminutive three-wheeler introduced in 1920. It cost £92 10s, a price that included a year's insurance policy. Manufactured by Tankettes Ltd in Finsbury Park, London, UK, the vehicle weighed 270lb. Despite its size it came equipped with a hood, screen, small electric lights and a long cushion seat with a padded back that could accommodate two people. Fitted with a 2.75bhp, two-stroke, air-cooled Union engine, it was capable of 30mph (48km/h). The engine sat vertically at the front part of the chassis in between the front two wheels and provided drive to the rear wheel by a chain through a two-speed gearbox that sat below the passenger's seat. Sprung by leaf springs at the front and back, the chassis was made from Ash with steel strips attached for the driving gear and to create a frame for the steel body panels. The front axle was telescopic and so the overall width of the vehicle could be narrowed to 2ft 11in at its widest part. Although the vehicle was classed as a three-wheeler, the single wheel at the back was actually two wheels that had been bolted together. Production of the Tankette is believed to have ceased in the same year as it was launched.

Tatra

1929 — Type 49 (Passenger/Commercial)

Manufactured in Kopřivnice, Moravia, Czechoslovakia, during 1929 and 1930 by Tatra, the Tatra 49 came in both passenger and commercial variants. It was an attempt by Tatra to offer a cheap utility vehicle. Fitted with a four-stroke, air-cooled, single-cylinder, 528cc engine that powered the single back wheel through a three-speed gearbox, the vehicle had a top speed of around 31-37mph (50–60km/h). Whilst the passenger version was a fully-enclosed four-seat vehicle with side doors, the commercial version was an open vehicle that had either one or two bucket seats at the rear (the passenger sitting behind the driver). A number of commercial bodies could then be fitted between the front two wheels. The chassis on both versions consisted of a central tube with a front rigid axle attached to it and a swing arm at the rear. The commercial version used the central tube of the chassis as an exhaust silencer. Around 200 vehicles were made, mostly in the commercial guise.

Despite its size the Tankette Runabout was fairly well equipped with electric lights, hood and a windscreen. Author's Collection

Most commonly seen in its commercial layout, the Tatra Type 40 was also available as a four-seat passenger version with a fully-enclosed body. Author's Collection

A 1958 Taylor R Trident; this was powered by a 24V electric motor.
Craig Thorness

Teilhol Voiture Électrique

1970 — Citadine

Manufactured in France from 1970 by Teilhol Voiture Électrique, the Teilhol Citadine was an electric vehicle powered by a 48V, 4kW electric motor. With its polyester body, tubular steel chassis and a bank of eight 12V batteries, the vehicle was able to run *circa* 25 to 40 miles (40-64km) on a single charge with a top speed of 31mph (50km/h). The vehicle had a single opening front door and seated two adults. It was manufactured until 1972 with 28 vehicles known to have been built.

1975 — Messagette

The Teilhol Messagette was introduced in 1975 and had an open body with back-to-back seating. Powered by an electric motor it had a range of 50 to 62 miles (80-100km). The vehicles were also available as a 'Handicar' designed for the disabled. Production of all models ceased in 1983.

Taylor-Dunn Manufacturing Co

1955 — PG

The Taylor Shop was founded in 1949 in California, USA, by R D Taylor Sr. At the time he built handcarts for carrying chicken feed. In 1951, F A Dunn joined the business, forming the Taylor-Dunn Manufacturing Co. In 1955 Taylor-Dunn produced a model PG, a three-wheel 24V electric chair.

1957 — Taylor R Trident

In 1957 the company produced the Taylor R Trident; this was another three-wheel vehicle designed for travelling around the neighbourhood. Powered by a 24V electric motor, the Trident had a top speed of 16mph (26km/h). With its batteries, the vehicle weighed 730lb and, to help reduce weight, had a fibreglass body that featured snap-in side curtains. The vehicle could be purchased with either a steering wheel or a tiller and also with either hand or foot controls. It was produced up until 1963 when the company built other vehicles. The company still exists at the time of writing, manufacturing commercial vehicles that include various three-wheel tow tractors for use in warehouses and on site.

Thompson Brothers (TB)

1919 — Cyclecar

Thompson Brothers (Bilston) Ltd was a manufacturer of a number of things, including galvanised baths and steam boilers. First established in 1810 in Bilston, Birmingham, UK, the company was acquired in 1882 by Enoch Stephen Thompson. It was in 1919 that the company started to manufacture the TB Cyclecar with the first vehicles being sold in 1920. Built on a patented tubular steel chassis the vehicle had an open two-seat body made of sheet metal. There were two engine options: an air-cooled, 8bhp JAP engine or a 10bhp JAP engine for £200. Both drove the single rear wheel via a two-speed with reverse gearbox. The wheels were wire spoke and fitted with discs. Lighting was an optional extra with other extras available, including a spare wheel, windscreen, hood, tools, jack and a pump

1920 — Sports

In 1920 a Sports model was introduced; this was a single-seat version that had the steering wheel positioned in the centre. It was

Although fitted with an emergency seat for a possible passenger, the TB Sports was essentially a single-seater. Author's Collection

A 1937 TB Mobile Refuelling Tender fitted with twin 500gall fuel tanks and a 50gall oil tank. This version was used at both military and civil airfields. Robert Knight

powered by an 8bhp, air-cooled, V-twin engine that drove the single rear wheel via a shaft drive through a two-speed with reverse gearbox. In case a passenger was required, it did have an emergency seat at the back. The wire wheels also had discs fitted to them to provide a sportier appearance. The Sports model received a number of changes, with 1922 and 1924 versions being produced.

1921 — Standard/Deluxe

In 1921 two new models in the form of the TB Standard and TB Deluxe were introduced. These now, in addition to the air-cooled engines, also used a water-cooled, 8bhp or 10bhp Precision engine that powered the rear wheel through a three-speed with reverse gearbox. The vehicles were updated in 1922 and then again in 1924.

1924 — Family

The Family version appeared in 1924; this was a four-seat version but was short-lived as production of all models ceased in the same year, when the company then decided to concentrate on commercial vehicles, with around 750 vehicles being manufactured.

1935 — Mobile Refuelling Tender

A three-wheeler did reappear in 1935; however, this was a single-seat commercial vehicle designed purely for airports for delivering petrol to aircraft, lubricating oil and towing aircraft. The vehicles were also fitted with an air compressor for pumping up tyres. It was powered by a Ford Ten 1,172cc engine and fitted with two x 500gall petrol tanks as well as a 50gall oil tank. The model was manufactured until the mid-1940s.

Thoroughbred MotorSports

2006 — Stallion

Built by Thoroughbred MotorSports and its sister company, Motor Trike, the Thoroughbred Stallion first appeared in 2006. The concept was to create an automatic vehicle to meet customer demand for such a vehicle. Around 800 vehicles were built before production ceased in 2010 as a result of the state of the economy with few orders being received. As the economy picked up again, the company announced in May 2012 plans to build another 150 Stallions, with the first models reaching dealerships in October 2012. Designed and built in Texas, USA, the Stallion is fitted with a four-cylinder, 2,300cc Ford engine that provides drive to the rear wheels through a Ford five-speed automatic with reverse gearbox. The vehicle has a tubular and box frame made from steel with an open injection moulded body with low cut sides and no doors. The standard model includes a number of features, including power front and rear disc brakes, on-board air compressor to adjust the patented air ride suspension, air conditioning, cruise control and

The Thoroughbred Stallion was created with the intention of building an automatic vehicle. Thoroughbred MotorSports

adjustable pedals. Weighing in at 1,736lb, the Stallion has a fuel consumption of 35mpg (8-litre/100km) in the city and 45mpg (6.2-litre/100km) on the highway. From 2013 a number of options became available; including wing deflectors, air wings and paint-on wood grain. The Thoroughbred Stallion remains in production at the time of writing and the sister company, Motor Trike, manufactures a number of motorcycle-type trikes.

Thurlow & Co

1914 — Cyclecar

Manufactured by Thurlow & Co in Wimbledon, London, UK, the first Thurlow prototype appeared in 1914 and used an 8bhp, air-cooled JAP engine. With the start of World War 1 plans for production were halted and did not start until after the war in 1920. The production version of the Thurlow Cyclecar was powered by a 10bhp, V-twin Precision engine. This drove a chain to a three-speed Sturmey-Archer gearbox that provided drive via belts to the front wheels. Unlike a number of vehicles at the time, the engine could be started from the driver's seat as the starter was connected to the exhaust valves that were automatically lifted during the first half of the lever's travel. The vehicle had a tubular steel chassis with the body being made from sheet steel. Production ended a year later, in 1921.

The Thurlow Cyclecar was amongst the very few vehicles of its time where the engine could be started from the driver's seat. Kerry Croxton

Tiger Truck

2005 — Liger

Primarily manufacturing four-wheel trucks, Tiger Truck was founded in 1999 in Texas, USA. In 2005 the three-wheel Electric Liger was introduced as a lightweight pick-up truck. Fitted with a 72V dc electric motor, it used 12 6V batteries (two banks wired in parallel). Weighing 2,967lb when empty, the vehicle could carry up to 4,500lb with a maximum speed of 20mph (32km/h). In December 2010 Tiger Truck closed down and ceased production of all vehicles. The company reopened its doors as Tiger International in January 2012 with a new range of vehicles but this no longer included a three-wheeler.

Toby Industries

1976 — Trivator

The Trivator was built in Ruidoso, New Mexico, USA, just west of the alleged UFO crash in Roswell in 1947. It was manufactured by a company called Toby Industries in 1976 and was sold in a number of kit forms or as a turnkey product. The body of the Trivator was a one-piece fibreglass shell attached to a steel frame. The body incorporated two seats that were side-by-side. Entrance to the vehicle was by a central canopy that tilted forward and could also be removed if required. As standard the Trivator used a Volkswagen engine giving speeds of up to 100mph (161km/h) and achieving 45-60mpg (6.2-4.7-litre/100km). Other engines were also installed, including a Porsche four-cylinder, Corvair six-cylinder, Buick V6 and the Mazda Rotary RX2 unit. These were all used with a Volkswagen transaxle although each engine required different conversion adapters. In addition to being a turnkey product, the Trivator was sold in three kit forms; these included a Basic kit that consisted of a one-piece fibreglass body, seat insert, belly pan, canopy and jig welded steel frame with front suspension. A Deluxe kit included the Basic kit plus all templates and patterns, wiring harness, continental wheel kit, fuel tank, trim accessories and steering assembly. Finally, there was a Complete kit; this was the same as the Deluxe kit plus all non-Volkswagen parts needed to bring the vehicle to a finished road machine. It is believed that the rights to build the body were sold on to someone in Arizona after 12 vehicles were built.

Sold in three kit forms or as a turnkey product, the Trivator was able to use a variety of engines. Bill Fiddler

Torpelle

1914 — Torpelle

Manufactured in France in 1914, the Torpelle was a tandem-seated vehicle that had a steel chassis and a metal body with a fold-down hood. The engine drove the single rear wheel via a chain. Production is believed to have been very brief and ceased in the same year with the start of World War 1.

Available with either an open or a fully-enclosed body, the Tourist was not fitted with a reverse gear as a result of its exceptional turning circle. Author's Collection

Tourist Automobile-Werk GmbH

1907 — Tourist

Although a three-wheeler, the Tourist was much more than a Cyclecar compared with other three-wheelers at that time. Built by the Tourist Automobile-Werk GmbH in Berlin, Germany, from 1907, the vehicle had a steel chassis and a large four-seat metal body that included side doors both at the front and at the back for passengers in the rear. The vehicle was available with either an enclosed or an open body fitted with a collapsible hood for bad weather but no windscreen. It was powered by a front-mounted, 7bhp, air-cooled, V-twin engine that had exhaust valves suspended over the cylinders. Drive was sent to the rear wheels by chains from a secondary shaft. A fan was also mounted in front of the engine to aid cooling and two dog clutches, which engaged with the high or lower gear, provided a number of speeds. A reverse gear was not fitted as the Tourist was able to turn around in a road that was only 10ft wide. The vehicle had both a hand- and a footbrake along with a steering wheel that steered through a pair of bevels by wheel and pillar.

1911 — Torpedo

In 1911 the Tourist was sold to George Beck & Co in Berlin and manufactured as the Berliner Automobilfabrik Torpedo until 1920 with only minor changes being made.

Toyota

2013 — i-Road

Unveiled at the Geneva Motor Show in March 2013, the Toyota i-Road is a concept vehicle with Active Lean technology. It is powered by two 2kW electric motors that are mounted in the front wheels and use a lithium-ion battery with a range of up to 30 miles (49km) on a single charge and can be fully charged from a domestic power point in three hours. With a top speed of 28mph (45km/h), the i-Road is classified by Toyota as a PMV (Personal Mobility Vehicle) and is a fully enclosed two-seater with the passenger sitting in tandem. Being no wider than a conventional motorcycle, the i-Road is able to lean into corners by using a lean actuator and gearing that is mounted above the front suspension member and linked via a yoke to both front wheels. An ECU then calculates the degree of tilt required based on steering angle, gyro sensor and road speed whilst steering is done by the single rear wheel via a conventional steering wheel. Due to its compact size — 2,350mm in length and 1,445mm in height — Toyota states that four i-Road vehicles can be parked in a single car parking bay. It is believed that, at some point in 2014, a vehicle developed from the i-Road will enter some form of production.

Fitted with a 2kW electric motor in each front wheel the Toyota i-Road is a two-seater with rear-wheel steering. Yasuo Taskahashi

Trevithick

1801 — Puffing Devil

On Christmas Eve 1801 in Camborne, Cornwall, UK, an engineer called Richard Trevithick took his new steam vehicle out for its first test run. After a number of years research, Trevithick had developed a high-pressure engine powered by steam. His vehicle — or *Puffing Devil* as it became known — was no more than a boiler on three wheels, but it took Trevithick and a number of his friends half-a-mile up a hill. The vehicle's principal feature was a cylindrical horizontal boiler and a single horizontal cylinder let into it. The piston propelled back and forth in the cylinder by pressure from the steam. This was linked by piston rod and connecting rod to a crankshaft bearing a large flywheel.

The vehicle was used for several journeys until it turned over on the unsuitable tracks that were used for packhorses in Cornwall at that time. After having been righted, the vehicle was driven by Trevithick and his crew back to Camborne where they retired to a public house. The water level dropped in the boiler and the fusible plug melted, sending a jet of steam into the furnace where it blew embers all around, setting fire to the surroundings and the wooden parts of the engine. *Puffing Devil* was the world's first passenger car.

1803 — London Steam Carriage

Undeterred, despite the disaster of losing his first vehicle, Trevithick built a three-wheel steam carriage that he called the *London Steam Carriage*. However, this time it was complete with seats and had a real carriage-like appearance. The vehicle had two large wheels measuring eight feet in diameter at the back with the boiler

mounted just behind them and a smaller, single front wheel with steering controlled by a tiller. In 1803, he drove it through London's Oxford Street on demonstration runs and reached speeds of 8-9mph (13-14km/h). With a chassis made of wrought iron and wood, the vehicle weighed around 1.9 tons and was large enough to carry eight passengers. Despite the runs through London, passengers found the vehicle uncomfortable and nobody was really interested with the result that, when he ran out of funds, Trevithick sold the power unit to a local miller. Trevithick's vehicle was the first self-propelled carriage in the capital and in essence the first London bus.

TR Hog

2002 — TR Hog

Designed in 2002 by Charles Valentine in Arkansas, USA, the TR Hog was a three-wheel Harley built for paraplegics. Charles Valentine created over 30 hot-rods and motorcycles and so knew the design was functional. It was designed to permit a paraplegic to roll his wheel chair up and enter the vehicle, placing his folded chair on the rack behind him. Powered by a 750cc Yamaha engine, Dave Norton (see page 177) was involved and, after a number of engineering studies, believed that the TR Hog was a potentially fine machine. A US Patent Attorney has also commented that the reverse mechanism is patentable and that the whole machine is possibly also patentable as a concept.

Tri Car Corporation of America

1955 — TRI-CAR Suburbanette

The *TRI-CAR* Suburbanette was announced to the public in February 1955 at the Universal Travel & Auto Sports Show at Madison Square Garden, New York City, USA. Designed by Charles H Payne and believed to be based on the 1932 Martin Martinette (see page 150), only one working vehicle was built although there were plans to build a further two variations: one with a transparent panel above the seats and another with a fabric roof. With a top speed of 60mph (96.5km/h), the Suburbanette was fitted with an air-cooled, 30bhp Lycoming engine positioned in the rear, driving the single back wheel, and had a fibreglass body attached to a wooden frame. Able to seat two adults and a child, the vehicle also featured a hydraulic lift to raise the body from the chassis to ease maintenance.

1955 — TRI-CAR Kari-van

A light commercial version, in the form of the TRI-CAR Kari-van, was also created although, unlike the Suburbanette, the engine was fitted at the front. It had a burnished aluminium body riveted to a wooden frame and had large sliding doors. With a carrying capacity of 45cu ft, the vehicle was fitted with two single seats so that the passenger one could be removed if required to create more space. It was initially believed that this model was never built; however, a 1955 TRI-CAR Kari-van is now known to exist.

1955 — TRI-CAR Stationette

A light parcel delivery version, with a 32cc ft carrying capacity, was to also to be built. This was to have been called the TRI-CAR Stationette. It was planned to have a fibreglass body with the same front end as the Suburbanette and an enlarged rear section designed for carrying cargo. However, it is not known whether the Stationette was built. It is understood that the TRI-CAR project was sold to Fairchild Aircraft, which then sold it to Rohr Industries. No news about the TRI-CAR has appeared since.

The brochure for the 1955 Tri-Car Suburbanette claims that, amongst other things details, the body cannot be dented with a hammer. Lane Motor Museum

Tri-Mobile

1938 — Tri-Mobile

Designed by W F Mehl in 1938, the Tri-Mobile from Missouri, USA, is not thought to have reached production. Advertised as 'The Car of Tomorrow', the Tri-Mobile was an open two-seat vehicle, with the engine positioned behind the seats driving the single rear wheel. The body had a raked windscreen, wrap-around chrome bumpers and louvres in the rear section of the body to pull in and circulate air around the engine.

Advertised as 'The Car of Tomorrow', the Tri-Mobile is believed not to have reached production. Alden Jewell

Tri-Tech Autocraft Ltd

Tri-Tech Autocraft Ltd originally started as a company in the UK in 2000 manufacturing a range of unobtainable parts for the micro-car market. It was, therefore, a natural progression for the company to manufacture its own replica cars in 2003. The vehicles were available as complete cars or in a DIY kit form. It was estimated it would take 28 days to build one of the kits. Production of both models ceased in 2004.

2003 — Zetta 300

The Zetta 300 was a replica of the BMW Isetta although it had the advantages of modern technology with a 40mm box ladder frame construction and a Honda 250cc automatic engine. The engine sat in line over the rear swing arm assembly; this was claimed to give a better ride and increased stability over the original. The body of the Zetta was made from fibreglass, giving the vehicle an overall weight of approximately 300kg and a fuel consumption of 60-70mpg (4.7-4-litre/100km).

2003 — Schmitt

The Schmitt was also powered by a Honda 250cc engine and was an accurate representation of the Messerschmitt. The vehicle used a braking system from the Mini; however, in 2004, a recall notice was issued. This advised six purchasers of the vehicles to obtain and fit the necessary components to ensure the rear brake worked on application of the service brake. The Schmitt had a fibreglass body and an integral steel chassis frame in a monocoque construction. The total weight of the Scmitt was 270kg giving the vehicle an overall fuel consumption of 65-75mpg (4.3-3.7-litre/100km).

Tri-Wheel Motor Corporation

1948 — Thrift-T

The Thrift-T was designed and manufactured by the Tri-Wheel Motor Corporation, Springfield, Massachusetts, USA, from 1948. The company initially started in Oxford, North Carolina, USA. The original vehicle was designed as a three-seater for commuting; however, by 1955, the Thrift-T was also available as a pick-up, an enclosed delivery van or an open-top utility that could seat up to five people with additional room for luggage. With a top speed of 40mph

Built from 1948 the Thrift-T was available as either a three-seater or a delivery van. Mark Zalutko

(64km/h), it was fitted with a 10bhp, air-cooled, opposed-twin, Onan engine that was mounted under the seat and had a Crosley drivetrain with a three-speed gearbox. The body was made from steel and reportedly could be removed from the steel box chassis in less than 30min. Production ceased in 1955.

Tribelhorn

1918 — Tribelhorn

Dating originally to 1899, the electric-powered Tribelhorn was manufactured in Switzerland in numbers from 1902 by A Tribelhorn & Cie AG, although it was not until 1918, under the name of Electrische Fahrzeuge AG (EFAG), that the company introduced a three-wheeler when production moved from Feldbach to Alstetten. The vehicle had a steel two-seat body and the batteries were stored under the seat with the motor driving the rear two wheels. The company also produced a hybrid vehicle that used a petrol-electric generator that increased the range of the vehicles. A commercial variant was used by the Swiss Post Office; such was the demand that Tribelhorn was prevented from building many vehicles for private use, constructing only special orders until production ceased in 1920. From 1920 to 1937 three- and four-wheel vehicles were manufactured using the EFAG name.

Resembling a canoe on wheels, the Trident Cyclecar was supposed to have been built in the UK. Author's Collection

Trident

1919 — Cyclecar

The Trident prototypes were first built in France but, in August 1919, it was announced that the Trident would be manufactured in the UK by Federated Exporters Ltd of London. However, despite planned models of a one-passenger taxicab and delivery van, production in the UK is not believed to have started. The first Trident Cyclecar was powered by a 3.5bhp, twin-cylinder engine that was mounted on, and drove, the single front wheel; however, later prototypes also used either a 8bhp or a 10bhp, twin-cylinder engine. The engine was mounted on the nearside whilst the gearbox, clutch and magneto were mounted on the offside. The vehicle was a two-seater, seating two people in tandem — the passenger behind the driver — and had a steel body. The latter had no weather protection and was suspended by four laterally mounted and interconnected cantilever springs; these were said to have provided exceptional shock absorption qualities. Production of the vehicle, which cost £160, ceased in 1920.

Trident Motors Inc

1985 — Trident R-834

Located in Columbus, Ohio, USA, Trident Motors Inc, a division of KVV Enterprises, made a number of utility three- and four-wheel vehicles. The four-wheeler — the M-25 Multi-truck — was a diesel-powered vehicle that had over 20 quick interchangeable bodies to turn the vehicle into virtually everything, including a pick-up truck and a snowplough. The three-wheelers were, therefore, designed to match this versatility.

The three-wheel Trident R-834 range was also a work horse albeit using a smaller 848cc, four-stroke, four-cylinder, aluminium Reliant engine. The vehicles came in a number of guises; each had a steel box chassis that was a heavily modified version of the chassis fitted to the Reliant Robin. The vehicles carried various steel bodies, with an enclosed cabin that had seating for two. Each Trident had a 1,000lb payload capacity dump bed with a hydraulic tilting system and a 'quick pin disconnect system', which allowed components to be interchanged between various models. Early models of the Trident R-834 had a single headlight; however, in 1985, the vehicles received a number of changes, including dual headlights with indicators mounted either side.

1985 — Trident R-834/T

The Trident R-834/T was an open-top version that had a hydraulic back with hinged sides.

1985 — Trident R-834R/ Trident R-834P

The Trident R-834R was an enclosed-cab version that had a deep dumper body at the back, whilst the Trident R-834P was similar although fitted with a shallower pick-up body at the rear. Production of all Trident three-wheel vehicles is believed to have ceased in the late 1980s.

Using a Reliant 850cc engine and modified chassis, the Trident R-834 series was available with a number of commercial bodies. Author's Collection

With an excellent power to weight ratio, the Trifid proved to be an efficient vehicle for hill climbing and cross-country trials. Phil Wells

The Trifid next to an Austin Mini; a Mini was the donor of many of the parts required to build the three-wheeler. Phil Wells

Trifid

1990 — Trifid

Created in 1990 at Hopton, Norfolk, UK, the Trifid was an Austin Mini-based, two-seat, three-wheeler built by Phil Wells and Mark Spriddell. The original vehicle was created from an abandoned trials/autotest car that was basically a cut-down Austin Mini. It was cut down even further to just the floor pan and they built their superlegerra — tubes covered in sheet steel — body onto to it. The rear subframe was fabricated from a narrowed rear subframe with a tower to carry a single front rubber cone. Total construction time from Mini to MoT was just three weeks of evenings and weekends. A production model then came about when the team obtained a fibreglass floor pan made by Minus cars and, after a six-month on/off process of carving foam and filler, the two part moulds for the wings and body were made. From these, four bodies were created before the pair moved on to other things. The fibreglass tubs were a monocoque with plywood diaphragms. The Trifid was powered by numerous stock engines; that owned by Phil Wells had a 100bhp, 1,380cc engine with a 2.9:1 final drive ratio. With a total weight of *circa* 360-380kg, the vehicle was not short of speed. In all, five vehicles — including the prototype — were built, of which the prototype and two of the fibreglass-bodied vehicles are known to survive at the time of writing.

Powered by a 50cc engine, the Trigger 50 is becoming a popular vehicle when rented out to tourists in a number of countries. Bob Kranenburg

Trigger Technics BV

1990s — Scooter Car/Trigger 50

The Trigger Scooter car is manufactured by Trigger Technics BV in the Netherlands. The president of the company, Jeroen Boekhoorn, first conceived the idea of a three-wheel sports car in 1987 and, a few years later, produced the first Trigger. The vehicle was powered by a Yamaha FZR1000 motorcycle engine and had a fibreglass body attached to a steel chassis. Its low weight gave the Trigger a 0-60mph (0-96km/h) time of 5.8sec and a top speed of around 140mph

Introduced in 1979, the Triking has consistently developed over the years with the latest versions being powered by a 950-1,200cc Moto-Guzzi engine. Alex

(225km/h). At that time the market was full of four-wheel sports car, like the Mazda MX5 and Lotus Elise, and so the Trigger was not a commercial success. Only one Trigger was built; this is now referred to as 'Big Trigger'. As a result of the Big Trigger's commercial failure, Jeroen Boekhoorn started thinking about a new venture after visiting Italy. In 1999 this became the Trigger Scooter Car and later the Trigger 50. This two-seat vehicle is powered by a one-cylinder, two-stroke, 50cc moped engine that provides drive to the single rear wheel through an automatic gearbox and has a maximum speed of 30mph (48km/h). It has a coloured polyester body attached to a steel cage construction, which also features a stainless steel roll bar. The controls are the same as on a moped with steering being via handlebars. It has successfully entered the US market and has a European Type and DOT approval. Due to increasing demand, production capacity was increased in October 2005. In 2006 Trigger Technics became a subsidiary of the Fox Group, becoming Trigger Cars BV. At the time of writing, the Trigger 50 is in production and exported to many countries worldwide, being employed in a number of places as a vehicle that can be hired by tourists.

Triking Cyclecars Ltd/ Triking Sports Cars Ltd

1979 — Triking

Generally recognised by many as one of the best trikes around, the Triking was introduced in 1979 in Norfolk, UK, by Tony Divey. Being a long-term Morgan enthusiast, he was inspired by three-wheel Morgans and, as a result of the high prices of Morgan three-wheelers at the time, decided to design and build his own car, which would be in effect a modern Morgan. Divey built his first car, the 'Old Lady' as it became known, between February and September 1978. Whilst building the car, Divey had several enquiries about making others, and decided to build 10 to recoup his extensive costs. Unfortunately, as he himself says: 'I didn't have the sense to stop there!' The first production car, at the time of writing based in Germany, was constructed in 1979. The vehicles have developed fairly constantly over the years, absorbing new technologies as they appear. However, a major revamp was made in 1990 when chassis 100 was built. Divey redesigned the body and chassis with a new tubular front end, and a one-piece fibreglass body with removable bonnets front and rear. Before this, the Triking had

alloy side panels and fibreglass bonnet, rear end and wings fixed to a steel space frame. In addition to road use, the Triking also has an extensive competition history, having competed in MCC Classic Trials continuously for 21 years. The 'Old Lady' also has the distinction of being the only car to compete in all three classic trials and the MCC Silverstone race meeting in one year. She had completed over 600,000 miles (965,000km) at the time.

A choice of Moto-Guzzi V-twin engines could be fitted to the vehicle, with either an 850cc or 950cc option. Fitting the 950cc engine provided the Triking with 71bhp and a top speed of 121mph (195km/h) with 0-60mph (0-96km/h) possible in 7.8 seconds. Costing £4,500 in 1982 for a complete vehicle, a 1,000cc engine was also available for an additional supplement of £250. In a kit form the price was £2,580 or £3,780 (excluding VAT) if the engine was included. By 1992 the 100th Triking had been made, with a number of variants available, including a 'Super Light' racing version and a supercharged example. Following Divey's retirement Triking Cyclecars Ltd was dissolved in 2006. The company was then taken over by Alan Layzell, who had joined Triking in 1989. Laysell formed Triking Sports Cars Ltd in 2009

The latest form of the Triking uses an air-cooled, V-twin, 950-1,200cc Moto-Guzzi engine that develops 70-100bhp and provides a top speed — 'in the most conservative state of tune' — of *circa* 100mph (161km/h). The chassis remains a tubular welded steel space frame that is epoxy powder coated and has an unstressed fibreglass body. With ventilated disc brakes on all wheels, the vehicle's suspension consist of a polyurethane bushed independent, fully adjustable tubular wishbone, with an inclined adjustable coil-spring damper. At the rear it uses a taper roller bearing swing arm with an inclined adjustable coil spring damper. Triking vehicles remain in production at the time of writing and are available in either kit form or full turnkey product.

Available with a number of body options, the Trimak had a two-seat cabin, which incorporated a heater. RUMCar News

Trilux

1986 — Trilux

Built in 1986 the Trilux was based on a 1920s Morgan Supersport Aero. Originally designed as a kit car, only one vehicle was ever produced and was described as one of the 'most professional one-off trikes ever built'. The Trilux was built on a homemade chassis and used parts from the Citroën Ami, the Renault 12 and the Morris Marina.

Trimak

1952 — 600/700/800

Designed by aeronautical engineer Estanislao Makowiecky Pomian, the Trimak was manufactured in Madrid, Spain, from 1952. It was a commercial three-wheeler that was available with a number of bodies — model 600 (pick-up); model 700 (van body); and, model 800 with concertina type sides — and had a payload of 700kg. A variety of other custom bodies were also available, including a dump truck and a

tanker. The vehicles had a two-seat cabin with standard car-type controls, with a steering wheel and creature comforts, including a heater. The vehicles were generally fitted with an air-cooled, single-cylinder, 14bhp, 250cc Lew engine, which was made under licence in Poland, although some models were equipped with a diesel engine. The engine was mounted under the seat and provided power to the rear axle through a propeller shaft. In 1967 the company went bankrupt and, after being seized by the creditors, was moved to Barcelona, Spain, where it continued production until 1974 although the vehicles were now fitted with a Seat 250cc engine.

1963 — Publicity car

In 1963 Trimak prepared a car version; this used the same commercial chassis and engine but was fitted with a car body that resembled that of an aircraft. It had a narrow body with a cockpit-type canopy and a large fin behind the passenger compartment. The rear wheels stuck out from the sides with small horizontal wing type fins over them. The vehicle was made for the 1963 Barcelona Exhibition and built purely as a publicity vehicle; it was, however, able to reach 84mpg (3.4-litre/100km)

The original Trio used parts from numerous vehicles and later went on to be sold as a set of plans.
Steve Bowers

Trio Cars

1983 — Trio

Using parts from numerous vehicles, the Trio was designed and built by Ken Hallet of Wareham, Dorset, UK, in 1983. It was based around a Mini sub-frame and A series engine, whilst using Austin Metro drive shafts, Austin Allegro steering column, Austin 1100 disc brakes and rear radius arm, a Reliant Robin coil/spring damper unit, Renault 5 radiator and Morris Ital wheels. This was all held together in a steel box chassis with a two-seat body made from marine plywood skinned in aluminium and vinyl with fibreglass bonnet and wings. The Trio was sold as a set of plans for £25; these were available until 2000 and consisted of two manuals — one for the chassis and another for the body — though five chassis kits are also believed to have been made.

Tripolino

1950s — Tripolino

The Tripolino was designed by Alois Wolf and created in Czechoslovakia in the 1950s. Vehicle production in post-war Czechoslovakia was very limited and did not fulfil the demand for personal transport. As a result, a number of vehicles were built by amateurs either as one-offs or as a small run; one of these was the Tripolino. With a body that tapered off towards the rear and was designed for high speed, this two-seat vehicle was powered by a Jawa 350cc, two-cylinder, two-stroke, air-cooled engine. This was fitted behind the passenger seat and provided power to the single rear wheel via a chain. The back section of the vehicle was hinged and lifted up to provide access to the engine. The 350cc engine gave the vehicle a top speed of around 71mph (114km/h) although there were plans for a 500cc version with an estimated top speed of around 93mph (150km/h). Only the prototype vehicle is known to exist at the time of writing, although this has its engine missing.

TriVette

1974 — TriVette

Designed by Bob Keyes, a physicist with 30 years of experience in the aerospace and defence business, the TriVette was introduced in 1974. The original vehicles used the Fiat 850cc engine, which gave sporty performance and three-wheel economy at 50-65mpg (5.6-4.3-litre/100km), whilst later models used a Honda Civic engine. With a tubular steel chassis and a fibreglass body, the vehicle had two seats, with the passenger sitting behind the driver. However, the vehicle was optimised to carry only a driver most of the time. Unlike many contemporary three-wheelers, which were built as low performance vehicles, the physics of the TriVette meant that it actually became more stable as its speed increased. In 1980 the Department of Transportation determined that the TriVette had a theoretical tip-over limit of 1.28 lateral 'G' or a 0.5 lateral 'G' safety margin over what the tyres could deliver. This meant the TriVette would slide long before it reached the tip-over limit and that, theoretically, the car

Bob Keyes with the TriVette. This was a vehicle that, as a result of its design, was said to out corner many four-wheel sports cars of its time. Bob & Diana Keyes

Pictured here with Diana Keyes, the TriVette featured a lift-up canopy to gain access to the vehicle. Bob & Diana Keyes

actually out cornered many four-wheel sports cars, like the Alfa Romeo, BMW 530i, Fiat X1/9, Lotus Elite and Porsche 911S. This, combined with the excellent braking of the vehicle, led to orders being placed for TriVettes with more powerful engines.

1975 — Turbo TriVette

The Turbo TriVettes used a high performance 220bhp engine whilst still maintaining the weight at 1,140lb. This allowed the vehicle to travel from 0-60mph (0-96km/h) in 3.5sec. Because of its characteristics, a high-speed pursuit vehicle capable of 160-165mph (257-265.5km/h) was made for the California Highway Patrol under a grant from the National Science Foundation. An enhanced version of the TriVette was created in 1993 with the 200mph (322km/h) Vigillante (see page 270).

2004 — TriVette Two

Introduced in 2004, the TriVette Two was available in a kit form starting at $12,500. This included all parts needed except for those from a donor vehicle. The donor vehicles provided the necessary drive trains required. There was a choice of five possible donor vehicles: a 1992-1995 Honda Civic; third-generation Volkswagen Golf; Ford Taurus (3.0-litre V6); Cadillac NorthStar V8; and, a small block 350 Chevrolet. The TriVette 2 had a mild steel tubular subframe at the front, whilst the rear of the vehicle used the entire front end from the donor vehicle. The passenger compartment was made from a tubed

aluminium structure that had aluminium bulkheads and floor skins, whilst the bodywork was a composite of aircraft fibreglass. The vehicle also featured an optional lift-up canopy that could be used. This came from the same mould as the canopy used on the Vigillante. Since Bob Keyes' death in July 2006 no further kits have been created to date.

Trojan

1961 — Trojan 200 (Model 601/603)

Having produced motor vehicles with the Trojan name since 1914, it was in 1961 that Trojan of Croydon, UK, took over the Heinkel plant (see page 115). Production of the vehicle was switched to Croydon, where the company continued to make the model under a new name — Trojan 200 — using a single-cylinder, four-stroke, 10bhp, 198cc engine that continued to be made by Heinkel in Germany. The Trojan — denoted Model 603 for a left-hand drive version — was later modified to be right-hand drive — Model 601 — for the UK market. Production continued until 1964 but competition from the Austin Mini undermined sales. Although the last vehicle was made in 1964, the Trojan was selling very slowly and some new vehicles were not actually registered until 1966.

After taking over Heinkel in 1961, Trojan continued to make Heinkel vehicles under the new name of the Trojan 200. Wilfried Dibbets

1961 — Trojan 200 (Model 605)

The Trojan 200 was also available; this was a van designated as Model 605. Around 19 vans were built; however, it is believed that production soon ceased when Customs & Excise refused to exempt it from Purchase Tax. Historically, exemption from Purchase Tax was something that many three-wheel vehicles benefited from.

Tryon Viper

1980s — Tryon Viper

Designed and built by Sci-Fi enthusiast Ric Murphy in the USA, the Tryon Viper landed in the mid-1980s. It resembled a Colonial Viper spacecraft from the television series *Battlestar Galactica*. The vehicle was sold as a kit and was also available at every stage of completion up to a turnkey model. Thanks to its futuristic design, the Tryon Viper had an extremely low drag coefficient of .193 — computer tested at the Northrop Aerospace Facility, Palatine, Illinois, USA — giving the vehicle a petrol consumption of around 45-48mpg (6.2-5.8-litre/100km). The body itself was colour-impregnated, impact-resistant fibreglass with an inner laminate of core mat whilst the chassis was made from a 1.5in (3.8cm) x 3in (7.6cm) box steel tubing frame that surrounded the perimeter of the body. This was bonded inside the mould, resulting in a stronger body. A canopy at the centre of

With its futuristic looks, the Tryon Viper resembled a futuristic spaceship both inside and out. Ric Murphy

the vehicle, hinged at the back, lifted up electronically allowing access from either side to the interior. The latter had two seats in tandem style, with the passenger seat being directly behind the driver's. Behind the passenger seat was space for 8cu ft of luggage. The interior continued the spacecraft-type design with a vast array of switches, gauges, and LED bar graphs to relay information to the driver. The equipment also included a backup computer, radio and CB radio. To start the Viper, the driver had to enter a five-digit code and, instead of a standard steering wheel, an aircraft type yoke was fitted. The passenger had access to a backup computer, radio and CB communications system.

For a three-wheeler the Tryon was quite large. It measured 15ft 4in in length, 4ft 3in in height and 7ft 6in in width at the stern narrowing to 3ft 4in. The standard vehicle used a Volkswagen 1,600cc or 1,835cc, dual-port, air-cooled engine, which gave the Viper a top speed of around 120mph (193km/h). More power could be added by fitting an adapted 250bhp rotary RX-7 motor. In addition to the Volkswagen engine, the running gear and rear suspension were also from a 1969 — or newer — type 1 Volkswagen; the front suspension was a motorcycle type that incorporated dual spring over shocks with a leading arm over an 800 x 815 x 8 tyre. In total five vehicles were built.

Trylon Inc

1988 — Trylon Viper

In 1988 the Tryon Viper was marketed as the Trylon Viper by Dale H Fox. Manufactured by Trylon Inc at Starfleet Headquarters of Arlington Heights, Illinois, USA, the vehicle was again sold either as a kit starting at $8.000 and or at every stage of completion up to a turnkey model for $18,000. It had the same specifications as the Tryon Viper, though in addition also included fender grilles, rear grilles, fin extensions, skirt details and front canard wings. An electric version was also offered; this was said to be able to reach speeds in excess of 90mph (145km/h) and a range of over 100 miles (161km).

1988 — Shuttle

Although it does not appear to be as heavily publicised, a Trylon Shuttle was also available with prices starting at $6,000 for a kit to $16000 for a turnkey vehicle. Whilst this had the similar specifications to the Viper it differed in that the body did not have the grilles, fin extensions and front canard wings.

Tuk-Tuk

1960s — Tuk-Tuk

The Tuk-Tuk — or auto rickshaw as it is also known — was first manufactured in Thailand in the 1960s as an answer to the samlor that had been outlawed in Bangkok in 1960. The first rickshaw appeared in Bangkok in 1871 and many forms of human-powered vehicles were devised. These led on to the development of the samlor ('three wheels'). The samlor was often a three-wheel bicycle or similar powered by a human. A driver sat astride a bicycle whilst the passengers sat at the rear under a canvas roof. As petrol-powered vehicles became more popular, the numerous samlors present on the roads of Bangkok began to cause increasing congestion and health hazards and so, as a result, the samlor was outlawed in the Thai capital in 1960. The Tuk-Tuk is in effect a motorised samlor but with enough power to keep up with modern traffic.

Tuk-Tuks come in many different shapes and sizes; this one — a Coco Taxi — was spotted by the author whilst in Cuba. It has a fibreglass body and is fitted with an air-cooled, two-stroke, 75cc engine. Author's Collection

The Tuk-Tuk is built by a number of companies. Whilst the structure is initially the same there are many combinations of vehicle, including various forms of a taxi, van or open-top truck. The vehicles are built from a steel frame; taxi versions have either a steel hard top or a retractable canvas roof. Initially most taxis are designed to carry the driver and up to three passengers; however, larger versions can carry up to seven people. As with the bodies, the vehicles are also powered by a vast range of engines — from two-stroke, 125cc engines up to larger Harley Davidson engines in custom-built machines. The Tuk-Tuk is used widely in Thailand and, until recently, in India; however, the increasing number of them on the road in certain countries has caused issues with noise and pollution. In 1990 Harley-powered taxis in New Delhi, India were banned. This resulted in thousands of taxi drivers losing their jobs instantly. Pakistan has also banned Tuk-Tuks in certain areas. The Sri Lankan government banned two-stroke Tuk-Tuks in 2007 in a bid to reduce air pollution. As a result of this and increasing legislation concerning the vehicles

In 2006 two women, Jo Huxster and Antonia Bolingbroke-Kent, drove a custom-built Tuk-Tuk 12,500 miles from Thailand to the United Kingdom to raise money for charity. Fitted with a 550cc engine, the vehicle had raised suspension, a 50-litre fuel tank, roll bars and an accelerator pedal rather that a twist grip control. Jo Huxster

in other countries, a large number of Tuk-Tuks are now powered by four-stroke engines with many running on natural gas. Electric versions also being created in order to combat noise and pollution; however, due to their cost and range, these are not widespread. Numerous attempts have also been made to ban the Tuk-Tuk in Bangkok but, to date, these have all been unsuccessful.

Tula Motorzikly Zavod (TMZ)

1960S — Zaika

Produced in the 1960s by Tula Motorzikly Zavod (TMZ) in Russia, the Zaika is believed to have never got beyond the prototype stage. Formed in 1955, TMZ was a manufacturer of scooters and motorcycles and so the same Tula engine was used to power the Zaika. This resulted in a fuel consumption of *circa* 31mpg (9.1-litre/100km). With a single wheel at the rear the vehicle had an open metal body with a fabric hood.

1967 — Muravey TMZ 5403

From 1967 the company also produced a more motorcycle trike-like three-wheeler called the Muravey TMZ 5403 — Muravey meaning ant — that was a cargo scooter powered by an air-cooled, 199cc engine. Built on a double tube frame, the Muravey was available in four versions, ranging from a base model to a model with a canvas top, steel cargo area and a double seat. Production ended in 1989.

Twentieth Century Motor Car Corporation

1974 — Dale

The Dale was a prototype vehicle designed in the USA in 1974 by Dale Clift and was to be sold by Twentieth Century Motor Car Corporation, California, USA. The 70mpg (4-litre/100km) Dale was powered by a rear-mounted, air-cooled, BMW 850cc engine. A 1975 brochure for the vehicle claimed that was constructed of 'rocket' structural resin that would withstand the heaviest blow from a sledgehammer. The two-seat body was also constructed from resin the same colour as the final paintwork and so minor scratches would not be visible. In addition the vehicle was also said

Left: *The brochure for the Dale noted that, amongst other things, the vehicle contained no electrical wires.* Author's Collection

Below: *Claimed to be capable of 70mpg, the Dale gathered much interest. However, only one vehicle capable of running was built.* Alden Jewell

Twike Ltd

1986 — Twike/Twike II

The Twike was first developed by a group of Swiss students for the 1986 World EXPO in Vancouver, Canada. It won the Functionality Award for the best ergonomic design in the Innovative Vehicle Design competition and first prize in the International Human Powered Vehicle Speed Championships. The first Twike was driven by human power via pedals. In 1991 an electric version — Twike II — was created. This featured a belt pedal drive with variable mechanical transmission and a dc motor powered by NiCd batteries to help power the vehicle. A year later the newly founded Twike Ltd developed the vehicle into a production vehicle with manufacture beginning in 1995. In 1998 a production line was launched in Germany by FINE Mobile GmbH, which became the exclusive producer of the Twike after taking over the rights of the Swiss LEM AEG in 2002. The latest Twike, the Lion Twike, is fitted with a 5kW electric motor powered by a LiIon Mn 353 20Ah battery pack and has a range of 125 miles (201km) with speeds up to 53mph (85km/h) and 0-40mph (0-64km/h) in 9sec. The body is covered by covered by Luran S, a thermoplastic resin made by BASF attached, to an aluminium frame to give a total weight of 170kg (without batteries; the batteries weigh 35-100kg). At the time of writing the Twike remains in production.

to contain no electrical wires, with all components plugging directly into a printed circuit board. The project was marketed by Liz Carmichael, who claimed to be the wife of a NASA structural engineer, although she was actually Jerry Dean Michael. He had undergone sex reassignment surgery as previously he was on the run from the FBI on forgery charges. No vehicles are believed to have been manufactured apart from three prototype vehicles and only one of those was able to run under its own power. It is alleged that there were rumours of fraud and the authorities began to investigate. At Carmichael's trial on charges of grand theft, fraud and securities violations, Dale Clift said he still believed in Liz Carmichael. He claimed he stood to receive $3 million in royalties once the Dale went into production. In all, he received $1,001, plus a $2,000 cheque that bounced. Liz Carmichael was sent to prison.

Fitted with a 5kW electric motor the Twike is capable of 125 miles on a single charge. Twike Ltd

IT'S A PLANE..?

IT'S A CAR..?

IT'S *UNISPORT*
A revolutionary new sensation in driving!

Unicar Corporation

1974 — Unisport Streaker

Detailed as the ultimate motorcycle accessory, the Unisport was manufactured in California, USA, from 1974 by the Unicar Corporation. It was half a car that you bolted a motorcycle into to produce a three-wheeler in less than two hours. Designed by Walter and Ray Caston along with Grant Ryan, the Unisport Streaker was available in kit form. It had car-like controls with a steering wheel, foot brake pedals and a gear lever. It was built around a tubular steel frame that could seat two adults. The Streaker had a narrow fibreglass body and a small rounded Plexiglas windscreen. The vehicle was able to tilt, with buttons on the steering wheel to allow the driver to control the amount of tilt produced. It had a 6-Free point banking suspension that was controlled by linear actuators, which allowed the driver to bank the vehicle, including the wheels, into a turn. Any motorcycle larger that 450cc was suitable and the conversion required no structural changes. This meant it could be converted back to a motorcycle if required.

1974 — Unisport Streaker XE

The Unisport Streaker XE was introduced at the same time as the Streaker and, whilst having the same mechanical layout, it was fitted with a slightly wider fibreglass body. It also had a much higher windscreen with an optional — hard or soft top — canopy designed by Bruce Meyers. The XE version also had an optional SuperSport package; this included rear sides and a top tonneau cover to hide the motorcycle rear end. After its release, the Unicar Corporation was producing 50 units a month and was unable to keep up with demand. Production is, however, believed to have ceased in the early 1980s.

Above left: *The cover of the Unisport brochure shows a glimpse of how the whole vehicle and its wheels tilt into a corner.* Earl E Mohr

Above right: *The Unisport Streaker XE was also available with a SuperSport package that extended the body further backwards to cover the motorcycle rear end.* Earl E Mohr

vision. A fourth person remotely operated various effects around the vehicle, such as fog machine and a flame-thrower through the exhaust. In 2009, the vehicle was sold off by the Volo Auto Museum in Chicago, USA, for $300,000.

Utopian Motor Works

1914 – Utopian

Created as a one-off, the Utopian was built by the Utopian Motor Works, Leicester, UK, in 1914. The vehicle was powered by a two-cylinder, water-cooled engine that was mounted under the seat. Steering the Utopian was achieved by a side tiller that worked along the same principle as early steam cars. It was believed to have been manufactured for a local clergyman. The company also made bicycles.

Universal Studios

2003 — SLOW

Created by Universal Studios for the 2003 film *The Cat in the Hat,* based on a book by Dr Seuss, the SLOW (Super Luxurious Omnidirectional Whatchamajigger) was a three-wheel car that cost $1.2 million to build. The vehicle was custom-built from the ground up and powered by 12 12V batteries attached to an electric motor that gave a top speed of 47mph (76km/h). It had a fibreglass body, which was 23ft long, sprayed aluminium with African mahogany panelling at the rear. In the film the SLOW is actually driven by a second person concealed behind the front seat, whilst the rear-view mirror was a camera connected to a monitor next to the driver so they could see where they were going. In addition, a third person outside the vehicle would communicate with the driver, warning of any objects outside the camera's field of

The 1914 Utopian was a one-off vehicle made for a clergyman. Author's Collection

Featuring an egg-shaped body the Vallée Chantecler was an open two-seater. Wikipedia — Butch T

Vallée

1950 — Tri-scooter Utilitaire

Founded in France in 1949, Paul Vallée manufactured motorcycles; however, from 1950, the company made three-wheel utility trucks. Powered by either a 125cc or air-cooled, two-stroke, single-cylinder, 175cc engine, the Tri-scooter Utilitaire was an open vehicle with a motorcycle rear end on which the driver sat on a saddle and controlled the vehicle with handlebars. In between the front two wheels were various forms of trays and boxes for cargo.

1954 — Chantecler

In 1954 the design was modified to create a vehicle that was more car like. Powered by the same 125cc or air-cooled, two- stroke, single-cylinder, 175cc Ydral engine, the Vallée Chantecler had an open fibreglass body that was attached to a square tube chassis. With a hood for protection against the elements, the interior had a bench seat that was able to sit two adults. Production ceased in 1957 with around 200 vehicles being made.

Above right: *The Carver One: this particular example was a demonstration vehicle and was test-driven by the author in Holland during 2003.* Author's Collection

Vandenbrink/Carver Europe

1997 — Carver

Vandenbrink first started to look at Man Wide Vehicles (MWV) in 1989 when Chris van den Brink put together a team of designers. In 1994 he and Harry Kroonen invented the basic concept of Dynamic Vehicle Control (DVC), whereby input to a car-type steering wheel resulted in optimal 'motorcycle-type' tilt of the vehicle's chassis. Over the next couple of years, two Carver prototypes were built with constant improvements to the hydraulic tilting system and, in 1997, the vehicle was approved by the Dutch Government Road Authority for driving on public roads. Manufactured in Holland, the Carver was a tilting three-wheeler that, unlike ordinary vehicles, tilted the same way as a motorcycle when cornering. The DVC system varied depending upon

With its DVC system, the Carver was able to tilt up to 45° each side when cornering. Harry Kroonen

Velorex

1943 — Oskar

The Oskar — 'kára na ose' ('cart on an axle') — was introduced in 1943 at Parník (near Ceské Trebové) in Czechoslovakia. Brothers František and Mojmír Stránský had, for a number of years, serviced bicycles in their shop — Moto-Velo Sport, Bicycle Service — when, in 1936, inspired by the Morgan three-wheeler, they thought about an economical car that would fill the gap between motorcycles and four-wheel vehicles. In 1943 the brothers constructed their first prototype — the Oskar. The vehicle was based on a steel tubular construction covered with a thin dural layer — similar to leather — that was attached to a steel frame by turnbutton fasteners. The mechanics of the vehicle were taken from bicycles that were then substituted for motorcycle parts. In post-war Czechoslovakia there was a need for cars, but there was a shortage of vehicle production and a problem with the state's conception of motorisation. It was, therefore, easier and quicker to build your own vehicle using any mechanical parts available than wait for a mass-produced factory car.

When the Oskar was introduced to the public, many people became interested in it; this led the Stránský brothers to build more of them. The mechanical parts, including the wheels originally taken from a motorcycle, were changed and improved upon as new parts became available and numerous types of engines were used. In 1945 the brothers bought a small shop in Ceská Trebová and produced the first series of Oskar vehicles with a tubular frame. The first cars were two-seaters, covered with the material used for work clothes though this was later changed for polyurethane. Three different models were created: the standard version used an air-cooled, 150cc CZ engine; the '3' used a 300cc PAL engine that had been originally designed for agricultural use; and the '6' had a 250cc JAWA engine. All three provided power to the single rear wheel via a chain.

1951 — Oskar 54

The Stránský brothers moved their workshop to a manufacturing company called Hradec Králové in 1950. The Oskar 54 was introduced in 1951 with six workers producing 120 vehicles a year; by 1954 this had increased to 80 workers building 40 vehicles a month. The 54, which

the speed of the vehicle. Turning whilst going slow kept the Carver almost upright but, with increased speed, the Carver tilted further in the same way that a motorcycle does. The tilting system also meant that a car just 1.30m in width could reach cornering speeds of Porsches and Ferraris as it is able to tilt up to 45° each side. Furthermore, within one second, the Carver could tilt from full left to full right.

The vehicle was powered by a 660cc, four-cylinder engine that also featured a turbo intercooler. This, combined with a lightweight steel chassis and a two-seat (monocoque design) body covered by composite panels, gave the Carver a top speed of around 120mph (193km/h). As a result of passing EU homologation test, the Carver was allowed all through the EU; this resulted in the company changing its name from Vandenbrink to Carver Europe. However, due to its price — around £45,000 (€50,000) — sales of the vehicle were not as high as hoped for and, in July 2009, the company filed for bankruptcy and ceased producing vehicles. The company behind the technology behind the Carver's innovative leaning technology — Advanced Technology Licensing Co — is still in business and, in 2010, the technology was licensed to Persu Ventures (see page 186) in the USA with manufacture expected to start in 2014. Whilst the original Carver could achieve up to 65mpg (4.3-litre/100km), a new hybrid version called the Persu Hybrid is being designed with a body that produces a lower drag coefficient. Combined with an electric motor, this is expected to achieve around 100mpg (2.8-litre/100km) through 75+mpg (3.7-litre/100km) on fuel and an electric range of around 20 miles (32km).

used the same single-cylinder, 250cc JAWA engine, consisted of a tubular steel frame with fabric bodywork stretched over the cage. Following František Stránský's death in 1954 and his brother's refusal to join the Communist Party of Czechoslovakia, the vehicle's name was changed to Velorex-Oskar in 1956 and, by 1959, just the Velorex. At this time 120 vehicles were being manufactured each month and production moved to a new plant in Rychnov nad Kněžnou.

1963 — Velorex 16/175/ Velorex 16/350

The type 16 model was introduced in 1963 and was a redesigned version of the Oskar though now powered by either a 175cc CZ engine (Velorex 16/175) or a 350cc JAWA engine (Velorex 16/350) that had a top speed of 53mph (85km/h). The vehicle received further updates until 1968. Production of three-wheelers ceased in 1971 in favour of a four-wheel version, the Velorex 453-0. In the 1980s a company in India tried to obtain a licence to produce the Velorex three-wheeler; however, the deal fell through as the original tooling no longer existed. An updated version of the Velorex was announced in 2010 called the Velor-X-Trike (see page 172).

The Velorex used a tubular steel frame with fabric stretched over the frame to form the bodywork. Johan Schoenmaker

Perhaps one reason the Velorex was so easy to maintain was that the body could be unfastened and removed, exposing the engine and transmission, and then simply reattached. Sam Glover

Left: *The Gordon was a four-seat family car though, as a result of the position of the engine on the driver's side, there was no door for the driver.* Author's Collection

Right: *For its time the Gordon was the cheapest car in Britain, being priced at £269 17s 9d including Purchase Tax.* John Lloyd

Vernon Industries Ltd

1950 — Invacar/Invacar Mk 8

Associated with the company that produced football pools, Vernon Industries Ltd, Cheshire, UK, started to manufacture the Invacar (see page 123) under licence in 1950. In 1952 the Invacar Mk 8 was introduced and the licence for Vernon Industries to build it was cancelled. As a result, Vernon decided to build its own invalid car in 1955.

1954 — Gordon

The Gordon first appeared in December 1954 and, with a price tag of £269 17s 9d including Purchase Tax, was at the time the cheapest car on the British market. It had a tubular steel chassis with an open body built from aluminium and was able to seat two adults with two children at the rear. Power came from a single-cylinder, two-stroke, air-cooled, 197cc Villiers 8E/R engine that was mounted on the offside of the car. It had a large air intake on the side of the body that was designed to help keep the engine cool. Due to the position of the engine, there was no door on the driver's side of the vehicle, with the sole door being on the left-hand side. As a result of the engine being offset, only one of the two wheels at the rear was actually powered by the chain via a three-speed with reverse gearbox. In 1957 a deluxe model was introduced; this had the same standard specification but featured a modified body trim with two-tone paint and white wall tyres. Production continued until 1958.

1955 — Vernon Invalid Car/ Vernon Invalid Car Mk 2/Mk 3

The Vernon Invalid Car — or Vi-Car as it is often incorrectly called — was introduced in 1955 and was similar to the Invacar Mk 8. It was powered by a Villiers 8E engine placed at the side of the vehicle, which powered one of the rear wheels. The vehicle was built with aluminium panels attached to a hardwood frame. The vehicle received several updates, with a Mk 2 in late 1955 that had a modified all-metal body and Mk 3 version in 1957 that bought the vehicle in line with the new Ministry Standard Specification, being powered by a Villiers 9E engine and Dynastart. Around 1,500 vehicles were built before production ceased in 1958.

Designed by Vernon Industries, the Vernon Invalid Car used a Villiers 8E engine fitted to the side of the vehicle. RUMCar News

Vidal & Sohn Tempo-Werke GmbH

1928 —T1/T2/T6/T10

Also known as just Tempo, Vidal & Sohn Tempo-Werke GmbH was founded in 1928 by Oscar Vidal with its first vehicle being the Tempo T1. At that time the law in Germany stated that a vehicle with fewer than four-wheels and fitted with an engine less than 350cc was licence and tax free. Built in 1928 out of house by a third party, the T1 model was powered by a 5bhp, air-cooled, two-stroke, single-cylinder, 196cc Ilo engine that drove the single rear wheel. The vehicle was an open single-seater with a steel chassis and a large box positioned between the two front wheels that provided a payload of 500kg. The driver sat on a sprung saddle over the rear wheel, controlling the T1 via handlebars. A T2 model was announced in 1928; this was powered by a larger 9bhp, single-cylinder, two-stroke, 440cc Hamor engine that provided a payload of 600kg including the driver. The T6 of 1929 was the first production model to be built in-house and, whilst resembling the T1, it had been completely redeveloped to become an extremely reliable vehicle. This was followed by a T10 model in 1930; this was powered by a single-cylinder, two-stroke, 349cc Ilo engine that now provided the vehicle an increased payload of 750kg, including the driver; this was built until 1936.

1932 — Pony

Introduced in 1932 and built alongside the T6 and T10, the Pony was an open delivery vehicle. It was a cheaper model with a payload of 500kg including the driver. It was powered by a 6bhp, single-cylinder, two-stroke, 198cc Ilo engine. The steering was via handlebars, with the whole front load area of the vehicle pivoting as the handlebars were turned. It was manufactured until 1936.

1933 — Front 6/ Front 7 (D200)/ Front 14 (D400)

The Tempo Front 6 in 1933 was the first Tempo to feature a fully-enclosed, two-seat passenger cabin. Powered by the same 198cc Ilo engine,

the vehicle had a payload of 500kg and was manufactured until 1935. In 1934 both the Front 7 (or D200) and Front 14 (or D400) models were introduced. Still with a two-seat cab plus a pick-up type rear end, the Front 7 was fitted with a 6.5bhp, single-cylinder, two-stroke, water-cooled Ilo engine and offered a payload of 600kg. The Front 14 was fitted with a larger 12.5bhp, 400cc Ilo engine and provided a payload of 750kg. Both versions were built until 1936.

1933 — Front 10 (Kabriolet)/E200/E400

The Tempo Front 10 was fitted with a cabriolet body to form a passenger vehicle. Introduced in 1933, the it had a steel body with a fabric roof and two seats. It was powered by a 10bhp, single-cylinder, two-stroke, water-cooled, 300cc Ilo engine. It was also available with a van body, with a payload of 650kg. In 1936 the E200 and E400 models were introduced; these had a larger body equipped with four seats. Whilst the E200 was powered by a 7bhp, single-cylinder, two-stroke, water-cooled, 200cc Ilo engine, the E400 was fitted with the larger 12.5bhp, 400cc version. The Front 10 was manufactured until 1935 whilst both the E200 and E400 were built until 1937.

Announced in 1933, the Tempo Front 10 was a two-seat passenger vehicle that was also available with a van body. Author's Collection

Available with a number of commercial bodies, the Tempo Hanseat, with a payload of 750-850kg, was a very popular vehicle.
Eduard Hattuma

1950 — Boy

The Tempo Boy was the last Tempo three-wheeler and was introduced in 1950; it was built until 1956. It was in essence a junior version of the Hanseat and was powered by either a 7.5bhp, twin-cylinder, two-stroke 198cc Ilo engine or a slightly larger 9.5bhp, 250cc engine. These provided a payload of 400-500kg. Like the Hanseat, the Boy was available in a range of commercial bodies. From 1956 Tempo concentrated on four-wheel vehicles, vehicles that it had been building since 1935.

Vigillante

1993 — Vigillante

In 1993 the first Vigillante prototype appeared and was announced as 'The World's Quickest Street-Legal Exotic' when compared with the Ferrari F40. The latter, according to *Road & Track* magazine at the time, was the quickest street legal production vehicle it had tested. Sprinting from 0-60mph (0-96km/h) in just three seconds and with a top speed of over 200mph (322km/h), the Vigillante was claimed to be quicker on acceleration and braking than both the Ferrari F40 and a McLaren F1 road car and comparable in cornering. Designed by Bob Keyes, a physicist with 30 years of experience in the aerospace and defence business, the Vigillante was powered by a 700bhp Chevrolet engine. The car had a maximum theoretical tip-over limit that was calculated to be 3.27 lateral 'G' and so the car would slide long before it reached its tip-over limit. It also had exceptional braking power and, with high-performance tyres, would stop at one 'G' with approximately 66% of the vehicle weight on the rear tyres, behind the centre of gravity (CofG).

The vehicle was an enhanced version of the TriVette (see page 257) and had a tubular steel sub-frame. It used a lightweight aluminium, honeycomb, foam and composite tub, whilst the bodywork was a composite of aircraft fibreglass, Kevlar and carbon fibre in an epoxy matrix. Aluminium wheels also helped to keep the weight of the Vigillante down to 1,480lb. With two seats in tandem, the passenger sitting behind the driver, entrance to the vehicle was via a lift-up canopy. It was anticipated that the Vigillante would be hand built to customer's order, with one vehicle taking a year to build by hand; however, following Bob Keyes' death in July 2006, no further vehicles have been built at the time of writing.

1938 — A200/A400/ A400 Athlet

The Tempo was refined further in 1938 with the A200 and A400 models; these followed the same recipe with a two-seat cabin but now had a whole range of commercial bodies, including pick-up, van and low flatbed. The A200 was fitted with a 7.5bhp, single-cylinder, two-stroke, water-cooled, 200cc Ilo engine that had a 600kg payload and was made until 1940. The A400 was fitted with the larger 12.5bhp Ilo engine and had a payload of 750kg. Whereas the A400 had a wheelbase of 2,870mm, the A400 Athlet was available with a longer wheelbase (3,170mm); both versions were manufactured until 1948.

1949 — Hanseat

Powered by a 14bhp, 400cc, twin-cylinder, two-stroke, water-cooled Ilo engine, the Tempo Hanseat was introduced in 1949. Again following the design of a two-seat cab with a commercial rear end, the Hanseat had a payload of 750-850kg. A number of bodies were available, including a low flatbed, cattle truck, panel van and pick-up. 37,131 vehicles were produced before production ceased for the domestic market in 1956; between 1956 and 1962 a number of vehicles were built and sold to India before production was moved there in 1962. The model was built by Bajaj until 2000.

Above: *Tom Karen (at the wheel) and Andrew Waddicor with their Vimp — a cross between an Imp and a Vamp.* RUMCar News

Vimp

1954 — Vimp

The Vimp was a small two-seat vehicle created in Kingswood, Surrey, UK in 1954, by Tom Karen and Andrew Waddicor. Tom Karen called the vehicle a Vimp as it was a cross between an Imp and a Vamp. The vehicle had a fibreglass open body with a single headlight at the front and a single wheel at the back. To access the vehicle, the windscreen and part of the bonnet hinged forward. Tom Karen later went on to join the Ogle design team and, amongst other three-wheelers, designed the Bond Bug.

Above left: *Powered by a 700bhp Chevrolet engine the 1993 Vigillante is said to have a top speed of over 200mph (322km/h).* Bob & Diana Keyes

Left: *Access to the Vigillante is via a lift up canopy with the passenger sitting in tandem behind the driver.* Bob & Diana Keyes

Vintage Reproductions Inc (VRI)

1977 — Gamma Roadster

Vintage Reproductions Inc (VRI) in Florida, USA, was founded on 23 May 1972 and was primarily engaged in the manufacture and sale of horseless carriage-type vehicles modelled after those of the early 1900s. Alongside the carriages, VRI spent 18 months researching, developing and creating a prototype of the Gamma Roadster at a cost of $120,000. The Gamma Roadster was first manufactured in 1977. It was a three-wheeler that incorporated a complete motorcycle for the power train. This was hidden under the rear of the body and was readily accessible with the rear section of the body lifting up. The body was a fibreglass shell attached to a tubular steel main frame. It included as standard a full fold-away top and side curtains. Standard power came from either a 750cc Honda or an optional water-cooled, shaft driven, 1,000cc Honda engine. This was combined with Volkswagen parts, including steering, brake and suspension system. Available in kit form. Production is believed to have ceased in the late 1980s.

The Gamma Roadster was based around a complete motorcycle, which was covered under the rear bodywork. John Massegee

Vincent

1932 — Bantam

The Vincent motorcycle company was founded in the late 1920s by Phil Vincent. In 1932 the company's first three-wheeler — the Vincent Bantam — was introduced. Powered by a 293cc, side-valve JAP engine, which was later replaced by a 250cc Villiers engine, the vehicle was a 2.5cwt delivery van that, unusually, used a car-type seat and steering wheel rather than a motorcycle saddle and handlebars favoured by some three-wheelers produced by motorcycle manufacturers. The standard van was priced at £57 10s 0d though for an extra £5 10s 0d a windscreen and hood could be purchased. Production of the Bantam ceased in the mid-1930s.

1954 — Polyphemus

In 1954/1955 a prototype Vincent three-wheeler was produced in Stevenage, UK. The vehicle was powered by a Vincent Rapide 998cc engine and was unofficially named *Polyphemus** by its owner Roy Harper. Prior to this the vehicle was named *Locomotion*. The new name was as a result of the single large cooling opening in the nose panel. A duct ran from the mouth at the front of the body, directly onto the front cylinder of the engine. Additional vents at the side of the Vincent helped cool down the engine further. In addition to the engine, the vehicle used a number of Vincent motorcycle parts, including clutch, power transmission, gearbox and monoshock rear suspension system from the company's Series D model. The 14in

The Vincent pictured at the racetrack in Snetterton in 1954 with the headlamps reversed, as it was not permitted to race with the glass outward. As a result of mechanical problems, it was unable to complete the race. Photographed by Ernie Allen, the lady on the bonnet is his then girlfriend Maisie, who is now his wife.
Ernie & Maisie Allen

Powered by a 50cc engine, the Vitrex Riboud was started in a similar way as a petrol lawnmower with a pull cord. Michel Humbert

wheels came from a Morris Minor. The two-seat body was made of 16-gauge aluminium panels bolted onto a four-inch steel tube chassis. The tail section of the car was hinged to allow good access to the rear wheel and engine, whilst another panel had to be removed to reach the kick-starter.

With the standard Rapide engine, the Vincent could reach 90mph (145km/h). In 1955 the engine was replaced with a Vincent Black Lightning engine that could reach 117mph (188km/h), a speed that beat sport MGs of the same era. After several prototypes, the Vincent three-wheeler was offered to the public in 1955 at £500. Despite the interest, the price put many people off as the Vincent was not a practical vehicle as it had no self-starter, reverse gear or hood. The whole project therefore came to an end.

* In Greek Legend Polyphemus was the son of Poseidon and Thoosa and was a Cyclops (meaning 'round eye').

Vitrex Industrie (Riboud)

1970 — Hanneton

The Hanneton was first built in France in 1970. It was based on an idea by Jacques Riboud who, at the time, was the chairman a society that built houses. A lot of his customers were living in Paris and, as a result of overcrowded roads, suffered intense traffic problems which were compounded by strikes of public transport workers. Riboud thought that a small vehicle would be excellent for his customers as its tiny size would mean increased manoeuvrability through the overcrowded streets. In

addition, he also wanted to build a vehicle to avoid his new town clients needing to purchase a second car. As his facilities were able to take care of the body and the engine, Riboud set to work on the project and gave everything to his designer and engineer to build a prototype. When the car was completed Riboud called it le Hanneton ('the Bug'). He was, however, disappointed as the vehicle was not what he had hoped for.

1974 — Riboud

An interesting opportunity came up a couple of years later when a company called Marland, which was well known for its buggies, was contacted by Riboud to create another project based on the Hanneton. This new project was a success and Riboud was very pleased with it, as this was the type of vehicle he wanted from the start. Many other prototypes were built and presented to the car press, before the car was finally considered as a microcar — voiturette sans permis ('without driving licence car'). The Riboud was powered by an air-cooled, 47cc Fichtel & Sachs engine. The homologation papers were given by the service des mines — where all French cars had to go to be homologated — at the end of June 1974, with a 'type mine' of 'M.R.1.' (or Marland-Riboud first version). Marland decided to build the cars in its factories situated in the Eure district of north-west France. Some cars were direct sales whilst others were delivered to Riboud's houses.

During 1975, a company called Vitrex Industrie, which specialised at first in manufacturing window panes, bought the Marland factories in the Eure to build new Riboud cars. The difference between the old and the new model was insignificant mechanically although the car had a new body, new wheels and new accessories, including a complete hood and electric windscreen wiper. The vehicles were powered by the same 47cc engine started from a hand-starter very similar to that found on a lawnmower. Vitrex Industrie also imported microcars from Italy, inheriting the licence previously held by Marland. By 1980 the third generation of the Riboud had arrived; It was now a four-wheeler, thus bringing production of the three-wheel versions to an end.

Fitted with gull-wing doors, the Volkswagen Scooter was a two-seat concept vehicle dating from 1986. Volkswagen

Volkswagen

1986 — Scooter

The German manufacturer Volkswagen is one of the list of major car manufacturers that are no strangers to three-wheelers. In 1986 Volkswagen revealed the Volkswagen Scooter; this was a concept lightweight urban commuter vehicle weighing 635kg. The Scooter's fibreglass body had a drag coefficient of 0.25 and was equipped with gull-wing doors that allowed access to the two-seat cabin. Power came from a 90bhp, 1,400cc engine that could take the vehicle from 0-60mph (0-96km/h) in just 8.5sec with a top speed of 136mph (219km/h).

2006 — GX3

The sporty Volkswagen GX3 was announced at the Greater Los Angeles Auto Show in 2006. It was a concept three-wheeler designed by project Moonraker at Volkswagen in California, USA. The vehicle was described as a 'crossover between sports car and motorcycle'. As a result of its tubular space frame chassis construction and open body made from fibreglass panels with no doors or windscreen, the vehicle weighed just 570kg. It was able to reach 0–60mph (0-96km/h) in 5.7sec using a transverse-mounted, 1,600cc engine from a Volkswagen Lupo GTi and a six-speed gearbox. In the same year, Volkswagen revealed that a production version of the GX3 might follow depending on the public reaction to it. However, despite an 'overwhelming' positive response and further chassis development by Lotus Cars, the project was shelved in late 2006 as, along with cost and complex redesigns, Volkswagen believed that possible safety issues might lead to product-liability lawsuits.

Above: *Described as a 'crossover between sports car and motorcycle', the Volkswagen GX3 used an engine from the Volkswagen Lupo GTi.* Volkswagen

Above top: *Volkswagen's GX3 concept vehicle in 2006 was considered for production; however, the project was shelved before manufacture commenced.* Volkswagen

W J Barker

1919 – Barker

Designed and constructed by W J Barker in 1919 London, UK, the two-seat Barker was powered by an 8bhp, water-cooled JAP engine. It had a two-speed plus reverse gearbox that provided drive to the single rear wheel by chain. The rear wheel was fitted with a chain drive on one side and a stout hand brake on the other; these components were easily detachable so that the wheel was interchangeable with the others. The vehicle had an Ash frame with a body that was built up with sheet metal along with an aluminium bonnet leading onto the radiator whilst the petrol tank was situated under the dashboard. Perhaps the most unusual feature of the Barker was that it was fitted with a special back axle that meant it could be turned into a four-wheeler for an extra cost of £27. Production is believed to have ceased in the early 1920s.

If you fancied the best of both worlds, the Barker was a fairly unique three-wheeler as an alternative back axle was available to convert the vehicle into a four-wheeler. Author's Collection

Whilst the Omega had a top speed of 60mph (96km/h), brakes on the front wheels were optional extras. Kerry Croxton

W J Green

1925 — Omega

Named after the its founder, William James Green, the company was formed in 1919 at the Omerga Works in Croft Road, Coventry, UK. Initially building motorcycles and sidecars, the Omega three-wheeler was introduced in 1925. With a top speed of around 60mph (96km/h), the Omega held a number of world speed records during the 1920s. The vehicle was fitted with a water-cooled, 980cc JAP engine that drove the single rear wheel by dual chains. The single rear wheel had a sprocket either side each driven by a chain. Despite the high speed of the Omega — especially when compared with contemporary vehicles — brakes were optional extras on the front wheels. With a two-seat body and a hood, there were a number of models to choose from, including one that had an aluminium polished body. The Omega was also noted for its excellent electric lights. Production of the Omega ceased in 1927.

W R Pashley

1949 — Portsmouth/Superior

Based in Aston, Birmingham, UK, W R Pashley — founded by William 'Rath' Pashley — produced bicycles and delivery tricycles from 1926 and then motorcycles from 1949. In the same year it also introduced a three-wheel commercial range. The driver sat at the rear of the body on a motorcycle-type saddle though steering was through a conventional steering wheel. Both the Portsmouth and Superior models had enclosed bodies at the front although these differed in style and purpose. Whilst the Portsmouth was a closed body truck that had a steel body and lid built upon a tubular steel chassis, the Superior was designed for ice cream sales and so had a 10gall ice cream storage space with room for three full-size biscuit tins along with washing and sterilizing facilities. Whilst the Portsmouth had a steel lid, the Superior had a rounded Perspex lid so that the contents could be viewed. The vehicle also featured a windscreen that offered some form of protection against the elements. Both versions used an air-cooled, 197cc Villiers engine that drove the single rear wheel by a chain.

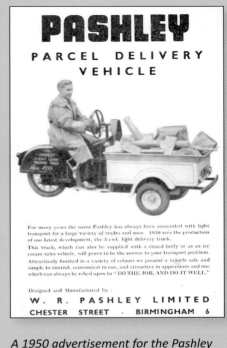

A 1950 advertisement for the Pashley 3cwt light delivery truck sees the driver completely exposed to the elements. Author's Collection

1949 — 3cwt Open Truck

Using the same engine, the 3cwt open truck also featured a saddle for the driver to sit on while controlling the vehicle with a steering wheel. As the name suggests, the open truck had a pick-up type flatbed between the front two wheels that was able to carry 3cwt. Production of all commercial vehicles ceased in 1962.

1953 — Prototype Car

Pashley created a prototype car in 1953; this used an air-cooled, 197cc engine and was different to earlier three-wheel vehicles produced by the company in that it had the single wheel at the front. The vehicle was a two-seater fitted with an open body that had no doors although it was provided with a collapsible hood. The car never progressed beyond the prototype stage.

Pashley created a two-seat prototype car in 1953; however, it was developed no further. RUMCar News

1953 — Pelican

Also introduced in 1953 was the Pashley Pelican rickshaw. This was more motorcycle-like with the vehicle having a motorcycle front end powered by a Royal Enfield or BSA engine and a rear end that utilised a tubular steel frame. This could accommodate two seats and was fitted with a canvas canopy over the frame. Production ceased in the late 1950s.

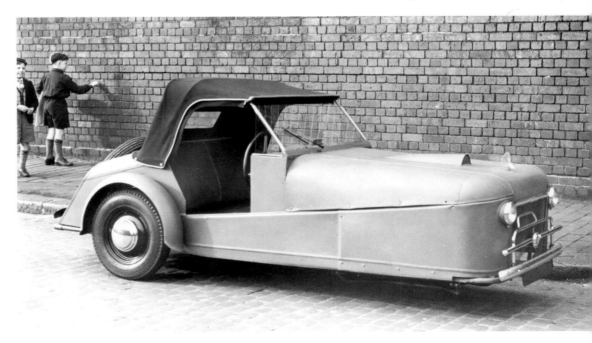

Wales & Edward Ltd

1951 — Milk Float

Well-known for its electric milk floats, Wales & Edward Ltd (W&E) of Wyle Cop, Shrewsbury, UK, was formed in 1918 by A C Wales. Initially it was a garage reconditioning and servicing used cars as well as distributing light aircraft. It was in 1951 that the company introduced its first three-wheeler designed as a milk truck. It was powered by an electric motor that drove the rear wheels via a chain. The vehicles were designed at the request or United Dairies — later Unigate — to replace horse-drawn trailers. The first vehicle was so well received that United Dairies placed an order for 1,500, with even larger orders then following. The vehicle became available on the open market from 1953. The milk float had a heavy steel chassis and an open steel cab. Early vehicles had tiller steering, which was later replaced by a conventional steering wheel. A number of body designs were used; some cabs featured no or single headlights with some very late models having twin headlights. The vehicles ran on electric motors; these ranged from 72V for a 4/40 model, 96V for a 4/60 model, 96V for a 6/75 model and 132V for the 6/60 model.

1961 — Loadmaster

Introduced in 1961 the W&E Loadmaster was an electric articulated truck capable of carrying 50cwt. The actual tractor unit was essentially the cab from a milk float with a bare chassis at the rear with a coupling device to attach it to a trailer. A total of 18 vehicles

Many of a certain generation in the UK will have, at some point, been stuck behind a Wales & Edward milk float as it trundled along with all the time in the world. This is a 25cwt example from 1962. Colin Pickett

were built, with 15 of those being supplied to Unigate Dairies, before production ceased in 1966.

1960s — Rangemaster

The W&E Rangemaster was introduced in the 1960s. It used a heavy gauge steel chassis and was generally built with a dairy-type body with a low-level, walk-through, single-seat, fibreglass cab to allow quick access into and out of the vehicle. Inside the vehicle, the driver's seat and steering wheel were positioned in the centre so that the driver could enter the vehicle from either side. The roof of the cab extended over the rear section; this was open sided. Rangemaster milk floats were powered by various electric motors, ranging from 30V for a Standard model, 44V for an Intermediate model, 60V for the Rangemaster model to 80V for the Major model. The top speed varied from 8mph to 16mph, whilst the range varied from 26 to 35 miles (42-56km). As a result of the weight of the batteries it carried, the Rangemaster weighed between 3.4 tons and 4 tons and was able to carry a payload of between 1.5 tons and 1.8 tons dependent on the model. The vehicle evolved several times, with an updated cab and more efficient mechanics although essentially keeping the same basic structure. In the 1970s W&E was said to be making around 1,200 milk floats a year; however, in the early 1980s price competition from the supermarkets resulted in a 70% drop in orders in one year. In 1989, as a result of falling orders, W&E was bought out by Smith's Electric Vehicles of Gateshead. In addition to three-wheelers, the company also made four-wheel vehicles.

Walter & spol

1908 — Walter

The Walter was first manufactured in 1908 in Jinonice, Czeckoslovakia, by Walter & spol. The company had built motorcycles and motor tricycles for a number of years before starting car production in 1908. The Walter was powered by a V-twin, 500c engine situated behind the single front wheel. Power was transferred to the back wheels by a shaft to the rear axle. The first models were open two-seat vehicles fitted with a tubular steel frame, tiller steering and minimal bodywork, which had a fold-down hood, whilst later models were closed four-seat bodies powered by a much larger 1,250cc engine. In 1912 the three-wheelers were replaced by a four-wheel model; production of the latter continued until 1936 when the company concentrated on making aero engines.

The Wendax Trivan that, unlike a number of similar vehicles of this type, offered a windscreen and a partial roof. RUMCar News

Wearwell Motor Carriage Co/Wolf Motors

1899 — Motette

The Wearwell Motor Carriage Co of Wolverhampton, UK, was established in 1896 as a cycle manufacturer — initially called the Wearwell Cycle Co — that, from 1899, produced motorcycles. In 1903 the company produced its first three-wheeler. The Motette was a 2.5bhp tricycle that was a modified bicycle. The front wheel of the bicycle was replaced with a two-wheel axle with an engine mounted in the frame. The vehicle was fitted with an upholstered wicker seat. The engine drove the rear wheel through a belt. In 1903 the Motette was revised and the engine uprated to a 3.5bhp, water-cooled, Stevens engine mounted vertically in the frame. The vehicle was sold as a conversion kit for two-wheel machines but proved to be unpopular.

1904 — Wolf

By 1904 the design had been altered and a new, sturdier model was launched as the Wolf. This vehicle was also fitted with the 3.25bhp Stevens engine. The engine was later uprated to 4.5bhp and then to 5bhp with a two-speed gearbox. From 1905 all vehicles manufactured used the Wolf name and were sold as Wolf Motors, although the company decided to concentrate solely on two-wheelers only from 1906.

Webster Motor Co

1990 — Bond Bug

It was in 1990 that brothers Mike and Gary Webster came across the original Bond Bug moulds made by the Reliant Motor Co; at the time Reliant was bankrupt and the official receivers sold the Bond Bug name, moulds and production rights to the brothers. After making the moulds serviceable, the Webster Motor Co (WMC) was formed in Hampshire, UK. Initially the company went into production with a modified four-wheel version of the Bond Bug called the WMC Bug. However, as there was so much interest in the original three-wheel version, they recreated it, selling it as the Bond Bug. The vehicle was sold in a kit form, with a similar steel ladder chassis to the original, and used a Reliant Robin/Rialto as a donor car. It used a large number of parts from the donor car, including the engine (either 748cc or 848cc). Whilst the vehicle could be made accurately to resemble the original, an updated version could also be chosen with folding fibreglass side screens and an updated dashboard. Around 12 Bond Bugs were made until *circa* 1995, when the Avonex Group, which had now taken over Reliant, purchased certain aspects of the design back with a view to creating an updated version.

1990 — Bug

The Bug was a sport version of the Bond Bug and, whilst using the same specifications as the Bond Bug, had a cut down canopy and aero screens. With the 41bhp, 848cc Reliant engine it had a top speed of 100mph (161km/h).

Wendax Fahrzeugbau GmbH

1931 — Trivan

Having built a prototype in 1931, it was not until 1935 that Wendax Fahrzaugbau GmbH of Hamburg, Germany went into production with a Trivan. However, production ended in the same year. Powered by a rear-mounted, air-cooled, single-cylinder, 200cc Ilo engine that drive the single back wheel via a chain, the vehicle had a tubular steel frame with a metal cargo storage box between the front wheels. The driver sat exposed on a saddle above the engine at the back of the vehicle; he was, however, offered some weather protection with a windscreen and a fabric roof that extended from it.

Western Front Inc

1981 — XK-1

Developed with assistance from Quincy-Lynn Enterprises, Inc, the XK-1 was announced in 1981 by Western Front Inc of Texas, USA. Styled upon Quincy-Lynn's Trimuter (see page 198), the XK-1 was built on a steel chassis and had an aerodynamic fibreglass body that had steel reinforcement at key stress points. Whilst the original plans featured a large lift-up canopy to gain access to the vehicle, some vehicles were modified and fitted with gull-wing-type doors. The XK-1 used a variety of rear-mounted engines, including a 16bhp Briggs & Stratton industrial engine, Volkswagen Beetle, Mazda rotary and a Porsche engine. It also used a number of other car parts, including a steering column from a Toyota Celica, rear suspension from a Datsun and a Honda Civic windscreen.

Based upon the Trimuter, the XK-1 was built with a variety of engines and featured either a lift-up canopy or gull-wing doors. Ron Will

The XK-1 was sold as a kit or as a set of plans and was available from both Western Front Inc and Quincy-Lynn Enterprises Inc until the former closed down in 1984.

Western Wheel Works

1892 — Electric Tricycle

In 1892 the Western Wheel Works of Chicago, Illinois, USA, built 'several hundred' electric tricycles for use at the 1893 Chicago World's Fair. This fair was held to mark the 400th anniversary of Christopher Columbus' arrival in the New World and was also known as the World's Columbian Fair. The vehicles, fitted with a steel tubular frame, had a smaller single wheel at the front; this was steered by a tiller. With two wicker seats positioned side-by-side, the tricycle was able to travel up to 14 miles (23km) per charge, with the battery being located under one of the seats. At the Fair, the tricycles were rented to visitors who did not want to walk.

1896 — Tri-Motor Crescent

Introduced in 1896, the Tri-Motor Crescent was produced by the company in order to enter the commercial motorised market. The two-seat vehicle with tiller steering featured an engine mounted above the front wheel; this drove the wheel via a chain. However, by 1901 production of the three-wheeler ceased and thereafter the company concentrated on bicycles; these also used the Crescent name.

Westward Industries Ltd

1989 — Go-4 Interceptor III — Parking Patrol

Westward Industries Ltd was founded in Canada during 1989 by Larry Mauws. He designed and built the first model of the Go-4 to fill a need in the marketplace for 'a reliable, manoeuvrable, comfortable and efficient vehicle for use by Police departments for parking patrol'. Over the years, the vehicle design has been modified to meet changing needs and demands for environmentally friendly products. The most popular model is the Parking Patrol; this has a body made of aluminium panels fixed to a tubular steel frame and has a cab with sliding metal doors. Power comes from a 61bhp fuel-injected engine with four-speed automatic transmission located behind the driver. The top speed is electronically governed from the factory at 40mph (64km/h). Whilst the vehicle has many accessories, including air conditioning and backup alarm to alert others that the vehicle is reversing. It also features an LTI (Lateral Thrust Indicator) unit as standard. Borrowed from the aerospace industry, the LTI unit measures lateral 'G' force and will notify the driver if the vehicle is driven at an unsafe speed around corners or is being operated on a dangerous cross slope.

1989 — Go-4 Interceptor III — Van

The van version is very similar in design, with the same front cab. However, the rear end has a van body with a lift-up hatch at the back.

1989 — Go-4 Interceptor III — Flat Bed

Again using the same single-seat cab, the flat-bed version has a large cargo loading area with a drop-down tail-gate and bars on the side to stabilise high loads. All vehicles are in production at the time of writing.

Whomobile/The Alien

1973 — Whomobile

The *Whomobile* was a vehicle once owned by a Time Lord. It was created in the UK in 1973, after being specially commissioned by Jon Pertwee — the third Dr Who in the BBC-TV series Dr Who — from designer Peter Farries. Farries at the time was chairman of the Nottingham Drag & Custom Club. In January 1973, Pertwee was opening a Ford main dealers branch in Nottingham, UK, and he saw a restored early Model T Ford called *The Californian Hot Rod* that could do 0-60mph (0-96km/h) in three seconds. After enquiring about the vehicle, Pertwee found out that it had been created by Peter Farries and so asked him to design a custom-built car that would suit Pertwee's time-travelling character in the Dr Who series.

The result was *the Alien;* this was a three-wheeler that was 14ft in length and 7ft in width with large fins extending five feet from the ground. Whilst the makers called the vehicle *the Alien,* Pertwee called it the *Whomobile* in his memoirs. The body was made from fibreglass and constructed in just two sections; this was a task considered impossible by other designers at the time. The body was then mounted on to a steel box section chassis that incorporated a sheet steel floor pan for added strength. An 8in rubber skirt was attached to the underside of the body that concealed the wheels — two at the back, one at the front — to create the illusion that the vehicle

was a hovercraft. The vehicle had no doors; to gain access you climbed in over the wing. The interior complemented the sci-fi look with a television screen and a fake computer bank of flashing lights as well as a silver radio cassette player. Both the radio and television were serviced by twin electric aerials that rose from the back of the car at the flick of a switch. Due to UK law, the television had a cover that had to be in place when the vehicle was in use on public roads. The engine was a 975cc Hillman Imp Sports engine specially prepared by Chrysler UK and the vehicle could reach 105mph (169km/h) and averaged around 50mpg (5.6-litre/100km).

By late September 1973 the *Whomobile* was written into the Dr Who series and was first featured in *Invasion of the Dinosaurs* in scenes where the Doctor would have been otherwise riding on a motorcycle. The car still lacked a proper roof and windscreens when filming took place; as a result a motorboat windscreen was used as a temporary measure to ensure the vehicle was legally roadworthy. By the time it made its second and last appearance in the series in *Planet of the Spiders*, it had been fully completed and was shown as a vehicle that could fly. On screen the word 'Alien', originally fitted on the rear wings, had been removed as the director wanted the vehicle to be nameless. In later years, Pertwee loaned the *Whomobile* to a bereaved fan whose mother had died in tragic circumstances and had an agreement that he would then borrow it back for special events. According to a BBC interview in December 2003, Farries stated that the car had been eventually sold at a car auction in the early 1980s for £1,700 and, since 1996, has been locked away out of sight at a secure location.

It's not only humans who drive three-wheelers but Time Lords too! The Whomobile *was a vehicle created for Jon Pertwee, who played the third Dr Who in the BBC series of the same name.* British Broadcasting Corporation

Sold by Wildfire Motors, the WF650-C is a fully-enclosed five-door vehicle, which was also sold as an open truck version with a two-seat cab.
Robert Woodard

Powered by a 1,070cc engine, production of the Williamson ceased during World War 1 and restarted again after the war with a smaller 771cc engine.
Author's Collection

Wildfire Motors

2008 — WF650-T/WF650-C

Made in China, the Wildfire WF650-T was first sold from 2008 by Wildfire Motors in Pennsylvania, USA. The Wildfire WF650-T was a pick-up truck that had a steel chassis with a two-seat steel cab. It was powered by a four-stroke, liquid-cooled, 650cc, high performance engine, with a four-speed with reverse gearbox, that provided a top speed of 65mph (105km/h). The vehicle had a payload of 1,000lb with collapsible bed sides. A WF650-C model was also available; this was a five-door passenger version with a fully-enclosed body. Both models were built until 2011.

2011 — Snyder ST600-C

Introduced in 2011, the Wildfire Snyder ST600-C is powered by a 34bhp, four-stroke, liquid-cooled, 586cc, high performance engine. The vehicle has a top speed of 50mph (80km/h) and a fuel consumption of up to 60mpg (4.7-litre/100km). The ST600-C has a four-speed with reverse gearbox and a steel body that has four seats and five doors (counting the rear hatch). These vehicles remain in production at the time of writing.

Williamson Motor Co

1912 — Williamson

With general lines that were somewhat similar to the Morgan three-wheeler, the Williamson was introduced in 1912 by the Williamson Motor Co of Coventry, UK. The company also manufactured motorcycles and was formed that same year when the founder, William Williamson, left the Rex Motor Manufacturing Co, where he had been Managing Director. The Williamson was fitted with a

horizontally-opposed, water-cooled, twin-cylinder, 1,070cc Douglas engine and a two-speed Douglas gearbox. Production ceased in 1916 as a result of World War 1 but resumed in 1919 although now powered with an air-cooled, twin-cylinder, 771cc JAP engine fitted with a three-speed Sturmey-Archer gearbox with chain drive to the single rear wheel. Manufacture of the vehicle ceased in 1920.

Witkar

1970s — Witkar

Designed for a car-sharing project in Amsterdam, the Witkar ('white car') was first created in the early 1970s by Luud Schimmelpennink. The Witkar was an electric two-seat car that had automatic transmission to the single rear wheel and, whilst having a short wheelbase, it had a tall body. With a top speed of 20mph (32km/h) the vehicles had a range of four miles (6km) and so charging stations were located at 2.4 miles (4km) apart from each other. Electric contacts were attached to the roof of the Witkar and, when it approached a charging station, the contacts automatically connected to an overhead gantry that started to charge the vehicle.

The idea was to reduce the amount of fossil fuel-powered vehicles within central Amsterdam by having Witkars at key locations. These could then be used by those who subscribed to the service and then left at the nearest Witkar station at that person's destination. The scheme was started on 21 March 1974 and ran until 27 October 1986, with over 4,000 registered users taking part. For its time, the system was exceptionally advanced and used specially developed technology controlled by a PDP-11 computer. A member would approach the charging station and access the system with a personal electronic key and then, from a map, dial in the number of his/her destination on a rotary phone. The computer would then check if there was a space for the vehicle at the destination and confirm this by illuminating a light. The driver wanting to hire the car would then press a button and all the vehicles in the rank would move forward until the front car was released, whilst the computer would debit the hire amount from that person's bank account. The driver would then open the vehicle door with an electronic key and drive off. Initially 35 vehicles were built as were five charging stations. The plan was ultimately to have around 150 stations and 1,000 vehicles; however, there were a number of issues and it did not take off as expected.

An advertisement aimed at encouraging people to car share and pick the Witkar for local journeys around Amsterdam thus easing congestion on the roads. Author's Collection

Wolseley Sheep Shearing Machine Co

1893 — Prototype

The Wolseley Sheep Shearing Machine Co in Australia was founded by Frederick Wolseley in 1887 after he invented a mechanical shearing machine powered by a petrol engine. The company moved to the UK in 1893. Prior to the move, Herbert Austin, who had earlier emigrated to Australia, was employed as Chief of Manufacturing and, having an interest in motor vehicles, he designed and developed a three-wheel vehicle based on the Léon Bollée. The rights to the Léon Bollée design had, however, already been sold to another company and so Austin went on to build his own design a year later.

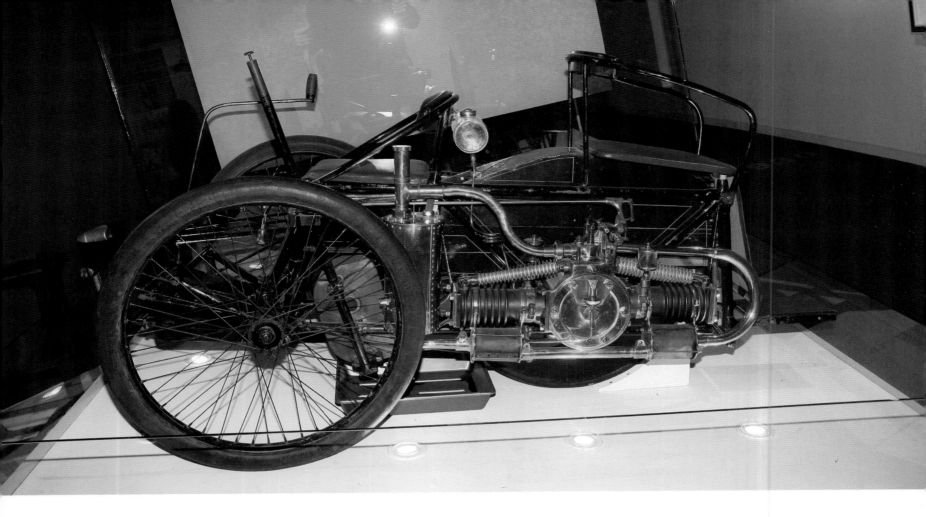

1890s – The Wolseley Autocar No 1

His second three-wheeler — The Wolseley Autocar No 1 — was a two-seater with back-to-back seating. Both models were to remain prototypes as, following a four-wheel prototype produced in 1900, the company went on to manufacture its first production four-wheeler under the new name of the Wolseley Tool & Motor Co.

With rather ornate pipework the Wolseley Autocar No 1 remained a prototype with the company then manufacturing four-wheelers.
Author's Collection

Wooler Motor Cycle Co

1919 — Mule

Having produced motorcycles since 1911 the Wooler Engineering Co Ltd of Middlesex, UK, announced the launch of a three-wheeler in February 1919. In the same year, the company was reformed as The Wooler Motor Cycle Co Ltd. Designed by John Wooler, the Mule was powered by a horizontally-opposed, air-cooled, twin-cylinder, 1,022cc engine that had the cylinders extending through the sides of the bonnet. The engine used rotary valves and, even though it was air-cooled, the vehicle had a circular dummy radiator. Whilst it was classed as a three-wheeler, the single wheel at the back was actually two wheels side-by-side. Only two Wooler Mules are known to have been made before the project ceased in 1921. No photographs of the vehicles are believed to have been published. After the Mule, the company continued to manufacture motorcycles, with production ending in 1956 when the founder, John Wooler, died.

Available as a set of plans, the Xzilarator uses the back end of a Honda Goldwing. Bob Kinney

Xtra Cars Ltd

1922 — Single-seater: Runabout/Touring

Resembling a three-wheel sidecar, the Xtra Cyclecar was first built in 1922 by Xtra Cars Ltd, of Chertsey, Surrey, UK. Designed by Cuthbert Clarke, the Xtra Runabout was very basic and was powered by a two-stroke, single-cylinder Villiers engine with a two-speed transmission mounted on the rear wheel. The Xtra had no front axle; instead the wheels were controlled by two transverse leaf springs. It was a single-seater — although there was also an occasional seat behind the driver on top of the engine — with a light steel chassis that had an Ash frame with light plywood attached to it. A Touring version was also built with all versions having acetylene lighting.

1922 — Two-Seater: Runabout/Touring

In 1922 a two-seat version of the Runabout was created; this was known as the Sociable and had a similar coach-built body and a bench seat for two. The two-seat version had front double transverse springs and was powered by a 3.5bhp, 270cc Villiers engine. A two-seat Touring model was also introduced; this was fitted with a larger 8bhp, V-twin JAP engine and, along with slightly larger tyres, had a hood and screen fitted as standard. Production of all models ceased in 1924 when the company went into voluntary liquidation.

The Xtra was a basic machine that, whilst having two wheels at the front, did not have an axle. Unknown

Xzilarator

2006 — Xzilarator

This reverse trike was first designed during 2006 in the USA by builder Bob Kinney, who has also created other vehicles, including a Hot Rod Helicopter. The Xzilarator is a build-it-yourself vehicle and available as a set of plans only. Using a 1,500-1,800cc Honda Goldwing as a donor, the vehicle utilises the back end of the Goldwing with drive going to the rear wheel, giving a top speed of around 130mph (209km/h) with the 1,500cc engine. The chassis and frame are made from tubular steel, whilst the body houses two seats that are side-by-side. Plans remain available at the time of writing.

Yamaha Motor Co Ltd

2004 — Pedicab

Whilst Yamaha of Japan is well known for a wide range of products, including musical instruments and vehicles, the company has also made ATV three-wheelers; however, these are not within the scope of this book. In 2004 Yamaha announced the Pedicab; this was a hybrid update of the rickshaw, which was powered by human pedal power and an electric motor that assisted the cyclist. The lightweight vehicle (160kg) had a single wheel at the front and a plastic cab that had open sides and front. The interior used natural materials, like hemp and wood fibres, and had a bench seat at the rear for two passengers with a single seat and handlebars for the driver. The vehicles were designed to ferry people around at the World Expo held in Japan in 2005.

York Noble Industries

1958 — Nobel 200

The Nobel 200 was the British version of the Fuldamobil (see page 90) that was built under licence. In the UK, the Nobel was financed by Cyril Lord and sold by York Noble (*sic*) Industries, being assembled by Harland & Wolff in Belfast, Northern Ireland. Unlike the original Fuldamobil, it had a fibreglass body courtesy of Bristol Aeroplane Co, which was attached to the steel chassis. The Nobel was powered by a two-stroke, 191cc Fichtel & Sachs engine that drove the rear wheel and gave a top speed of approximately 50-55mph (80-88.5km/h) with fuel consumption of 60mpg (4.7-litre/100km). The Nobel 200 was also available as an open pick-up type vehicle. Nobels were produced from 1958 to 1962; only some 30 vehicles are known to survive at the time of writing.

Yue Loong Motor Co

1960s – Heavy Trucks

Located in Japan, the Yue Loong Motor Co manufactured heavy three-wheel trucks in the 1960s. The trucks had a sturdy steel chassis fitted with a steel three-seat cab and a steering wheel. With double telescopic shock absorbers at the front, the vehicle had twin wheels either side at the rear to help take the weight and provide extra traction.

This Yue Loong truck from 1963 was an exceptionally wide vehicle compared with other three-wheel trucks of its time and, as such, was designed to carry heavy loads. Author's Collection

Built as both a five-door passenger version and as an open truck, the Zap Xebra is an electric vehicle with a range of up to 25 miles per charge. Stephen Smith

ZAP/ZAP Jonway

Zero Air Pollution (ZAP) was founded in California, USA, in 1994 and began by producing electric bicycles and scooters as an alternative means of transport to fossil fuel-powered vehicles. In January 2011, ZAP announced that it had completed the 51% acquisition of Jonway Automobile in China and, from that point forward, the newly combined company became ZAP Jonway. At the time of writing the company produces electric bicycles, scooters, four-wheelers and the following three-wheelers.

2006 — Xebra

Although ZAP had started to produce electric vehicles in 2003, it was in 2006 that its first three-wheeler arrived in the form of the ZAP Xebra. Since 2006 the Xebra has evolved through a number of versions as improvements are continually being made. Powered by an electric motor, the four-seat car is able to reach 40mph (64km/h) with a range of up to 25 miles (40km) per charge or up to 40 miles (64km) on the optional upgraded batteries. The vehicle has a 110V ac charger on board — with an optional 240V available — so that it can be recharged at any standard electrical point. The Xebra's body, made from steel, is a five-door hatchback that incorporates a luggage space behind the seats with a carrying capacity of 500lb (230kg). With a gross vehicle weight of around 2,805lb, a number of options are also available, including radio/CD, leather seats, solar charger, car cover and upgraded batteries.

2008 — Xebra Truck

The Zap Xebra Truck arrived in 2008 and is powered by the same electric engine as the car version of the Xebra. It features a two-seat cabin and a large dump bed at the rear, which has a cargo weight capacity of 1,000lb (460kg) and is fitted with fold down sides and a drop-down tail-gate.

2008 — Alias

The Zap Alias is a three-seat electric sports car that was announced in 2008. With a top speed of 85mph (137km/h) it is capable of sprinting 0-60mph (0-96km/h) in 7.8sec. Using an electric motor powered by Lithium batteries that drives the front two wheels, the vehicle is able to achieve up to 100 miles (161km) on a full charge. Made from a composite structure, the Alias features a number of creature comforts, including integrated GPS system, theatre satellite stereo, electric windows, power steering and solar panels to name but a few. Initially, it was planned to go on sale in the USA from 2011; however, at the time of writing it remains under development with a number of prototype vehicles being built.

When assembled, the Zascka was a folding car that had a tubular steel frame with a body consisting of fabric stretched over it. Author's Collection

Zaschka

1929 — Zaschka

The Zaschka was a folding three-wheel car that was built in 1929 in Berlin, Germany, with the aim of being cost effective and space saving. It was designed and built by Engelbert Zaschka who, amongst other things, was one of Germany's first helicopter pioneers. Zaschka's vehicle was designed so that it could be taken apart within 20min. It could be 'knocked down' into three main sections and so did not require a garage. Each section was built around a tubular frame with a canvas body stretched over the frame and clipped into position. The vehicle used a single-cylinder engine that had chain drive to the rear wheel and a top speed of around 30mph (48km/h).

Taken apart the Zashcka consisted of several major components, which, for those without a garage, could be kept in a garden shed. Author's Collection

Powered by a Honda engine, the Zoe Zipper was a single-seater manufactured in Japan and then shipped to the USA. Doug Tuttle

Zoe Motors Inc

1983 — Zipper

Introduced in 1983 by Zoe Motors Inc of Los Angeles, California, USA, the Zoe Zipper was a lightweight single-seat vehicle that weighed in at less than 400lb. It had been initially manufactured by Mitsuoka Motors in Japan in 1982. The vehicle was powered by a 5bhp, 49cc Honda engine that provided power to the single rear wheel and had a top speed of 45mph (72km/h) whilst offering 112mpg (2.5-litre/100km). The body was made of fibreglass and came in two versions — a hardtop and a convertible — that were sold until around 1985.

Actually a modified Reliant Rialto, the Zoe Z/3000 ST featured an extra wide axle and flared wheel arches to help entice the American market. Author's Collection

1985 — Zoe Little Giant

Powered by a 49cc Honda engine and sold from 1983 to approximately 1985, the Zoe Little Giant was a mini pick-up truck that was advertised as an 'all purpose mini-utility truck' that could carry a payload of half a ton.

1985 — Zoe

The Zoe first appeared in 1985 and was essentially a rebadged Ligier that had been imported into the USA from France. The company imported both three- and four-wheel versions until 1986 in both car and van form. All were fitted with diesel engines.

1985 — Zoe Z/5000

In 1985 the Zoe Z/5000 was an attempt by Zoe Motors to introduce the Reliant Rialto (see page 211) to the American market. Using the standard Reliant configuration with its 848cc engine, the interior was revamped with a more appealing dashboard and leather seats though the vehicle sold in very small numbers.

1986 — Zoe Z/3000 ST

In an attempt to make the Zoe Z/5000 more appealing, the Zoe Z/3000 ST version was introduced in 1986 with the rear axle and bodywork both considerably widened. Although extensively marketed, with both 'sedan/wagon' and 'panel van' variations offered, only six Z/3000ST prototypes were built, of which only three are known to exist today.

Zundapp Ges GmbH

1928 — Zundapp

Zundapp Ges GmbH of Nuremberg, Germany, was founded in 1917 and was a motorcycle manufacturer from 1928 to 1935. It made a number of three-wheelers that incorporated a motorcycle front with a number of rear sections. These ranged from open and enclosed passenger vehicles as well as, in 1933, a trivan. All were powered by either a 400cc or 500cc Zundapp motorcycle engine that drove both rear wheels. The company went bankrupt in 1984 and closed.

Built as either an open or an enclosed passenger vehicle, the Zundapp was also built with a van body. RUMCar News

Three-wheelers of the future

If there is one thing that this book has shown, it is that the three-wheeler is extremely versatile and, throughout its history, has constantly adapted to meet the demands of its time. For this reason, it has always served a purpose and found a following of devoted owners. In a world swamped with mass produced four-wheelers, a lot of people would be surprised at just how many manufacturers around the world are still producing three-wheelers today. Yet, if asked, many would be hard pressed to name just one of them. Changing times means that three-wheelers are not as common as they were; however, they are certainly not out for the count. There is no doubt that, in the years to come, variations of three-wheelers will continue to appear, especially as technologies improve and alternative energy sources become more reliable and indeed cheaper to manufacture. Who knows, perhaps one day flying three-wheelers may be common or wheels themselves may themselves become a thing of the past with hover cars becoming the norm. Until that happens, I think we can safely assume that three-wheelers will be around for many more years to come and, all being well, will be celebrating their 300th birthday in 2069.

Above: *The Atlantric is just one vehicle that is still in its infancy and being developed for the future. It is designed to have a planned fuel consumption of around 120+mpg (1.97-litre/100km).* Arak Leatham

Below: *Designed by Tom Karen (see also Bond Bug on page 210), the Buz is currently under development. It is a three-seater, with the driver sitting at the centre with two passengers behind. It has a space at the front large enough for a week's shopping with either an electric or internal combustion power pod at the rear.* Tom Karen

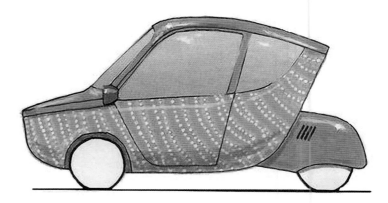

Acknowledgements

This book has been made possible thanks to a whole army of people who have provided photographs and information. My sincere thanks therefore go to the following people: A1 Classic Cars Maastricht; A U (Dan) Daniels; Ace Scott King; Adam Reif; AeroCycle Cars (Arthur Rayner); Alan Styles; Alden Jewell; Alan Pinnell; Allan Hailstone; Andreas Kukuljan; Andy Carter; Anthony Olway; Anthony Philllipson; Arak Leatham; Arseny Zhdanov; Arvil Shepherd; Autoblog.com (John Neff); Roderick Holland); British Broadcasting Corporation; Black Country Living Museum, UK (Geoffrey Payne); Blackjack Trikes (Richard Oakes); Bob and Diana Keyes; Bob Kinney; Bob Kranenburg; Bob Purton; B.R.A (David Wiles); Brian Snelson; Brian Thornton; Budd Steinhilber; Campagna Motors (Jean-Simon Goudreau); Carlo Lamattina; Caroline Payne; Chris Van Rooy; Chuck Andersen; Clive Sargeant; Coventry Transport Museum, UK (Damien Kimberley); Craig Thorness; Colin Pickett; Damiano Garro; Daniel Blow; Danny Higgins; Dave Norton; Dave Starr; Dave Stretton; Dave Stollery; Dave Vezina; Dave Womack; David Baker; David Buckley; David Suarez; Des Ferguson; Don Dennes; Donald Le Bihan; Doug Malewicki; Doug Tuttle; Drive Inc Ltd; Earl E Mohr; Eco-Fueler Corporation (Jerry Hendricks); Eduard Hattuma; Elio Motors (Chip Stempeck); Ernie and Maise Allen; Eva Håkansson; Ford Motor Co (Richard Weedn); Warren Crone); Frank Webster; FRS Motorsports (Fred and Jason Reeve, Lisa Swaine); Fuel Vapour Technologies (George Parker); Gabriel Grare, Gene Rodgers; General Motors (Kathleen Adelson); Georg Schwalbach; Gill Richardson, Peter Waller and everyone at Crécy Publishing; Grinnall Specialist Cars (Mark Grinnall); H Roy Jaffe; Hans Bodewes; Hal Schmidt; Hans van Os (DWAC — Nederlandse Dwergautoclub); Hans van Scharrenburg; Harry Kalsbeek; Harry Kraemer; Helen Sanders; Helena Belden; Hikaru Baba; Iain Ayre; IndyCycle (Jamieson Durette); Jan Barnier; Jaume Jubert; James Nichol; Jane Neil; Jeff Green; Jez Hildred; Jo Huxster; Joe Fajdich; Joe Turner; Joel Bradshaw; Joel Loiseau; Johan Schoenmaker; John Cleve Graham; John Lloyd; John Lucas; John Massegee; John Meadows; John Mulders; John Napper; John Robson; John Rothwell; Jonathan Poll; Joseph Hall; Joseph Lawrence; Jozef Tedjrasi; Justin Bruett; Ken Baker; Kerry Croxton; Kim Scholer; KKM Deliveries; Lane Motor Museum, USA (David Yando); Larry Fisher; Luis Pallás; Lovson Auto Division (Joanna); Malcolm Tait; Marc Le Beller; Mark Zalutko; Marlene Gaskin, Marotti Automotive (Markus Rogalski); Martin Strange; Markus Klett; Maserati Archive (Georgina Cox), Maurice de Boer; Maurizo Bol; Maximilian Busch; Maxwell Paternoster; Mian Muhammad Ali Hameed; Michael Barnard; Michel Humbert; Miller Technology (Chad Miller); Morgan Motor Co (Charles Morgan and Beverley Moore); MOSI: Museum of Science & Industry, Manchester, UK (Sarah Roe and Nick Fonder); Nagy Róbert; National Motor Museum, Beaulieu, UK (Jonathan Day); Nick Greatwood; Oliver Hartmann; Olivier Houllier; PAL-V Europe NV; Patrick Castelli; Peel Engineering Ltd (James Buggle); Pete Shirk; Pete Skinner (E300DSLR); Peter Edgley; Peter Frost; Peter Klensberg; Peter Smeaton; Peter Stanhope; Peugeot (Janet Brace); Phil Wells; Planet Engineering Ltd; Pol de Carnières; Predator Trikes (Allan Daniels); Razor Cars Ltd (David Chapman); Reliant Motor Co; Ric Murphy; Richard Lewis; Richard Robinson; Rik Borgman; Robert Grounds; Robert Iveson; Robert Kermode; Robert Knight; Robert Occhialini; Robert Pichon; Robert Woodard; Robert Q Riley; Rogerio Machado; Ron Will; Ronald Powers; Sam Glover; Samuel Hawley; author of *Speed Duel: The Inside Story of the Land Speed Record in the Sixties*; Sceadu Design (Dave Mounce); Scorpion Motorsports (Mark Margolis); Scott Merrill; Silvano Notaro; Simon Baynes; Spike; Stephen Smith; Steve Green; Steve Hole; Steve Maguire; Stratstone Morgan Stourbridge (Mark Townsend and Simon fox); Structural Plastics Inc (Larry Barker); Stuart Cyphus; Sub Motorsports; Subaru (Peter Tenn); Sverker P Zethelius; Terry Parkin; T3 Motion (Dan Ellis); Thom Taylor; Thomas Touw; Thomas Tutchek; Thoroughbred Motorsports Inc (Kacy Mills); Tom Carmody; Tom Karen; Tony Cox; Twike UK (Dr Andreas Schroeer); Tycho de Feyter; Unique Motor Co (Nigel Scarr); Ursula Haigh; Vandenbrink (Harry Kroonen); Velor-X-Trike (Pavel Brida); Volkswagen (Kate Thompson and Danielle Hutchinson); Walter B Statter; Warren Behler; Willem Alink; William Brandt; Wilfried Dibbets; William Fiddler; and, Yasuo Taskahashi. My sincere apologies to anyone I may have missed off the list.

Bibliography

Web-Sites:

3-wheelers.com: www.3-wheelers.com

Autoblog.com: www.autoblog.com

Autopassion: www.autopasion18.com

Car News China: www.carnewschina.com

Frisky: www.meadowsfrisky.co.uk

Grace's Guide: www.gracesguide.co.uk

Hemmings: www.hemmings.com

La Web de los Microcoches: www.grupo7.com/microcoches

Lambretta: www.lambro.plus.com

Lexikon der vergessenen Autotypen: www.autolexikon-thyssen.de

Wikipedia: www.wikipedia.org

Also manufacturers' web-sites as detailed below.

Books:

A-Z of Kit Cars; Steve Hole (2012)

Know your Bond; Bond Owners Club (1990)

Light Motor Cars and Voiturettes; John Henry Knight (1902)

Morgan 3 Wheelers 1909-1952; Eric Eadon (2012)

Peddling Bicycles to America: The Rise of an Industry; Bruce D. Epperson (2010)

On Three Wheels — The three-wheeler car in Britain; Rod Ward (2008)

Powered Vehicles Made in the Black Country; Jim Boulton (1990)

The Three-Wheelers Almanac John Cleve Graham (1997)

The Electric Vehicle; Gijs Mom (1997)

The Engineer's and Mechanic's Encyclopædia: Comprehending Practical Illustrations of the Machinery and Processes Employed in Every Description of Manufacture of the British Empire; Luke Herbert (1836)

The Reliant Three Wheeler 1935-1973; Stuart Cyphus & Elvis Payne (2011)

The Reliant Three Wheeler 1973-2002; Elvis Payne & Stuart Cyphus (2012)

The Vincent HRD Story; Roy Harper (1975)

Three-Wheelers; Chris Rees (1997)

Three-Wheelers; Ken Hill (1986)

Weird Cars; Stephen Vokins (2004)

Magazines and Newspapers (various editions 1900 onwards):

Autocar

Classic Motor Cycle

CycleCar

Daily Telegraph

English Mechanic Journal

Go-Go

Light Car & Cyclecar

Motor Cycle

Motor Cycling

Parade

Popular Mechanics

Practical Classics

Scooter and Three-Wheeler

TKC mag (Total Kit Car)

Mechanix Illustrated

The Commercial Motor

Further reading on current manufacturers

The following addresses and companies are known to exist at time of publication. The author and publisher accept no responsibility for any information or advice contained within these web-sites or their availability. This list details known web-sites only and not all current manufacturers.

Aero CycleCars: www.spitfireart.com

Bajaj: www.bajajauto.com

Blackjack Trikes: www.blackjackzero.com

Buckland B3 Mk II: www.penguinspeedshop.com

Campagna Motors: www.campagnamotors.com

Eco-Fueler Corporation: www.eco-fueler.com

Elio Motors: www.eliomotors.com

FRS Motorsports: www.frsmotorsport.com

Fuel Vapour Technologies: www.fuelvaporcar.com

Grinnall Specialist Cars: www.grinnallcars.com

J A Prestwich: www.japrestwich.com

JZR: www.jzrpa.com

Liberty Motors: www.cycle-car.com

Lovson: www.lovson.com

Malone Car Company: www.malonecar.eclipse.co.uk

Marotti Automotive: www.marotti.eu

Morgan Motor Co: www.morgan-motor.co.uk

PAL-V: www.pal-v.com

Peel Engineering Ltd: www.peelengineering.co.uk

Pembleton Motor Co: www.pembleton.co.uk

Predator Trikes: www.predatortrikes.com

Razor Cars: www.razorcars.co.uk

Rayvolution Cars: www.rayvolutioncars.com

Road Track Race Ltd: www.roadtrackrace.com

Robert Q Riley: www.rqriley.com

Sceadu Design: www.sceadu.com

Scott Coupe: www.scootcoupé.com

Scorpion Motorsports: www.scorpionmotorsports.com

Thoroughbred Motorsports Inc: www.thoroughbred-
    motorsports.com

Trigger Cars: www.triggers.nl

Triking: www.trikingsportscars.co.uk

Twike: www.twike.com

Velor-X-Trike: www.velor-x-trike.com

Index

Due to the vast number of model names, this index only details alphabetical model names (ie. Gordon) and not alphanumeric based models names. (ie. AA12)

The A-Z of Three-Wheelers